Sustainable Lessons from People-Friendly Places

Current planning and design modes of cities are facing challenges of philosophy and form. Past approaches no longer sustain new demands and call for innovative thinking. In a world that is becoming highly urbanized, the need for a new outlook is propelled by fundamental global changes that touch upon environmental, economic and social aspects.

The book introduces fundamental principles of timely sustainable urban design, paying attention to architecture, integration of natural features, public urban spaces and their successful use. Readers will learn how cities are transitioning to active mobility by placing the wellbeing of citizens at the heart of planning; making buildings fit nature; supporting local culture through preservation; and including community gardens in neighborhoods, among others. Written by a practicing architect, professor and author, the book is richly illustrated and features meticulously selected international case studies.

Avi Friedman received his bachelor's degree in Architecture and Town Planning from the Israel Institute of Technology, his master's degree from McGill University, and his doctorate from the University of Montréal. He is the director of the Affordable Homes Research Group at the McGill School of Architecture, where he teaches. He also holds a Visiting Professor position in Lancaster University in the UK. Avi is known for his housing innovation and for several demonstration projects. He is the author of 25 books and the principal of Avi Friedman Consultants, Inc. He is the recipient of numerous awards, including the Manning Innovation Award, Lifetime Achievement Award from Sustainable Buildings Canada, and the World Habitat Award.

Sustainable Lessons from People-Friendly Places

Avi Friedman

Routledge
Taylor & Francis Group
NEW YORK AND LONDON

Designed cover image: © Avi Friedman

First published 2024
by Routledge
605 Third Avenue, New York, NY 10158

and by Routledge
4 Park Square, Milton Park, Abingdon, Oxon, OX14 4RN

Routledge is an imprint of the Taylor & Francis Group, an informa business

© 2024 Avi Friedman

The right of Avi Friedman to be identified as author of this work has been asserted in accordance with sections 77 and 78 of the Copyright, Designs and Patents Act 1988.

All rights reserved. No part of this book may be reprinted or reproduced or utilised in any form or by any electronic, mechanical, or other means, now known or hereafter invented, including photocopying and recording, or in any information storage or retrieval system, without permission in writing from the publishers.

Trademark notice: Product or corporate names may be trademarks or registered trademarks, and are used only for identification and explanation without intent to infringe.

ISBN: 978-1-032-47128-0 (hbk)
ISBN: 978-1-032-47129-7 (pbk)
ISBN: 978-1-003-38468-7 (ebk)

DOI: 10.4324/9781003384687

Typeset in ITC Officina Sans Std
by SPi Technologies India Pvt Ltd (Straive)

Printed and bound in Great Britain by
TJ Books Limited, Padstow, Cornwall

Contents

Preface   vii
Acknowledgments   ix

CHAPTER 1   **A Call for Sustainable Cities**   1

CHAPTER 2   **Learning from the Past, Retooling the Future**   12

CHAPTER 3   **Denser Mixed-Use Communities**   23

CHAPTER 4   **Public Squares and Urban Life**   33

CHAPTER 5   **Planning Cities for Walkability**   41

CHAPTER 6   **Developing in Natural Settings**   50

CHAPTER 7   **Creating Urban Landscapes**   61

CHAPTER 8   **Cities as Farms**   71

CHAPTER 9   **Social and Economic Values of Markets**   84

CHAPTER 10   **The Culture of Places**   94

CHAPTER 11   **Planning for Wellbeing**   103

CHAPTER 12   **Places for Social Interaction**   114

CHAPTER 13   **Art and the City**   125

CHAPTER 14   **Streets and Sidewalks for Living**   138

CHAPTER 15   **Slowing Down Vehicular Traffic**   149

CHAPTER 16   **Urban Preservation**   159

CHAPTER 17   **Planning for Urban Evolution**   170

Contents

CHAPTER 18 **Designing Sustainable Buildings**   179

CHAPTER 19 **Powering Cities: Net Zero and District Heating**   191

CHAPTER 20 **Old Buildings, New Life**   203

Illustration Credits   216
References   217
Index   234

Preface

Cities are facing social, economic and environmental challenges that force policymakers, planners and architects to rethink current practices. The depletion of non-renewable natural resources, elevated levels of greenhouse gas emissions and climate change are a few of the environmental challenges that force designers to reconsider conceptual approaches in favor of ones that promote a better suitability between communities and nature. Consideration of overall planning concepts that minimize the development's carbon footprint, district heating, passive solar gain, net-zero buildings and preserving the site's natural assets are some of the contemporary strategies that architects and planners are integrating into their thought process and urban design practice.

Increasing costs of material, labor, land and infrastructure have posed economic challenges, with affordability being paramount among them. The need to do more with less brings about concepts that include higher density, mixed-use districts. Also, the need to reduce infrastructure costs gave rise to better building practices, which benefits both the environment and the citizens.

Social challenges are also drawing the attention of planners and policymakers. As the "baby-boom" generation is retiring, housing an elderly population will take priority. Walkable communities, aging in place and multigenerational living are some of the concepts considered. In addition, live–work environments, especially following the COVID-19 pandemic, have become part of the economic reality for those who wish to work from home – which has been made possible through digital advances.

A term commonly mentioned in the context of contemporary urban design is sustainability, which is another underlying principle of this book. The proliferation of the term sustainable development and the conditions that brought it about can be traced back several decades. In 1992, the United Nations

Conference on the Human Environment in Stockholm dealt with concerns that humanity is stretching the "carrying capacity of the earth" to its limits. The meeting served as a forum for the first international discussion on the relationship between ongoing environmental damage and the future of humanity. It was recognized then that population growth in some nations and overconsumption in others leave noticeable footprints in the form of land degradation, deforestation, air pollution and water scarcity. The three original pillars of sustainable development were social, economic and environmental aspects. However, it became clear that culture and governance must be part of any attempt to implement sustainability initiatives if the implementation process is to succeed.

The need to think innovatively about cities led to the idea to write this book. The intention is to offer contemporary information on urban and building design concepts and illustrate them with outstanding international examples. The objective is to outline principles and learn from places that already charted a sustainable course or practiced them for generations to affect the lives of the people who live or use them. Those places have lessons to offer through their appearance and make-up and by extension on other spots. The narrative of some places is rooted in their distant past. Other places' lessons and forms are relatively recent and defined by their locations. There are spots which have been crafted by the people who have inhabited them, which at one point, or over a prolonged period, have had to respond to a challenge to become resilient. Some places offer a lesson which makes one reflect upon humanity's current habits and helps draw lessons about the future.

At times it takes cataclysmic events and ominous signs to remind us that human existence is at the mercy of nature. Phenomena like prolonged periods of drought in one part of the world and floods in another, the melting of the ice caps, the increase in the cost of food and the depletion of natural

Preface

resources are some of these aspects. Socio-economic transformations have also brought to the forefront other issues such as the widening gap between rich and poor nations. These natural and social phenomena have forced us to rethink how future development should take place. We have begun to reflect on global issues that were once considered marginal, making them a central concern.

Over the years I have continued leaning about various subjects from places I visited and photographed as much as from other sources. At times, the lesson of a place reveals itself at once – it was right there. In other times, years passed before I recognized the hidden message of what the place wanted to tell. My travels took me to spots near and far. Some densely inhabited while others just natural. When there, I talked to people or simply recorded them with my camera.

Following my visits, I went on to investigate the distant and near histories of these locations, their effect on civilizations, the people that inhabit them, what made them special, and the lessons they offered. I wondered what made strolling through, sitting in, conversing with, rubbing shoulders or simply being in them memorable and thought-provoking. My training as a

planner and architect helps my study into the structure of their fabric.

The need to think innovatively about cities and retool them to become sustainable and resilient led to the idea to write this book. Each of the book's twenty chapters investigates a single topic that when combined illustrate the functioning of sustainable cities on their environmental, economic, social and cultural pillars. The intention is to offer information on planning, urban and architectural design principles and illustrate them with international cases. My quest for unique cases has taken me to locations around the world that offer valuable lessons. Neighborhood squares in several locations made me think about the importance of having "urban living rooms." A Scottish wind farm led to ideas about global use of renewable energy. The *Madonnelle* religious niches on the exterior walls in Italian cities led to reflect on the role of faith in social sustainability. The graffiti-painted laneways in Melbourne, Australia, made me think about spontaneous public art and local culture. It is a personal take on subjects that range from large- to small-scale aspects from which designers can learn. It is hoped that this book will help the reader reflect on the lessons that places want to teach us about sustainable existence.

Acknowledgments

Researching and writing on sustainable urban and building design was a subject of my work for years. It included collaboration with and contribution by numerous colleagues, assistants and students who directly and indirectly inspired my work. My apology if I have mistakenly omitted the name of someone who contributed to this book. I will do my best to correct such omissions in future editions.

This book could not have been written without contribution to the background research, compiling information and the writing by Ryan Cho, Callie Palmer, Charlotte Pink and Fanny Sachet. Contribution to background research and the writing of the case studies was also made by Brian McGinn, Jason Jorgji and Emmanuelle Bandia. Special thanks to Victoria Fratipietro for preparing the alternative text of the images and listing them for submission. The work of Yangaiyuan (Ariel) Lin in proofreading the bibliography is appreciated. The team's hard work, talent, dedication and punctuality is most appreciated. Thanks to Teagan Vincent for proofreading the text.

Special thanks are extended to Siqi (Natalie) Qiu for drawing many of the illustrations along with Lucy Anderson, Charles Grégoire, Elif Kurkcu, Elisa Costa, Jeff Jerome, Zhong Cai, Diana Nigmatullina, Rachel O, Jing Han (Jay), David Auerbach, Maria Teleman, David Cameron, Sorel Friedman, Rainier Silva, JJ Zhao and Nyd Garavito-Bruhn. Their talent and insistence on achieving excellence is truly appreciated and admired.

To Megha Patel, Editorial Assistant, Planning, Landscape, and Urban Design and Jake Millicheap, Editorial Assistant, Architecture at Routledge, many thanks for their guidance and support.

Finally, my heartfelt thanks and appreciation to my wife Sorel Friedman, PhD, who accompanied me to many of the places described in the book and children Paloma and Ben for their love and support.

CHAPTER 1

A Call for Sustainable Cities

Cities are facing social, economic and environmental challenges that force rethinking of current practices. It is vital to look at these changes as an evolution: recognizing the past, examining the present and pointing to the future. This chapter introduces *sustainability* as a framework for shaping an approach to urban design and combatting contemporary challenges. First, the chapter lists the current challenges faced by today's cities. Then, sustainability on its key pillars is presented and defined and indexes to measure it using carbon and ecological footprints as well as notable case studies are given.

1.1 Contemporary Urban Challenges

Among the challenges that cities are facing one can list rapid urbanization, climate change, aging populations, traffic congestion and food security that are shifting the ways town planning is practiced.

Recent statistics on urbanization suggest that 75 percent of the world's population resides in urbanized areas (Carneiro et al. 2019). Additionally, according to the United Nations Development Programme, over two-thirds of the world population will live in cities by 2050 (Palanivel 2017). Building the physical and social infrastructure to meet the needs of this population will be crucial.

Another challenge faced by today's cities is the result of global warming. According to Kumar (2021), urbanization intensifies the heating of cities, which are already warm. This is expected to further increase health risks in areas with poor air quality (Kumar 2021). As illustrated in Figure 1.1, urban heat islands (UHI) effect cities the most since soil cover and natural features such as forests is being built on (United States Environmental Protection Agency 2022).

Wildfires have increased significantly in size and number in places such as Australia and across North America over the past three decades (Schoennagel et al. 2017). While it is true that the ecosystem and several plants and species benefit and depend on periodic fires to regenerate, the burning and warming caused by fires is much more frequent and considerable than previously seen, which makes nature's replenishment unknown and to some degree impossible. The length of fire seasons has increased globally by 19 percent from 1979 to 2013, with the longest fire seasons being experienced in the western United States (Figure 1.2). There, anthropogenic climate change has been identified as causing more than 50 percent of the increase in forest areas burned by wildfires (Schoennagel et al. 2017).

In 2018, an incredibly damaging wildfire engulfed parts of southern California in fire and smoke, sparking an investigation into the effects of climate change on the intensity of these fires (Borunda 2018). Fifteen of the largest 20 fires in California's recorded history have taken place since the year 2000. Nearly each year California's climate becomes hotter and drier than that of the previous year, making these regular fires increasingly more powerful. Scientists believe that climate change contributed to an extra 4,046,856 hectares (10 million acres) of burning of forests in the west (Borunda 2018).

Extreme climate events such as hurricanes and flooding can also pose significant threats to cities. On August 29, 2005, a Category 5 hurricane slammed into the southeastern coast of Louisiana to take a direct hit on New Orleans (Amadeo 2020). It caused what is regarded as the most destructive natural disaster the United States has ever experienced. Winds, which reached a sustained speed of 225 kilometers per hour (140 mph), could be felt up to 160 kilometers (105 miles) from the center of the vortex (FEMA 2015). Sea levels rose to 6 and 9 meters (20 and 30 feet) above the norm, causing flooding to damage a large swath of land, widespread beach erosion and

1   **DOI: 10.4324/9781003384687-1**

A Call for Sustainable Cities

Figure 1.1 Urban heat islands (UHI) are created because soil cover and natural features such as forests were transformed to structures or roads.

Figure 1.2 The length of fire seasons has increased globally by 19 percent from 1979 to 2013, with the longest fire seasons being experienced in the western United States, as shown here in Yellowstone Park, US.

destruction to homes and infrastructure. Large holding tanks full of fuel were ruptured, contaminating water and soil.

Some 300,000 homes were either destroyed or made uninhabitable in the aftermath of Hurricane Katrina. Approximately 770,000 residents were displaced, and it is estimated that 75,000 residents returned only to find their homes gone (Figure 1.3) (Amadeo 2020). Eighty percent of New Orleans was flooded due to the city's levees which proved to have many engineering flaws, as some were not built high enough, were not supported by concrete pilings or were built on inadequate soil. Furthermore, 90 cubic meters (118 million cubic yards) of debris were left over after Katrina had run its course through the southeastern coast of Louisiana (Amadeo 2020).

Some argue that Katrina was no different than the storms that frequent the area yearly during hurricane season, just more ferocious. However, the data tells another story. In the past three decades the number of hurricanes classified as Category 4 or 5 has nearly doubled. The ocean surface, where hurricanes draw their energy, and the air just above it, has warmed almost 1 degree Celsius (33.8 Fahrenheit) from the pre-industrial era. As a result, these storms draw the ocean heat into the atmosphere in the form of moisture. The outcome is extreme winds, rainfall and rising sea levels which ravage communities causing damage in the billions of dollars (Gibbens 2019). Like Katrina, hurricanes that followed such as Harvey, Sandy and Florence left in their wake destruction which takes decades to rebuild.

Another challenge that nations like Canada and cities around the world are facing is aging population. Due to improvement in healthcare people are living longer than previous generations (Figure 1.4). The World Health Organization (WHO), as per a 2022 report, states that the population of people 60 and older will double, and those 80 years or older will triple, by the year 2050 (WHO 2022). As populations age, infrastructure that includes proper housing and easy access to social services, such as healthcare, need to be established.

Another challenge is traffic congestion. A study from the Texas Transportation Institute estimates that, in American cities, the cost of the average traffic delay costs each American commuter US$1,080 annually (Ashik et al. 2022). Traffic congestion has adverse effects on the environment, creating high energy usage, noise and air pollution (Figure 1.5). Additionally, it increases physical inactivity and negatively

A Call for Sustainable Cities

Figure 1.3 Some 300,000 homes were either destroyed or made uninhabitable in the aftermath of Hurricane Katrina.

Figure 1.4 A challenge that nations like Canada and cities around the world are facing is rapidly aging population.

affects the mental state of those commuting (Ashik et al. 2022). It is widely accepted that avoidance of car-centric infrastructure by increasing public transportation, bike lanes and walkability, while integrating all these latter factors within denser city structures, can prevent traffic congestion and its subsequent negative effects.

A Call for Sustainable Cities

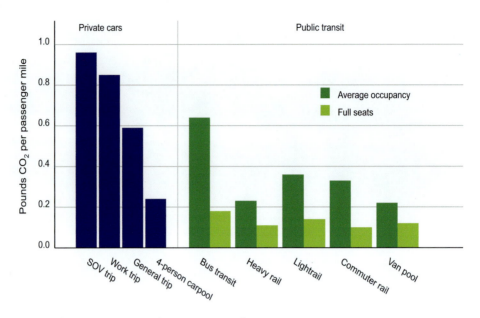

Figure 1.5 Tailpipe emissions of common transport modes per passenger mile.

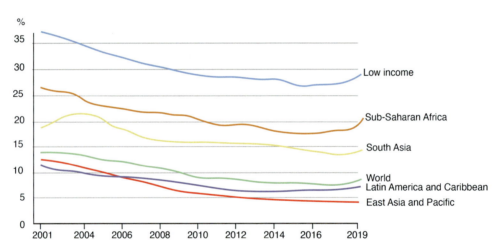

Figure 1.6 Share of the global population that is undernourished (after Food and Agricultural Organization of the United Nations).

Food security is another subject of concern. With the rapid growth of both the world's population and urbanization, alongside climate change impacting what food, and how much of it, can be grown, consideration must be given to ways to combatting hunger. The urban poor are most affected by this, faced with, in many cases, poor access to affordable, non-processed foods, time scarcity, and deficient access to electricity, clean water and refrigeration (Figure 1.6) (Ruel 2020).

The factors detailed above exemplify only some of the formidable obstacles facing cities and provide a distressing outlook of what is to come if society does not act promptly.

The need to reshape current urban design frameworks to meet this challenge is imperative to reach a livable future.

1.2 A Sustainable Mind-Set for Cities

The twentieth century was riddled with the emergence of suburban, car-centred, sprawling communities characterized by massive highways and wide roads, scattered residential developments, and large plots. A key factor in redirecting city development is uncoupling people from their cars.

When developing a project, planners could aim to offer infrastructure that encourage people to walk, bike or use public transit. As well, it makes the city and its resources much more accessible, especially for lower-income groups.

When planning a new development, designers need to consider the energy consumption of buildings and their maintenance. Cities should be using renewable energy that is replenished at a greater rate than it is consumed (UN 2016). Additionally, public green spaces should be central in these urban plans to positively benefit both a place's environmental and social health. These principles embodied the notion of sustainability which is central to this book.

The roots of sustainability, and more specifically, the term *sustainable development*, can be traced to the 1972 United Nations Conference on the Human Environment in Stockholm. The conference marks a turning point in the international discussion on environmental politics, delineating the environment as a major issue in present and future global development (UN 2022). It determined that overconsumption of natural resources and rapid population growth could not be reasonably sustained given the capacity of the environment and its resources. This conference led to the creation of important international organizations for environmental preservation, including the United Nations Environmental Programme and the International Union for the Conservation of Nature and Natural Resources (UN 2022).

These organizations put in place the idea that the earth is environmentally degrading and proliferated the message that non-renewable resources are finite. The creation of the World Commission on Environment and Development (WCED) in 1987, now known as the Brundtland Commission, harbored the latter message and solidified the view that taking the future effects of present actions into consideration was the predominant focus to secure a livable future. Their report, *Our Common Future*, echoed this concern in its definition of sustainable development as one that meets present needs without compromising the ability of future generations to meet their own needs (WCED 1987). However, this concern is not solely environmental, as sustainable development involves many intersecting and evolving pillars. Therefore, the WCED outlined a model for sustainable development to include conflict resolution for matters catalyzed by developmental and environmental pressures, social equity, as well as an equitable provision of resources both between and within countries (Figure 1.7).

The key pillars of sustainability have molded over time to fit the pressing needs and growing scholarship on sustainable development; once at three pillars – the environment, economy and society – more recent discussions have added the fourth and fifth pillars – culture and governance. It is important to recognize these five pillars as separate entities, while, at the same time, acknowledging their interrelationships with one another (Figure 1.8). A new UN agenda introduced eleven Sustainable Development Goals (SDGs) and identifies processes and policies, generation of finance frameworks and planning (Figure 1.9).

The first pillar is concerned with the environment. It is focused on keeping resource and energy use to a minimum. The use of a 'cradle-to-cradle' cycle assessment is vital to ensuring environmental sustainability; it targets not just the preliminary effects of, for example, certain material choices, but the long-term potential of this infrastructure, including its recyclability once its initial use has ended. An example of developing infrastructure to have a good cradle-to-cradle cycle assessment will be detailed below.

Figure 1.7 The three underlying principles of sustainable developments according to the authors of the United Nations' *Our Common Future* report.

A Call for Sustainable Cities

Figure 1.8 The key pillars of sustainable developments are environment, economy, and society, culture and governance.

The second pillar is the economy, which aims to prevent the transfer of costs to future generations. This situation is usually the result of poor planning decisions, such as the implementation of wide roads instead of narrow ones, which results in increased maintenance costs over time. Additionally, when a development is privately initiated, the cost of oversized roads will seep into the cost of the homes nearby, making them unaffordable.

Society is the third pillar of sustainability. An all-encompassing term, the social aspect of sustainability emphasizes that the wellbeing of people through the provision of their social needs and values when planning the city must be ensured. For example, the development of walkable, mixed-use neighborhoods, equipped with walkways and bike paths, ensures the health of the people and the environment. As well, the creation of public spaces, such as parks with outdoor gyms, squares and 'urban wilds', nurtures social interaction, a connection to the natural environment, and provides a space of tranquillity – especially in busy urban environments (Figure 1.10). These provisions improve both citizens' mental and physical health. In addition, a sustainable, equitable and accessible healthcare system is paramount to a healthy society, and it is essential that sufficient funds will be continually available to make this possible.

The fourth pillar, culture, emphasizes the need to recognize and promote the traditions of a given place. For example, the preservation of historic buildings helps to conserve histories that are vital to the culture of the place, such as maintaining the building's original facade, even with shifting uses. Additionally, the focused upkeep of buildings from the past tends to contribute to enhancing the quality of future buildings. As well, instead of erecting entirely new buildings, the conversion of old buildings into new uses helps reduce natural resource consumption and avoids the demolition that occurs in new construction processes (Figure 1.11).

Figure 1.9 A UN agenda introduced eleven Sustainable Development Goals (SDGs) and identified processes, policies, generation of finance frameworks and planning.

A Call for Sustainable Cities

Figure 1.10 A park with outdoor gym in Montreal, Canada contributes to improving public wellbeing.

The final pillar of sustainable development is governance. Innovative and sustainable urban design practices cannot be implemented without the assistance of municipal leadership. It is necessary to have the government enact appropriate policies, as well as produce and explain its long-term vision to its citizens. If the governance system is effective in creating sustainable systems, it will inspire citizens to participate in public service, creating a cyclical process of furthered sustainable development.

1.2.1 Measuring Sustainability

Indexes of sustainability provide a baseline for measuring a project's fulfillment of good environmental standards. These indexes include ecological and carbon footprints (Figure 1.12). First, a place's ecological footprint measures how rapidly humans will consume land and resources given the productive area and the size of the population using it. To put this in numerical terms, an ecological footprint is measured by the given productive area and divided by the number of people who will need to use it. This footprint will include the

Figure 1.11 The village of Pérouges, France adhered to strict restoration guidelines to conserve its visual history and its culture of place.

productive area of a given place, such as a crop and grazing land, that is essential to food production and additional resources the population consumes; additionally, it will consider a place's pollution emitted and waste production, and the equivalent area needed to absorb these latter factors. To have a low ecological footprint, especially in cities, designers should strive to develop strategies to ensure low resource use and efficient, sustainable land allocation for resource production. An example of this would be urban rooftop agriculture

Carbon Footprint	Ecological Footprint
Measures CO_2 generated by activities	Measures renewable and non-renewable resources used
Only includes carbon emission numbers	Includes both carbon emissions and environmental impact
Can be used for Carbon Credit Marketplace	Used to gauge global consumption
Directly impacts climate change	Directly impacts continuing life on Earth

Figure 1.12 Indexes of sustainability provide a baseline for measuring a project's fulfillment of good environmental standards and include ecological and carbon footprints.

A Call for Sustainable Cities

practices using renewable energy sources (Harada and Whitlow 2020).

The second measure important to determining a place's environmental standards is its carbon footprint. This is measured by singular individuals, households or industries, and the given amount of carbon dioxide they emit. For example, if a place's population has a long commute time and poor public transportation resources, it is likely to have a large carbon footprint.

1.3 Greening Singapore

More than a conservatory and a park, Singapore's Garden by the Bay is a lesson in how this city-state set a determined mind to follow a biodiversity path and educate its people about green living. The Cloud Forest Conservatory and the nearby Flower Dome structures are a stunning manifestation. In enormous tent-like buildings with a green mountain and the world tallest indoor waterfall, you get to see up close and read about the region's flora (Figure 1.13).

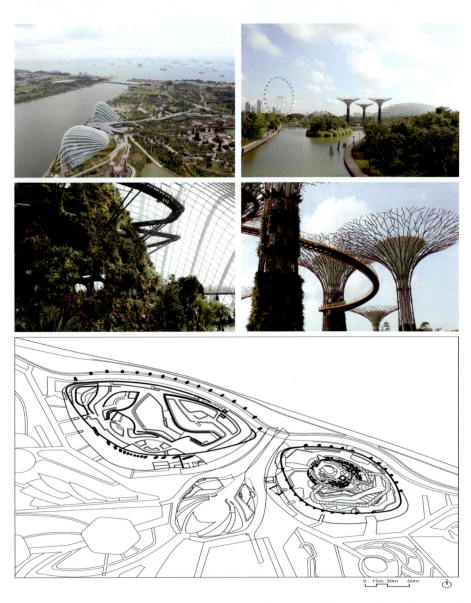

Figure 1.13 More than a conservatory and a park, Singapore's Garden by the Bay is a lesson in following a biodiversity path and educating people about green living.

A Call for Sustainable Cities

Upon exit, one sees another unusual garden. In a 101-hectare (250 acres) nature park of reclaimed land from the sea, tall metal-like tree structures are linked to each other with a suspended upper walkway. From up there you get to look down and see trees and other plants from a vantage point not commonly seen in a garden of this kind.

The greening of Singapore began in the 1960s, when it gained independence from Malaysia. From being an extremely polluted place it has become a global champion in urban environmentalism and cleanliness. To do so, the Singaporean government adopted the phrase "keep us clean, keep us green," which grew to shape many of the policies that led to the dramatic turnaround. The place's status as a city-state allowed for much easier implementation of policies as opposed to larger nations with more a cumbersome decision-making process.

The government determined that improved biodiversity was not a want, but rather a need. The sanitization of the Singapore River, which previously operated as the city's open sewer, took ten years and thousands of Singaporeans to complete. Through various agencies, like the National Parks Board, the government was able to create a treatment plan in every polluted area in the city. The greening did not stop there. As you walk the city's streets you notice plants hanging from the facades of many of the tall buildings and the lush green public parks.

Coupled with advanced urban planning techniques and continuous support from consecutive governments, Singapore has been able to achieve a relationship with nature that is incredibly rare in the industrialized world. It is a vivid example that when a nation sets its mind to embark on a green path, a combination of public education, innovative planning and disciplined action gets results.

1.4 Thinking like Norwegians

In Norway, architectural design is equally split between form, function and attention to the project's environmental context. The natural surroundings are regarded as an intrinsic part of every building. In fact, Norway's National Planning and Building Act plays an important role in guiding municipalities when it comes to safeguarding nature. For instance, one of the key targets of the act highlights the importance of integrating biodiversity into all developments and planning processes (Bertelsmann Stiftung 2019).

Many of the built areas in Norway are found in the lowlands or along the coast of fjords which are home to rich natural habitats (Figure 1.14). These green areas face a constant danger of destruction due to ongoing development pressure. Therefore, some innovative ideas which aim to prevent development from greatly compromising the natural landscape have been introduced. For instance, man-made habitats, which include green roofs and walls, have been used as biotopes for species in developed areas. In parallel, many towns have started to restore natural habitats through urban planning. For instance, culverted rivers and streams have been reopened to become a part of urban areas.

Figure 1.14 Many of the built areas in Norway are found in the lowlands or along the coast of fjords, which is home to rich natural habitats and therefore the subject of intense conservation.

The capital, Oslo, is known for having the highest species diversity compared to any other municipality in Norway. Nature is very much a part of the city, as open public spaces include calcareous islands, coastlines and meadows with a number of floral species. Maintaining ecosystems and biodiversity is therefore the capital's main concern as the city is experiencing a rapid population growth (Oppla 2019). Norway's initiatives demonstrate that when a country values its natural habitat and adapts a mind-set that regards biodiversity as a priority, it becomes part of every planning aspect and legacy.

1.5 The Archetype of Sustainable Preservation

Established in 1872, Yellowstone Park was the world's first national park and nature reserve. It stretches across the northwest corner of Wyoming, and spreads into parts of Montana and Idaho in the United States. The park was created by President Ulysses S. Grant after geologist Ferdinand V. Hayden, who surveyed the lands, had showed the authorities in Washington how beautiful the site was and argued why it needed to be saved. It covers up to 890,308 hectares (2.2 million acres) and welcomes up to 4.1 million visitors yearly (Yogerst 2019) (Figure 1.15).

Yellowstone's fauna and flora includes 67 species of mammals, 285 species of birds, 16 species of fish, more than seven aquatic invasive species, five species of amphibians, six species of reptiles and two threatened species, which are the Canada lynx and the grizzly bear. The park's flora includes nine species of conifers, more than 80 percent of the forest being lodgepole pine, more than a thousand species of native flowering species, 225 species of invasive plants and 185 species of lichens (Yogerst 2019).

Many of the species would have been extinct by now if it was not for the vision of a geologist and the determination of a president to preserve the place. The act is known to have set the tone for the creation of many similar nature reserves around the world. Such places are highly important in time of ever-increasing human encroachment on nature. Perhaps the most threatened area in the world is the Brazilian Amazon's burial forest which is subject to clearance to make room for farming often with government backing. More than a tourist attraction, Yellowstone is a statement that nature thrives when it is left alone and that we need to section more similar areas.

1.6 Final Thoughts

Faced with contemporary ongoing environmental, economic and social challenges, cities need to constantly adapt and be resilient. Planners must keep these challenges in mind while considering the future to make communities functional and livable. In addition, since the planet's resources are finite, planning cities to meet society's current needs without sacrificing the needs of future generations has to be a leading mind-set. It must be done in an equitable manner respectful of the socio-cultural conditions of a given place. Working with the key pillars of sustainability and understanding their interrelationships, as well as the four sustainable systems' principles should be paramount to any process and goal.

Figure 1.15 Yellowstone Park covers up to 890,308 hectares (2.2 million acres) and welcomes up to 4.1 million visitors yearly.

References

Amadeo, K. (2020). Hurricane Katrina facts, damage, and costs. *The Balance*. Retrieved July 5, 2023, from www.thebalance.com/hurricane-katrina-facts-damage-and-economic-effects-3306023

Ashik, F. R., Rahman, M. H. and Kamruzzaman, M. (2022). Investigating the impacts of transit-oriented development on transport-related CO2 emissions. *Transportation Research Part D: Transport and Environment* 105: 103227. Retrieved June 22, 2023, from www.sciencedirect.com/science/article/abs/pii/S1361920922000578

Bertelsmann Stiftung (2019). Norway. *Sustainable Governance Indicators*. Retrieved June 22, 2023, from www.sgi-network.org/2017/Norway/Environmental_Policies

Borunda, A. (2018). See how a warmer world primed California for large fires. *National Geographic*. Retrieved June 22, 2023, from www.nationalgeographic.com/environment/2018/11/climate-change-california-wildfire/

Carneiro, F., Sergio, M., Corban, C., Ehrlich, D., Florczyk, A., Kemper, T., Maffenini, L., Melchiorri, M., Pesaresi, M., Schiavina, M. and Tommasi, P. (2019). *Atlas of the Human Planet 2019*. Publications Office of the European Union. Luxembourg.

FEMA (2015). Hurricane Katrina overview. Retrieved June 22, 2023, from www.fema.gov/hurricane-katrina-overview

Gibbens, S. (2019). Hurricane Katrina, explained. *National Geographic*. Retrieved June 22, 2023, from www.nationalgeographic.com/environment/natural-disasters/reference/hurricane-katrina/

Harada, Y. and Whitlow, T. (2020). Urban rooftop agriculture: challenges to science. *Frontiers in Sustainable Food Systems* 4(76): 1–8.

Kumar, P. (2021). Climate change and cities: challenges ahead. *Frontiers in Sustainable Cities* 3(645613): 1–8.

Oppla (2019). Oslo biodivercity: maintaining ecosystem services in a rapidly developing but biodiversity rich city. Retrieved June 22, 2023, from https://oppla.eu/casestudy/19231

Palanivel, T. (2017). Rapid urbanisation: opportunities and challenges to improve the well-being of societies. United Nations Development Programme. Retrieved June 22, 2023, from https://hdr.undp.org/content/rapid-urbanisation-opportunities-and-challenges-improve-well-being-societies

Ruel, M. (2020). Growing cities, growing food insecurity: how to protect the poor during rapid urbanization. Center for Strategic and International Studies. Retrieved June 22, 2023, from www.csis.org/analysis/growing-cities-growing-food-insecurity-how-protect-poor-during-rapid-urbanization

Schoennagel, T., Balch, J. K., Dennison, P. E., Harvey, B. J., Krawchuk, M. A., Mietkiewicz, N., Morgan, P., Moritz, M. A., Rasker, R., Turner, M. G. and Whitlock, C. (2017). Adapt to more wildfire in western North American forests as climate changes. *Proceedings of the National Academy of Sciences of the United States of America* 114(18): 4582–4590. Retrieved June 22, 2023, from https://doi.org/10.1073/pnas.1617464114

UN (United Nations) (2016). Specifications for the application of the United Nations framework classification for fossil energy and mineral reserves and resources 2009 to renewable energy resources. In *United Nations Framework Classification for Fossil Energy and Mineral Reserves and Resources 2009 (UNFC-2009)*, pp. 1–21. United Nations. New York.

UN (United Nations) (2022). United Nations Conference on the Environment, Stockholm 1972. Retrieved June 22, 2023, from www.un.org/en/conferences/environment/stockholm1972

United States Environmental Protection Agency (2022). Reduce urban heat island effect. Retrieved June 22, 2023, from www.epa.gov/green-infrastructure/reduce-urban-heat-island-effect#:~:text=%22Urbanheatislands%22occurwhen,heat-relatedillnessandmortality

WCED (World Commission on Environment and Development) (1987). *Our Common Future*. Oxford University Press. Geneva.

WHO (World Health Organization) (2022). Ageing and health. Retrieved June 22, 2023, from www.who.int/news-room/fact-sheets/detail/ageing-and-health#:~:text=By2050%2Ctheworld'spopulation,2050toreach426million

Yogerst, J. (2019). Everything to know about Yellowstone National Park. *National Geographic*. Retrieved June 22, 2023, from www.nationalgeographic.com/travel/national-parks/yellowstone-national-park/

CHAPTER 2

Learning from the Past, Retooling the Future

When planning new communities, familiarity with the genesis of settlements and how their make-up informed their function is of value. In fact, a place's sustainability potential is, in large part, directly connected to its history. This chapter offers a brief overview of the historical evolution of cities, their main planning forms and its effect on contemporary urban design. The chapter also describes the proliferation of post-World War II suburbs and the consequences it begets. Lastly, strategies that can be used to ensure alternative development planning known as *Smart Growth* are presented.

2.1 The Genesis of Urban Settlements

In *The Economy of Cities*, Jane Jacobs challenges the "dogma of agricultural primacy" which argue that agriculture preceded the development of cities (Jacobs 1969). This argument explains that the very first human settlements evolved when primarily nomadic and self-sufficient groups began to cultivate grain and herd cattle, making agricultural settlements the forerunners of contemporary communities. Jacobs rather argues that agricultural intensification *followed* the creation of settlements to provide them with existential means (Jacobs 1969).

In *The City Shaped* (1991) Spiro Kostof also discusses the theories surrounding the origin of the urban settlement. He states that there is not an all-encompassing explanation and that a trading spot or a market was not always a prerequisite to or essential to the genesis of early towns. He instead argues that no singular factor can be pinpointed to the creation of the social, economic and political transformations that brought about settlements. Rather, the changes that occurred were due to the best interest of an authoritative body, and not a particular activity (Kostof 1991).

Kostof also suggests that cities developed because governing bodies would use them as an instrument to elicit their authority over their subjects. For example, the generating nucleus of the first cities in Japan, between the fourth and sixth century AD, was the palace-capitals which united various tribes (Kostof 1991). However, he agrees that processes – such as well-connected trading sites, favorable topographical conditions for defense and ecological conditions for agriculture, solid political structures, and intricate social process – are all necessary and relevant to explaining the inception of cities (Kostof 1991). One must consider these factors when explaining cities' genesis since these factors may be interdependent in some cities, meaning that many towns may only have developed to serve the purpose they burgeoned for.

Kostof identifies two distinct patterns that city development follows: "spontaneous" and "created" cities. Ville spontanée, or the *spontaneous city*, is not determined by any sort of master plan; rather, it evolves by means of the passage of time, its topographical nature and the everyday life of its citizens (Kostof 1991) (Figure 2.1). The result is an irregular, 'organic' city landscape, marked by curved streets and spontaneously evolved open spaces. This organic pattern was typical of medieval towns, like Volterra, Italy.

Stretched on a hill between the valleys of Cecina and Era, the walled Tuscan town of Volterra in Italy exemplifies this pattern. Volterra's defense walls acted as a containment mechanism, forcing growth within their confines. Narrow, winding streets cross the town's elongated shape to meet at squares. Piazza Del Priori, the main square, is framed by the town hall and the Duomo, the cathedral, serving as a main gathering place. Buildings were added to, and new ones were constructed on the footings of demolished structures (Friedman 2014). Land, naturally, was at a premium in these towns, which forced the narrowing of streets, while also permitting horse-drawn carriages to pass (Figure 2.2).

The other pattern identified by Kostof is the *created city*, which has a predetermined pattern that has been set out by an

DOI: 10.4324/9781003384687-2

Learning from the Past, Retooling the Future

Figure 2.1 Cities can be designated according to their geography and form.

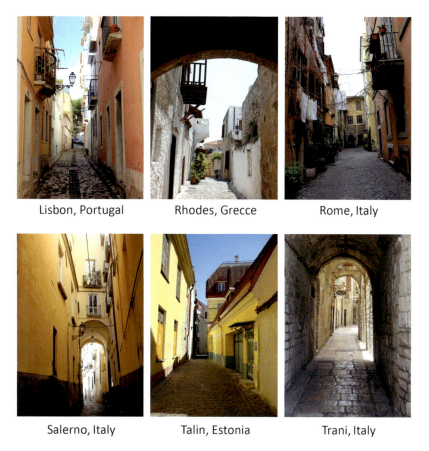

Figure 2.2 Land in organically evolved walled cities was at a premium, which forced the narrowing of streets.

Learning from the Past, Retooling the Future

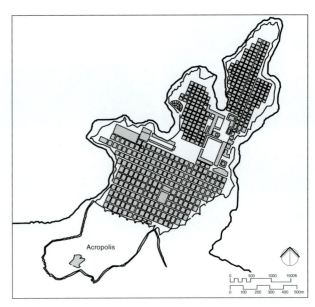

Figure 2.3 Diagram City, which tends to be a product of spectacle and utopian visions, is based on geometric rules as shown in the plans for Washington, D.C. (top) and Seaside, Florida (bottom).

overseeing authority (Kostof 1991). These places follow three typologies. The first is a *diagram city*, which tends to be a product of spectacle and utopian visions, based on very rigid geometric rules (Figure 2.3). They have rarely been built, but among those which were, one can name Brasilia, the modernist capital of Brazil. The second is a *grand manner*, which is where the planning of a city, its buildings, streets and public spaces, is constructed in a way that projects grandeur and sophistication. An example of this is Washington, D.C., where Pierre Charles L'Enfant's plan is characterized by its Baroque urban planning with wide boulevards leading to grandiose public buildings (Scott 2020). The last typology is the *grid plan*. This type of planning is very common today and typically occurs in a controlled fashion, as seen in the planning and evolution of San Francisco.

2.1.1 Greek and Roman Settlements

Ancient Greek and Roman towns depict the origin of town planning. Dating back to the early seventh century BC, the Greek city Miletus, in present-day Turkey, had a grid layout that historian Lewis Mumford (1961) traced to early Egyptian and

Figure 2.4 The Greek city Miletus, in present-day Turkey, had a grid layout with neighborhoods made up of clusters with narrow streets, squares and perimeter walls.

Chinse civilizations. Neighborhoods were made up of clusters with narrow streets, squares and perimeter walls (Figure 2.4).

Following the demise of the Hellenistic period and the rise of the Roman empire, the grid form was embedded into their settlements. Roman cities would typically have two main intersecting axes, the *Cardo Maximus* and the *Decumanus Maximus* that crossed in a square, with public buildings typically facing this space (Saddington 1972). These two main arteries were the places where commerce and residences existed side by side. For example, the Roman forum acted as the main gathering space, which was settled in between the two axes. This feature is still visible in European cities that were build on the ruins of Roman settlements.

The two streets are highly visible in Pompeii, an ancient Roman city that had a population of between 10,000 and 20,000. In 79 CE the city was covered with ash during the volcanic eruption of Mount Vesuvius. The six meters (18 feet) of ash preserved it for centuries and it now offers a near perfect glimpse of what an Ancient Roman city and life looked like. Walking along the *cardo*, the commercial hub, one can envision how life unfolded. People lived at the rear of their shops with the front opening to serve patrons (Figure 2.5). The distance between other homes and the two main streets was small. The 4.5-meter wide (15 feet) roads are paved with slabs of granite. Additionally, the streets had pedestrian crossings that cut through streets and stood 30 centimeters (11.8 inches) higher to prevent pedestrians from getting their feet dirty (Saddington 1972).

Learning from the Past, Retooling the Future

Figure 2.5 Roman cities like Pompeii typically had two main intersecting axes, the *Cardo Maximus* and the *Decumanus Maximus*, that met in a square, where public or religious buildings stood.

2.2 The Garden City and the Emergence of Suburbia

The Industrial Revolution that laid the foundation for contemporary planning was marked by a mass influx of people into cities in search of employment. Cities grew rapidly, despite the lack of appropriate infrastructure and services to support this shift to witness immense overcrowding, appalling sanitary conditions and poorly constructed homes.

These conditions planted the seeds of change for a new kind of living with a mix of attributes from both the country and the city. The shift towards this ideal was inspired by the *Arcadian myth*, which idealized the past, pastoral way of living close to nature (Schmitt 1990). Both the *Garden City movement* and the development of the mass produced suburbs, which will be discussed below, draw on this myth.

The Garden City movement was a critical node in the development of the suburb. In his book *Garden Cities of Tomorrow* (1902) British theorist Ebenezer Howard lays out a proposal for an exodus from the crowded, industrialized city into new communities. Howard proposed that the residential limit was capped at 30,000 people per town. The commerce in Garden Cities were meant to be community-owned, following socialist principles (Relph 1987). The Garden City had a concentric ring model, comprised of a central civic area, with green space around the center. The next ring was made of residences with attached gardens. Following was a Grand Avenue that separated residential from industrial areas, and at the periphery rail lines and farms were located (Figure 2.6).

Radburn, a New Jersey community that was planned by American planners Clarence Stein and Henry Wright drew on Garden City principles. The plan created a 'Garden Suburb' that foreshadowed the post-World War II mass produced suburb (Schoenauer 2000). Radburn embedded several of Howard's Garden City principles, however, did not utilize his plans verbatim and added additional features. For example, houses in Radburn were sold rather than leased, and the 'greenbelt', meant for the second ring of the Garden City, was never implemented. Radburn was characterized by elongated streets and culs-de-sac, limited housing types, and a neighborhood retail center. Like later post-World War II suburbs, Radburn was car-centric and mainly residential with single-family units (Figure 2.7).

The introduction of *Euclidean Zoning* in 1926 separated residential areas from other land use types, diminishing the benefits of mixed-use communities (Logan 1976). This led to a further separation of home, work and commerce, which has resulted in increased traveling distances and air pollution. It also eroded the social fabric of communities, with fewer opportunities to meet and an abundance of low-density single-family dwellings. The mid-twentieth century saw a massive urban sprawl that has brought with it a plethora of negative effects that have hindered sustainability.

Levittown, one of the post-World War II subdivisions, is an example of a mass-produced American suburb. Utilizing *Euclidean Zoning*, it contributed to the greater physical, and therefore ideological, separation of rural and urban areas.

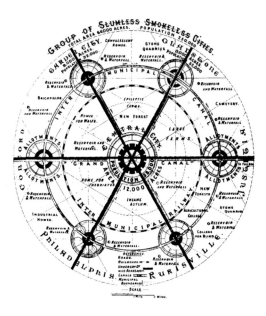

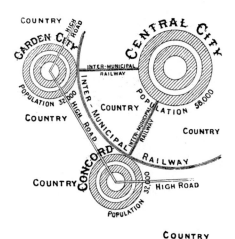

Figure 2.6 Ebenezer Howard's Garden City plan had a concentric ring model, comprised of a central civic area surrounded by green space.

Figure 2.7 Radburn, a New Jersey community that was planned by American planners Clarence Stein and Henry Wright, was characterized by elongated streets and culs-de-sac, limited housing types and neighborhood retail centers.

Learning from the Past, Retooling the Future

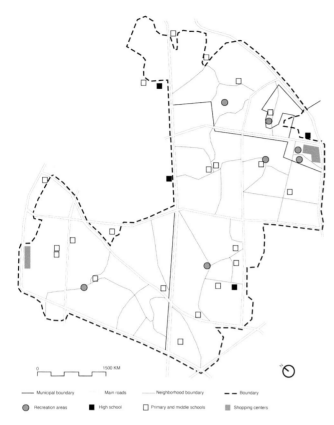

Figure 2.8 A plan of Levittown, one of the post-World War II subdivisions, an example of a mass-produced American suburb.

Levittown's carefully staged image, with uniform homes on their driveways, epitomized the suburban dream (Figure 2.8). At the time, the Federal Housing Association, which offered mortgages to Levittown's buyers, engaged in redlining: refusing mortgages to people of color (Ruff 2007). Hitherto, every rental lease and homeowner's contract in Levittown prohibited those who were "not member(s) of the Caucasian race" to maintain its appeal to the traditional white Protestant and keep the neighborhood value high (Ruff 2007).

Apart from being a method of racial exclusion, suburbia embedded unsustainable planning mechanisms for the suburbs that would proliferate for decades. The very merit of such neighborhoods was built around reliance on privately owned vehicles. Residents needed to access services and workplaces and the low density and residential nature of the suburb meant that the use of cars become essential supported by wide roads (Figure 2.9). With the proliferation of private vehicles, the need of homeowners to have a garage arose – thereby widening lots to accommodate them. The suburban dream included detached single-family homes a distance away from their next-door neighbors with manicured front and rear lawns. As a result, the cost, as well as the maintenance, of homes grew parallel to their environmental footprint.

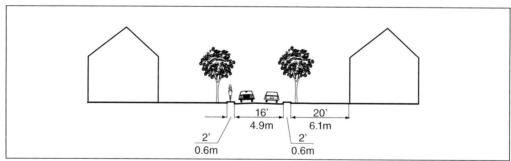

Hampstead Garden Suburb, 1905

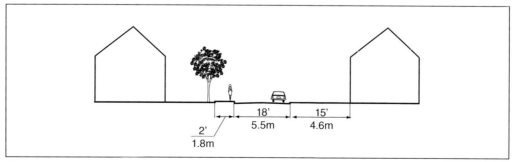

Radburn, New Jersey, 1927

Figure 2.9 The width of highways and streets across North America kept expanding to consume more land.

Learning from the Past, Retooling the Future

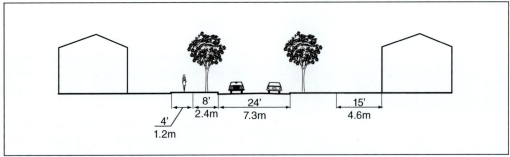
FHA Standards, 1936

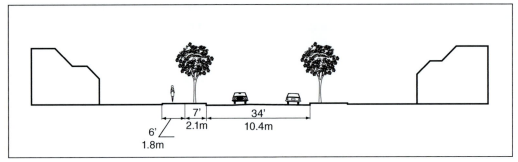
ITE Standards, 1965

Figure 2.9 (Continued)

2.3 Smart Growth Planning

The nature of low-density communities and their negative environmental consequences provides strong argument for densification. Additionally, those who live in higher-density settings with smaller dwellings tend to drive less than those in low-density places. These factors, coupled with recent trends that indicate the size of the average household is decreasing and the affordability gap between rising house prices and the slow growth of incomes, means that a call for denser, smaller-sized living must take place.

By employing *Smart Growth* principles when planning communities, a place can sustainably strengthen its economy, environmental conditions, cultural attributes and social interactions. Smart Growth encourages planning places where residents can live, work and play in the same location. It enables people to walk to the corner store, reach work by public transit, and children bike to school. To achieve these attributes, Smart Growth adopts density of at least 70 units per hectare (35 units per acre). The dwellings are typically made up of townhouses or apartments, rather than single-family homes (Figure 2.10).

When planning higher density communities, one needs to consider the wellbeing of the residents and design efficacy of day-to-day living. The creation of open spaces, such as parks, is necessary for recreation and social interaction. Homes should face these parks to reduce the negative effect that might be associated with dense areas (Figure 2.11). To ensure physical and social integration, as well as to reduce driving, communities should have mixed-land use with businesses placed at the ground floor of taller buildings. Variety of housing types will contribute to having residents across different ages and economic backgrounds. Additionally, integrating light industries will ensure live-work opportunities that will also help communities be economically autonomous and support local products and services.

Smart Growth see densification of existing areas rather than planning new ones on virgin land with amenities making up the core of a development. The center acts as a public meeting place for social gathering and, preferably, is framed by taller buildings and has a transit stop (Figure 2.12). Additionally, land should be allocated to green public spaces with walkable safe access.

2.4 The Stone Dwellings of Matera

In *Architecture without Architects: A Short Introduction to Non-Pedigreed Architecture* (1965) Bernard Rudofsky introduced readers to architecture produced not by specialists but by

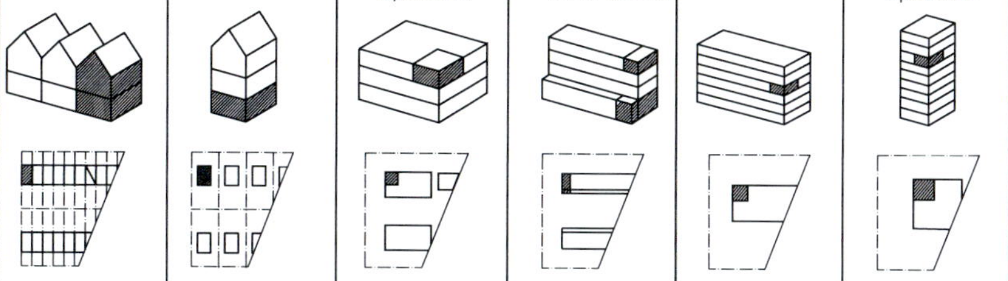

Learning from the Past, Retooling the Future

Dwelling type	Row house	Triplex	3-story walk-up apartment	Combined apartments & row houses	Slab block apartment	High rise point block apartment
Isometric						
Plot plan						
Dwelling units/acre (dwelling units/hectare)	19 (47)	21 (52)	65 (160)	84 (207)	90 (222)	120 (296)
Floor area ratio % open space	0.56 72%	0.60 80%	1.36 55%	1.92 62%	1.78 62%	2.62 87%
Unit area in square feet (unit area in square meters)	1200 (111.5)	1200 (111.5)	800 (74.3)	800 & 1200 (74.3 & 111.5)	800 (74.3)	800 (74.3)
Number of floors/unit	1 or 2	1	1	1 and 2	1	1

Figure 2.10 Smart Growth adopts density of at least 70 units per hectare (35 units per acre). The dwellings are typically made up of townhouses or apartments.

Figure 2.11 In denser communities, homes should face green open spaces to reduce the negative effect that might be associated with crowdedness.

spontaneous continuing activity of people with common heritage whose knowledge is passed on from one generation to the next. Matera in Italy's southeastern region of Basilicata is such a place and was evolved by accretion in layers. Inhabitants added to and built dwellings on top of previous ones to give the place a highly organic look. Each of the stone structures with clay tile roofs was of different size and height, yet they all seemed to correspond to the same hidden language that offered some order to the chaos. It was clearly a product of architecture without architects. What guided construction here was common sense, intuition and the skills of local master builders.

The city had a population of roughly 10,000–20,000 residents into and beyond the Middle Ages (Charles 2011). Until the eighteenth century, Matera was predominantly isolated and little affected by the outside world. A global surge in trade eventually brought Matera into the spotlight and, with that, the city saw a rise in its population which strained its food sources and led to overcrowding. From then until the mid-twentieth century, Matera became a hotbed of disease and food shortages until the Italian government intervened to fix the city's problems by forcefully abandoning the cave dwelling (Figure 2.13).

Learning from the Past, Retooling the Future

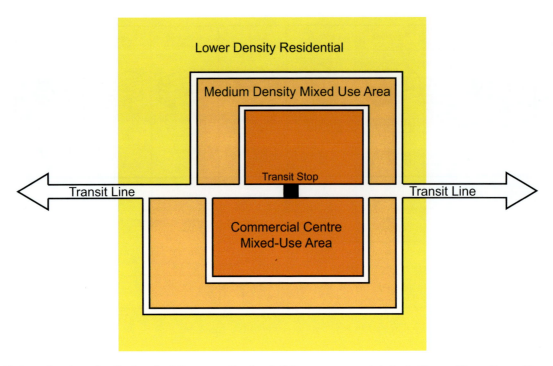

Figure 2.12 Smart Growth see densification of existing areas rather than building new ones on virgin land with amenities making up the core of a development surrounded by residences.

Figure 2.13 The Sassi, a cave dwelling in Matera, Italy.

The place seems to have grown almost naturally out of the mountains. In fact, curved into it. The only building material was the local Tufa limestone harvested from the curving of homes into the cliff. The Sassi stone cliff dwellings are the city's hallmark, which in 1996 earned the place a UNESCO World Heritage Site recognition. A typical cave had a kitchen, bed area and even a small stable. With cisterns built under the Sassi, the inhabitants collected rainwater for used in the dry summer season.

Matera had classic marks of traditional sustainable living. It followed several principles: integration of natural geography and water systems; provide a comfortable, long-lasting habitation; and it grew its own food. It was all done naturally without central planning and regulations to create a highly sustainable existence.

2.5 Adaptable Narrow Living in Bruges

Four- and five-story structures with brick, stone and stucco facades and tall, narrow windows are set back from the water in Bruges, Belgium. Occasionally, in between wider homes stand very narrow ones, about 3 meters (10 feet) wide (Figure 2.14). The buildings, which were built in the sixteenth and seventeenth centuries, seems to have weathered the ages well. As buildings in walled cities like Bruges were taxed according to their width, it was in the best interests of builders to restrict the size of the front (Friedman 2010). Area could only be gained by increasing the depth and, therefore, plots and structures grew long and narrow.

As for the interior, the ground floor had a few steps and was entered through a vestibule. The front parlor was the first room one would enter. Behind the parlor was the dining room, followed by the kitchen, with a view of the backyard. Underneath the ground floor was, typically, a cellar. The second floor, with high ceilings, contained two additional parlors, the front one for men, and the one at the back for women. The third floor was occupied by master and children's bedrooms. Finally, the attic was occupied by servants.

These buildings were the subject of constant adaptations. The narrow width spared the need to have interior support walls since wooden joists spanned from one end wall to the next. The position of the stairs was another contributor that simplified adaptability. Located parallel to the side walls, they didn't stand in the way of changes. Having a skylight on top of the stairs created a well of natural light that brightened the heart of each floor. The bathrooms were placed in the middle of each storey, making it unnecessary to be relocated. Pipes and plumbing fixtures nonetheless were introduced with time. Finally, both front and rear facades had plenty of windows to illuminate the rooms.

As contemporary city planners are contemplating halting urban sprawl, the narrow houses of Bruges demonstrate that width need not to be a barrier to creativity and that good sustainable design can stand the test of time.

Figure 2.14 Between the wider homes in Bruges, Belgium, there are very narrow ones, about three meters (ten feet) wide, four- and five-story tall structures with brick, stone and stucco facades.

2.6 Final Thoughts

Cities' built environments, in large part, reflect their ability to be sustainable. The planning principles of ancient cities and contemporary ones provide ideas that one can utilize for future development. Recognizing a place's form and how it affects its sustainability is paramount. One must utilize densification principles to create walkable and public transit-centric places that improve citizens' wellbeing and the environment. Smart Growth strategies would ensure the creation of places where citizens can comfortably work, live and play while avoiding urban sprawl.

References

Charles, R. W. (2011). Lessons from Italy's Matera, the sustainable city of stone. *The Atlantic*. Retrieved June 22, 2023, from www.theatlantic.com/international/archive/2011/09/lessons-from-italys-matera-the-sustainable-city-of-stone/244622/

Friedman, A. (2010). *Narrow Houses: New Directions in Efficient Design*. Princeton Architectural Press. New York.

Friedman, A. (2014). *Planning Small and Mid-Sized Towns: Designing and Retrofitting for Sustainability*. Routledge. London.

Howard, E. (1902). *Garden Cities of Tomorrow* [original 1898 title: *Tomorrow: A Peaceful Path to Real Reform*]. Swan Sonnenschein & Co. London.

Jacobs, J. (1969). *The Economy of Cities*. Random House. New York.

Kostof, S. (1991). *The City Shaped: Urban Patterns and Meaning Throughout History*. Thames & Hudson. London.

Logan, T. (1976). The Americanization of German zoning. *Journal of the American Institute of Planners* 42(4): 377–385.

Mumford, L. (1961). *The City in History: Its Origins, Its Transformations, and its Prospects*. Harcourt. New York.

Relph, E. (1987). The invention of modern town planning: 1890–1940. In *The Modern Urban Landscape*, pp. 49–75. The Johns Hopkins University Press. Baltimore.

Rudofsky, B. (1965). *Architecture without Architects*. Doubleday & Company, Inc. New York.

Ruff, J. (2007). For sale: the American dream. *American History*, 29–42. Retrieved July 3, 2023, from www.bartleby.com/essay/For-Sale-The-American-Dream-Analysis-FJAJJ5WGUFV

Saddington, D. B. (1972). The city in classical antiquity. *Akroterion* 17: 14–22. Retrieved June 22, 2023, from https://hdl.handle.net/10520/AJA03031896_147

Schmitt, P. J. (1990). *Back to Nature: The Arcadian Myth in Urban America*. The Johns Hopkins University Press. Baltimore.

Schoenauer, N. (2000). *6,000 Years of Housing*. W. W. Norton. New York.

Scott, J. C. (2020). The high modernist city: an experiment and a critique. In *Seeing Like a State*, pp. 103–146. Yale University Press. London.

CHAPTER 3
Denser Mixed-Use Communities

Important aspects of planning sustainable cities lie in the choice of a place's density and land use. This chapter analyzes the history of zoning and the negative effects that segregating planning according to land uses have had on contemporary urban and suburban places. It lays out a counterargument in favor of higher density living that merge the benefits of low density, such as open space and privacy, without the associated negative effects of high cost and excessive driving. The chapter introduces key density indexes, types of dwellings that can be included in denser sustainable development and discusses how to generate relevant urban forms. Lastly, the chapter outlines how higher density will benefit the social, cultural and environmental make-up.

3.1 The Contemporary History of Zoning

Zoning is the process of dividing a city, town or borough into different functional uses. Each area, called a *zone*, has a designated set of rules that planners and developers, among others, must abide by when using the land. As listed in Figure 3.1, there are variety of measures by which governments exercise control over land in their jurisdictions.

Zoning is a relatively new invention. It was institutionalized in the United States in 1926 following the *Euclid v. Ambler* decision (*Euclid v. Ambler* 1926) which gave way to what is known as *Euclidean Zoning* – separating large, exclusively residential areas from all other forms of land use. It had negative ramifications on contemporary urban and especially suburban areas – increasing the separation between home and work, and, subsequently, the distance traveled to and from the latter. It has also further divided those who live in urban and suburban spaces along socio-economic and racial lines.

The first zoning regulations in North America attempted to limit the spread of commercial and industrial areas into

neighborhoods. Through height limitations and minimum setback requirements within sections of the city, early zoning rules contributed substantially to determining the character of neighborhoods. The most far-reaching zoning control, and the continent's first comprehensive zoning law at the beginning of the twentieth century, was drafted in 1916 by the Heights of Buildings Commission of New York City. An appeal to the residents of New York City drafted by the commission is shown in Figure 3.2. Reform activists joined members of the commission, most of whom were real estate investors, in the interests of saving their city from the detrimental impact of the Manhattan skyscraper.

The institutionalization of suburban zoning for single-family homes instead of multi-family units was utilized among others as a lucrative tactic to extract taxes. Embedding commercial activities such as corner stores, offices or dry cleaners, was barred due to the fear that it would attract out-of-area visitors and generate noise. Municipalities and citizens also believed that these commercial spaces would lower the economic value of homes.

The judges in the *Euclid v. Ambler* case argued that single-family zoning policies were deemed essential to protecting the American home. This idea was backed by the notion that the nuclear family was the natural order, thereby supporting an orderly nation (Frisch 2002). Those in favor of single-family zoning laws saw multi-family housing, in the form of duplexes, apartments or communal housing, as sites of immoral activity. The supreme court ruled that the apartment house is a "mere parasite" favoring people with indulgent lifestyles (Frisch 2002). These tenants were known as 'households': the immoral antithesis of the family.

As touched on above, zoning was founded upon discriminatory principles. Contemporarily, zoning continues to be a contentious practice, as it tends to divide places by class and racial barriers depending on the type of buildings allotted to that

Denser Mixed-Use Communities

Type	Description	Application	Enforcement
Land Subdivision Control	• Regulate the development of vacant or undeveloped areas • Create a high-quality physical environment • Ensure voicing of concerns of interested parties	Applied to new deveopments	Enforced by municipality
Building Code	• Protection of public health, safety, and property • Establishment of minimum construction standards	University applied in a jurisdiction (town, city, province)	Enforced by local buildings departments
Zoning Ordinances	• Regulate land usage and building construction • Ensure public access to light, air, and open space • Protection and stability of property values • Protection against aesthetic nuisances	Applied over an entire municipality (not site specific)	Enforced by city, town, or village municipalities
Deed Restrictions	• Regulate land usage and building construction • Regulate visual environment and building form • Protection and stability of property values • Protection against aesthetic nuisances	Applied on an individual lot basis	Privately imposed by developer/ neighbourhood association
Design Review	• Monitor the overall design process • Advise and approve architectural design based on the judgement of individual board members	Applied on an individual lot basis	Enforced by authority of a review board
Design Guidelines	• Establishment of minimum construction standards • Regulate land usage and building construction • Protection and stability of property values • Protection against aesthetic nuisances • Regulate visual environment and building form	Not necessarily applied to a specific site (can be theoretical and generically based)	Not enforceable or legally binding

Figure 3.1 Measures by which governments exercise control over land use in their jurisdictions.

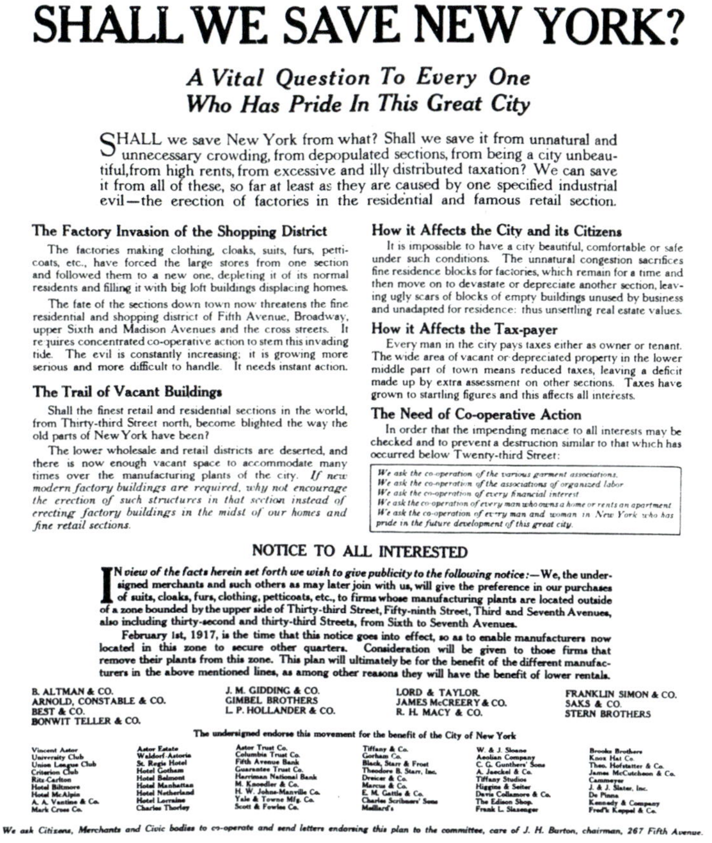

SHALL WE SAVE NEW YORK?

A Vital Question To Every One Who Has Pride In This Great City

SHALL we save New York from what? Shall we save it from unnatural and unnecessary crowding, from depopulated sections, from being a city unbeautiful, from high rents, from excessive and illy distributed taxation? We can save it from all of these, so far at least as they are caused by one specified industrial evil—the erection of factories in the residential and famous retail section.

The Factory Invasion of the Shopping District

The factories making clothing, cloaks, suits, furs, petticoats, etc., have forced the large stores from one section and followed them to a new one, depleting it of its normal residents and filling it with big loft buildings displacing homes.

The fate of the sections down town now threatens the fine residential and shopping district of Fifth Avenue, Broadway, upper Sixth and Madison Avenues and the cross streets. It requires concentrated co-operative action to stem this invading tide. The evil is constantly increasing; it is growing more serious and more difficult to handle. It needs instant action.

The Trail of Vacant Buildings

Shall the finest retail and residential sections in the world, from Thirty-third Street north, become blighted the way the old parts of New York have been?

The lower wholesale and retail districts are deserted, and there is now enough vacant space to accommodate many times over the manufacturing plants of the city. *If new modern factory buildings are required, why not encourage the erection of such structures in that section instead of erecting factory buildings in the midst of our homes and fine retail sections.*

How it Affects the City and its Citizens

It is impossible to have a city beautiful, comfortable or safe under such conditions. The unnatural congestion sacrifices fine residence blocks for factories, which remain for a time and then move on to devastate or depreciate another section, leaving ugly scars of blocks of empty buildings unused by business and unadapted for residence: thus unsettling real estate values.

How it Affects the Tax-payer

Every man in the city pays taxes either as owner or tenant. The wide area of vacant or depreciated property in the lower middle part of town means reduced taxes, leaving a deficit made up by extra assessment on other sections. Taxes have grown to startling figures and this affects all interests.

The Need of Co-operative Action

In order that the impending menace to all interests may be checked and to prevent a destruction similar to that which has occurred below Twenty-third Street:

We ask the co-operation of the various garment associations.
We ask the co-operation of the associations of organized labor
We ask the co-operation of every financial interest
We ask the co-operation of every man who owns a home or rents an apartment
We ask the co-operation of every man and woman in New York who has pride in the future development of this great city.

NOTICE TO ALL INTERESTED

IN *view of the facts herein set forth we wish to give publicity to the following notice:*—We, the undersigned merchants and such others as may later join with us, will give the preference in our purchases of suits, cloaks, furs, clothing, petticoats, etc., to firms whose manufacturing plants are located outside of a zone bounded by the upper side of Thirty-third Street, Fifty-ninth Street, Third and Seventh Avenues, also including thirty-second and thirty-third Streets, from Sixth to Seventh Avenues.

February 1st, 1917, is the time that this notice goes into effect, so as to enable manufacturers now located in this zone to secure other quarters. Consideration will be given to those firms that remove their plants from this zone. This plan will ultimately be for the benefit of the different manufacturers in the above mentioned lines, as among other reasons they will have the benefit of lower rentals.

B. ALTMAN & CO.
ARNOLD, CONSTABLE & CO.
BEST & CO.
BONWIT TELLER & CO.
J. M. GIDDING & CO.
GIMBEL BROTHERS
L. P. HOLLANDER & CO.
LORD & TAYLOR
JAMES McCREERY & CO.
R. H. MACY & CO.
FRANKLIN SIMON & CO.
SAKS & CO.
STERN BROTHERS

The undersigned endorse this movement for the benefit of the City of New York

Vincent Astor
University Club
Union League Club
Criterion Club
Ritz-Carlton
Hotel Biltmore
Hotel McAlpin
A. A. Vantine & Co.
Mark Cross Co.
Astor Estate
Waldorf-Astoria
St. Regis Hotel
Hotel Gotham
Hotel Belmont
Hotel Manhattan
Hotel Netherland
Hotel Lorraine
Charles Thorley
Astor Trust Co.
Columbia Trust Co.
Fifth Avenue Bank
Guarantee Trust Co.
Harriman National Bank
M. Knoedler & Co.
H. W. Johns-Manville Co.
Yale & Towne Mfg. Co.
Scott & Fowles Co.
Tiffany & Co.
Gorham Co.
Black, Starr & Frost
Theodore B. Starr, Inc.
Dreicer & Co.
Marcus & Co.
E. M. Gattle & Co.
Charles Scribners' Sons
Maillard's
W. & J. Sloane
Aeolian Company
C. G. Gunthers' Sons
A. Jaeckel & Co.
Tiffany Studios
Higgins & Seiter
Davis Collamore & Co.
The Edison Shop.
Frank L. Slazenger
Brooks Brothers
Knox Hat Co.
Theo. Hofstatter & Co.
James McCutcheon & Co.
Cammeyer
J. & J. Slater, Inc.
De Pinna
Kennedy & Company
Fred'k Keppel & Co.

We ask Citizens, Merchants and Civic bodies to co-operate and send letters endorsing this plan to the committee, care of J. H. Burton, chairman, 267 Fifth Avenue.

Figure 3.2 An appeal to the residents of New York City drafted by the Heights of Buildings Commission of New York City.

area. Zoning can be used to deter poorer residents from moving into wealthier neighborhoods, therefore unable to reap the benefits of the latter, such as better transit, services and education. These wealthier communities block multi-family housing from being built, preventing lower-income folks from obtaining access to these dwellings. An example of these discriminatory practices is in San Francisco where, in 2021, 82 percent of the land in the Bay Area was allocated to single-family zoning. Some towns, like Atherton, California, do not allow any multi-family housing in their boundary (Chakraborty and Demsas 2021). Additionally, by usually disallowing mixed-use development, such as residential buildings set atop small businesses, zoning restricts crucial economic activity as well as social interactions among residents.

3.2 Key Density Indexes

To begin a discussion on density, one must consider key indexes that help measure the latter. As the definition of *urban density* may vary depending on locations and varying cultures, this section offers common density indexes of communities. Density indexes also help determine what a high- or low-density place may look like and finding a density that balances sustainability and liveability.

Low and high are two distinct designations of densities in planning. *Low density* is typically 17 units per hectare (7 units per acre). The large size of lots in them contributes to high land and infrastructure costs per unit and leads to suburban sprawl and car dependency. On the other hand, *high density*, typical of populous urban areas, tends to be around 77.5 units per hectare (35 units per acre). This density may be unpopular with some who wish for more private, family-oriented living with ample public green spaces (Figure 3.3).

To find a common medium between the two, the author suggests an in-between density that veers toward the high-density side of the spectrum. This community combines aspects of both densities, such as having minimal widths separating homes typical of higher-density areas and including central open green spaces. The desired sustainable development would have a density of around 9 units per hectare (22 units per acre), including private parking and rear yards.

Denser Mixed-Use Communities

	Old historic centres	High density	Low density	Suburban
Number of dwelling per hectacre	475	155	21	8
Number of residents per hectacre	2000	280	42	17
Average household size	4	1.8	2	2.2
Average dwelling area per occupant, m²/sq.ft	10/110	60/650	60/650	60/650
Floor to area ratio	200%	200%	25%	20%

Figure 3.3 Examples of building types and their respective densities.

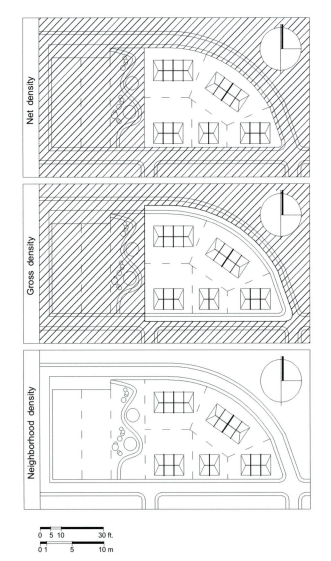

Figure 3.4 Net, gross and neighborhood density indexes.

Another key density index is *gross density*. It divides the number of dwellings by the development's land – this land includes streets and parks. Another index is the *floor-area ratio*. This index measures how efficiently a lot is used by dividing a building's habitable enclosed floor space on every floor of a structure by its lot area. For example, a skyscraper in a massive urban center will have a much higher floor-area ratio than a suburban shopping strip, despite having a similar footprint (Figure 3.4).

Just as a neighborhood density can be measured by the number of dwelling units per area, densities can also be measured by the number of people who reside in a given area. In a common North American suburb, the average density is around 1,350 people per square kilometer (3,500 per square mile). Additionally, in a larger, denser area such as Montreal, Canada, there will be around 3,900 people per square kilometer (10,000 per square mile) – three times that of a suburban place. In comparison, a large metropolitan area, such as Tokyo, Japan will have around 39,000 people per square kilometer (100,000 per square mile). A place with especially high density in Shanghai, China, is described below.

3.3 Sustainable Urban Densities and Mixed Land Uses

As noted above, to lower a place's footprint a recommended density for residential development is around 44 to 70 units per hectare (22 to 35 units per acre). This allows the combination of dense housing that includes sought-after features of the low-density suburban home, such as private parking and a backyard for private gatherings and for children to play. This design ensures that higher-density communities remain attractive and livable.

Denser Mixed-Use Communities

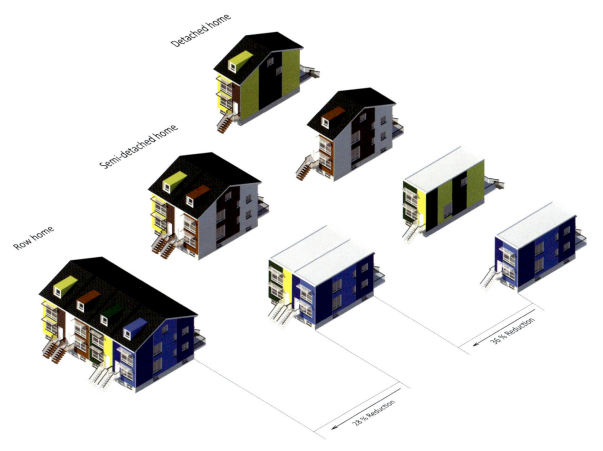

Figure 3.5 By joining units and decreasing the exposed wall area, energy consumption for heating and cooling can be reduced by 64 percent in townhouses.

Economists argue that some consumers often begin their search for a home with the "suburban ideal" in mind (Aurand 2010). Therefore, townhouses act as a middle ground between the suburban home and the apartment. To plan for this density, housing units should be clustered to lessen unused space and create a variety of building types for mixed households. By joining units and decreasing the exposed wall area, energy consumption for heating and cooling can be reduces by 64 percent in townhomes (Figure 3.5). This will also contribute to creating a diverse social neighborhood dynamic and allow for higher number of units making the area more affordable (Aurand 2010).

When designing townhouses, it is important to include front or back yards to increase curb appeal and create private space for residents to enjoy. Additionally, designing high-density housing, such as townhouses, should include adjacent and clearly demarcated communal open spaces. Jacobs (1961) states that clear demarcation between public and private spaces, with proper landscaping around them, is essential within higher-density development. This creates a public meeting space between neighbors to ensure a community feel (Figure 3.6). The larger number of residents in higher density neighborhoods can also ensure that commerce, places of employment, public transit and schools will be viable.

Figure 3.6 Accessible public spaces in higher-density development creates meeting spaces that foster a sense of community.

Denser Mixed-Use Communities

Figure 3.7 Taller buildings should be placed along main roads with public transit lines for easy access to commerce and amenities.

Figure 3.8 Small commercial centers should be integrated into areas with low-rise residences to lessens the need of residents to commute to the city center to access amenities.

To ensure livability and human scale of high-density environments taller buildings should be placed in commercial areas and utilize a higher density with a minimum of 70 units per hectare (35 units per acre) to concentrate activities in one location. Taller buildings should also be placed along main roads where public transit lines are situated (Figure 3.7).

Lower-rise residences should be located on the periphery of the city's center. These areas should have a lower density of 44 units per hectare (22 units per acre) for both livable and sustainable urban density. Although the main commercial center should remain in the middle with wider roads and taller buildings, stores should still be integrated into areas with low-rise residences. This promotes the creation of mixed-use communities and lessens the need for residents to commute to the city center to access amenities. People who live in these neighborhoods, however, should be able to easily access the center by bike, walking or public transit (Figure 3.8).

When situating buildings, planners can consider that roads may not be used exclusively by cars. Burden (2001) suggests that streets are also a place of people's gathering and should be safe for children to play. Having narrower roads and shorter blocks will also slow traffic. Additionally, avoiding wide roads decreases frequent and costly servicing, which, in turn, benefit each resident financially.

In contemporary planning, the advantages of mixing land uses are many. For instance, locating different dwelling types near institutions makes reaching them on foot easier. Mixing a variety of housing types and amenities encourages social diversity as well. A neighborhood's density, maximized through mixed land use, affects its economy, its social fabric, and as a result increases its potential to become sustainable. Having stores, workplaces and schools in the same location ensures walkability. Mammen and Iancovich (2015) suggest that children who walk or ride to school have higher academic performance with increased attentiveness, and enhanced numerical, verbal and reasoning abilities.

Designing for walkability has many health benefits. Baobeid et al. (2021) state that those in walkable neighborhoods have lower rates of obesity, diabetes and cardiovascular diseases. Additionally, walking and biking help build and maintain social skills and fitness (Baobeid et al. 2021) (Figure 3.9).

The integration of various establishments, such as stores, cafes, public open spaces and community centers, will lead to opportunity for more social interactions. Additionally, having mixed types of dwelling brings together people of different ages and socio-economic backgrounds to foster a more cohesive and open community.

3.4 Living Above the Store in Saint-Valery-sur-Somme

In Saint-Valery-sur-Somme, population 2,700, in France, the main street looks similar to the ones one finds in the heart of Europe's small old towns (Figure 3.10). The place's genesis is the remains of an old Roman settlement which drew settlers and grew by accretion. In the densely populated town, citizens lived above their businesses, be it a workshop or a store (Hohenberg 2004). Things have not changed much since. Merchants are closing their businesses for the mid-day break and heading to their apartment above the store. The place can teach lesson on how contemporary cities can be planned.

Denser Mixed-Use Communities

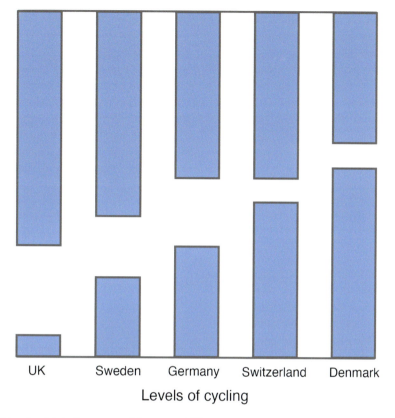

Figure 3.9 Cycling helps build and maintain fitness, especially among children.

Figure 3.10 In Saint-Valery-sur-Somme, France, some live above their shops.

Denser Mixed-Use Communities

North America has undergone fundamental changes that make it necessary to re-evaluate archaic bylaws. Driven by the information revolution, homes can be places for more than one activity. Zoom and email have enabled people to run a business from home without anyone noticing. Professionals such as translators, illustrators and bookkeepers are running their businesses from the heart of many suburban neighborhoods. But according to current bylaws, it's hard to determine whether their activities are legal. One hopes that municipal legislators will change their minds and that some stores will pop up on the lower level of homes in denser new residential development and offices in others.

3.5 An Upper Neighborhood in Vancouver

In the evolution of commerce, location always played a key role in a place's success. From having a store under or in front of a residence on a busy street, over the past half-century, commercial development saw the birth of the shopping strip, the shopping mall, and in recent years the "big box" retail concept. Whereas the mall provides an enclosed space for people to stroll and meet, the big box store has turned shopping into a highly efficient and profitable venture. The cheaply built, two-story-tall stores resemble utilitarian warehouses simple in form and devoid of style. Seen from above, a vast expanse of roofs and parking dominate the landscape. Building a residential floor above the stores is often prohibited. Local zoning ensures that residential and commercial uses won't mix. When asked why not build more floors on top, public officials and developers respond that no one would want to live there anyway.

The Rise is a city block size contemporary 56,206 square meter (605,000 square foot) mixed-use complex near downtown Vancouver, Canada. The 92 apartments are built on top of large retailers such as Home Depot, Winners, HomeSense, Save-On-Foods and other small retailers, offering a convenient shopping experience for residents and visitors. When one stands on the residential level atop the stores it feels like being in the heart of a neighborhood. Townhomes surround an 1,858 square meter (20,000 square foot) green roof and community garden, to form a pleasant courtyard. Designed by Nigel Baldwin Architects Ltd. with Integral Group, the building consumes 31 percent less energy, 67 percent less potable water and 52 percent lower greenhouse gas emissions than the Model National Energy Code of Canada for Buildings (The Rise n.d.) (Figure 3.11).

The design got the city's go ahead once the developer allocated more area to the dwelling units instead of retail. The Rise demonstrates that large-scale commerce and housing can be mixed to the benefit of both. At times, being creative and challenging convention is necessary.

3.6 High Density Living in Shanghai

The Ludi Xiangianaqino Chang on the outskirts of Shanghai was built as a residential showpiece to demonstrate China's resettlement initiative of those who had traded their rural home or land for an apartment. From a rooftop of a twenty-story tower one can spot air conditioning units affixed to most apartments' exterior walls. There were 30 towers in an area of approximately 16.2 hectares (40 acres). With eight units per floor, the project had about 4,000 apartments. If three people on average reside in each apartment, the project's population count stood at 12,000 people, the size of a small Canadian town (Figure 3.12).

Figure 3.11 In The Rise, a city block size mixed-use complex in Vancouver, Canada, homes are built above large "big box" stores.

Denser Mixed-Use Communities

Figure 3.12 The high-density Ludi Xiangianaqino Chang project on the outskirts of Shanghai demonstrates China's resettlement initiative.

Rural-to-urban migration within China became an important initiative in the mid-1980s. Prior to that, more than 80 percent of the Chinese population lived in the countryside under China's Communist Party rule. Economic reforms started in the late 1970s, and by the mid-1980s, rural underemployment became a serious concern as agricultural productivity had greatly increased. Rural-to-urban migration was at first quite limited, as it was heavily restricted by the government who wanted to keep people in the countryside. The authority eventually relented to the demand for unskilled labor in the limited Special Economic Zones. By the mid to late 1990s, economic activities grew significantly in cities, and it is therefore not surprising that China's urban areas are very densely populated (Li 2011).

China's population density is roughly 150.51 people per square kilometer (58 people per square mile), which is quite high relative to other countries such as Mexico and South Africa, with population densities of 65.64 and 48.65 people per square kilometer (25.3 and 18.7 people per square mile) respectively (Li 2011).

The Ludi Xiangianaqino Chang project demonstrates how can nations need to learn to leave within their means and that urban sprawl has many negative ramifications to society and the environment to be avoided.

3.7 Final Thoughts

Denser mixed-use neighborhoods are essential to sustainable planning. Denser dwellings, such as townhouses, allow private backyards while being environmentally friendly. They can be incorporated in an urban form that is mixed-use, to enable residents to easily walk or bike to amenities. By concentrating high-density buildings in a city center and maintaining high to middle density, those on the periphery will still benefit from being away from the bustle of the central city, while able to easily access it via walking, biking and public transit.

References

Aurand, A. (2010). Density, housing types and mixed land use: smart tools for affordable housing? *Urban Studies* 47(5): 1015–1036. Retrieved June 23, 2023, from https://journals.sagepub.com/doi/pdf/10.1177/0042098009353076

Baobeid, A., Koç, M. and Al-Ghamdi, S. G. (2021). Walkability and its relationships with health, sustainability, and livability: elements of physical environment and evaluation frameworks. *Frontiers in Built Environment* 7(721218): 1–17. Retrieved June 23, 2023, from www.frontiersin.org/articles/10.3389/fbuil.2021.721218/full

Burden, D. (2001). Building communities with transportation. *Transportation Research Project*, 1773(1). Retrieved June 23, 2023, from https://journals.sagepub.com/doi/abs/10.3141/1773-02

Chakraborty, R. and Demsas, J. (2021). How the US made affordable homes illegal. *Vox*. Retrieved June 23, 2023, from www.vox.com/videos/2021/8/17/22628750/how-the-us-made-affordable-homes-illegal

Euclid v. Ambler, 272 U.S. 365 (1926). *Justia Law*. Retrieved June 23, 2023, from https://supreme.justia.com/cases/federal/us/272/365/

Frisch, M. (2002). Planning as a heterosexist project. *Journal of Planning Education and Research* 21(3): 254–266. Retrieved June 23, 2023, from www.researchgate.net/publication/238430139

Hohenberg, P. M. (2004). The historical geography of European cities: and interpretive essay. In J. V. Henderson and J. F. Thisse (eds.), *Handbook of Regional and Urban Economics*, pp. 3021–3052. Retrieved June 23, 2023, from http://citeseerx.ist.psu.edu/viewdoc/download?doi=10.1.1.112.3064&rep=rep1&type=pdf

Jacobs, J. (1961). *The Death and Life of Great American Cities*. Vintage Books. New York.

Li, Y. (2011). The impact of China housing reform on residents' living conditions. University of Oregon. Retrieved June 23, 2023, from https://scholarsbank.uoregon.edu/xmlui/bitstream/handle/1794/11498/Li_Yao_mpa2011sp.pdf?isAllowed=y&sequence=1

Mammen, G. and Iancovich, V. (2015). Why walking to school is better than driving for your kids. University of Toronto. Retrieved June 23, 2023, from www.utoronto.ca/news/why-walking-school-better-driving-your-kids#:~:text=walking%20to%20school%3F-,Children%20who%20walk%20to%20school%20have%20been%20found%20to%20have,on%20the%20journey%20to%20school

The Rise (n.d.). Integral Group. Retrieved June 23, 2023, from www.integralgroup.com/projects/the-rise/

CHAPTER 4
Public Squares and Urban Life

Over centuries, public squares played an important urban and social role in cities. Their use has evolved with the cultural and political necessities of the time. Understanding the functions of public squares is crucial to planning sustainable urban environments. This chapter will touch on the historic role that squares have played, their typology and how their different types and functions morphed. Furthermore, it will delve into how the public square can alleviate the effects of high-density in contemporary planning. Lastly, the chapter will touch on the important civic function of public squares as gathering places that facilitate a plethora of meaningful activities.

4.1 Evolution and Functions of City Squares

Open spaces devoted to public gathering has formed an integral part of the urban and cultural heritage of many societies throughout history to play a critical role in the genesis of commerce, the emergence of democracy and the vitality of civic life. Bearing different names, the square is known as *plaza* in cities of Spanish origins, *piazza* in Italy, *village green* in settlements with feudal pasts, and *market square* in others. The names all mean a physical clearance in the heart of a built place which can be of any shape – including a square.

Similar to the emergence of present-day cities from former trading posts, military camps or sprawling castles, which for various reasons expanded to become full-fledged communities, some squares were the outcome of accidental conditions. Others were purposely planned into a city's fabric, perhaps at the intersection of two arterial thoroughfares running perpendicular to each other. Yet, other squares came to be when existing edifices were demolished, or new ones were erected.

Squares evolved by accretion. Once defined, over time the place took on a life of its own. New buildings replaced old ones, dirt floors were paved, entry gates under which victorious armies might pass were erected, and monuments built in the center to mark special occasions or commemorate persons of note. In fact, squares distinguish themselves according to several features: the nature of the surrounding structures – their height, materials and uses, the nature of their floor coverage, their location in and relation to the city's urban pattern, and their proportions, which determined their scale and affect the spatial impression by relating their height to their width and length.

The first formal and public squares can be traced to early Greek and Roman towns. The *agora* is regarded as one of the original public squares, dating back to 479 BC in Miletus in present-day Turkey. The agora is notably marked by open space and colonnades, which protected citizens from harsh weather. The colonnade facilitated a place of civility, in which it was easy to stroll along and greet strangers and friends. It included businesses and leisure centres, as well as easy access to the theatre, a gymnasium and a stadium. Another early example of the city square is the *forum* in ancient Rome. As the Roman empire became the political center of the Mediterranean, the forum replaced the Greek agora as the main gathering place (Figure 4.1).

Present in the square was often a civic or religious building of note, such as a city hall or a church. This defined the public square as a tool of democratic and religious activities, sometimes overlapping as the church acted as a powerful, pseudo-governmental body (Figure 4.2). The religious element also made the public square a place where spirituality was embedded, giving it a sacred association. Additionally, it was a place where statues of important historical religious or political figures were erected, recognized and revered by the citizens.

DOI: 10.4324/9781003384687-4

Public Squares and Urban Life

Figure 4.1 When the Roman empire became the political center of the Mediterranean, the forum became the main social gathering place.

George Square
Glasgow, Scotland

Plaza de la Reina
Valencia, Spain

The Markt
Bruges, Belgium

Town Hall Square
Esslingen am Neckar, Germany

Figure 4.2 Present in main squares was often a civic or religious building, such as a city hall or a church as shown in these cities.

4.2 Typology of Squares

When considering contemporary planning of public squares, it is important to touch on their typology. One needs to note that the usage and form of the public square differed in chronological and geographical contexts. The delineation between *spontaneous* and *created* growth, terms coined by Spiro Kostof that have been discussed in Chapter 2, is central to understanding the planning of public squares. Over time, many public squares developed as an outcome of accidentally occurring open spaces in the urban fabric while other squares were purposefully and strategically conceived into the city's schema (Kostof 1991).

There are also different archetypes that can characterize the built form of a square. Paul Zucker, in his 1970 book *Towns and Squares: From Agora to Village Green*, describes four types of public squares: the closed square, the nuclear space, grouped squares and amorphous squares. The *closed square* is recognized by Zucker as the perfect form of a public square (Figure 4.3). It is demarcated by the repetition of equal-height buildings surrounding the square, and its design dates back to the Hellenistic and Roman eras, utilized in the original public square, the agora (Zucker 1970). The 'closed' element of the square came from its comfortable, human scale and its ability to create social vitality.

The *nuclear square* is a large square of any form that has a very dominant and central feature, such as a statue. These squares are usually regarded as very dissimilar to the closed square, as they tend to be impressive in scale, but do not fit the human scale necessary for the everyday needs of the citizens, such as being suitable for small gatherings and open markets (Figure 4.4).

Zucker describes the third typology, *grouped squares*, as several independent squares that are in proximity to one another that tend to have unique sizes and forms that distinguish them

Figure 4.3 Closed squares in Italy's Lucca (left) and Siena (right).

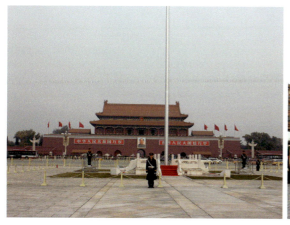 

Figure 4.4 The nuclear square is a large space with a dominant central feature as is the case in Beijing's Tiananmen Square (left) and Warsaw's Old Town Market Place (right).

Public Squares and Urban Life

from one another; nonetheless, they are usually linked by large buildings or other prominent features. Finally, *amorphous squares* are oddly shaped squares that are usually the result of urban transformations that left behind large tracts of land merged with arterial roads (Zucker 1970). A prominent example of this is New York's Times Square (Figure 4.5).

The impact of Spanish colonial powers dispersed the Roman typology of the square widely. In 1573, the Spaniards created the *Laws of the Indies*, which implemented a planning guide on colonial towns reminiscent of the Renaissance. A grid layout was implemented on the 'barren land' inherited by the Conquistadors, forming rectangular shapes known as *barrios*. Reflecting the design of Roman settlements, two main arterial roads intersected in the public square known as a *plaza*. Places like *Plaza de Armas*, which is the term for many of Latin America's main public squares, have this layout (Figure 4.6). Similar to many European cities, public buildings faced the plaza and the church usually acted as a focal point.

The onset of the Industrial Revolution shifted the built form and function of the public square, as it prioritized exclusive spaces, such as the British residential square, that were the first expressions of class segregation and privatization of open space. This would characterize twentieth and twenty-first century planning structures, leading to the creation of suburban development that placed residential isolation and private spaces over the public square. The design of the suburbs rejected density and grid development in favor of large lots and free-flowing streets, therefore, the

Figure 4.5 Amorphous squares are oddly shaped spaces that are usually the result of urban transformations that left behind large tracts of land as is the case in Times Square, New York (left), and Esslingen am Neckar, Germany (right).

Figure 4.6 Plaza Constitucion in Santiago de Querétaro, Mexico.

characteristics of the old urban square could not be implemented into these developments (Figure 4.7).

4.3 The Squares' Importance in High-Density Settings

Neighborhood squares are a shared living room of sorts. Nestled between buildings, they play a vital role in strengthening social networks and establishing new relations. They offer places to sit, dine, display artwork and include play structures, water features, promote local identity, a sense of belonging, and support democratic engagement.

Neighborhood squares are distinct from one another thanks to the variety of features related to their location, the nature of the surrounding structures, and their small area and proportions (Figure 4.8). Well designed squares are framed by housing with a mix of commercial and public amenities under apartments within walking distance of all parts of the neighborhood.

When planning high- density communities, it is crucial to include open spaces to ensure a place's livability. Neighborhoods with a density of 87 homes per hectare (35 homes per acre) can have a public square. When creating a public square, the Project for Public Space (2009), a non-profit initiative that has helped support the creation of public spaces across the United States since 1975, has delineated that easy access is a key aspect in the creation of a successful public square. For example, a survey

Figure 4.7 Leicester Square in London, a former British residential square, was an expression of class segregation and privatization of open space.

Copenhagen, Denmark

Frascati, Italy

Montreal, Canada

Venice, Italy

Figure 4.8 Neighborhood squares are distinct according to features related to their location, the nature of the surrounding structures and their area.

Public Squares and Urban Life

of public square usage by Thompson (2002) states that the majority of users will reach the space by foot if the public space is within a three- to five-minute walk of their residence. Therefore, the creation of dense urban spaces is necessary to facilitate the functions of the public square. Additionally, having high-density buildings face a public square ensures that the neighborhood will not seem as dense.

Public squares can act as green spaces while having social benefits. They provide fresh air and open space to engage in outdoor activities. A 2010 study by the *Journal of Environmental Psychology* indicates that having even just 15 minutes of time outdoor a day was enough to significantly improve a person's mood (University of Rochester 2010). Sunlight exposure also assists in regulating circadian rhythm and providing vitamin D, which is linked to lower rates of heart disease and cancer (Mead 2008).

4.4 The Civic Functions of Squares

As public squares acted as civic centers, their use was shifted toward places of democratic activity – such as protests. Arguing that public open space plays a crucial role in a democratic society, Thompson (2002) states that the public square is the place where democracy is worked out, quite literally, on the ground. For example, Plaza de Mayo in Argentina was home to the famous Madres de Plaza de Mayo, who protested their disappeared children during the Argentine military junta in the 1970s to 1980s (Navarro 1989).

The 1999 Urban Task Force report, under the guise of architect Richard Rogers, stated that to experience full social integration in an urban space, one must think of the public square not as a static or isolated unit, but rather as working with its surrounding neighborhood and those who live and work within it, as well as existing with its own individual set of functions (Rogers and Urban Task Force 1999). These places act as gathering spaces for all walks of life and are essential to eliminating feelings of isolation for urban residents.

On festive occasions, in a public square, one can watch formal performances or street entertainment. Additionally, public squares can be utilized as a place to relax and enjoy the outdoors. Benches and other seating should be placed in public squares to ensure increased accessibility to older populations or those with disabilities (Figure 4.9). There is also often a central monument which allows citizens to learn more about local history and creates an appealing aesthetic.

Figure 4.9 Public squares' contribution to communities is by being sites of many social activities.

Public Squares and Urban Life

Figure 4.10 Vibrant public squares often have residences over ground-level commerce.

Additionally, public squares can have commerce on the ground level. There are often restaurants and cafes that line the streets, therefore engaging diners with the vibrancy of the place. This also allows visitors to enjoy while experiencing the location. Atop the public buildings are typically residents, which provide local businesses with patrons (Figure 4.10).

4.5 The Living Room of Kameiros

Kameiros, on the Greek island of Rhodes, is a Hellenistic city from 226 BC. Its easily defensible location, coupled with the rich soil in the green valley below, explained why this spot was originally settled. The well-preserved sloping excavations have three zones. The first is the Acropolis, Temple of Athena, the place of worship. The second, with dense waist-high stone structures, housed people and their domesticated animals. The last, marked by an open space and a colonnade, was the agora, an open public area (Figure 4.11).

A planning method which led to the creation of squares and the agora was developed by the ancient Greek architect and town planner Hippodamus, who designed the rebuilding of the Ionian city Miletus in 479 BC. Hoping to challenge the urban hegemony of Athens, with its well-known Panathenaic Way, he developed a grid plan system, where the streets were uniform in width and the city blocks of equal dimensions. The plan intentionally called for voids in the grid, creating large public spaces around which important edifices were constructed.

The Athenian agora is perhaps the most famous as it is widely discussed in literature through the ages. This important area provided the Greeks and later the Romans with spaces to debate, arbitrate and socialize in an important urban spot. There the locals were both the actors and audience constantly judging each other's behavior. It was also the place where the classes mixed and citizens could listen to present and future leaders articulate their vision and where social ideas and ideals formed. Historians have described the agora as the ideal public space, and its invention is cited as an important milestone in the creation for urban life and to be maintained in contemporary planning.

Public Squares and Urban Life

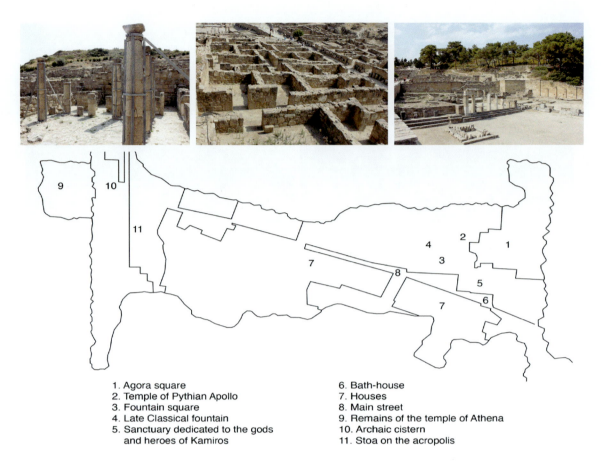

Figure 4.11 The excavated settlement of Kamiros in Greece has three zones. The first is the Acropolis (top left), the second housed people and their domesticated animals (top middle), and the last, marked by an open space and a colonnade, was the agora (top right).

4.6 Final Thoughts

Public squares are essential to the creation of people-friendly sustainable places. The public square, throughout all its usages and forms, is at its very core a social gathering place. When planning denser environments, they are essential in eliminating feelings of isolation. They provide places for people to meet, relax and take a break from their daily life and engage in democratic activities. Public squares also support local commerce and help uplift the place's local economy. Finally, it is a place where people can celebrate holidays, events and festivals.

References

Kostof, S. (1991). *The City Shaped: Urban Patterns and Meaning Throughout History*. Thames & Hudson. London.

Mead, N. (2008). Benefits of sunlight: A bright spot for human health. *Environment Health Perspectives* 116(4): 160–167.

Navarro, M. (1989). The personal is political: Las Madres de Plaza de Mayo. In *Power and Protest: Latin American Social Movements*, pp. 241–258. University of California Press. Berkeley and Los Angeles.

Project for Public Space (2009). 10 benefits of creating good public spaces. Retrieved June 23, 2023, from www.pps.org/article/10benefits

Rogers, R. and Urban Task Force (1999). *Towards an Urban Renaissance: Final Report of the Urban Task Force Chaired by Lord Rogers of Riverside*. Department of the Environment, Transport and the Regions. London.

Thompson, C. W. (2002). Urban open space in the 21st century. *Landscape and Urban Planning* 60(2): 59–72. Retrieved June 23, 2023, from www.sciencedirect.com/science/article/pii/S0169204602000592

University of Rochester (2010). Spending time in nature makes people feel more alive, study shows. Retrieved June 23, 2023, from www.sciencedaily.com/releases/2010/06/100603172219.htm

Zucker, P. (1970). *Town and Square: From the Agora to the Village Green*. MIT Press. Cambridge, MA.

CHAPTER 5
Planning Cities for Walkability

People-friendly places are often defined by their sense of place and walkability. Important to health, wellbeing and the environment, there are physical features and measures that can be introduced to enhance walkability. This chapter discusses what 'sense of place' is, how it can be achieved and how it can enhance walkability. Additionally, it investigates why the creation of human-scaled neighborhoods is crucial. Lastly, macro measures that ensure safe and pleasant experiences that support walkable places are listed.

5.1 Establishing a Sense of Place

The term *sense of place*, although at times vague or abstract, generally describes the ways people feel in places, how they perceive them and, ultimately, the meanings they attach to them (Hashemnezhad 2013). It is hard to pinpoint how to plan for sense of place, as the term itself is complex. Nonetheless, the concept's general framework also provides room for planners to create places that are likely to be widely enjoyed. It is also a vital aspect of the planning of walkable neighborhoods.

Since sense of place is a person's subjective quality, it is important to discuss a wide range of strategies when relating sense of place to walkable cities, as these traits can vary between individuals and communities. A conceptual framework by Ewing and Handy (2009) delineates the objective to subjective scale of walkability in neighborhoods. It shows how objective features, such as sidewalks and street width, tree canopy and building height, and urban design qualities, like enclosure and 'human-scale' – which will be discussed below – lead to the subjective feeling of sense of place, delineated by a sense of safety and comfort and the level of interest felt by pedestrians (Figure 5.1). Ultimately, their framework leads to the most subjective aspect, a place's overall walkability and its effect on someone's behavior. Therefore, to achieve sense of place, and ultimately to enhance walkability, planners can first focus on creating the objective physical features that may lead to more subjective qualities of urban design.

Given the above noted framework, to support a walkable neighborhood, a place must exhibit traits that ensure a sense of place. Generally, this includes elements that make walking

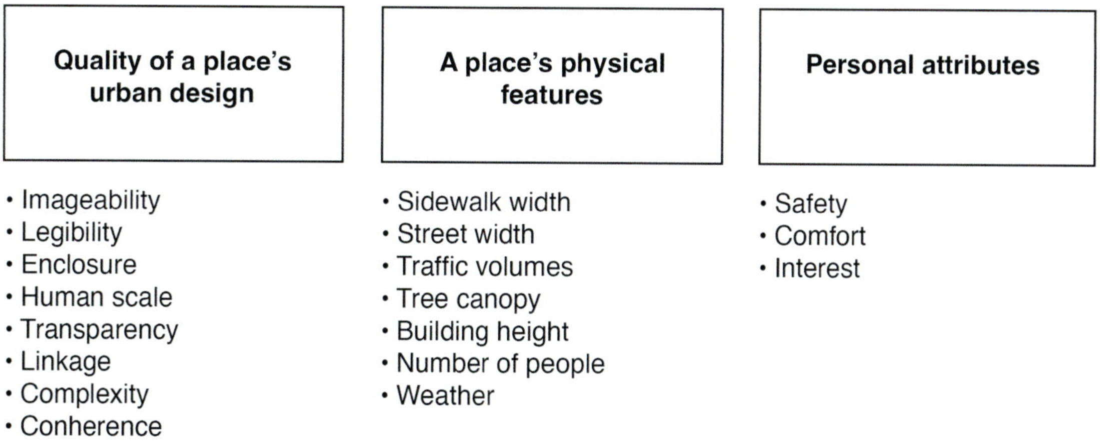

Quality of a place's urban design	A place's physical features	Personal attributes
• Imageability • Legibility • Enclosure • Human scale • Transparency • Linkage • Complexity • Conherence	• Sidewalk width • Street width • Traffic volumes • Tree canopy • Building height • Number of people • Weather	• Safety • Comfort • Interest

Figure 5.1 Objective and subjective attributes that affect a place's walkability (after Ewing and Handy 2009).

DOI: 10.4324/9781003384687-5

Planning Cities for Walkability

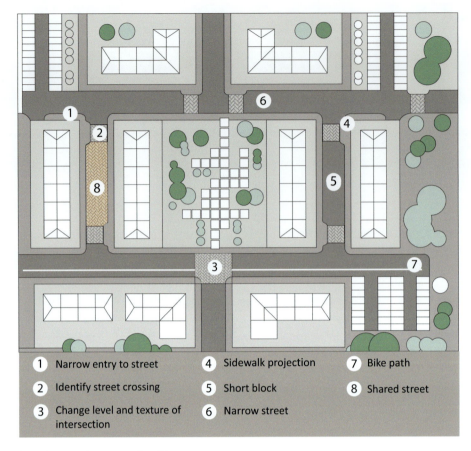

①	Narrow entry to street	④	Sidewalk projection	⑦	Bike path
②	Identify street crossing	⑤	Short block	⑧	Shared street
③	Change level and texture of intersection	⑥	Narrow street		

Figure 5.2 Measures that enhance and promote safe walking.

more pleasant and inhibits feelings of safety and enjoyment (Figure 5.2). Installing walking paths next to a busy street, especially without ample protection for the pedestrian, invokes a negative, unsafe walking experience – disincentivizing individuals to walk. Therefore, walkways should be designed with the antithesis of the North American model in mind.

To develop walkable environments, while achieving sense of place, planners need to ensure well-proportioned relation between buildings and streets, ample greenery, and safety. Once these features are achieved, a sense of place can be enhanced, thereby incentivizing people to participate in increased walking behavior.

5.2 Human Scale and Walkability

Planning for walkable cities need to consider a place's *human-scale*. Being one of the key yardsticks of creating a sense of place, human-scale refers to how our surroundings are proportioned in accordance with a person's height (Figure 5.3). A comfortable human-scale includes streets with well-proportioned width, that can be shared with vehicles. It also includes structures set back from the street, their height, presence of trees and streetlamps.

Commonly, human-scaled environments are the features of old towns characterized by a unique human- scale and material that make for a pleasant walking experience. However, following World War II, planning regulations prioritized roads and vehicles over walkability and cycling (Figure 5.4). That followed a proliferation of developments with wide roads and increased space for parking to make people feel disconnected from their environment.

Proper human-scale was a topic of study by planners who have proposed 'ideal' proportions. Austrian city planner and theoretician, Camillo Sitte, suggested that the minimum dimensions of a square should be equal to the height of the main building within it, while its maximum height should not be more than double the former. This is based on the

Planning Cities for Walkability

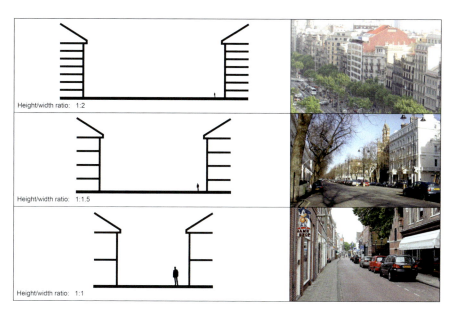

Figure 5.3 Height to width ratio that illustrates different proportions in accordance with a person's height and, as a result, a human-scale.

Figure 5.4 Human-scaled environments were common in old cities. That changed in new subdivisions after World War II when driving was prioritized over walking.

conviction Sitte had that a person's line of vision is between 27 and 45 degrees (Burke 2016). Human-scale can also be created vis-à-vis placemaking, rather than bounded dimensions delineated by planners. As illustrated in Figure 5.5, placemaking can be the outcome of activities by people who have strong emotional connections to a place – rather than the outcome of zoning regulations (Burke 2016). Therefore, it is increasingly important to welcome the voices of locals into the future of planning processes (Burke 2016).

It is also important to consider planning for people with disability. At times, designers may disregard the needs of those who have more difficulty in walkable environments. It is important to consider the 'social model' of disability – which sees people as being disabled by their environment, rather than having disabilities – to adhere to planning principles that minimize 'disability' (Burton and Mitchell 2006) (Figure 5.6). Therefore, designers must make accessible urban design, such as curb-cut, ramps, benches and comfortable rest-stops, a priority.

Planning Cities for Walkability

Figure 5.5 Placemaking is, among others, the outcome of activities by people who have strong emotional connections to a place.

Figure 5.6 It is important to consider the "social model" of disability, which sees people as being disabled by their environment, rather than having disabilities.

5.3 Macro Measures for Walkability

With the concepts of sense of place and human-scale in mind, and how these two interact and contribute to neighborhood planning, one must consider the macro measures planners can utilize to achieve these concepts.

A measure that can support walkability is *shared streets* used by both pedestrians and cars, to foster diverse forms of mobility and social interaction (Figure 5.7). An example of a shared street is the Netherlands' *woonerf*, meaning "streets for living" in Dutch. The street has no distinction between the sidewalks and the street which are on the same level. To do this, planners utilize narrower streets and slight curves and a low-speed limit to slow down traffic. This helps to encourage

Planning Cities for Walkability

Figure 5.7 A measure that can support walkability is shared streets for use by pedestrians and vehicles.

safer walkable areas in places with some vehicular activity, as well as network connectivity, and includes trees and benches.

To create successful, walkable places measures must be taken to ensure the safety of pedestrians. Designated streets should include buffer spaces between the sidewalk and the street. A desirable buffer zone is between 1.2 to 1.8 meters (4 to 6 feet) with the adjacent sidewalk being around 1.5 meters (5 feet) – with larger sidewalks installed in areas with higher pedestrian traffic (U.S. Department of Transportation n.d.). These buffer zones preferably incorporate small green spaces to foster a more safe, comfortable environment and encouraging a sense of place (Figure 5.8). Another form of buffer zone includes incorporating parking or bike lanes, which helps pedestrians feel much safer as they are distant from moving vehicles.

Another key to creating walkable cities is simultaneously enhancing the 'bike-ability' of places. Cycling is becoming a more prominent means of getting to school, work and other amenities, as cities prioritize pro-bike policies. For example, since Portland, Oregon, began introducing a high-quality,

interconnected network of bike pathways after the 1990s that link major destinations with residential and mixed-use areas, they have managed to increase their levels of cycling sixfold by 2018 (Pucher et al. 2021). Additionally, cities should include well-marked bike paths and traffic signs, to encourage cycling while discouraging driving. Other ways of encouraging cycling include bike-share programs, public awareness campaigns, and equitable access to bike paths (Figure 5.9).

Another measure to ensure a safe and pleasant pedestrian environment is narrower streets. Like the *woonerf* that was discussed above, the width of local streets preferably should not exceed 6 meters (20 feet). Additionally, pedestrian crossings should be incorporated every 80 to 100 meters (262 to 328 feet) to help stop pedestrians from crossing more unsafe spots and incentivizing vehicles to drive slower (Global Designing Cities Initiative 2016).

Reducing or even eliminating vehicular traffic loads in city centers has become a way to reclaim streets, as Danish planner Jan Gehl advocates in his practice and writing (Gehl 2010).

Planning Cities for Walkability

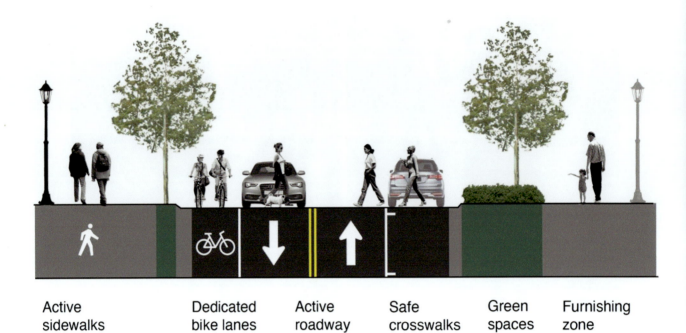

Figure 5.8 A green buffer between the sidewalk and the street makes walkability safer.

Figure 5.9 Amenities for cyclists' safety and convenience like special traffic lights, dedicated lanes, bikes on public transit and a stand with maintenance tools will encourage more people to cycle.

Planning Cities for Walkability

Figure 5.10 Making the heart of cities walkable by limiting vehicular traffic is a change that caught on internationally.

Making the heart of cities walkable by limiting vehicular traffic is a change that caught on internationally (Figure 5.10).

Like many current sustainable initiatives having walkable cities is not new. Ancient streets were planned and used by people, their domesticated animals and horse-drawn carriages. The car naturally came much later. Yet, blocking car entrance to the heart of cities was not easy to introduce. Delivery of goods to businesses, accessibility and parking by local inhabitants all posed a challenge. Protest was also voiced by local merchants who argued that patrons will not come if they cannot park in front. But these claims were proven wrong. In fact, more people came to visit and shop since it was fun and safe to be there.

There are different kinds of car-free cities. Some cities bar cars due to the narrow streets which make driving very difficult. Other cities, with historic centers, banned cars in an attempt to reduce pollution and increase tourism. Some are rural with smaller populations and can afford to rely on bicycles to get around. There are also canal cities, such as Venice, which rely on boats for transportation. In all cases, to make being car-free a success, cities have to provide good alternatives to private vehicles, so that people can still make their way into

these areas. Creating clustered parking outside districts is one of the strategies.

5.4 Sense of Place in Sun Juan del Zur

The main street of Sun Juan del Zur, a surfers' mecca on Nicaragua's southwest coast, is lined with single-story colorful buildings of many styles, making it look as if zoning did not apply to this place. Souvenirs are sold in some stores, while others cater to the locals with food stalls. In one of the rows there was a restaurant with a sign that read Simon Say with an interior courtyard.

The courtyard was partially roofed by an intricate web of native flora and natural light flowed through, creating sunny marks on the pavement. Other dense tropical plants fill the place. The brick wall on one side was painted purple to which an assortment of local artwork was affixed. The furnishing was improvised with an unmatched collection of items (Figure 5.11). The ensemble created a unique space unlike anything I have seen before that lent the place an authentic and relaxed atmosphere.

Planning Cities for Walkability

Figure 5.11 Street view and the court in Sun Juan del Zur on Nicaragua's southwest coast.

Patrons were sitting on sofas having animated conversations. A man nodded to me and pointed to an empty corner sofa. I sank into it and stretched my feet and cherished the moment. A waiter came and took my meal order which was served shortly after.

Sitting there, I wondered why this spot has a unique sense of place? Was it the sounds and sights? Was it the culture in which I had been embedded? Looking at the court, I recognized that time and an absence of formal design had shaped it and contributed to its appearance. It was clear that the place took years to evolve by accretion to reach its markings and the owners let it happen to the benefit of the patrons.

5.5 Human- Scale in Haarlem

Roofs with orange clay tiled and pointy dormers are common features in Haarlem, the Netherlands. The tall Grote Kerk gothic church and the Grote Markt – the market square – are among the most visited places. The Dutch city, whose roots date back to well before medieval times, was known as a place of tolerance. In the fifteenth century, it welcomed immigrants who had fled neighboring countries, making it a center of linen and silk production.

With meandering narrow streets, walking in the Botermarkt neighborhood, as the place is called, near rows of traditional red-brick townhouses that lined a narrow 4.9 meter (16 foot) street, provided a unique sense of place (Figure 5.12).

The street had been built during the horse-and-carriage era. Many of the townhouses had businesses on their lower levels. Wooden benches stood next to black-painted entry doors, flowers spilled over from pots on windowsills and bicycles rested on walls. Both the hidden and the overt make-up of the neighborhood – its materials, its domestic touches, its corner stores – made you feel as if you had known the place for a long time. What is most visible is the ratio between the width of the streets and the height of the buildings that edge them. The scale made it comfortable being there.

At times, people failed to question the rationale behind regulations that govern the planning of contemporary cities and streets. Some fall into the habit of leaving things to the way they have been done for long. Despite changing modes of transit, Haarlem's streets kept serving their occupants for centuries, teaching us that we can design and build similar places to serve us as long.

Planning Cities for Walkability

Figure 5.12 The Botermarkt, an old neighbourhood in Haarlem, the Netherlands teaches lessons about human-scale and car-free environments.

5.6 Final Thoughts

When planning communities, there should be a proliferation of streets that share space between pedestrians, cars, public transit and cyclists, making way for diverse interactions and equitable access to the environment around them. These streets should be designed at the human-scale, with buildings, streets and sidewalk widths of appropriately sized buffer zones to keep pedestrians safe and for the integration of green spaces and tree canopies. They should be mixed-use, allowing for the support of local commerce and diverse interactions, leading to a vibrant atmosphere. Having walkable cities will also help to lower vehicular traffic, which contributes heavily to the global climate crisis.

References

Burke, S. (2016). Placemaking and the human scale city. *RSS*. Retrieved June 23, 2023, from www.pps.org/article/placemaking-and-the-human-scale-city

Burton, E. and Mitchell, L. (2006). *Inclusive Urban Design: Streets for Life* (1st ed.). Elsevier. Amsterdam.

Ewing, R. and Handy, S. (2009). Measuring the unmeasurable: urban design qualities related to walkability. *Journal of Urban Design* 14(1): 65–84. Retrieved June 23, 2023, from www.tandfonline.com/doi/full/10.1080/13574800802451155

Gehl, J. (2010). *Cities for People*. Island Press. Washington, D.C.

Global Designing Cities Initiative (2016). *Global Street Design Guide*. Island Press. Washington, D.C. Retrieved June 23, 2023, from https://globaldesigningcities.org/publication/global-street-design-guide/

Hashemnezhad, H., Heidari, A. A. and Hoseini, P. M. (2013). "Sense of place" and "place attachment". *International Journal of Architecture and Urban Development* 3(1): 5–12. Retrieved June 23, 2023, from https://ijaud.srbiau.ac.ir/article_581_a90b5ac919ddc57e6743d8ce32d19741.pdf

Pucher, J., Buehler, R., Geller, R. and Marqués, R. (2021). Implementation of pro-bike policies in Portland and Seville. In *Cycling for Sustainable Cities*, pp. 371–399. MIT Press. Cambridge, MA.

U.S. Department of Transportation (n.d.). *The Walking Environment*. Retrieved June 23, 2023, from https://safety.fhwa.dot.gov/saferjourney1/library/countermeasures/01.htm

CHAPTER 6
Developing in Natural Settings

An environment's natural features are essential to its ecosystem and biodiversity. Disrupting this ecosystem will have negative effects on organisms and humans. Threats to biodiversity also increase a place's vulnerability to climate change and natural disasters. Therefore, when developing in natural settings, it is crucial to protect a place's ecological features. While there is a dire need to meet population development demands, it must be done in a sustainable manner. This chapter investigates the conflict between new development and the preservation of natural environments to bridge the gap between them.

6.1 Natural Features

Natural features refer to environmental aspects, including topography, vegetation and soil, wildlife and ecosystems, and weather systems, among other features. It plays a major role in a location's future vitality, the wellbeing of its residents, and the community's potential to become sustainable. Any fundamental changes to natural landscapes, through structure or spatial organization, are often permanent and almost impossible to restore (Sonko et al. 2021).

Biodiversity refers to the variety of life on Earth, ranging from the micro-scale, such as genes, to the macro-scale within ecosystems (Figure 6.1). It can be interpreted in evolutionary, ecological, social or cultural processes, and is a vital source in sustaining life (American Museum of Natural History n.d.). Biodiversity has been found to have direct effects on human wellbeing, health, and quality of life (Apfelbeck et al. 2020). Over the past decades, humans have posed threats to the Earth's biodiversity, through resource depletion, land development and pollution, among many other acts. The removal of even a single species from an ecosystem can disrupt its entire functioning, leading to a 'domino effect' on the entire ecosystem (Sonko et al. 2021). Ecosystems offer free commodities to users of space. However, through the negative consequences of human development, the loss of these benefits and commodities become increasingly prevalent (Morano et al. 2020). Despite biodiversity being fundamental to allowing cities to remain healthy and livable places, it is often not considered a fundamental goal of city planning, urban design and housing development (Apfelbeck et al. 2020).

Over centuries, humans have modified nature to cater to societal needs. Although this has some benefits, such as societal progress, it irreversibly changes natural features of the environment and often negatively impacts the biodiversity of ecosystems. Land take, being the conversion of untouched land into "human developed" land, often leads to the

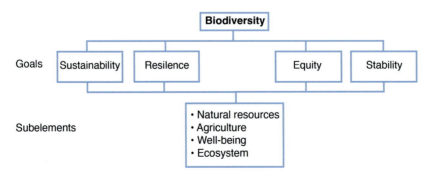

Figure 6.1 Biodiversity refers to life on earth, ranging from micro to macro scales. It can be interpreted as evolutionary, ecological, social or cultural processes.

DOI: 10.4324/9781003384687-6

irreversible loss of many natural features and exosystemic processes of the environment (Morano et al. 2020). Research shows that humans have converted 40 percent of Earth's land into agricultural land, and have used approximately half of the Earth's freshwater, mainly to irrigate crops in the agricultural industry (Myers and Frumkin 2020). Furthermore, human practices have already reduced the number of animal species by over 50 percent since 1970, and continually place millions of species at risk of extinction (Myers and Frumkin 2020). Increased development has had many consequential effects, including increasing frequency and magnitude of natural disasters, the gradual loss of biodiversity and climate change (Sonko et al. 2021).

Urban sprawl, urban development outside the traditional city centers, produces an irregular and dispersed development pattern and has been associated with negative environmental impacts (Morano et al. 2020). Not only does this residential development pattern take up more land, harming its natural features and threatening its biodiversity, but it also intensifies reliance on private automobiles, increases traffic congestion, requires more infrastructure and increases greenhouse gas emissions, among others (Morano et al. 2020).

6.2 Human Practices, Pollution and Resource Availability

It is believed that global agricultural production can feed between 500 million and 1 billion people without harming the planet (Sonko et al. 2021). However, increased development leading to the destruction of the environment's natural features and biodiversity greatly impacts the food resources that ecosystems are able to provide. Not only does decreased biodiversity lead to decreased resource availability, resulting in poverty and food insecurity, but it has also been found that poverty and food insecurity are primary drivers of biodiversity loss (Rondeau et al. 2020). This clearly illustrates the need to preserve natural features in an attempt to maintain biodiversity. With increased urbanization, diets have shifted to more unhealthy and processed foods, leading to health concerns such as obesity, diabetes, heart disease and stroke, cancer, and hypertension (Myers and Frumkin 2020).

For centuries human civilization and culture have been closely interconnected with nature (Bridgewater and Rotherham 2019). Specifically, the Declaration of Belem in 1988 stated that there is an inextricable link between cultural and biological diversity (Bridgewater and Rotherham 2019). Sense of place is important in maintaining both community cohesion and mental health

(Jennings and Bamkole 2019). When the physical space is altered, it also modifies the cultural and social aspects associated with it. Therefore, it is important to preserve natural environmental features, to not only protect biodiversity, but to also conserve the rich cultural practices connected to nature as was practiced in the region of Tuscany, in Italy for centuries (Figure 6.2). Particularly, certain groups such as indigenous peoples, have a very strong and sacred cultural connection to the natural features of the environment, viewing nature as a provider to their society, instead of a resource to exploit (Hatala et al. 2020). These groups have lived synonymously alongside nature, growing their civilizations and developing without harming the ecosystem's biodiversity. However, this cultural connection between these communities and nature becomes increasingly threatened by the degradation of the environment, loss of biodiversity and climate change, which are amplified by modern development practices.

6.3 Typology of Natural Features

The typology of natural features refers to the categorization of features, such as forests and vegetation, topography and land formations, water, and soil. The way in which natural features are classified can influence how they are regarded, subsequently impacting their preservation, maintenance or destruction. This section describes the typology of some natural features pertinent to urban development, such as topography, sun and wind, soil, wildlife, and trees.

6.3.1 Topography

The natural topography of a site should be retained as much as possible. This is to avoid disturbing natural features, maximize the uniqueness and integration of design into the natural features of the site, and lower construction costs associated with drastically changing natural features. Preserving the natural topography of an area involves building alongside its natural contours, reducing the destruction of trees and natural drainage ways, and limiting changes to the grading of land (Figure 6.3). The environment exists with certain natural mechanisms, such as natural drainage ways, natural wind and sun path patterns, and species of flora and fauna existing at certain elevations and in various conditions, which helps to maintain the area's biodiversity. Therefore, disrupting these natural mechanisms through development disrupts the area's biodiversity, either directly through physically disrupting habitats, or indirectly by altering sunlight and wind patterns, or causing flooding or soil erosion.

Developing in Natural Settings

Figure 6.2 It is important to preserve natural and man-made features in order to conserve the rich cultural practices connected to nature as is the case in Tuscany, Italy.

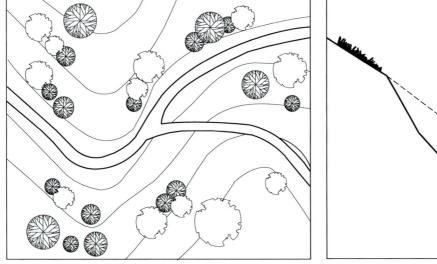
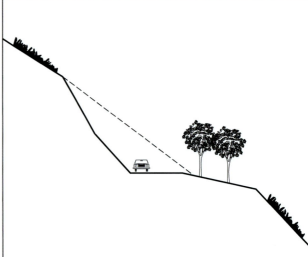

Figure 6.3 Preserving the original topography of an area involves building alongside its natural contours.

52

6.3.2 Sun Path and Wind Direction

Although sunlight is not per se a "natural feature" in the same sense as vegetation, rock formations and water, it can be used to maximize a community's sustainability. The orientation of a development in relation to the sun path can substantially affect its energy consumption, impacting both costs and negative environmental impacts such as energy usage (Figure 6.4). This orientation will vary depending on the location of the proposed urban development. To maximize the advantage of the sun in the northern hemisphere, structures should be oriented toward the south. Additionally, rectangular buildings are advantageous as they maximize sun exposure, reducing the need for heating and cooling by approximately 85 percent. The presence of existing trees, shrubbery and other natural features may also impact this sun exposure into a home, which should be considered during the design process.

Prevailing winds can also be used in the design process to maximize energy efficiencies of a home. For example, wind direction considerations can be applied to prevention strategies for soil erosion, or applied to reduce heating requirements, by orienting a structure's windows to prevent snow build-up on doors or windows during the winter. Trees, particularly coniferous trees which maintain their foliage year-round, can also be used to shield against cold winds. However, the effectiveness of wind blockage depends on the foliage density and spacing between trees. Typically, 40 to 60 percent of cold prevailing winds are blocked by a single row of coniferous trees, and 60 to 80 percent of winds can be blocked by multiple rows (Friedman 2018). In the summer months, wind directions can be utilized to reduce heating needs by positioning windows and arranging vegetation to permit cross-ventilation (Figure 6.5).

6.3.3 Wildlife

Wildlife forms a large part of our environment, and is fundamental to our ecosystems. However, increased urbanization and land area taken over by human development decreases biodiversity through the quantity and diversity of species which can survive (Apfelbeck et al. 2020). Wildlife-inclusive urban design is fundamental to ensuring that the needs of animals are accounted for in design and development of urban areas (Apfelbeck et al. 2020). In urban design, inclusion of ample green space does not always occur, leading to extremely limited suitable habitats for wildlife. Increasing the amount of green space, particularly through the preservation of natural green space, not only provides habitat for these species, preserving biodiversity of the ecosystem, but it also improves quality of life for urban residents and promotes connections between people and nature (Apfelbeck et al. 2020). Additionally, developing along the environment's natural topography, as previously discussed, limits the amount of habitat change for species, providing them with better chances of being able to continue to live in the area.

6.3.4 Trees

Trees are a very critical natural feature of the environment. They are important in stabilizing ground cover, improving soil filtration, preventing soil erosion and absorbing carbon dioxide. Trees are often cleared to allow for development, leading to many negative effects and the destruction of the

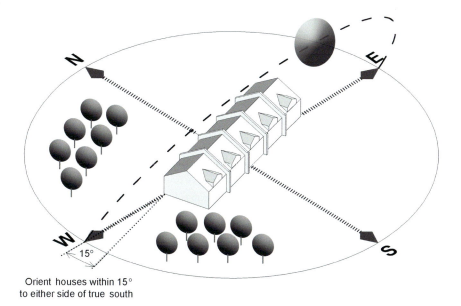

Orient houses within 15° to either side of true south

Figure 6.4 The orientation of a development in relation to the sun path can substantially affect its buildings' energy consumption.

Developing in Natural Settings

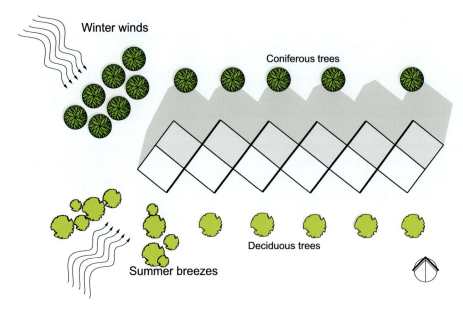

Figure 6.5 Typically, 40 to 60 percent of cold prevailing winds are blocked by a single row of coniferous trees, and 60 to 80 percent of winds can be blocked by multiple rows.

natural benefits which trees provide. It is estimated that the average American has a carbon footprint of 16 tons of carbon dioxide per year, and that 640 trees would need to be planted per person, or 200 billion trees for the entire US population, to be able to offset these emissions (Moseman 2022). Research has also predicted that to offset the carbon emissions from the use of an automobile for one year, fifteen trees are needed, and forty trees are needed to offset emissions from a single home (Friedman 2018). Additionally, the roots of trees absorb water to prevent flooding and promote proper filtration of soil, as well as help stabilize ground cover (US Environmental Protection Agency 2022a).

Trees also help to reduce temperatures, which is especially beneficial in urban areas where there may be urban heat islands (US Environmental Protection Agency 2022a). An urban heat island (UHI) is a phenomenon in urban areas leading to significantly higher temperatures in the city center as natural land is replaced with artificial land such as pavement and buildings, which absorb and retain large amounts of heat (US Environmental Protection Agency 2022b). Therefore, it is recommended that mature trees be preserved, and only be removed if they are dying or causing any major obstructions. Mature trees are trees which have reached 75 percent of their full canopy growth, which varies depending on the tree species (Figure 6.6).

6.4 Integration of Natural Features in Urban Design

Efforts toward the conservation of biodiversity in urban design are often lost to priorities of economic growth, transportation, infrastructure and housing development, which are at times viewed by decision-makers as more important (Apfelbeck et al. 2020). A focus on these latter priorities may be perceived as greater benefits in the short term. However, in the long term, lack of preservation of biodiversity and the environment's natural features have cumulative negative impacts. These contribute to decreased mental and physical health, decreased community cohesion, decreased resource availability, and environmental degradation leading to climate change and natural disasters.

There are minimal ways around development that do not involve developing on land with natural features, which almost guarantees the disruption to some degree of these features and the environment. Even "man-made" developments such as new master-planned cities in the Global South such as BiodiverCity in Malaysia, and Floating City in the Maldives, marketed as being sustainable, have been ridiculed for potentially disrupting biodiversity and natural features to an even greater degree than normal development, as despite

Developing in Natural Settings

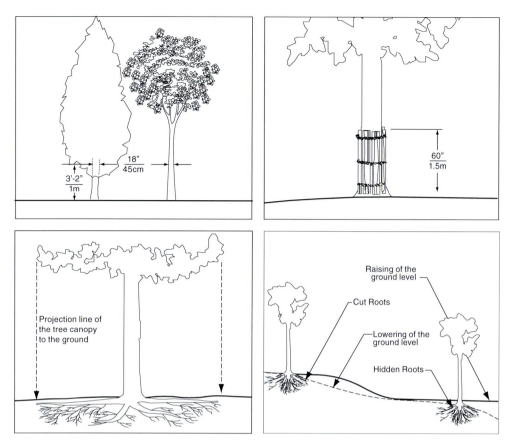

Figure 6.6 It is recommended that mature trees be preserved, and only be removed if they are dying or causing major obstructions.

being built on "man-made" land in oceans they destroy marine ecosystems (Ren et al. 2020).

6.4.1 Preserving Flora and Fauna

Not only does design which preserves and integrates natural features of the environment help to benefit the environment and its ecosystems, but it also improves design, way of life for people living in and using the area, and fosters a unique sense of place.

In development, builders often clear land of all flora and fauna, to create an empty site on which to build. Not only does this destroy the existing ecosystem composed of flora and fauna, but it also disrupts the site's natural uniqueness, leading to a uniform and sometimes "lifeless" environment. It can also decrease the site's natural processes, leading to soil erosion and reduced water retention and shifting sunlight and wind patterns. Trees and other plants naturally act as agents to prevent soil erosion and absorb stormwater runoff, which positively impacts the environment and decreases the built infrastructure needed in developments. It may be beneficial to build an interdisciplinary design team including wildlife and ecosystem specialists, to ensure that the preservation of flora and fauna is occurring adequately and comprehensively (Apfelbeck et al. 2020) (Figure 6.7).

Preserving and implementing plant species which are native to the area being developed is also beneficial to ensuring maintenance of biodiversity (Landi et al. 2020). Not only will these plant species be more suited to the climate conditions of the area, requiring less upkeep and having better chances of survival, but they will also be suitable habitats for native wildlife species. The implementation of perfectly maintained grass lawns with non-native plant species is not a sustainable vegetation choice, and is very energy-intensive to maintain, and may have an adverse effect on an ecosystem's biodiversity (Landi et al. 2020).

The incorporation of public green spaces, community gardens, nature conservation areas, backyard gardens, green roofs and greenery along streetscapes into urban design is a strategy to protect biodiversity and natural features, and also directly improve people's lives. It allows for places of leisure and socialization, and increases connection with nature and physical activity, which have been found to improve both mental and physical health (Jennings and Bamkole 2019) (Figure 6.8).

Developing in Natural Settings

Figure 6.7 In sites endowed with trees designers must ensure their preservation and protection during construction.

Figure 6.8 Incorporating greenery in design protects biodiversity as is the case in this path in Singapore.

6.5 An Alternative Design Process

Progressive change in urban design, due to changes in the needs of users, is certain to occur. It is not realistic to design a building to last indefinitely. For example, the materials themselves may only have a certain lifespan before they are no longer suitable and safe. Also, the needs and desires of consumers and society change over time along with technological and material advances. Although it cannot be exactly predicted or always designed for in advance, spaces can be designed to accommodate change whenever it may occur. This can involve using vernacular materials which can be easily repurposed, and construction methods for ease of disassembly and rearrangement.

Conserving natural soil is crucial to maintaining the biodiversity and natural features, as it is the base on which vegetation and life relies. The following methods can be applied in existing urban green areas and when implementing new green spaces; however, it is preferable to preserve natural, pre-existing spaces.

An innovation called "precision agriculture" aims to decrease resource consumption and environmental degradation of the agriculture industry. This method involves tractors equipped with computers and GPS systems which collect data on soil and land conditions and precisely track where each crop seed is planted and monitor the amount of resources it needs at each growth stage (Myers and Frumkin 2020). This helps to limit resource consumption, therefore limiting the effects of pollution on biodiversity and limiting the amount of change to the environment's natural features. Furthermore, "no-till agriculture" can be used to minimize soil disturbances and soil erosion (Myers and Frumkin 2020). This involves growing vegetation without disturbing the natural soil surface and topography by not creating tillage or ridges in the surface (Regeneration International n.d.).

6.6 The Rose Bushes of Gerberoy

Preservation of existing shrubbery was a main feature in Gerberoy, a small village in northern France that is listed among the country's most beautiful villages. Known as *the village of a thousand rose bushes*, the flower is planted and blossoms along roads and near the old colorful houses. In the sixteenth and seventeenth centuries, a plague outbreak occurred in Gerberoy, and the village was abandoned for the following two to three hundred years. In 1901, Impressionist painter Henri le Sidaner came across Gerberoy and was impressed by its charm. He settled there and played an active part in the place's restoration. He went on to establish a terraced garden on 4,000 square meters (43,056 square feet), and gradually started to shape the village to his liking, adding three more gardens on the old site and covered remains of an old castle. The inclusion of a variety of flowers, especially roses, became a key feature of Gerberoy's landscape. The painter encouraged all residents to plant flowers in front of their houses. Le Sidaner was also responsible for initiating "La fête des roses" in 1928, which is an annual event that takes place on the third weekend of June (Duhamel n.d.) (Figure 6.9). The roses of Gerberoy offer a lesson in how the preservation of plants can change the fortune of a small place, to make it livable, internationally recognized, contribute to the place's exceptional beauty and help the plant too.

Figure 6.9 Preservation of rose bushes is a main feature in Gerberoy, a small village in northern France, that made it a tourist attraction.

6.7 Weaving Development and Water in the Netherlands

Some 29 percent of the Netherlands' land mass of 41,865 square kilometers (16,164 square miles) is below sea level, making it prone to flooding from overflowing rivers. As a result, water management is one of the country's main preoccupations to make canals and rivers a prominent part of the country's city and rural planning (Breukers 2001).

Since the thirteenth century when the Regional Water Authorities were created, water governance kept most of its territory dry by efficiently combining natural and man-made infrastructure and successfully reclaiming land from the sea. Canals that historically played an important role in water management have also been used for travel, irrigation and water removal. The canals of Amsterdam, for example, resulted from successful city planning, and the ones found in cities such as Leiden and Delft were designed to become transportation arteries. Designing waterways is therefore an integral part of Dutch town planning with a long tradition of using a collaborative process between different branches of government such as transportation, landscaping and urban design.

A recent approach to water management in the Netherlands calls for *room for the river* and supports the idea of combining innovative architecture, urbanization and landscape to design and build landscapes which embrace water's natural course. This approach moves away from adopting a defensive approach to water management which work against rather than with water, such as the Delta Works project, which was initiated after the Netherlands suffered from major flood damage in 1953. Delta Works is the largest flood protection scheme in the world, comprising of infrastructure such as storm surge barriers, dikes, dams and sluice gates (Figure 6.10).

It is impressive how the Netherlands, a small nation of 17.6 million people, was able to cope with and turn a menacing natural phenomenon into an advantage of sorts, making the most out of a bad situation. It offers lessons to other nations that may live with apparent natural disadvantage. Innovation and collaborative effort can turn these seemingly unfortunate cases into a source of national pride and even wealth.

6.8 Planning with Nature in Morgan's Rock

Morgan's Rock near Sun Juan Del Sur in Nicaragua is an example of integration of nature and development in a dense forest. Established in 2004 by the Poncon family, it is home to a variety of exotic animals, including spiders, howler and capuchin monkeys, and deer, as well as native and migrant birds and reptiles. Nearly half of the 1.61-hectare (4-acre) property was turned into a private reserve. The rest is El Aguacate, a low-impact agricultural land and sustainable tropical forest where endangered species are cultivated and planted. The design and construction of the lodges followed vernacular traditions using sustainably locally sourced wood for furniture and palm leaves for roof coverings.

Near the ocean shore, there is minimalist design intervention. Looking up the hill, one could hardly notice the lodges in between the tall trees. They merged nicely with their surroundings. Reflecting on common North American residential design, poor development practices saw agricultural land and forested landscape cleared to make room for wide roads and houses. Vast, green natural lands were covered with sod and required large amounts of fresh water during the dry summer months. Morgan's Rock is a demonstration of what sensible development needs to stand for. Of course, one could not

Figure 6.10 The Delta Works in the Netherlands is the largest flood protection system in the world, comprising of storm surge barriers, dikes, dams and sluice gates around which communities are built. It comprises existing cities like Amsterdam (left) and new ones like Almere (right).

Developing in Natural Settings

Figure 6.11 Morgen's Rock stands as a demonstration of what sensible development needs to stand for: protection of flora and fauna, planting native spices, and seamlessly combining natural and man-made environments.

Figure 6.12 In Alberobello, a small town in southeastern Italy, local stones have been used as roofing material for centuries.

compare a resort to a residential project, but the basic principles still apply – not harming flora and fauna, using native spices, and combining natural and man-made environments seamlessly (Figure 6.11).

6.9 Using Local Stone in Alberobello

Material choice for structures can have a significant impact on the development's sustainability and its impact on the biodiversity of its environment. It is beneficial to use local materials, when possible, as not only does this decrease costs associated with transportation and construction, but it also allows the structure and sense of place to more closely connect to the natural environment in which it resides. Local materials which are natural, renewable and have a minimal negative environmental impact are most desired.

An historical manifestation of such practice can be seen in the Trulli (singular Trullo), limestone buildings in Alberobello, a small town in southeastern Italy. In 1996, the place was recognized by UNESCO as a World Heritage Site for its urbanity and architecture (UNESCO 2019). Made of long thin slabs of limestone, shaped in a pyramidal dome with a rectangular base, the construction of the buildings began in the mid-fourteenth century, and they are still inhabited and used as dwelling or stores. Their dry stone, applied without mortar, construction technique is several thousand years old. It was initiated by the settlers to evade taxes since conventional homes were highly taxed. The walls are made of two layers of stacked stone slabs sandwiching a layer of rubble, and the roofs are made with an outer waterproof layer of corbelled stone slabs, and an inner layer of wedged stones. The walls and top of the roofs are typically white, with ornamentations at their peak and painted religious symbols (Figure 6.12). Additionally, the interior is a single room, with a fireplace, and space for a bed and furniture. The centuries-long endurance of the Trulli is a demonstration that when constructed properly with local materials good architecture can be built to last.

6.10 Final Thoughts

There has commonly been conflict between contemporary urban development and the natural environment. This conflict can often lead to destruction of natural features and biodiversity loss, which impacts mental and physical health, resource availability and cultural heritage. The destruction contributes to cycles of environmental degradation, involving the exacerbation of climate change and natural disasters and weather events. Actions such as building an infill development and relying on existing amenities, preparing for change, using local materials, preserving natural soil surface, and government action and policy must be taken to ensure the preservation and protection of natural features.

References

American Museum of Natural History (n.d.). What is biodiversity? Retrieved June 24, 2023, from www.amnh.org/research/center-for-biodiversity-conservation/what-is-biodiversity

Apfelbeck, B., Snep, R. P., Hauck, T. E., Ferguson, J., Holy, M., Jakoby, C., Scott MacIvor, J., Schär, L., Taylor, M. and Weisser, W. W. (2020). Designing wildlife-inclusive cities that support human-animal co-existence. *Landscape and Urban Planning* 200: 1–11. doi:10.1016/j.landurbplan.2020.103817

Breukers, C. P. M. (2001). Creating water management strategies for the northern part of Holland using a collaborative planning process. In *Integrated Water Resources Management*, pp. 427–452. IAHS. Wallingford.

Bridgewater, P. and Rotherham, I. D. (2019). A critical perspective on the concept of biocultural diversity and its emerging role in nature and heritage conservation. *People and Nature* 1(3): 291–304. doi:10.1002/pan3.10040

Duhamel, G. (n.d.). Historique. Les Jardins Henri le Sidaner. Retrieved June 24, 2023, from www.lesjardinshenrilesidaner.com/

Friedman, A. (2018). *Smart Homes and Communities: Fostering Sustainable Architecture*. Images Publishing. Victoria.

Hatala, A. R., Njeze, C., Morton, D., Pearl, T. and Bird-Naytowhow, K. (2020). Land and nature as sources of health and resilience among indigenous youth in an urban Canadian context: a photovoice exploration. *BMC Public Health* 20(1): 1–14. doi:10.1186/s12889-020-08647-z

Jennings, V. and Bamkole, O. (2019). The relationship between social cohesion and urban green space: an avenue for health promotion. *International Journal of Environmental Research and Public Health* 16(3): 452. doi:10.3390/ijerph16030452

Landi, S., Tordoni, E., Amici, V., Bacaro, G., Carboni, M., Filibeck, G., Scoppola, A. and Bagella, S. (2020). Contrasting patterns of native and non-native plants in a network of protected areas across spatial scales. *Biodiversity and Conservation* 29(6): 2035–2053. doi:10.1007/s10531-020-01958-y

Morano, P., Tajani, F. and Anelli, D. (2020). Urban planning decisions: an evaluation support model for natural soil surface saving policies and the enhancement of properties in disuse. *Property Management* 38(5): 699–723. doi:10.1108/pm-04-2020-0025

Moseman, A. (2022). How many new trees would we need to offset our carbon emissions? Retrieved June 24, 2023, from https://climate.mit.edu/ask-mit/how-many-new-trees-would-we-need-offset-our-carbon-emissions

Myers, S. S. and Frumkin, H. (eds.) (2020). *Planetary Health: Protecting Nature to Protect Ourselves*. Island Press. Washington, D.C. Retrieved June 24, 2023, from www.researchgate.net/publication/343426449_Planetary_Health_Protecting_Nature_to_Protect_Ourselves

Regeneration International (n.d.). What is no-till farming? Retrieved June 24, 2023, from https://regenerationinternational.org/2018/06/24/no-till-farming/

Ren, P., Zhu, H., Sun, Z. and Wang, C. (2020). Effects of artificial islands construction on the spatial distribution and risk assessment of heavy metals in the surface sediments from a semi-closed bay (Longkou Bay), China. *Bulletin of Environmental Contamination and Toxicology* 106(1): 44–50. doi:10.1007/s00128-020-03032-3

Rondeau, D., Perry, B. and Grimard, F. (2020). The consequences of covid-19 and other disasters for wildlife and biodiversity. *Environmental and Resource Economics* 76(4): 945–961. doi:10.1007/s10640-020-00480-7

Sonko, S., Maksymenko, N., Vasylenko, O., Chornomorets, V. and Koval, I. (2021). Biodiversity and landscape diversity as indicators of sustainable development. *E3S Web of Conferences* 255: 01046. doi:10.1051/e3sconf/202125501046

UNESCO (2019). The Trulli of Alberobello. Retrieved June 24, 2023, from https://whc.unesco.org/en/list/787/

U.S. Environmental Protection Agency (2022a). Soak up the rain: trees help reduce runoff. Retrieved June 24, 2023, from https://www.epa.gov/soakuptherain/soak-rain-trees-help-reduce-runoff

U.S. Environmental Protection Agency (2022b). Reduce urban heat island effect. Retrieved June 24, 2023, from https://www.epa.gov/green-infrastructure/reduce-urban-heat-island-effect

CHAPTER 7
Creating Urban Landscapes

This chapter examines the importance of effective planting and landscaping in promoting biologically diverse and sustainable cities. It investigates the ecological, economic and social importance of biodiversity and provides planners with practices of integrating planting and landscaping to counteract the urban heat island (UHI) effect and conserve water. Special emphasis is placed on *xeriscaping* techniques that promote water conservation through a thorough understanding of regional weather patterns and local climates. Additionally, the importance of green roofs is highlighted for their ability to improve human wellbeing and lower the dwelling's carbon footprint. Placemaking through planting is additionally observed in the consideration of community spaces, such as community gardens and parks. The chapter concludes with recommendations for planners, through the implementation of these various methods, to design in harmony with biodiversity rather than against it.

7.1 Fundamentals and the Importance of Biodiversity

Biological diversity, which was also touch upon in Chapter 6, simply refers to the abundant existence of a variety of plant and animal species in their natural environment (Verma et al. 2020). Biodiversity encompasses three distinct levels: genetic, species and ecosystem, all of which interact to shape the tapestry of life on Earth (Verma et al. 2020). The importance of biodiversity is rooted in its centrality to the maintenance of ecosystem health and resilience, along with its provision of a vast range of resources and services essential to human wellbeing (Marselle et al. 2021) (Figure 7.1). Efforts in urban planning can be made to conserve and protect biodiversity, which is being significantly impacted by extractive human activities such as habitat destruction, overexploitation and pollution. Overall, the significance of biodiversity can be evaluated in three comprehensive dimensions: ecological, economic and social.

Biodiversity is the ecological foundation for the functioning of ecosystems, where individual species perform different roles, and the loss or decline of one species can ripple to affect the entire ecosystem (Hung et al. 2018). For instance, urbanization and excessive use of pesticides, among other factors, have resulted in a decline of pollinating insects such as honeybees. The decline of this single species has an impact on the food resources for a large number of animals and can seriously affect global human food security (Ullah et al. 2021). Considering this example, the loss of biodiversity can be compared to a game of Jenga, where each species is a block in the tower. As blocks are removed and species diminish, the tower becomes less stable and more likely to crumble. Similarly, as biodiversity is threatened, ecosystems are made less stable and more sensitive to disruption, ultimately affecting the survival of all species, including humans, who depend on the functions of such ecosystems. Biodiversity is indispensable for the mutual existence of all living beings and for the maintenance of ecological balance (Verma et al. 2020). In the face of increasing climatic pressures driven by climate change, preserving biodiversity in cities can help to mitigate the negative effects of urbanization on surrounding natural areas as well as the UHI effect, a phenomenon in which urban areas become substantially warmer than their rural surroundings. This is due to factors such as the substitution of natural landscapes with heat-absorbing pavements and buildings, the release of heat from vehicles and other industrial processes, and an absence of vegetation to provide shade and cool the air (Tan et al. 2021) (Figure 7.2). These conditions lead to increased energy consumption, air pollution and negative health consequences for city residents, which urban biodiversity can help counteract.

Research also points toward a clear picture of the positive links between nature and human mental health and wellbeing in urban spaces (Bratman et al. 2019). Green space and urban parks can improve air and water quality, provide opportunities for recreation and exercise, relieve stress, and the

DOI: 10.4324/9781003384687-7

Creating Urban Landscapes

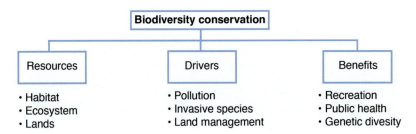

Figure 7.1 The importance of biodiversity is rooted in its centrality to the maintenance of ecosystem health and resilience, along with its provision of a vast range of resources and services essential to human wellbeing.

Figure 7.2 The replacement of natural landscapes with heat-absorbing pavements and buildings contributes to the urban heat island (UHI) effect, as seen in Melbourne, Australia.

accompanying mitigation of UHI can improve public health by reducing the risk of heat-related illness (Tan et al. 2021). Urban biodiversity provides pest control and flood protection, which can enhance the livability of cities. Excessive noise in cities has been shown to impact the cardiovascular, respiratory, immune and metabolic systems of city residents (Recio et al. 2016). In fact, acoustic research reveals how structural elements of vegetation buffers noise and suggests that dense and diverse vegetation are particularly effective sound barriers (Ow and Ghosh 2017). Given its ecological, economic and social importance, urban biodiversity conservation can be considered a public investment (Marselle et al. 2021).

7.2 Retooling Cities

The practical strategies and methods for the creation of biodiverse urban environments can be observed through green infrastructure, connectivity and sustainable development by using environmentally favourable building techniques. Protection of a location's biodiversity is key to creating a livable city. Planning for nature in development can look like integrating sunlight, wind paths, fauna and flora into design. It is suggested to use strategies as proposed by Victor Olgyay, that work with and not against natural forces and make use of their potential to create better living conditions (Gutiérrez and de la Plaza Hidalgo 2019). Placemaking through planting can be used to create community spaces, such as community gardens, orchards and green roofs (Figure 7.3). Such spaces can be used for socialization, relaxation and recreation, but also to grow food, provide habitat for wildlife, and reduce the impact of the built environment on the natural environment. This can not only enhance the aesthetic appeal of an area but also serves a functional purpose by utilizing plants to define spaces, add visual interest, provide shade and privacy, and promote biodiversity. Incorporating native plants and other species that thrive in the local environment supports ecosystem functions and ensures the sustainability of the landscape (Gutiérrez and de la Plaza Hidalgo 2019).

Creating Urban Landscapes

Figure 7.3 Placemaking through planting can be used to create attractive urban gardens.

Some cities have employed strategies of incorporating green spaces to serve as gaps in the urban fabric, which not only improves human health and wellbeing but also allows for opportunities such as Biodiversity Sensitive Urban Design (Kirk et al. 2021). Such approaches enable the development of urban areas that benefit native species and ecological communities by providing essential habitat and food resources (Kirk et al. 2021). By creating the opportunity for individuals to consistently immerse themselves in urban nature, planners can foster a renewed connection to biodiversity, increase the regularity and intensity of interactions with plants and animals in urban settings, and cultivate a sense of place (Kirk et al. 2021). For instance, a strategy was implemented in Paris to strategically place numerous green spaces throughout the urban landscape, including large peripheral parks. This approach allows residents easy access to nearby green areas for daily use, while also contributing to improved air quality in the city (Urbano Gutiérrez and de la Plaza Hidalgo 2019). In contrast to Paris, Manhattan, New York lacks ample green spaces. To compensate for this, a large urban park is strategically situated in the heart of the city, providing easy access for residents from all areas. Furthermore, Central Park's vast size allows citizens to fully immerse themselves in a natural environment (Figure 7.4).

Planting diverse vegetation in these spaces is vital to help future-proof cities (Tan et al. 2021).

In order to minimize long-term ecological, social and economic impacts, urban development and infrastructure projects can also incorporate green building techniques (Urbano Gutiérrez and de la Plaza Hidalgo 2019). As noted in Chapter 1, Singapore serves as a shining example of thriving urban biodiversity, as the great majority of interactions between people and wildlife in modern Singapore occur in urban areas. Property developers are required to replace any greenery lost during construction and are provided with financial assistance to install green roofs and walls on existing buildings. As a result, the city's rooftop gardens and green walls are projected to triple by 2030 (Figure 7.5). These, along with ample green spaces such as parks and park connectors, not only reduce the city's heat-island effect, but also assist in stormwater absorption, provide recreational areas and ultimately increase urban biodiversity (Hwang et al. 2015).

Working with nature rather than against it can also look at the very construction of buildings. For example, a building's orientation is one of the most important factors affecting

Creating Urban Landscapes

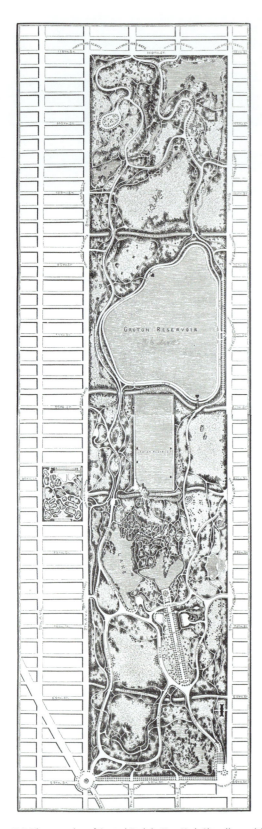

Figure 7.4 The vast size of Central Park in New York City allows citizens to immerse themselves in a natural environment.

Figure 7.5 Property developers in Singapore are required to replace any greenery lost during construction and are provided with financial assistance to install green roofs and walls on existing buildings.

Figure 7.6 The siting of buildings in accordance with the yearly sun path will lead to substantial passive solar gain to save on energy costs.

energy consumption (Elghamry and Azmy 2017). In the early stages of planning, it is critical to consider the position of the sun over the day and year, as it can supply natural heat and energy (Elghamry and Azmy 2017) (Figure 7.6). Using trees and other vegetation as shading devices in the summer can help keep the house cool, while in the winter, when the leaves fall, the sun's rays can penetrate the house, increasing the room temperature and ultimately saving energy and lowering heating costs.

Creating Urban Landscapes

7.3 Planning for Water Conservation

In light of climate change and increasing populations, water scarcity is becoming a critical issue for cities worldwide (Filali et al. 2022). Effective management and conservation of water, which is essential for all aspects of urban life such as industrial production, outdoor recreation and residential consumption, is another key for achieving sustainable urban environments (Figure 7.7). Urban planners seeking to create sustainable, low-maintenance and water-efficient outdoor spaces can turn to xeriscaping, an innovative method of landscaping that prioritizes the efficient use of natural resources. By implementing xeriscaping techniques, planners can achieve significant water savings, reduce the need for chemical use and prevent soil pollution (Çetin et al. 2018). This approach not only benefits the environment, but also helps to create beautiful, functional outdoor spaces that require minimal upkeep.

The use of xeriscaping landscape design increases the efficiency of watering by using slow-growing, drought-tolerant plants, focusing on indigenous species which have deeper roots and are adapted to the local climate (Yari et al. 2020). This approach allows for the conservation of water resources and relieves strain on municipal water systems while mitigating the UHI effect and improving air quality. Xeriscaping incorporates a select number of basic principles of landscaping to achieve optimal water conservation (Yari et al. 2020). First, the design of a xeriscape landscape must be founded on the mapping of water and energy conservation strategies, which must be tailored to the unique regional environment and microclimate. This means that plant placement and selection must be chosen based on what will thrive in the specific climatic conditions.

The ultimate goal of xeriscape landscapes is to minimize turf surfaces, particularly by reducing the use of bluegrass turf, which requires excessive amounts of supplementary watering (Figure 7.8). Although it requires more water, turf provides a functional activity area that xeriscaping does not offer. Therefore, it may be worthwhile to retain a portion of the land for turf, if necessary. Designers are encouraged to consider a substitute turf that uses less water than bluegrass. Equally important is the use of proper soil, which allows for better water absorption and promotes deeper roots, along with the use of mulches that keep plant roots cool, minimize evaporation, prevent soil crusting and curb weed growth (Yari et al. 2020).

Finally, the installation of efficient irrigation in xeriscapes is essential to facilitate maintenance and maximize water use efficiency, but equally essential to all urban landscaping. Water from natural sources, such as rainwater runoff, is most effectively used to reduce the use of water from pipes for irrigation. Collecting water runoff from downspouts, outbuildings and paved areas, and directing it to a retention pond or rain barrels, can conserve a significant amount of water (Filali et al. 2022). Domestic wastewater from showers, sinks, laundry, washing machines and kitchen waste, or greywater, is also an alternative method that can reduce the drain of resources, as recycling greywater through a proper management system is both an economical and ecologically sound approach to water management and conservation (Filali et al. 2022). Low-consumption taps and showers, toilet flushes, and washing machines have been developed and can also aid in the reduction of individual consumption. By implementing water-saving measures at home and replacing traditional lawns with drought-resistant landscapes, residential water use can be reduced by 40 to 60 percent (Yari et al. 2020) (Figure 7.9).

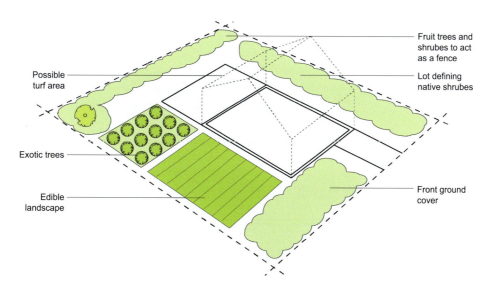

Figure 7.7 Effective management and conservation of water, such as having water zones, is key for achieving sustainable urban environments.

Creating Urban Landscapes

Figure 7.8 The ultimate goal of xeriscape landscapes is to minimize turf surfaces which requires excessive amounts of supplementary watering.

Figure 7.9 By implementing water-saving measures at home and replacing traditional lawns with drought-resistant landscapes, residential water use can be reduced by 40 to 60 percent.

Creating Urban Landscapes

This not only makes urban environments more resilient to drought conditions, but also saves energy, reduces greenhouse gas emissions, and ultimately lowers the cost of water treatment and engineering.

7.4 Green Roof

A green roof is a roofing system that is partially or completely covered with vegetation. Two common categories of green roofs are intensive and extensive. The former resembles traditional gardens, with the greatest diversity of plants, deep soils and high maintenance cost and labour, while the latter requires less maintenance, lower cost and doesn't allow for as much plant diversity (Cascone 2019; Friedman 2015) (Figure 7.10). Both types of green roofs offer a variety of benefits. Given that roofs account for a large percentage of surfaces in urban areas, the implementation of green roofs in cities is an opportunity to harmonize the relationship between nature and urban spaces. Not only do they enhance the visual landscape of buildings, but they also generate significant ecological, social and economic benefits for a community.

Green roofs can create habitats for a variety of plant and animal species, which can in turn aid in maintaining biodiversity in urban areas (Francis and Jensen 2017). Enhancing biodiversity through the use of green roofs is once again closely connected to the choice of plant species and habitat or vegetation used (Friedman 2015). Extensive roofs can be an excellent site of thriving, undisturbed local and non-local vegetation, as they are not designed to be stepped on (Cascone 2019). Where conventional garden space may be limited, rooftop space can also allow for community gardens and the cultivation of fruits, herbs and vegetables, thereby providing social value by amplifying the sense of community, as well as the aesthetic benefits that nature brings to people's wellbeing: reducing stress, lowering blood pressure, and generally increasing positive feelings and mental health (Marselle et al. 2021) (Figure 7.11).

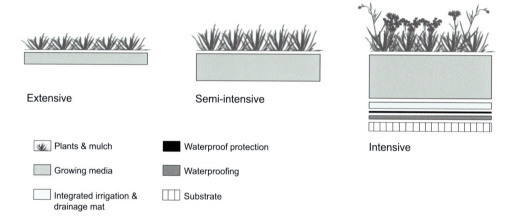

Figure 7.10 Two common categories of green roofs are intensive and extensive roofs; the former resembles traditional gardens, with the greatest diversity of plants, deep soils and high maintenance cost and labor; the latter requires less maintenance, lower cost and doesn't allow for as much plant diversity.

Figure 7.11 Green roofs can create habitats for a variety of plant and animal species, which can in turn aid in maintaining biodiversity in urban areas.

Creating Urban Landscapes

By slowing down currents, providing shade, releasing moisture into the air and filtering air pollution, green roofs help mitigate the negative impacts of the UHI effect to the mutual benefit of wildlife and the urban population (Mayrand and Clergeau 2018). Furthermore, they are inherently energy efficient and help insulate buildings, reducing energy costs and carbon emissions (Francis and Jensen 2017). A green roof prevents heat from both escaping overhead in cold weather climates and entering the building in the summertime and, when designed and constructed effectively, also have a longer life expectancy than traditional roofs by providing a layer of protection from UV rays and extreme temperatures, also contributing to water resistance.

7.5 Lemon Orchards in Positano

Clinging to the Amalfi mountains, the town of Positano, population 4,000, in southern Italy edges a popular, breathtaking coastal road. Seen from afar, one wonders why have people chosen to settle here in the first place. The answer, no different than other settlements of this kind, is rooted in the place – easy to defend against attacking enemies, access to trading roots and food. Positano experienced a golden age as an important port and trading hub in the eighteenth century, and today it is a humble fishing village and a tourist destination (Encyclopedia Britannica 2020).

When one walks uphill and across the narrow meandering roads it is easy to admire not only the industriousness but the knowledge it took to build this place. The rocky terrain was curved along the cliff's contours to make walking easy and minimize steep climbs all without dynamiting and bulldozing. The builders were also aware of microclimate aspects. They knew that sites on slopes of ridges are subject to year-round breezes and lower humidity which cools the place on hot summer days. Designing narrow streets of varying heights, and placing buildings along them, shade the rows below when the sun was high in summertime. The structures' southern sun exposure helped keep them warm in the winter as well.

Nestled between the homes are lemon orchards. An urban agriculture of sorts to which the inhabitant need not walk far. The region is known for its cultivation of lemons, which started in the nineteenth century when an unproductive rural landscape from the towns of Positano to Vietri sul Mare were transformed into lemon orchards. The region is the hub of a lemon liqueur called Limoncello (Curnow 2010) (Figure 7.12).

Positano teaches that regardless of challenging topography cities can weave nicely in with nature. Sustainable places are

Figure 7.12 Nestled between the homes in the town of Positano, Italy are lemon orchards.

achieved when generations of builders adhere to simple common-sense rules for centuries. Agriculture from which people will draw their livelihood can also be made part of urban areas. These attributes can become vital in fueling a tourist industry which draws people to admire it all and support the local economy.

7.6 A Garden in a Victoria Quarry

Along the paths of the 22-hectare (55 acres) Butchart Gardens near Victoria, in British Columbia, Canada, there are low-lying beds of flowering plants, bushes and exotic trees. There is a Japanese section, followed by an Italian with its Renaissance style landscape, and a Mediterranean garden as well as the sunken garden with a fountain.

Established in 1904 by Jennie Butchart, who decided to rehabilitate a scarred industrial wasteland into a lush and beautiful garden, the site was a former limestone quarry and a cement plant at the rear of Butchart's home. With time, the cement production depleted the limestone, and the Butcharts

Creating Urban Landscapes

Figure 7.13 Butchart Gardens near Victoria, Canada teaches a lesson about the vision and perseverance needed to transform an abundant quarry into a place of beauty that also educates many about landscaping.

were left with a useless site that called for a new use. Since 1912, they transferred topsoil onto the quarry, a process that started humbly – with just a few pea seeds and a rose bush (Dick 2004).

Whereas Jennie had envisioned the garden to serve her own pleasure and that of the community, the Butchart Gardens is today a private and commercialized tourist attraction with 900 varieties that attracts roughly 1.3 million visitors yearly and a National Historic Site of Canada. The place teaches a lesson about the vision and perseverance that it takes to transform a disfigured place into a place of beauty, that mesmerises and educates many (Figure 7.13).

7.7 Final Thoughts

Considering the numerous benefits that they provide, green roofs can indeed play a crucial role in the overall concept of sustainable development and can aid in the attainment of creating truly sustainable cities. Using natural weather patterns to mitigate the UHI effect, conserve water and reduce energy consumption, green building and landscaping techniques, such as xeriscaping, can advance cities toward sustainability. Effective sustainable design starts with a deep understanding of the natural environment, specifically the climate and weather patterns of a region. By incorporating this knowledge into the planning process from the outset, planners can design in harmony with nature rather than against it. Furthermore, regarding the promotion and protection of biodiversity as essential to the health of the planet, people and cities is critical to creating sustainable cities that promote healthy natural and social ecosystems.

References

Bratman, G. N., Anderson, C. B., Berman, M. G., Cochran, B., de Vries, S., Flanders, J., Folke, C., Frumkin, H., Gross, J. J., Hartig, T., Kahn, P. H., Kuo, M., Lawler, J. J., Levin, P. S., Lindahl, T., Meyer-Lindenberg, A., Mitchell, R., Ouyang, Z., Roe, J., Scarlett, L., Smith, J. R., van den Bosch, M., Wheeler, B. W., White, M. P., Zheng, H. and Daily, G. C. (2019). Nature and mental health: an ecosystem service perspective. *Science Advances* 5(7). Retrieved June 24, 2023, from https://doi.org/10.1126/sciadv.aax0903

Cascone, S. (2019). Green roof design: state of the art on technology and materials. *Sustainability* 11(11): 3020. Retrieved June 24, 2023, from https://doi.org/10.3390/su11113020

Çetin, N., Mansuroğlu, S. and Önaç, A. (2018). Xeriscaping feasibility as an urban adaptation method for global warming: a case study from Turkey. *Polish Journal of Environmental Studies* 27(3): 1009–1018. Retrieved June 24, 2023, from https://doi.org/10.15244/pjoes/76678

Curnow, P. (2010). Story of the Amalfi coast lemon. *Delicious Italy*. Retrieved June 24, 2023, from www.deliciousitaly.com/campania-naples-food/story-of-the-amalfi-coast-lemon

Dick, L. (2004). Butchart Gardens. *The Public Historian* 26(4): 88–90. DOI: 10.1525/tph.2004.26.4.88

Encyclopedia Britannica (2020). Amalfi. *Encyclopedia Britannica*. Retrieved June 24, 2023, from www.britannica.com/place/Amalfi

Elghamry, R. and Neveen Youssef Azmy, N.Y. (2017). Buildings orientation and its impact on the energy consumption. *Al Azhar 14th International Conference (AEIC) on Engineering, Architecture & Technology*. Retrieved December 4, 2023, from www.researchgate.net/publication/327623184

Filali, H., Barsan, N., Souguir, D., Nedeff, V., Tomozei, C. and Hachicha, M. (2022). Greywater as an alternative solution for a sustainable management of water resources: a review. *Sustainability* 14(2): 665. Retrieved June 24, 2023, from https://doi.org/10.3390/su14020665

Francis, L. F. and Jensen, M. B. (2017). Benefits of green roofs: a systematic review of the evidence for three ecosystem services. *Urban Forestry & Urban Greening* 28: 167–176. Retrieved June 24, 2023, from https://doi.org/10.1016/j.ufug.2017.10.015

Friedman, A. (2015). Design strategies for integration of green roofs in sustainable housing. *Vitruvio – International Journal of Architectural Technology and Sustainability* 1: 57. Retrieved June 24, 2023, from https://doi.org/10.4995/vitruvio-ijats.2015.4475

Hung, K.-L. J., Kingston, J. M., Albrecht, M., Holway, D. A. and Kohn, J. R. (2018). The worldwide importance of honey bees as pollinators in natural habitats. *Proceedings of the Royal Society B: Biological Sciences* 285(1870): 20172140. Retrieved June 24, 2023, from https://doi.org/10.1098/rspb.2017.2140

Hwang, Y. H., Lum, Q. J. and Chan, Y. K. (2015). Micro-scale thermal performance of tropical urban parks in Singapore. *Building and Environment* 94: 467–476. Retrieved June 24, 2023, from https://doi.org/10.1016/j.buildenv.2015.10.003

Kirk, H., Garrard, G. E., Croeser, T., Backstrom, A., Berthon, K., Furlong, C., Hurley, J., Thomas, F., Webb, A. and Bekessy, S. A. (2021). Building biodiversity into the urban fabric: a case study in applying Biodiversity Sensitive Urban Design (BSUD). *Urban Forestry & Urban Greening* 62: 127176. Retrieved June 24, 2023, from https://doi.org/10.1016/j.ufug.2021.127176

Marselle, M. R., Lindley, S. J., Cook, P. A. and Bonn, A. (2021). Biodiversity and health in the urban environment. *Current Environmental Health Reports* 8(2): 146–156. Retrieved June 24, 2023, from https://doi.org/10.1007/s40572-021-00313-9

Mayrand, F. and Clergeau, P. (2018). Green roofs and green walls for biodiversity conservation: a contribution to urban connectivity? *Sustainability* 10(4): 985. Retrieved June 24, 2023, from https://doi.org/10.3390/su10040985

Ow, L. F. and Ghosh, S. (2017). Urban cities and road traffic noise: reduction through vegetation. *Applied Acoustics* 120: 15–20. Retrieved June 24, 2023, from https://doi.org/10.1016/j.apacoust.2017.01.007

Recio, A., Linares, C., Banegas, J. R. and Díaz, J. (2016). Road traffic noise effects on cardiovascular, respiratory, and metabolic health: an integrative model of biological mechanisms. *Environmental Research*. Retrieved June 24, 2023, from https://pubmed.ncbi.nlm.nih.gov/26803214/

Tan, J. K. N., Belcher, R. N., Tan, H. T. W., Menz, S. and Schroepfer, T. (2021). The urban heat island mitigation potential of vegetation depends on local surface type and shade. *Urban Forestry & Urban Greening* 62: 127128. Retrieved June 24, 2023, from https://doi.org/10.1016/j.ufug.2021.127128

Ullah, A., Tlak Gajger, I., Majoros, A., Dar, S. A., Khan, S., Kalimullah, Haleem Shah A., Nasir Khabir, M., Hussain, R., Khan, H. U., Hameed, M. and Anjum, S. I. (2021). Viral impacts on honey bee populations: a review. *Saudi Journal of Biological Sciences* 28(1): 523–530. Retrieved June 24, 2023, from https://doi.org/10.1016/j.sjbs.2020.10.037

Urbano Gutiérrez, R. and de la Plaza Hidalgo, L. (2019). *Elements of Sustainable Architecture*. Routledge. London. Retrieved June 24, 2023, from https://doi.org/10.4324/9781351256445

Verma, A. K., Rout, P. R., Lee, E., Bhunia, P., Bae, J., Surampalli, R. Y., Zhang, T. C., Tyagi, R. D., Lin, P. and Chen, Y. (2020). Biodiversity and sustainability. In *Sustainability*, pp. 255–275. Wiley. Basel. Retrieved June 24, 2023, from https://doi.org/10.1002/9781119434016.ch12

Yari, A., Eslamian, S. and Eslamian, F. (2020). *Urban and Industrial Water Conservation Methods*. CRC Press. Boca Raton. Retrieved June 24, 2023, from https://doi.org/10.1201/9781003081531

CHAPTER 8
Cities as Farms

The current food system faces many challenges, including food insecurity, environmental degradation and unhealthy eating habits. To address these issues, this chapter delves into the concept of urban agriculture, an innovative approach to boosting agricultural production while minimizing its impact on the environment. The chapter covers three key areas: the first, a critical evaluation of the challenges faced by the current food system; second, an exploration of the design principles behind creating sustainable and productive edible landscapes; and finally an examination of the benefits of farmers' markets. With a focus on promoting a more sustainable and resilient food system, this chapter provides valuable insights for urban planners, designers and policymakers.

8.1 The Challenges of the Current Urban Food System

Prior to COVID-19, the world was already faced with a significant problem of food insecurity, affecting an estimated 25.9 percent of the population in 2019 – an increase from 22.4 percent in 2014 (United Nations Department of Economic and Social Affairs 2022). However, the pandemic has only exacerbated this issue, causing disruptions in production and access to safe and nutritious food, therefore threatening food systems already impacted by threats and vulnerabilities such as natural hazards, pests, armed conflicts and violence (Dona et al. 2021). The impact of COVID-19 and the subsequent revelation of flaws in our food system indicate food resilience in cities should be a priority for social and ecological wellbeing. Approximately 55 percent of the global population lives in cities, with a projected increase to 68 percent by 2050 (UNDESA 2018) (Figure 8.1). The pandemic brought to public attention the need to question the level of food sovereignty we would like to see in urban and peri-urban areas (Langemeyer et al. 2021). This presents an opportunity to re-examine our food system, and its relationship to cities and address its

shortcomings, considering factors such as environmental impact, negative health outcomes and accessibility.

The industrialization of agricultural production has drastically increased food production, following the rate of an ever-increasing population. Although this is a positive development to counteract food insecurity, it comes at the cost of pollution, resource depletion and overconsumption, causing large social and ecological externalities. Coal, mined phosphorus, oil and natural gas are all non-renewable or slowly renewable resources, meaning they take much longer than a person's lifespan to be replaced. The current food system and its sub-elements (i.e., growing, distribution, retail) relies heavily on many of these finite resources (Figure 8.2). Increasing demand for diverse food products has led to transportation emerging as a key link in food supply chains, in turn increasing the distance traveled by the food we consume (Friedman and Pollock 2022). As reductions in transportation cost drive the rapid growth of the food trade, the concept of 'food miles' is being increasingly employed to account for the extensive distance traveled by food products from points of production to consumption (Li et al. 2022). Although an imperfect form of measurement, the idea seeks to demonstrate the associated environmental impact that transportation has on the environment, such as energy use and emissions, considering that some 30 percent of food system emissions are due to transport (Li et al. 2022). The transportation of food due to extended food supply chains requires the use of vehicles such as trucks, ships and airplanes, which emit greenhouse gases like carbon dioxide, methane and nitrous oxide. Along with the by-product of other processes in the system, these emissions contribute to saturating the environment with pollutants, leading to long-term environmental damage and climate change (Bricas 2019) (Figure 8.3). Although it is feasible to streamline industrial production methods to reduce resource waste and decrease environmental pollution, the foundation still lies on non-renewable resource use, which in itself is fundamentally unsustainable.

71 **DOI: 10.4324/9781003384687-8**

Cities as Farms

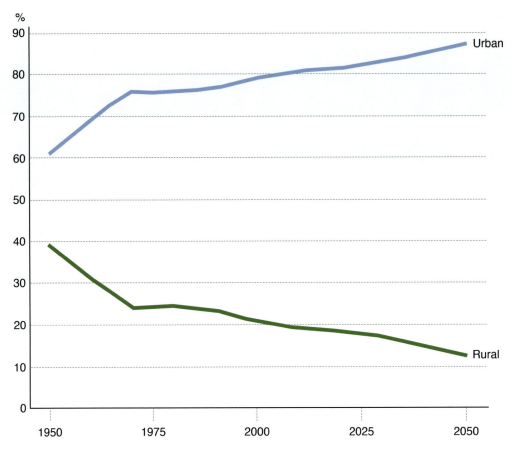

Figure 8.1 Approximately 55 percent of the global population live in cities with a projected increase to 68 percent by 2050.

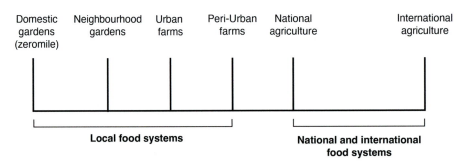

Figure 8.2 The current food system on its sub-scales.

The excessive use of chemical inputs in production agriculture is having a devastating impact on soil health, biodiversity and human wellbeing (Campbell et al. 2017). It has resulted in the evolution of pesticide-resistant pests and a heightened risk of disease spread (Connolly et al. 2020). Additionally, the adoption of practices such as genetic engineering as a response to unfavourable environmental conditions due to climate change and pests has also been observed as potentially having negative characteristics like toxicity, allergenicity and genetic hazards (Chekol 2021). Equally, pesticide exposure has been shown to have substantial impacts on human health, including reproductive, neurological and cancerous outcomes (Sanford et al. 2015). One's environment also plays a crucial role in determining health. Access to nutritious food is a major concern and the extremes can be divided into two categories: food deserts and food swamps. *Food deserts* are found in communities that lack access to healthy and affordable food options, such as supermarkets and farmers' markets (see section 8.3). Conversely, *food swamps* are areas with an abundance of fast food and unhealthy food choices, directing individuals to poor dietary habits and an increased risk of obesity (Figure 8.4). Unfortunately,

Cities as Farms

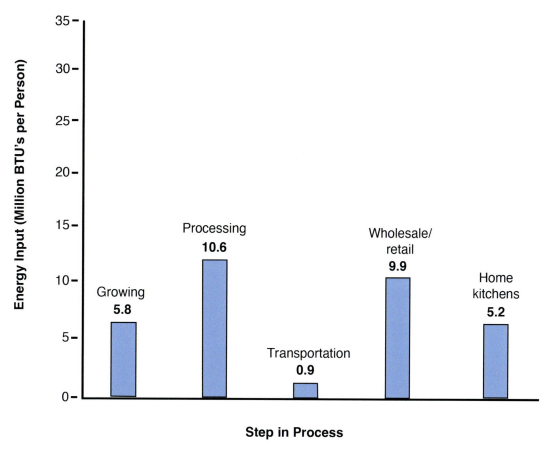

Figure 8.3 Energy input in the various phases of food consumption and production.

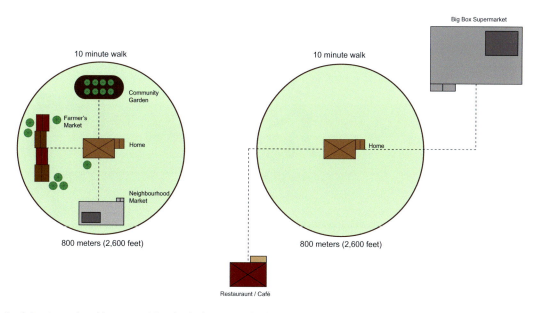

Figure 8.4 Food deserts are found in communities that lack access to healthy and affordable food options. Food swamps are areas with an abundance of fast-food and unhealthy food choices (after HB Lanarc).

Cities as Farms

low-income communities and communities of color are disproportionately affected by these unhealthy food environments. The challenge of accessibility and cost is becoming increasingly prevalent in our current food system. As the COVID-19 pandemic made it more difficult to produce and transport fruits and vegetables, we have seen supply chain disruptions leading to an enormous rising cost of food prices compounded with the loss of income that considerable amounts of people experienced during the pandemic. (Mead et al. 2020; Stoevska 2020). This underlines the social and ecological insecurities and instabilities of urban environments and their residents in relation to food scarcity under different scenarios of change (Langemeyer et al. 2021).

There has recently been a trend of revitalizing urban markets through the promotion of locally sourced production supplies. This not only helps to mitigate the risk of price fluctuations caused by reliance on imported goods but also creates job opportunities and income streams in rural areas, preventing the rapid migration of people to cities. By connecting cities with their surrounding regions, society can create a more balanced and sustainable economic landscape (Bricas 2019).

8.2 Creating Edible Landscapes

Due to a growing reconsideration of production agriculture (PA) as the dominant method of food supply, attention has turned to local food systems (LFS): a collaborative approach that integrates sustainable food production, processing, distribution, consumption and waste management to reimagine the current global PA model (Buchan et al. 2019) (Figure 8.5). LSF presents a solution to enhance the economic, ecological and social health of particular areas through spatial and non-spatial planning, for instance, land use plans as well as food procurement policy and governance strategies. Urban planning plays a significant role in discourses surrounding community sustainability and resiliency. Furthermore, planning principles such as Agricultural Urbanism (AU) are important to consider in the face of rapidly growing city populations, considering that out of all the food produced in the world, 80 percent is destined for consumption in urban spaces (Dona et al. 2021).

With a focus on LFS, AU integrates a sustainable food and agriculture system into urban environments, covering concerns related to growing food. The term encompasses a range of activities aimed at improving food security, nutrition and income generation through practices ranging from animal agriculture to aquaculture, beekeeping and horticulture. It aims to bridge the gap between individual consumers and autonomous producers, promoting a more conscious approach to food choices and the consumption of locally sourced products. The principles of AU encourage the creation of a community-based food system, from personal gardens to urban farms, transforming urban landscapes into productive, edible ones. Many cities are now taking the lead by establishing community-farming projects that foster collective food production and support the growth of local agriculture (Lohrberg et al. 2016). Shortening complex, costly and resource-intensive supply chains allows for smaller amounts of

Figure 8.5 The current global production agriculture (PA) model.

Cities as Farms

Figure 8.6 Urban agriculture differentiates itself by varying its priorities, where growing flowers, for example, can be the main activity.

food to spoil on long trips, less nutritional value lost due to long travel times, and a decline in demand for genetic modification to help preserve produce during transportation (Friedman 2017). Production often divides urban from rural agriculture, as the latter focuses on production as the immediate goal. AU differentiates itself in this regard by varying its priorities, where non-production aspects such as aesthetic landscapes, recreational opportunities, educational programming and health initiatives can be emphasized by certain urban farms (Lohrberg et al. 2016) (Figure 8.6).

To have a significant positive impact on people's diets, cities must prioritize the reorganization and optimization of their green spaces for urban agriculture. This starts, first, with the surrounding environment and farmers in the rural regions, and, second, with parks and nature reserves. Ultimately, the potential for growth must be considered in all urban spaces, including roofs, medians and other unused areas (Figure 8.7). Urban planners and landscape designers should collaborate to carefully choose access points that limit the space between the sidewalks and the urban gardens while designing a pathway through the garden without obstructing plant growth. Urban gardens should be situated in easily accessible locations near transit stops and other local amenities with the surrounding areas featuring elements like covered outdoor spaces, playgrounds and businesses to foster a vibrant street life and promote the culture of agriculture (Greytak et al. 2019). By investing in AU, individuals and communities can reap numerous benefits, including improved health, increased social cohesion and the reduction of environmental problems such as the heat island effect.

Figure 8.7 Locations of small-scale food growing can include sidewalks and rooftops.

8.3 Community Gardens and Domestic Agriculture

Social scientists have incorporated shared gardens into the discourse surrounding food sovereignty, community food security, environmental justice and multifarious socio-economic power relations (Furness and Gallaher 2018). While making use of unused urban space, community gardens can improve social cohesion and connect populations to their food sources and the larger community while providing local nutritious food to a neighborhood (Furness and Gallaher 2018). Community gardens entail a particular type of urban agriculture where farming

Figure 8.8 Community gardens like the one shown here contribute to social, mental and physical wellbeing.

objectives are equally connected with social, mental and physical wellbeing and resilience goals at the individual, communal and environmental levels (Tapia et al. 2021) (Figure 8.8). It promotes LFS and socially engages a community in sustainable city practices, promotes learning about local sustainability, facilitates social connections across generations, and advances a sense of community belonging.

Community gardens can be optimal spaces for the growth of leaf crops, vine crops and culinary herbs. These include spinach, lettuce, salad greens, tomato, cucumber, pepper, basil, parsley, chives and much more (Specht et al. 2013). Unused urban spaces often include rooftops, where the implementation of gardens may help mitigate the urban heat island effect. Ample rooftop space for rooftop greenhouses and gardens can be found on top supermarkets, hotels, convention centers, hospitals, schools, apartment blocks, prisons, warehouses and shopping malls, all which may provide ideal settings for rooftop greenhouses (Granchamp 2019). These practices can be a significant push forward for greater accessibility to nutritious food, fighting against food deserts and food swamps.

Another facet of AU can include optimizing space in homes, offices and other similar buildings. Vertical farming is an innovative solution for businesses or individuals in high-density areas where space is limited. If implemented indoors, vertical farms can be added as interior walls, space separators or partitions for privacy (Figure 8.9). As well as providing food, studies have shown that vertical gardens have the potential to improve the quality of life for urban dwellers by lowering stress levels (Lotfi et al. 2020). Exteriorly, vertical gardens can be incorporated into buildings to create a "green envelope" of edible plants. Additionally, urban cultivators can be useful in this regard. Urban cultivators are indoor gardening systems that use LED lights to grow plants indoors and can be used in a similar setting where outdoor space is scarce. They are designed for use in urban areas where outdoor gardening may not be feasible or convenient. The LED lights in an urban cultivator serve as a substitute for natural sunlight, providing the plants with the necessary light they need to grow and thrive. They can also be used indoors in individual households.

On the other hand, for households with outdoor space, various home production practices can be adopted as means of adjustment to consume local, in-season produce and grow food without chemical inputs (Granchamp 2019). Vegetable gardening has been studied as having a strong symbolic meaning for individuals beyond just eating locally and it can represent a means of concrete action with regard to the problems of climate change (Granchamp 2019). Food production and distribution have become so industrialized and complex that individuals often feel a loss of control. Meanwhile, climate change presents a massive global risk that is often disconnected from everyday life. Growing vegetable gardens allows people to bridge the gap between knowledge and action, connecting the theoretical with the practical. Studies have shown that vegetable gardening in a family setting can raise environmental awareness, leading individuals to become more invested in addressing climate issues (Granchamp 2019).

The vegetable garden symbolizes an eco-friendly lifestyle and is the center of a comprehensive set of practices. To optimize the effectiveness of rectangle gardens for hosing and

Cities as Farms

Figure 8.9 Spots for small-scale growing activities by individuals.

harvesting, it is crucial to choose well-adapted native species that are in harmony with local conditions in terms of soil, water and sunlight requirements. Additionally, to minimize maintenance and ensure optimal growth, it is advisable to divide the plants into separate zones based on their water usage and fertilizer needs. By planting native species and implementing this zoned approach, you can avoid the use of harmful chemicals that pose a threat to human health, while also maximizing the success of a garden (Friedman and Pollock 2022). Other small initiatives can have a positive impact. For instance, grocery stores and farmers' markets have begun to offer a variety of greens, such as lettuce, kale and herbs, with the root attached for customers to grow back and enjoy at home, creating a sustainable and eco-friendly method of producing fresh greens.

8.4 Promotion of Artisan Food Production

A sustainable food system should strive to strike a delicate balance between maximizing profits and preserving the livelihoods of all stakeholders, while promoting social sustainability and minimizing any adverse environmental impact.

To achieve this, it is crucial to embrace diversity in the food system (Furness and Gallaher 2018). The promotion of artisan food producers and the support of farmers' markets are key elements in this effort. Acting as an intermediary between farms and the city, these small-scale, resilient and diverse markets offer a promising approach to building a sustainable food system (Connolly et al. 2022) (Figure 8.10). An Australian study highlights the multiple benefits of farmers' markets (Ripoll González et al. 2022). Not only do they encourage conscious consumption, they also support local businesses and their products, preserve cultural and gastronomic traditions, and contribute to the sustainability of local food systems. Furthermore, they offer a unique and authentic social experience, making them a great addition to sustainable tourism (Ripoll González et al. 2022).

8.5 Gardening in a Heart of a Montreal Community

The planners of the Benny Farm neighborhood in Montreal set their sight on local food production (Goldie 2017). The uniqueness of the redeveloped plan lies in a central community garden for agriculture. In the garden, residents could grow the

Cities as Farms

Figure 8.10 Acting as an intermediary between large local farms and the established food chains, small-scale, resilient and diverse farmers' markets, as seen here in Hamburg, Germany, are part of the sustainable food system.

produce of their choice on their assigned lots (Figure 8.11). The place forms part of the city's community gardens network, which encourages people to grow nutritious food close to home while fostering social interaction. The city built a tool shed and provided water throughout the site, and some lots were designated for the use of the local community food bank. More than a place to grow food, it became the community's social hub and a wait list currently exists for lots due to its popularity. It is a very active place with a wide variety of produce and flowers. Since the community is ethnically diverse, the food is also a reflection of the cultural origins of residents.

8.6 The Pots of Matera

Dating back to the Paleolithic times, Matera, a city of 60,000 residents, evolved in layers. The first inhabitants of the place built their homes into or under a thick layer of rock. Those who followed them built dwellings on top of the rock to give the place a highly organic look (Figure 8.12).

Outside each home on the hard surface that was the roof of the dwelling below there were clay pots of all types and sizes.

In large pots there were fair size fig, apricot and pear trees, and in smaller ones, varieties of vegetables. In one yard a tomato plant clung to strings affixed to a wall. In low flat rectangular containers, green onions and basil plants were growing. There were also grapevines that formed the roof of outdoor seating or the partition between two adjacent homes. The scene was replicated near every home, making the whole look like an improvised growing operation.

Not having soil near their homes for planting forced the people of Matera to use pots. This resulted in local production that not only supplied some of their basic daily food needs but softened the hard outdoors. The pots of Matera demonstrate that our supermarkets can be outside our homes if we just make an effort.

8.7 Gardening in the Negev Desert

For centuries Israel's Negev Desert was an inhospitable home of nomad bands and caravans who cross the place en route to markets in the north. When visiting, in the distance one notices a row of vaulted structures. Reaching closer, a few

Cities as Farms

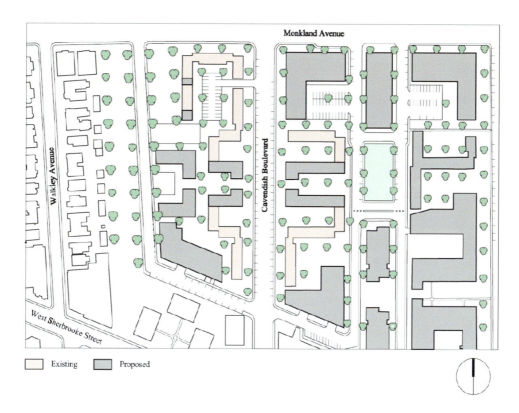

Figure 8.11 The uniqueness of Benny Farm's redeveloped plan in Montreal, Canada, lies in having a central community garden.

Cities as Farms

Figure 8.12 On the hard surfaces outside each home in Matera, Italy, there are clay pots and planters for food growing.

dozen are covered with transparent plastic sheets. Inside, there are columns of plants from which green bell peppers were hanging. No one was around and only the dripping sound of automated irrigation could be heard (Figure 8.13).

For years, Israel invested in developing agricultural technologies to improve farming. Israel's Negev Desert, a place with poor soil, a challenging climate and rocky terrain, has proven to be a great location for testing new types of agriculture. Considered one of the most arid places on earth, the Negev is part of the Sahara-Arabian desert belt. It was initially thought to be uninhabitable, but Ben-Gurion, Israel's first prime minister, wanted it to be part of the Jewish state when the country boundaries were discussed, envisioning the potential of the land to serve the new state. His prediction was right, as the arid land conditions of the Negev have been overcome, and many fruits, vegetables and flowers are now being produced in the region (Leichman 2020).

The cultivation of cherry tomatoes has been especially successful, with up to 75 percent of exports making their way to international markets. New methods allow farmers to use brackish (salty) water, which is partially responsible for this, as the place has very little access to fresh water. Furthermore, creating optimal growing conditions for crops is important to consider. The use of the greenhouses has been instrumental, as they may increase yield crops during the wintertime to allow year-round gardening. They also give plants the ideal growth environment by controlling temperature and exposure to solar radiation. For instance, solar collectors can be used to generate heat when outdoor temperatures are below freezing, so that the inside of greenhouses are cool, but allow spring vegetables to survive. During the summer, fans or other cooling devices can be used to protect more sensitive plants from perishing due to scorching heat (Fedler 2011).

As many parts of the world are coping with the ravaging effects of climate change, drought and hunger, it is necessary for new and innovative agricultural techniques to be tested and shared. The greenhouses of the Negev demonstrate that even regions where growing crops is unthinkable due to adverse conditions can turn into gardens.

Cities as Farms

Figure 8.13 The greenhouses in Israel's Negev Desert.

8.8 Final Thoughts

A cultural entity may need to change to revise the values and norms that shape our current food system. This change must involve a wide range of actors, including individuals, communities, governments and businesses. Collaboration between these sectors is essential to create a successful and sustainable food system. The cultural shift toward urban agriculture and local food systems requires a multi-faceted approach, including education, community involvement, collaboration, supportive policies and regulations, and an embrace of new innovations. Urban planners play a vital role in creating supportive environments for urban agriculture. They can work with communities, governments and other stakeholders to develop policies, regulations and infrastructure that support food production, and ensure that urban agriculture is integrated into broader land-use and planning goals. Practices can include vertical farming, widespread community gardens and the promotion of farmers' markets in the effort to diversify food supply and revitalize urban markets through the rise of locally sourced produce.

References

Bricas, N. (2019). Urbanization issues affecting food system sustainability. In *Designing Urban Food Policies*. Springer. Cham. Retrieved June 24, 2023, from https://doi.org/10.1007/978-3-030-13958-2_1

Buchan, R., Cloutier, D. S. and Friedman, A. (2019). Transformative incrementalism: planning for transformative change in local food systems. *Progress in Planning* 134: 100424. Retrieved June 24, 2023, from https://doi.org/10.1016/j.progress.2018.07.002

Campbell, B. M., Beare, D. J., Bennett, E. M., Hall-Spencer, J. M., Ingram, J. S., Jaramillo, F., Ortiz, R., Ramankutty, N., Sayer, J. A. and Shindell, D. (2017). Agriculture production as a major driver of the Earth system exceeding planetary boundaries. *Ecology and Society* 22(4). Retrieved June 24, 2023, from https://doi.org/10.5751/es-09595-220408

Chekol, C. (2021). The health effects of genetically modified foods: a brief review. *International Journal of Nutritional Sciences* 6(1). Retrieved June 24, 2023, from https://doi.org/10.26420/intjnutrsci.2021.1047

Connolly, C., Keil, R. and Ali, S.H. (2020). Extended urbanisation and the spatialities of infectious disease: demographic change, infrastructure and governance. *Urban Studies* 58(2): 245–263. Retrieved June 23, 2023, from https://doi.org/10.1177/0042098020910873

Connolly, R., Bogue, J. and Repar, L. (2022). Farmers' markets as resilient alternative market structures in a sustainable global food system: A small firm growth perspective. *Sustainability* 14(18): 11626. Retrieved June 24, 2023, from https://doi.org/10.3390/su141811626

Dona, C. G. W., Mohan, G. and Fukushi, K. (2021). Promoting urban agriculture and its opportunities and challenges: a global review. *Sustainability* 13(17): 9609. Retrieved June 24, 2023, from https://doi.org/10.3390/su13179609

Fedler, J. (2011). Agriculture in Israel: coping with population growth. *Jewish Virtual Library*. Retrieved June 24, 2023, from https://www.jewishvirtuallibrary.org/agriculturally-coping-with-population-growth

Friedman, A. (2017). *Designing Sustainable Communities*. Bloomsbury Academic. London.

Friedman, A. and Pollock, A. (2022). Food production and distribution. In *Fundamentals of Planning Cities for Healthy Living*, pp. 83–94. Anthem Press. London.

Furness, W. W. and Gallaher, C. M. (2018). Food access, food security and community gardens in Rockford, IL. *Local Environment* 23(4): 414–430. Retrieved June 24, 2023, from https://doi.org/10.1080/13549839.2018.1426561

Goldie, J. (2017). Benny farm redevelopment: maintaining community while greening affordable housing. *Sustainable Heritage Case Studies*. Retrieved June 24, 2023, from https://sustainableheritagecasestudies.ca/2017/12/08/renewing-social-housing/

Granchamp, L. (2019). Adjusting food practices to climate prescriptions: vegetable gardening as a way to reduce food-related greenhouse gas emissions. *Review of Agricultural, Food and Environmental Studies* 100(1–4): 1–25. Retrieved June 24, 2023, from https://doi.org/10.1007/s41130-019-00087-7

Greytak, N., Bartholow, M., Dryke, J., Powell, M., Olson, M., Davis, E., Prendergast, C., Schlegel, C., Kalenberg, C., Lindner, C., McQuillan, K., Servais, M., Wege, A., Berg, H., Khan, N., Jung, S., Lee, V., Gallahue, S., Yentzer, B., Bascom, M., Druziako, S. and Monnens, A. (2019). Creating an edible landscape: policy and ordinances, best practices, sustainability, budget, and plant data. Resilient Communities Project (RCP), University of Minnesota. Retrieved June 24, 2023, from https://hdl.handle.net/11299/206729

Langemeyer, J., Madrid-Lopez, C., Mendoza Beltran, A. and Villalba Mendez, G. (2021). Urban agriculture: a necessary pathway towards urban resilience and global sustainability? *Landscape and Urban Planning* 210: 104055. Retrieved June 24, 2023, from https://doi.org/10.1016/j.landurbplan.2021.104055

Leichman, A. K. (2020). Why the future of agriculture lies in Israel's desert. *Israel 21c*. Retrieved June 24, 2023, from www.israel21c.org/why-the-future-of-agriculture-lies-in-israels-desert/

Li, M., Jia, N., Lenzen, M., Malik, A., Wei, L., Jin, Y. and Raubenheimer, D. (2022). Global food-miles account for nearly 20% of total food-systems emissions. *Nature Food* 3(6): 445–453. Retrieved June 24, 2023, from www.researchgate.net/publication/361432691_Global_food-miles_account_for_nearly_20_of_total_food-systems_emissions

Lohrberg, F., Lička, L., Scazzosi, L. and Timpe, A. (2016). *Urban Agriculture Europe*. Jovis. Berlin.

Lotfi, Y., Refaat, M., El Attar, M. and Salam, A. (2020). Vertical gardens as a restorative tool in urban spaces of New Cairo. *Ain Shams Engineering Journal* 11(3): 839–848. Retrieved June 24, 2023, from www.sciencedirect.com/science/article/pii/S2090447919301856

Mead, D., Ransom, K., Reed, S. and Sager, S. (2020). The impact of the COVID-19 pandemic on food price indexes and data collection. Retrieved June 24, 2023, from www.bls.gov/opub/mlr/2020/article/the-impact-of-the-covid-19-pandemic-on-food-price-indexes-and-data-collection.htm

Ripoll González, L., Yanotti, M. B. and Lehman, K. (2022). Local focus: farmers' markets as an approach to sustainable tourism. *Tourism, Hospitality & Event Management*, 95–113. Retrieved June 24, 2023, from https://doi.org/10.1007/978-3-030-92208-5_7

Sanford, C., Sabapathy, D., Morrison, H. and Gaudreau, K. (2015). *Pesticides and Human Health*. Retrieved June 24, 2023, from www.princeedwardisland.ca/sites/default/files/publications/cpho_pesticide_part_1.pdf

Specht, K., Siebert, R., Hartmann, I., Freisinger, U. B., Sawicka, M., Werner, A., Thomaier, S., Henckel, D., Walk, H. and Dierich, A. (2013). Urban agriculture of the future: an overview of sustainability aspects of food production in and on buildings. *Agriculture and Human Values* 31(1): 33–51. Retrieved June 24, 2023, from https://doi.org/10.1007/s10460-013-9448-4

Stoevska, V. (2020). COVID 19 is driving up food prices all over the world. *ILOSTAT*. Retrieved June 24, 2023, from https://ilostat.ilo.org/covid-19-is-driving-up-food-prices-all-over-the-world/

Tapia, C., Randall, L., Wang, S. and Aguiar Borges, L. (2021). Monitoring the contribution of urban agriculture to urban sustainability: an indicator-based framework. *Sustainable Cities and Society* 74: 103130. Retrieved June 24, 2023, from https://doi.org/10.1016/j.scs.2021.103130

United Nations Department of Economic and Social Affairs (2018). 68% of the world population projected to live in urban areas by 2050, says UN. United Nations Department of Economic and Social Affairs. Retrieved June 24, 2023, from https://www.un.org/development/desa/en/news/population/2018-revision-of-world-urbanization-prospects.html

United Nations Department of Economic and Social Affairs (2022). *The Sustainable Development Goals: Report 2022*. UN. Retrieved June 24, 2023, from https://unstats.un.org/sdgs/report/2022/The-Sustainable-Development-Goals-Report-2022.pdf

CHAPTER 9
Social and Economic Values of Markets

Markets have long been recognized as important venues for local businesses to sell their products and services. They not only provide consumers with access to unique and locally sourced goods, but also promote local economic growth. However, the impact of markets extends far beyond their economic benefits. Markets play a crucial role in reducing the carbon footprint associated with the transportation and packaging of food and other products by supporting local farmers and producers. They also serve as vital community spaces that foster social connections, build relationships and promote a shared sense of belonging. This chapter explores the various ways in which markets contribute to the social fabric of a community, and how they can facilitate the adoption of healthier dietary practices. Additionally, urban market design principles are outlined for supporting socialization, inclusion and economic benefit, and their importance in building vibrant and resilient communities.

9.1 Genesis and Evolution of Markets

From the Greek agora to the bazaars of Persia, humans have been selling and purchasing food and goods at markets for thousands of years (Figure 9.1). However, markets are seldom studied as actual, physical places within cities in history. Instead, they are typically thought of in terms of their institutional meaning as abstract concepts of commerce and exchange, whether involving commodities, labor, cash or shares (Stobart and Van Damme 2015). Yet, an explanation of the origins and functioning of cities can be thought of as very closely linked to the existence of a 'central market' – a physical core of the exchange of goods between buyers and sellers (Stobart and Van Damme 2015). To understand the evolution of markets throughout history to the present day, one needs to reflect on how and why they came to be.

In a time when hunters and gatherers lived and survived on what nature could provide, people congregated in bands whose size was determined by food supply. Patterns shifted as humans began to settle down, and while bands still relied on their hunting and gathering skills, animals started to be domesticated, seeds were planted and crops harvested. The earlier food supply chain no longer limited the group's size, which expanded rapidly, and there was sufficient food for the farmer's household and leftovers for trade. Societies then began to pack themselves in a different social order where trade was commonplace. Exchanges took place in public areas, often in the heart of a settlement. Communities continued to increase in the following centuries and trading became more important and formalized in location and process. Weekly days were chosen for buying and selling livestock and other commodities, an activity named *market* from *mercatus* in Latin, meaning "a regular gathering of people for the purchase and sale of provisions, livestock, and other commodities" (Oxford Languages 2023). Along with the evolution of commerce and the invention of currencies, the physical form of markets varied and progressed.

Markets and cities are commonly understood to have emerged in tandem as distinct economic environments, where the existence of surpluses, such as in vegetables, facilitated the differentiation of society into communities of citizens (Janssens and Sezer 2013). Markets have played a vital role in the growth and transformation of local economies and the social fabric of communities. With the rise of monetary systems, farmers could obtain currency instead of exclusively trading goods or services. For example, Kelley argues that London's street markets played a crucial role in the city's urbanization and economic development during the period of 1850 to 1939 (Kelley 2015). The author highlights the social and economic importance of street markets, as they provided affordable goods to working-class people and served as a platform for small businesses to thrive.

DOI: 10.4324/9781003384687-9

Social and Economic Values of Markets

Figure 9.1 These markets in Bruges, Belgium (left) and Beuvron-en-Auge, France (right) served patrons for centuries.

Figure 9.2 Markets played a pivotal role in European cities' economies, and they were commonly embedded in the heart of neighborhoods, such as this one in the region of Normandy, France.

Urban sociologists acknowledge the market's pivotal role in European cities' growth and development, as it served as the hub of the central business district and was surrounded by concentric circles of flourishing neighborhoods (Stobart and Van Damme 2015) (Figure 9.2). With the expansion of cities came the realization that markets are valuable sources of tax revenue and permanent markets started taking place. For example, Istanbul's Grand Bazaar is a large, covered structure with 1,500 shops and 15,000 tradesmen in 80 streets and alleys (Friedman 2016). Congregating similar types of merchandise was common and specialty areas were prominent in this market, with goldsmiths, clothing and footwear, and furniture divisions (Figure 9.3). However, markets served a greater purpose beyond just economic exchange – they were also

Social and Economic Values of Markets

Figure 9.3 Istanbul's Grand Bazaar is a covered structure with some 1,500 shops and 15,000 tradesmen in 80 streets and alleys.

social hubs where people gathered, interacted and shared cultural experiences (Crespi-Vallbona and Dimitrovski 2017). It also allowed for subsidiary social institutions, such as pubs and inns, to thrive. Moreover, it was the hub of information exchange, the ancestor of today's print and electronic media. In the nineteenth and early twentieth centuries, the farmers' market served as both a food source and a focal point for interaction between urban and rural dwellers.

The twentieth century saw the emergence of supermarkets that coincided with the birth of suburbia. In 1935, there were only around 300 supermarkets operating in the United States, a number that soared quickly to 6,175 by 1940 (Friedman 2016). The need for a constant large supply of food triggered the replacement of family-run farms with larger industrial operations that supplied wholesalers and manufacturers. With the rise of supermarkets, many consumer habits began to shift away from shopping in local and farmers' markets toward the more convenient and centralized locations of supermarkets that were more competitive. Likewise, the rise of supermarkets also had a significant impact on the agriculture sector globally. Small-scale farmers were often unable to compete with larger industrial operations that supplied supermarkets. This led to a

decline in the number of small-scale farms in Europe and the United States. However, in recent years, there has been a growing trend in Europe toward supporting local agriculture and sustainable food systems. This has led to a resurgence of in-person markets and small retailers, as consumers increasingly value locally sourced and sustainable goods.

9.2 Urban Functions of Markets

Urbanization, shifts in work pattern and changes in family structures have also led to the elongation of the food supply chain, resulting in a greater distance between agricultural production and food consumption (Connolly et al. 2022). Unfortunately, major vulnerabilities exist in the economic, social and environmental sustainability of long food supply chains, as evidenced by the recent shocks of the COVID-19 pandemic, the war in Ukraine and extreme weather events (Connolly et al. 2022). In response to these vulnerabilities, farmers' markets have emerged as a vital solution, offering market access and livelihoods to local small-scale producers while also preserving traditional practices and creating a sense of collective identity that stands in opposition to the dominant forces of mass production (Figure 9.4). Today, markets may not be as prominent as they once were during certain periods in history, but they continue to prosper as essential parts of towns and cities worldwide. This is due to the innumerable economic, social, urban and ecological benefits of successful public markets. Although markets and their food retailing functions have been regarded as fundamental elements for developing compact and livable cities, their economic and social impact has often been underestimated (Navapan and Charoenkit 2022). Economically, they foster connections between urban and rural economies, expand access to affordable and healthy food, and provide low-risk business opportunities for vendors and farmers. Socially, markets are the original civic centers and remain key public gathering places that shape social norms and activities (Figure 9.5).

These markets serve as more than mere economic hubs. They act as moral pillars for the community, promoting socially just and environmentally sustainable practices while offering opportunities for social interaction and inclusion (Navapan and Charoenkit 2022). The lively atmosphere created by face-to-face trading distinguishes these markets from the sterile environments of supermarkets, providing richer and more authentic experiences. As such, they serve as vital components of a city's urban fabric, attracting both local residents and tourists (Ripoll González et al. 2022). Well-managed markets can serve as a catalyst for urban renewal, connecting city centers with their rural surroundings and fostering multicultural interactions. Markets are known for their ability to create social spaces that promote proximity, creativity, identity and diversity. This social atmosphere has been shown to enhance safety and friendliness in urban areas. Moreover, markets play a critical role in shaping a city's identity and contributing to its livability, sustainability and vibrancy (Navapan and Charoenkit 2022). Their sociable and interactive character also draws tourists, promoting sustainable tourism and travel practices like proximity and slow tourism. Research indicates that farmers' markets play a crucial role in promoting conscious consumption and sustainable tourism behaviors (Ripoll González et al. 2022). These markets encourage support for local businesses and products, preservation of cultural and gastronomic heritage, and the promotion of slow and proximity tourism as alternatives to mass tourism and other unsustainable tourism activities (Figure 9.6).

Figure 9.4 Farmers' markets offer a vital support to local small-scale producers while also preserving traditional practices and creating a sense of collective identity.

Social and Economic Values of Markets

Figure 9.5 Markets can be regarded as "social magnets" and public gathering places on their many activities.

Figure 9.6 In many cities markets have become tourist destinations.

Consolidation and increased market concentration have led to the loss of jobs in agriculture and local food production. However, these jobs serve as crucial pillars of rural society by providing social and cultural values. This loss of jobs contributes to a migration of people to urban areas, further exacerbating the issue (Francis and Griffith 2011). The contributions of local markets to the economy are invaluable, as they not only drive spending in nearby shops and generate tax revenue, but also create employment opportunities for agricultural and local food-producing jobs. They foster new businesses, strengthen and diversify regional agriculture, and increase farm profitability (Connolly et al. 2022). Additionally, urban markets can serve as a stepping-stone for entrepreneurship. Lowering barriers to entry in these markets would enable citizens to invest and seize opportunities that would otherwise be out of reach due to a lack of access to capital (Hergül and Göker 2021). Along with creating dynamic local economies, supporting local growers reduces the need for food to travel long distances, and thereby lowers emission levels. Furthermore, locally sourced produce reduces the need for chemical treatments to extend shelf life, leading to improved overall public health.

9.3 Markets Typologies and Design

It is essential to acknowledge the significant variation that exists among markets, both locally and globally. Depending on their location, markets can be situated in bustling city centers, suburban areas or specific neighborhoods. These markets can be found in a range of settings, including public squares, streets and semi-open or covered market halls. Markets may specialize in a diverse selection of goods or focus on particular commodities, such as fish or fruit. Additionally, some markets may cater to specific consumer groups or serve the broader urban population. Every market is unique, with its distinct character and appeal that stems from its individual features (Stobart and Van Damme 2015). There are different types of markets, including temporary markets and those that operate year-round, indoor and outdoor markets, and other farmers' markets that come in various forms (Figure 9.7). By understanding the differences that exist among markets, consumers

Social and Economic Values of Markets

Figure 9.7 Markets can be categorized according to their content (top row), their location (middle row) and their time of operation (bottom row).

can make informed decisions about where and when to shop for goods that meet their needs (Stobart and Van Damme 2015).

Some markets have permanent structures located on a daily route for growers who sell items like dairy products or honey. Others are seasonal and only operate during the summer and autumn months. These types of markets are often less formal, and products are sold from the backs of trucks or makeshift stalls. For example, the Talad Tai market in Thailand is a temporary street market that is set up early in the morning and taken down later in the day. The open-plan design of the market building also allows for future redesign or development (Stobart and Van Damme 2015).

If a market wants to establish permanency, investing in thoughtful landscape design such as entry structures, gazebos, fountains, market pavilions, mature groves of trees, plazas and pedestrian-scaled lighting can help ensure its long-term success and stability (Francis and Griffith 2011). This can elevate the market from being merely a temporary event in public space to a more significant fixture in the community (Figure 9.8). Yet, considering the plethora of market variations that exist around the world, design must be grounded in local knowledge, customs and traditions. Thriving markets are those that prioritize the needs and characteristics of the surrounding community in their planning, design and operation. This involves a thoughtful integration of local culture and community groups into the market's layout and services. Additionally, effective markets often connect with adjacent civic institutions and retail activities through well-planned pedestrian walkways, bicycle routes and open space networks, creating a vibrant, interconnected community. Planning a successful market also involves considering regional transportation systems, public transit, overflow parking and other relevant aspects of the regional landscape, to ensure accessibility and convenience for all (Francis and Griffith 2011).

Understanding the role of markets in urban areas requires considering their relationship with demographic changes in the city structure, evolving traffic patterns, public transport availability, conflicts with other land uses, and the location of the residential population they serve. The physical characteristics of the marketplace, such as its accessibility, size, amenities and layout, affect its social appeal. Providing benches to sit on, small restaurants in the area to grab a snack, other shops to investigate, or winding alleys and

Social and Economic Values of Markets

Figure 9.8 The decorative ceiling of Mercat Central de Valencia made the place a significant fixture of the community and the city.

Figure 9.9 Markets often include dining areas like the ones in Singapore (left) and Lisbon, Portugal (right).

corners to explore can increase the sociability of the market (Janssens and Sezer 2013) (Figure 9.9). When it comes to location, urban markets, especially street markets, are best placed at right angles to the main traffic arteries, with linkages to pedestrian routes and parking areas located behind them. This way, cars can pull off the main road without entering the market area, minimizing congestion and safety hazards. To reduce their environmental footprint, parking areas should be kept small and covered by plants or walls (Hergül and Göker 2021). It is also a good idea that these spaces contain shade trees, protective structures and an assortment of seating arrangements that are located within parks, along pedestrian paths and in plazas (Francis and Griffith 2011). Moreover, it is necessary to follow accessible building standards to make sure everyone can enjoy the market. This means providing wide door openings and easy-to-use doors, sufficient space for wheelchair users to open and close doors, and enough maneuvering room. Unimpeded transport and access should be provided to at least one entrance of the buildings, and all accessible route points should be at least 90 cm (35.43 inch) wide with ramps no steeper than 8 percent (Hergül and Göker 2021).

Special design attention should be given to supporting socialization. Francis and Griffith (2011) identify several important elements to consider in designing markets, including the promenade, working market and market landscape. The promenade is a central pathway where visitors can browse products and interact with one another. Typically, this pathway is 3 to 6 meters (10 to 20 feet) wide and lined with colorful displays of goods. In more intimate settings, the aisle width may be reduced to encourage social interaction between

Social and Economic Values of Markets

visitors that are less prevalent in contemporary public spaces. To further enhance the experience, the promenade can be adorned with features such as pedestrian lights, tree plantings and outdoor furniture to punctuate moments along the way (Francis and Griffith 2011).

When planning a working market, it's crucial to consider the distinct areas within the space, such as prepared foods, value-added products, arts and crafts, and fruits and vegetables. However, ensuring vehicle access for loading, unloading and parking is also a key consideration for its functionality. Beyond these practical needs, a well-balanced working market should also offer spaces for entertainment, such as music and theater performances, as well as food courts and other open areas for social programs (Francis and Griffith 2011). These spaces are typically located at the end of a promenade. To further support vendors and ensure their success, it is important to provide accessible parking and easy access to electricity and water (Hergül and Göker 2021). By taking these factors into account during the planning process, a working market can truly thrive and serve the community it is designed for.

Furthermore, the market landscape consists of the open space surrounding the working market and promenade, offering more than just buying and selling opportunities (Francis and Griffith 2011). Similar to well-designed urban spaces, a successful market landscape provides comfortable seating options such as benches, movable chairs, steps and lawn areas for leisure. To ensure an inclusive social space, it is important to accommodate a diverse range of ages, genders and cultural backgrounds. This can be achieved by integrating children's play and activity needs into the design. Employing a participatory design process can be beneficial in meeting these goals. By providing opportunities for leisure and relaxation, a market landscape creates a welcoming and inviting atmosphere that enhances the overall experience.

9.4 Turnips in Dalian

Walking in Dalian, China, in the early morning, I noticed loaded pushcarts and people entering and exiting a yard. I followed them and saw an open day market framed by four-story, shabby-looking apartment buildings (Figure 9.10).

Agricultural produce was arranged in improvised parallel lines on the ground, in no apparent order. Vendors – local farmers, it seemed, and other traders – sold to urban dwellers who resided nearby. Celery, turnips, green onions and leeks looked freshly harvested. Buyers holding cotton bags pointed, asked for a price and, at times, bargained. The seller grabbed the item and

Figure 9.10 The morning market in Dalian, China, offers a sense of place that brings visitors closer to the food and culinary culture of the locals.

placed it on a handheld scale. Money was exchanged. Fried food and dumplings were cooked and sold in a corner. Sea creatures were tucked in between fruits and vegetables. Unshaven, tired-looking fishermen snatched handfuls of crabs and shrimp, shoved them into folded newspaper and handed them over to customers.

I wondered what made this market unique. Was it the raw quality of the place: a mercantile act stripped of the trappings that Westerners are used to? Perhaps it was the produce, some of which I did not recognize, and the feeling of being a foreigner in an unexpected spot. I was clearly experiencing a sense of place that brought me closer to the food and the culinary culture of people who minutes ago were total strangers.

Western urban dwellers have become accustomed to a formal food trade with little or no information about the produce or the grower. The increased popularity of the farmers' market has changed that. More needs to be done to make these markets a regular feature of our neighborhoods to the benefit of everyone.

9.5 Mixing Market and Housing in Rotterdam

The Market Hall in Rotterdam is the Netherlands' first covered mixed-use market and apartments. It successfully addresses the need for high-density housing while significantly contributing to the local economy and nicely integrating with the

Social and Economic Values of Markets

surroundings. The firm MVRDV designed the project to expand the current open-air market with a covered addition due to stricter European rules forbidding the open-air sale of fresh and chilled food (Figure 9.11).

The building's facade, a cable net structure, deftly balances transparency with the practical necessity of protecting the interior from the winter winds. Constructed of natural stone, the facade subtly complements the more exuberant hues of the

Figure 9.11 Rotterdam's Market Hall has apartments built over a market.

building's interior, which takes center stage in terms of aesthetics (Aguilar 2014).

The building's unique structure incorporates a massive market floor under an arch of apartments, separating different activities across varying levels while also increasing the efficiency of interior space. The main ground floor entrance leads to the commercial area, which includes a fresh food market, dry food shops, restaurants and a supermarket. Notably, the supply chain of the building is located underground, mitigating the impact of early-morning delivery activities on inhabitants. From the third to the eleventh floor, there are 228 apartments housed in the horseshoe-shaped arch. Some apartments feature triple-glazed windows overlooking the market to minimize noise and odor intrusion.

Sustainability is paramount in the design of Market Hall, which boasts city heating, a thermal storage system and a natural ventilation system. The building also features an intelligent sanitation system designed to conserve water. As a commitment to future sustainability goals, the building's tenants have signed a Green Lease Agreement outlining sustainable performance requirements.

Market Hall became a new icon of Rotterdam and successfully integrates housing, shopping and dining. Its innovative design solidifies its status as an architectural marvel and a thriving hub of urban life and a model for other cities to emulate.

9.6 Final Thoughts

Markets provide a platform for local businesses to showcase their products and services, allowing consumers to directly promote economic growth. Additionally, supporting local farmers and producers can help reduce the carbon footprint associated with the transportation and packaging of food and other products. Markets are not just places to shop, but also play an important role in building a sense of community and strengthening social bonds. By their very nature, markets foster a unique identity for a community, which goes beyond a simple commercial exchange. This social aspect of markets creates opportunities for people to connect and interact with one another, building relationships and a shared sense of belonging. Therefore, the impact of markets extends far beyond economic transactions, and can greatly contribute to the social fabric of a community. Finally, many markets offer an array of fresh and nutritious food choices, thereby facilitating the adoption of healthier dietary practices and enhancing overall wellbeing in the community.

References

Aguilar, C. (2014). Markthal Rotterdam / MVRDV. *ArchDaily*. Retrieved June 24, 2023, from www.archdaily.com/553933/markthal-rotterdam-mvrdv

Connolly, R., Bogue, J. and Repar, L. (2022). Farmers' markets as resilient alternative market structures in a sustainable global food system: A small firm growth perspective. *Sustainability* 14(18): 11626. Retrieved June 24, 2023, from https://doi.org/10.3390/su141811626

Crespi-Vallbona, M. and Dimitrovski, D. (2017). Food markets from a local dimension: La Boqueria (Barcelona, Spain). *Cities* 70: 32–39. Retrieved June 24, 2023, from https://doi.org/10.1016/j.cities.2017.06.011

Francis, M. and Griffith, L. (2011). The meaning and design of farmers' markets as public space: an issue-based case study. *Landscape Journal* 30(2): 261–279. Retrieved June 24, 2023, from https://doi.org/10.3368/lj.30.2.261

Friedman, A. (2016). *A Place in Mind: The Search for Authenticity*. Véhicule Press. Montreal.

Hergül, Ö. C. and Göker, P. (2021). Determining the suitability level of urban markets to the urban planning and design criteria: case of Bilecik, Turkey. *Environment, Development and Sustainability* 23(12): 18443–18470. Retrieved June 24, 2023, from https://ideas.repec.org/a/spr/endesu/v23y2021i12d10.1007_s10668-021-01454-5.html

Janssens, F. and Sezer, C. (2013). 'Flying markets' activating public spaces in Amsterdam. *Built Environment* 39(2): 245–260. Retrieved June 24, 2023, from https://doi.org/10.2148/benv.39.2.245

Kelley, V. (2015). The streets for the people: London's street markets 1850–1939. *Urban History* 43(3): 391–411. Retrieved June 24, 2023, from https://doi.org/10.1017/s0963926815000231

Navapan, N. and Charoenkit, S. (2022). Local markets: how the ordinary public places can support urban sustainable development. *GMSARN International Journal* 16(3): 308–313. Retrieved June 24, 2023, from http://gmsarnjournal.com/home/wp-content/uploads/2021/10/vol16no3-12.pdf

Oxford Languages (2023). Definition of market. *Oxford Learners Dictionaries*. Retrieved June 24, 2023, from www.oxfordlearnersdictionaries.com/definition/english/market_1

Ripoll González, L., Belén Yanotti, M. and Lehman, K. (2022). Local focus: farmers' markets as an approach to sustainable tourism. *Tourism, Hospitality & Event Management*, 95–113. Retrieved June 24, 2023, from https://doi.org/10.1007/978-3-030-92208-5_7

Stobart, J. and Van Damme, I. (2015). Introduction: markets in modernization: transformations in urban market space and practice, c. 1800–c. 1970. *Urban History* 43(3): 358–371. Retrieved June 24, 2023, from https://doi.org/10.1017/s0963926815000206

CHAPTER 10
The Culture of Places

This chapter delves into the relationship between local culture and place, investigating how the unique characteristics of a place can be reflected in its design. Connectedness and participation in a city are then emphasized in the design process, followed by a discussion on "place narratives." The chapter provides principles for urban design that go beyond mere technicalities of form and function. Instead, the focus is on creating places that reflect the identity and aspirations of the community and contribute to their social sustainability and quality of life, thereby promoting local culture. Overall, the chapter aims to illustrate how urban design can promote meaningful, unique and culturally relevant spaces that enhance a sense of place.

10.1 The Elements of Culture and Place

Culture serves as the collective memory and history of a city, and reflects the layering of its architecture, topology, topography and social heritage (Mellano 2017). It enriches humanity and provides a framework for ideas, norms, experiences and a common identity that shapes expected behavior and rules. When it comes to urban places, the quality that distinguishes them clearly from any other place is their unique identity. Place can be thought of as a physical space that has assumed a particular identity and set of properties, both in a physical form and in human expression. This identity is closely related to one's self-identity, derived from everyday experiences of places and the built environment. The sense of place identity is related to the meaning of that place to someone, as places make memories cohere in complex ways (Gieseking et al. 2014). Culture among people in a place contributes to building a sense of local identity and solidarity. It encompasses the unique way of life, beliefs, customs and values that a group of people share and pass on from one generation to the next (Salman 2019). These shared practices and traditions are then reflected in various aspects of the community, such

as its social, political, educational and economic institutions, as well as its languages and artifacts. Therefore, the culture of a community serves as a foundation for its sense of identity and cohesion, belonging to the people's collective imagination (Salman 2019).

One of the most fascinating and defining aspects of cities is their architectural, material and spatial stratification over time, in other words, their history (Mellano 2017). Burano, a charming island nestled in the Venice lagoon, is a vivid representation of a place with a particularly distinct identity through its history (Figure 10.1). This small, 21 hectare (52 acres) Venetian island with a population of around 3,000 people was first settled in the fifth century by the Romans. Other than fishing, since the sixteenth century much of its economy was supported by the lace industry. The Punto di Burano lace become renowned worldwide, and the city capitalized on this by founding a lacemaking school in 1872. The island's unique character is manifested by the brightly colored houses that adorn its streets. Legend has it that the fishermen who once inhabited the island painted their homes in vibrant hues to help them navigate through the thick fog that often enveloped the area. Today, Burano's vibrant houses have become a signature feature, attracting visitors from around the world who marvel at the island's colorful beauty.

Burano illustrates how modern buildings can be seamlessly integrated with the historical context of a place, creating a unique and memorable environment. As Bonesio (1997) reasons, there is no one-size-fits-all solution when it comes to designing and developing spaces within a particular culture or location. However, this does not mean that subjective creative judgment has free reign over the design process. The dimension of a place and its essence or spirit has implicit rules that need to be respected in order to achieve good form and stable harmony. These rules are based on the unique characteristics and context of the place, such as its historical, social and cultural background (Mellano 2017). In other words, every

DOI: 10.4324/9781003384687-10

The Culture of Places

Figure 10.1 Burano, an island nestled in the Venice lagoon with colorful homes, is a vivid representation of a place with a particularly distinct identity that lasted centuries.

place has its own distinctive character and identity that must be considered when designing or developing it. This character is shaped by the people, history and physical features of the place, and it must be respected to create a design that is in harmony with the environment. When the design is successful, it enhances and complements the place's identity rather than detracting from it. Accordingly, the harmony achieved in the design process should not disfigure or mask the place's physiognomy, but rather make it recognizable in every intervention (Bonesio 1997). It is crucial for designers to pay attention to and incorporate unique cultural values and artifacts (Figure 10.2). By doing so, they can harness the power of culture as a tool for sustainable and equitable development in cities. In this way, culture serves as a powerful driver of positive change and progress in urban areas.

10.2 Urban Design for Culture

Public spaces in cities play a vital role in fostering social cohesion and cultural exchange. It is imperative that urban planners prioritize designing spaces that are built at a human scale and encourage interaction among residents. By prioritizing social attributes and fostering connectedness, planners can create vibrant and livable cities that reflect the culture and traditions of their residents. In the pursuit of meaning and a sense of belonging, it is important to establish linkages between people and places, present and past, and local and regional communities. Creating vibrant and livable cities that reflect the unique culture and traditions of their residents requires designing interconnected urban areas that make social engagement and participation the convenient choice.

The implementation of urban and architectural design features that promote social interaction between people is imperative for the promotion of culture in a place. The front porch is such a feature. Sitting on a front porch seems to be a relic of the past. With the invention of air conditioning, porches seem to have disappear form the vocabulary of modern residential design. Parking garages and large front lawns took their place instead. Additionally, the "eye on the street" and a chat with a neighbor was replaced by television viewing and other digital means. They, however, experienced resurgence with the introduction of neo-traditional design of the 1980s which

The Culture of Places

Figure 10.2 It is crucial for designers to pay attention to and incorporate unique cultural artifacts in new planning, as was the case in these cities.

Figure 10.3 The front porch offers opportunities to keep an "eye on the street" and foster interaction between neighbors.

attempted to draw form the past (Figure 10.3). The porch offers opportunities for interaction between neighbors. It is what designing for civility is all about. When such features are put in place, the chance for a healthy evolution of a neighborhood is set in motion. Ultimately, the goal should be to design interconnected cities that facilitate social engagement and participation, thereby strengthening the sense of community and belonging among residents.

The concept of *fourth places* holds significant value in fostering a cohesive society, particularly in the context of contemporary cities that are increasingly diverse and multicultural as a result of globalization and human migration (Aboutorabi 2018). The emergence of multiple cultural communities within urban areas has made it imperative to overcome the barriers that create social clusters and impede social interactions (Brittion et al. 2015). Furthermore, research has demonstrated that promoting participation in practical everyday activities can significantly enhance the quality of life for individuals and the neighborhoods in which they reside (Brittion et al. 2015).

10.3 Culture and Economy

Cultural expression and display are pivotal to fostering identity and sense of place. Relaying on and cultivating local economy is also critical for a place's wellbeing. A winning combination happens when both are fused. Fairs and public exhibits can play a crucial role in shaping a place's identity and contributing to its culture. They serve as a catalyst for connecting city centers with their rural surroundings and fostering multicultural interactions (Navapan and Charoenkit 2022). Fairs also encourage support for local businesses and products, preservation of cultural and gastronomic heritage, and the promotion of slow and proximity tourism as alternatives to mass tourism and other unsustainable tourism activities (Figure 10.4). Furthermore, fairs and markets can be great places to promote local art and culture by integrating public art, cultural events and performances. Public gathering places, such as local markets, play a significant role in shaping social and cultural norms. Designing communities with these kinds of social spaces at the center makes them a convenient choice. In addition to social spaces, key amenities such as services and transit nodes should also be placed in the center. This ensures that all residents are equidistant from these essential services, making the community more accessible and increasing its overall walkability. A community where art contributes to the local economy is described below.

10.4 The Narrative of Places

Cities are not only shaped by their physical features, but also by the stories and narratives that are created in them. In turn, stories can also shape urban form by serving as a means to communicate ideas and values to the users of an environment. To achieve good urban design, it is essential to understand both the physical and cultural dimensions of urban space. According to urban designer Dennis Frenchman (2021), a new approach to city design is necessary; one that integrates archaeology, history, museums and modern media to create interpretive landscapes within cities. Places should tell a story, using design elements to create a sense of place and a connection to the community's history and culture. By bringing the stories and events of the past to life in public spaces, cities can attract a diverse range of activities and become more vibrant places to live (Diao and Lu 2022). Heritage places, in particular, are valuable as they offer a wealth of narratives that can be leveraged to create a sense of place and community (Frenchman 2021). By preserving cultural resources throughout the city and using them to bridge the gap between heritage and contemporary issues such as sustainability, competitiveness and creativity, promoting local culture can be facilitated (Diao and Lu 2022).

Frenchman (2021) proposes several design principles for creating successful urban places, including contextualism, identity, connectivity, social and environmental sustainability, adaptability, narrative and collaboration. He argues that these principles can help urban designers create places that are not only functional and aesthetically pleasing but also socially and culturally meaningful. These principles outline how urban

Figure 10.4 Fairs support local businesses and products, preservation of cultural, gastronomic heritage and the promotion of tourism.

The Culture of Places

design should be more than just a technical exercise in form and function and should instead be focused on creating places that reflect the identity and aspirations of the community and contribute to their wellbeing and quality of life. The narrative approach to urban design emphasizes the importance of collaboration between designers, stakeholders and the community. By involving the community in the design process, planners can ensure that the design responds to their needs and aspirations and reflects their values and culture. This collaboration can also help build a sense of ownership and pride in the place among the community, which can contribute to the long-term success and sustainability of the place.

10.5 Places of Faith in Italy

Placed on a building's corner and covered by a small canopy to protect them from the elements, they contain figurines or paintings. Called *Madonnelle*, these ancient street shrines play an important part in the soul and the belief of the locals. They have been part of Italy's cultural landscapes for centuries and Rome alone has thousands of them and as many in other cities (Sagredo 2013) (Figure 10.5).

The tradition of placing religious imagery on streets dates to an ancient Roman custom where a statue or painting of a domestic deity would be placed at crossroads and lit up at night, to guard passers-by from evil spirits which were thought to frequent the area. Throughout the centuries, the Madonnelle have been used as a means of spiritual protection, and they are also lit by small lanterns when the sun sets. The shrines have even been said to perform miracles, and some observers have claimed to have seen Madonnelle cry, bleed, move their eyes and even take vengeance.

Spiritual moments often find us unexpectedly. The Italians ease their coming by building Madonnelle, reminding passers-by to leave a place for faith in their lives.

10.6 Paying Homage to the Past in Edam

When designing facades of buildings in already built areas the designer must negotiate a compromise between the new and the old. When such balance is reached, places become visually pleasing to form a unique sense of place where locals are paying homage to the past and respect cultural traditions that evolved over centuries.

The Dutch town of Edam, population 7,400, is such a place. Renowned for its cheese-making, which dominated the local economy for centuries, it draws tourists to its daily and weekly markets. Walking in Edam, near the rows of townhouses along its canals and through the neighborhoods' narrow streets, you notice a blend of new and old buildings. Yet, the new does not overpower the old nor does it attempt to replicate it.

To avoid mimicking the old, designers of Edam's contemporary buildings created a vocabulary of a fixed number of elements based on the form and the geometry of the existing structures that when combined offer diversity yet retain the spirit of the past (Figure 10.6). In some structures, varying the dormers' shapes, or color of window frames, gave the homes character. In others, shades of bricks or the color of roof tiles sets them apart from the one nearby. You can still spot the old, which dates back centuries, yet appreciate the mixed ensemble that reinforces a distinct identity.

In Edam it was clear that the locals respect their heritage. They understood that the cumulative effect of ignorance will result in an unattractive town and no cultural legacy to leave to future generations.

10.7 Bringing Cultures Together in Superkilen

Superkilen is a 0.8 km (0.5 mile) long park located in Norrebro, one of the most culturally diverse neighborhoods of Copenhagen, Denmark. Its designers were tasked with improving the infrastructure of the park. In addition, their design functions to foster a sense of community and make an urban statement (Figure 10.7).

Superkilen is divided into three sections, organized by color: red, black and green. Each section serves a different purpose, featuring fun and interesting visual cues. As a response to the neighborhood's cultural diversity, the designers chose to include objects found in 60 different countries from which residents in the area had immigrated. In addition, trees reflecting these various geographical origins have been planted on islands throughout the park, placed closely to the aforementioned cultural artifacts.

The first section of the park is the Red Square, which serves as a cultural, sporting and market destination. It is in fact an outdoor extension of the existing sports and cultural center. Its vast recreational area provides a place for locals to meet one another through games and activities. Its entire surface is covered in an extremely durable rubber allowing for a variety of activities including a winter skating rink. A marketplace is held here every weekend, a popular destination for the residents of Copenhagen and those of its suburbs. It is also a

The Culture of Places

Figure 10.5 Placed on a building's corners of Italian cities and covered by small canopy these ancient street shrines play an important part in the culture and the belief of the locals.

The Culture of Places

Figure 10.6 Designers of Edam's contemporary buildings created a vocabulary of a fixed number of elements based on the form and the geometry of the existing structures that when combined offer diversity yet retain the spirit of the past.

Figure 10.7 The Superkilen project in Copenhagen, Denmark, demonstrates how creative open spaces that celebrate culture can revitalize struggling communities and create a sense of place

popular spot for screening open-air movies and sporting events. Facades, painted red, have been incorporated to fit the design theme of the area. At times, these form a curved surface with the ground, to create a truly three-dimensional space. The limits of the square are marked by streets at each end and fences along the side.

The second section, the Black Square, is meant to function as an urban living space. Features here are similar to the interior furnishings of a house. There are several benches, tables and even grilling facilities. The bike lane has been shifted to the east of this section in order that it intersect conveniently with another bike lane and avoid the square's hills. A mound in the

The Culture of Places

north serves as a popular relaxation point for residents and offers a great view overlooking the square. The designers and residents did not want this section to end in a street, and thus decided to fold the northeast corner up, thus creating a shelter.

The final section, Green Park, is a direct response to residents' wishes for more green space. The area consists of a mostly grass-covered landscape and offers access to several sports and workout facilities. Soft hills and its location adjacent to a local school make Green Park a popular place for children and families.

Superkilen demonstrates how creative open spaces that celebrate culture can revitalize struggling communities. The addition of a park creates a more communal feel in the neighborhood while simultaneously improving the urban context.

10.8 Fusing Art and Economy in Val-David

Founded by Kinya Ishikawa, 1001 Pots in Val-David, population 5,000 in the province of Quebec's Laurentian Mountains in Canada, is the largest pottery fair in North America (Figure 10.8). Originally from Tokyo, Kinya moved to Montreal where he worked as a janitor in a pottery studio and soon became passionate about making pottery himself. In 1988 he moved into the village of Val-David to collaborate with other potters. Promoting the culture of pottery rather than displaying his work became a cause and the reason behind his motivation to found 1001 Pots (Sage 2011).

The first 1001 Pots pottery exposition took place was in summer of 1989 when Kinya invited 50 other potters to exhibit their work. The name of the exposition comes from the nearly 1,000 pieces of pottery that were showcased that summer. Today, a variety of displays and activities take place, such as

Figure 10.8 Variety of displays and activities such as workshops, a children's ceramic show, a tearoom discussion, as well as several beautifully landscaped gardens combining art take place in Val-David, Canada.

The Culture of Places

workshops, a children's ceramic show and a tearoom discussion, alongside several beautifully landscaped gardens combining art. The works are shown in a variety of styles and formats through both indoor and outdoor displays. The month-long exposition attracts some 100,000 visitors every year and includes work from more than 100 local and international potters. The fair is also an important contributor to Val-David's local economy and hospitality industry, as the village benefits from revenue generated by the tourists drawn to the place.

10.9 Final Thoughts

Urban design can promote cultural identity in cities by recognizing the permanence of the past and reinterpreting it in a contemporary context. Technology facilitates connecting different cultures and parts of the world, and while this exchange of ideas and information can lead to cultural blending and new forms of cultural expression in cities, globalization in technology can also lead to the homogenization of cultures in cities. Urban planners can combat this by recognizing the unique characteristics of each place and approaching each project as a unique story (Mellano 2017). By valuing specificity and storytelling, urban design can break free from the constraints of a globalized world and create cities that celebrate their cultural heritage while embracing modernity. Any project for a city should be capable of defining a strategy by getting local players involved to reimagine how projects can communicate with what was there before in a valuable way. By taking a collaborative and strategic approach to urban development, projects can create a positive impact on culture, its residents and the surrounding environment. At the heart of this approach lies the vital role of citizen-to-citizen and citizen-to-city interaction (Urb Cultural Planning 2020). By engaging all members of the community in the cultural evolution of their city, the strategy fosters an inclusive and participatory process. Focusing on these human-centred design principles will guide planners who can help create socially sustainable communities.

References

Aboutorabi, M. (2018). Culture, space, and place: an inquiry into the urban landscape of multicultural cities. *Journal of Engineering and Architecture* 6(2). 10.15640/jea.v6n2a2. Retrieved June 23, 2023, from www.researchgate.net/publication/330510624_Culture_Space_and_Place_An_Inquiry_into_the_Urban_Landscape_of_Multicultural_Cities

Bonesio, L. (1997). *Geofilosofia del paesaggio*. Mimesis. Milan.

Brittion, T., Billings, L., Beunderman, J., Alexander, M., Johar, I., Specht, M., Oliver, M., Owczarek, M., Walding, E. and Bowen, R. (2015). Designed to scale mass participation to build resilient neighbourhoods. academia.edu. *Open Works*. Retrieved June 23, 2023, from www.academia.edu/26403441/Designed_to_Scale_Mass_participation_to_build_resilient_neighbourhoods

Diao, J. and Lu, S. (2022). The culture-oriented urban regeneration: place narrative in the case of the inner city of Haiyan (Zhejiang, China). *Sustainability* 14(13): 7992. Retrieved June 23, 2023, from https://doi.org/10.3390/su14137992

Frenchman, D. (2021). Narrative places and the new practice of urban design. In *Imaging the City*, pp. 257–282. Routledge. London.

Gieseking, J., Mangold, W., Katz, C., Low, S. and Saegert, S. (2014). Section 3: place and identity. In *The People, Place, and Space Reader*, pp. 68–77. Routledge. London.

Mellano, P. (2017). Regaining the culture of cities. *City, Territory and Architecture* 4(1). Retrieved June 23, 2023, from https://doi.org/10.1186/s40410-017-0063-3

Navapan, N. and Charoenkit, S. (2022). Local markets: how the ordinary public places can support urban sustainable development. *GMSARN International Journal* 16(3): 308–313. Retrieved June 23, 2023, from www.researchgate.net/publication/355874127_Local_Markets_How_the_Ordinary_Public_Places_Can_Support_Urban_Sustainable_Development

Sage, A. (2011). Kinya Ishikawa, potter-1001 pots founder. *Kickass Canadians*. Retrieved June 23, 2023, from https://kickasscanadians.ca/kinya-ishikawa/

Sagredo, A. M. (2013). The "madonnelle" in Rome. *Italian Ways*. Retrieved June 23, 2023, from www.pinterest.fr/pin/532058143482675717/

Salman, M. (2019). Sustainability and vernacular architecture: rethinking what identity is. *Urban and Architectural Heritage Conservation within Sustainability*. Retrieved June 23, 2023, from https://doi.org/10.5772/intechopen.82025

Urb Cultural Planning. (2020). Urban cultural planning as a method. *Urbcultural*. Retrieved June 23, 2023, from https://urbcultural.eu/urban-cultural-planning-as-a-method/

CHAPTER 11
Planning for Wellbeing

Obesity and inactivity are growing global public health challenges evident particularly in Western societies. Urban design holds the potential to lessen the negative effects of these challenges and introduce healthier living. This chapter explores urban planning concepts that promote healthy and active lifestyles. To frame the issue, the chapter first explores obesity, inactivity and mental health problems in the context of urban design. Alongside these challenges, solutions for retooling cities are suggested, including designing outdoor play areas for children, adolescents, adults and seniors.

11.1 The Challenges of Obesity, Inactivity and Mental Health

Health is defined by the World Health Organization (WHO) as a state of one's mental, physical and social wellbeing. Wellbeing integrates both mental and physical health, and measures objective and subjective quality of life aspects (CDC 2018). This section will clarify issues related to obesity, inactivity and mental health and their relation to urban environments.

Obesity is defined by the WHO as abnormal or excessive fat accumulation that presents a risk to health. Body mass index (BMI), based on the proportion of body weight to height, is used to determine obesity and to determine whether an individual is at a "healthy" weight (World Health Organization n.d.). Obesity, which saw a rise in nations around the world, is a health problem which impacts people globally, exacerbated by lifestyle choices such as inactivity and poor diet (Monteiro and Martins 2020) (Figure 11.1). Although obesity is associated with an excess consumption of food, it is considered a form of malnutrition, as the foods consumed are often lacking in nutrients, leaving the individual nutrient-deficient (World Health Organization n.d.). Obesity is associated with many poor health outcomes, particularly diabetes and cardiovascular disease, alongside many other diseases, as well as increased mortality risk (Monteiro and Martins 2020). Although there are

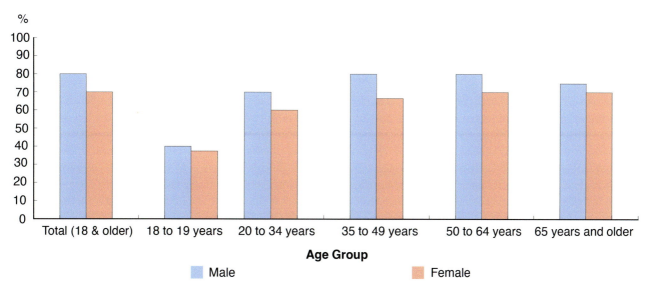

Figure 11.1 Overweight or obese by age group and gender population 18 and older (after Statistics Canada, 2018).

Planning for Wellbeing

genetic predispositions to obesity, it is largely impacted by lifestyle choices, beginning in childhood, highlighting the importance of promoting outdoor healthy living, through urban design.

Inactivity is found to be both a precursor and consequence of obesity, reflecting the interconnected nature of these issues, further exacerbating the problems, and making them a challenge to resolve (Woessner et al. 2021; Monteiro and Martins 2020). Inactivity refers to lack of physical activity undertaken in everyday life. With technological advances over the past century, including the use of private automobiles, overall physical activity levels have decreased and sedentary lifestyles have increased (Woessner et al. 2021). It is estimated that, globally, 3.3 million people die from inactivity every year, making it the fourth leading cause of non-communicable death (Jansson et al. 2019).

Additionally, over the past three decades, rates of childhood inactivity have been increasing at alarming rates, deeming this a public health concern (Brusseau et al. 2020). Specifically, in the United States, in 2015 and 2016, less than 30 percent of adults and 20 percent of adolescents were meeting recommended levels of physical activity (Woessner et al. 2021). It is very concerning, as childhood inactivity often becomes ingrained within one's lifestyle, continuing into adulthood, leading to accumulating health and societal burdens (Brusseau et al. 2020).

Mental health disorders have been found to account for most health-related disabilities worldwide, but they are a particular concern in North America (Mental Health Disorder Statistics n.d.). Specifically, in the United States, it is estimated that 26 percent of individuals aged 18 years and older suffer from a diagnosable mental disorder every year, and many suffer from multiple comorbid disorders (Mental Health Disorder Statistics n.d.). Unfortunately, many who need it are not receiving treatment, illustrating the need for urgent prevention (Alkermes and Otsuka America Pharmaceutical Companies n.d.).

Furthermore, since the beginning of the COVID-19 pandemic, the prevalence of mental health problems has increased dramatically, exacerbated by decreased physical activity, increased stress and, at times, using technology, which were all related to COVID-19 lockdown policies (Reid et al. 2022). However, studies have found that people with access to views of green space, private or indoor green space, and urban parks, during the COVID-19 pandemic, had decreased stress compared to individuals who could not access green space (Reid et al. 2022).

The World Health Organization's *Global Action Plan for Physical Activity 2018 to 2030* illustrated the need for policies that improve road safety, promote compact urban design, and prioritize access by pedestrians, cyclists and users of public transport to destinations and services and decrease private vehicle use (Brusseau et al. 2020). Indeed, proper urban design can be used as an agent for improving mental and physical health. For example, active transportation is associated with higher levels of physical activity, maintenance of a healthy body weight, better cardiovascular fitness and enhanced mental health (Brusseau et al. 2020) (Figure 11.2).

11.2 Designing Outdoor Play Areas

With the growing global population and higher density of cities, the importance of outdoor public spaces can at times be neglected, which increases the risk of obesity, inactivity and mental health. Past urban planning theorists and movements, including Ebenezer Howard's Garden City and the Parks Beautiful Movement, prioritized public green space, recognizing their importance to wellbeing.

Through child development research, it has been found that 'play' is an important facet of children's development. It allows children to explore their natural curiosity and environments, develop social skills, establish a sense of self and independence, and guide learning. The act of play needs to involve aspects of physical, perceptual, emotional and social stimulation. It has been estimated that in the United States 71 percent of parents played outdoors as children, however, only 21 percent of their children currently do so, depicting societal changes in outdoor healthy living over time (Friedman 2018). It is crucial that urban design helps to develop outdoor areas where children are encouraged to promote their development and contribute to their mental and physical health and wellbeing.

Playgrounds are mostly outdoor areas, which are designed for recreation and typically cater for children. They were invented in the late nineteenth century, alongside specialized play equipment such as swings, rocking horses and bicycles. However, the introduction of playgrounds in North America had an ulterior motive of acting as a deterrent against juvenile crime and as a "melting pot," being a way of integrating immigrant children into society and instilling them with "American" values. In 1906, the Playground Association of America was founded, representing an important milestone in the implementation and development of playgrounds (Friedman 2018). This also represented a shift from playgrounds being initiated by private philanthropic organizations to public municipal authorities. Increased implementation of

Planning for Wellbeing

Figure 11.2 Active mobility, as seen here in the Netherlands, is associated with higher levels of physical fitness, healthy body weight, better cardiovascular condition and enhanced mental health.

playgrounds coincided with the incorporation of playtime and physical activity in the school curriculum.

As children grow older, they transition out of playgrounds as outdoor places for physical activity. Therefore, other urban facilities catering to the increased development and evolving interests of adolescents are needed to promote physical activity and community cohesion. Outdoor sports and activity facilities, such as skateboard parks, basketball courts, soccer and football fields, and skating rinks, among many others, offer opportunity for both activity and community interaction and socialization for adolescents (Figure 11.3).

Outdoor sports and activity facilities cater to adults as well as adolescents. These facilities make important contributions to social cohesion in many ways, through increasing community interaction, as well as through increasing mental health and physical activity, which decreases risk for obesity and other inactivity-related health challenges.

In addition to these activities or sports-focused outdoor facilities, the implementation of outdoor gym equipment in public parks helps promote equal access to exercise facilities and physical activity among adults. Outdoor gyms are facilities that typically consist of simple and durable exercise apparatus that require no electricity and are usually installed in open spaces such as outdoor park areas, and often utilize the user's own body weight to create resistance and movement in the equipment (Jansson et al. 2019). Outdoor gym equipment has been installed in many public green spaces globally and is composed of both static strength-focused equipment and mobile cardio equipment (Exercise Equipment in Parks (Outdoor Gyms) n.d.) (Figure 11.4). Some nations like Finland made active lifestyle and the play of children near homes a priority in community planning, as illustrated below.

11.3 Engaging Seniors

Inactivity is a great concern among seniors, as they often have decreased physical mobility, which can leave them feeling socially isolated and increase their susceptibility to health concerns. Obesity among the elderly is also a significant concern, as it only further increases the risk of disease and other health concerns (Monteiro and Martins 2020).

Planning for Wellbeing

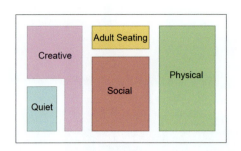

Linear space

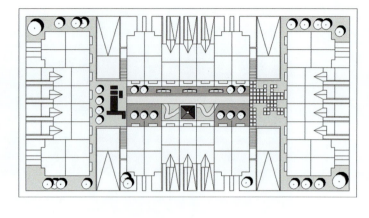

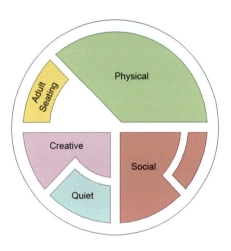

Circular space

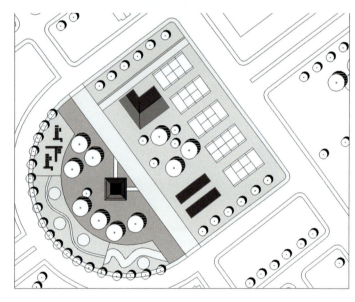

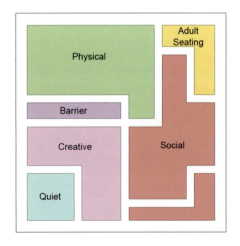

Square space

Figure 11.3 Suggested site plans for play spaces.

Planning for Wellbeing

Figure 11.4 Outdoor gym equipment is being installed in many public green spaces globally, composed of both static strength-focused and mobile cardio equipment.

The senior population, those aged 60 years old and older, worldwide is expected to increase to 22 percent of the population by 2050, from 12 percent of the population in 2015, which represents nearly 2 billion people (Loke et al. 2020; Goethals et al. 2020). Therefore, there is a dire need to provide outdoor spaces to this cohort to promote healthy aging. Implementing facilities to engage seniors and promote active aging is particularly important in urban areas with high proportions of seniors (Figure 11.5). Active aging refers to the continuous process of participation in various activities, including social, economic, cultural, spiritual and civil affairs to maintain a high quality of life (Loke et al. 2020). Urban design initiatives, such as implementing outdoor public areas and designing urban spaces to promote active transportation is a method to promote outdoor healthy living among seniors. Falling represents a major source of morbidity and injury among the elderly; however, it has been found that physical activity is the most effective method for preventing falls, by improving physical mobility, strength and balance (Goethals et al. 2020).

Outdoor public spaces, including plazas and parks, are beneficial for promoting physical activity among seniors and aiding them in community and social engagement. It has been found that outdoor sports and activities among the elderly are associated with the maintenance of physical performance, as well as increased positive engagement, revitalization, tranquility and improved mood (Eigenschenk et al. 2019). Additionally, the introduction of public outdoor gym equipment in these public spaces may also be beneficial for improving physical activity in seniors. These spaces help to bring elderly individuals out of their homes and into public space where there are opportunities for physical activity and social interaction. This is crucial for the elderly, as they often face social isolation (Ali et al. 2022). Additionally, outdoor exposure to the sun helps to maintain vitamin D levels, which is especially important for the elderly who often spend more time sedentary and indoors, compared to other age groups (Eigenschenk et al. 2019) (Figure 11.6).

Community gardens provide an outdoor area to the public at large, including seniors, and can provide nutritious food, light to moderate physical activity and an outlet for social connections (Scott et al. 2019) (Figure 11.7). In terms of physical health, studies have also found an association between partaking in gardening and decreased BMI, and therefore decreased obesity prevalence (Kunpeuk et al. 2019). An association between gardening and improved pulse pressure and lung functioning, bone mineral density, hand function and dexterity, total cholesterol, blood pressure, and grip and pinch force was also established (Kunpeuk et al. 2019). Gardening has been found to reduce the risk of certain cancers, Type 2 diabetes, depression and heart disease among older adults (Scott et al. 2019).

Community gardens also help increase food security and healthy diets among community members including seniors who are experiencing financial challenges, which indirectly decreases obesity prevalence. Food insecurity is the inability to acquire enough food to meet the nutritional demands of all individuals in a household, often either due to insufficient income or accessibility (Coleman-Jensen et al. 2022) (Figure 11.8). Community gardens are a way to obtain fresh, healthy produce for free, while also fostering social connections.

Planning for Wellbeing

Figure 11.5 Building facilities and activities to engage seniors and promote active aging like the one shown here is particularly important in urban areas with a high concentration of elderly population.

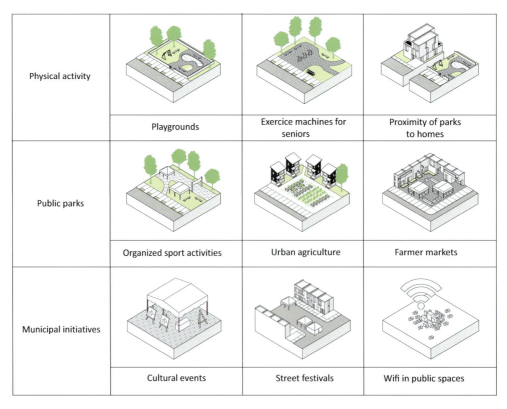

Figure 11.6 Initiatives that help draw seniors into public space where there are opportunities for physical activity and social interaction.

Planning for Wellbeing

Figure 11.7 Community gardens provide an outdoor area to the public at large, including seniors, for nutritious food, light to moderate physical activity and an outlet for social connections.

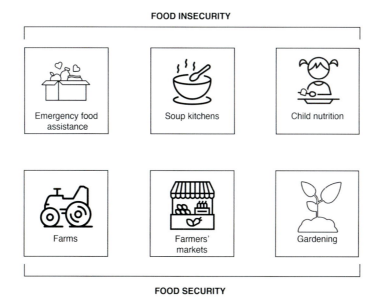

Figure 11.8 Food insecurity is the inability to acquire enough food to meet the nutritional demands due to insufficient income or accessibility.

Planning for Wellbeing

11.4 Slow Life in Trani

Trani, a fishing port city in the Puglia region in southern Italy with a population of 56,000, was established by the Romans and later developed under the kings of Sicily as a trading hub. The place is one of several Italian cities who formed an association known as Cittaslow (slow city). The association was founded in 1999 in Orvieto by four mayors, who advocated the positive benefits of slowness, sustainability and social justice, and grew to become a worldwide network. They support a way of life that encourages people to reduce traffic, noise and crowds while adhering to local traditions (Slow Movement 2020) (Figure 11.9).

Slow cities ignore the fast-paced modern city and avoid speculative unsustainable developments. Their main objective is to maintain community spirit while passing on cultural heritage to new generations. The association developed a manifesto which sets out the underlying principles, a charter which cities wanting to qualify must sign, and an annual gathering that representatives must attend. Among the 55 pledges in the manifesto, one reads: "We are looking for towns where men are still curious about old times, rich with theatres, squares, cafes, workshops, restaurants and spiritual places." To become a slow city and be allowed to use the snail logo, cities are vetted and regularly checked to make sure they continue to respect those standards. Cittaslow engages in a variety of different projects and initiatives touching on or related to agriculture, tourism, urban planning, education, markets, the crafts and industry.

The city of Trani demonstrates that to appreciate a place and live a healthy life one needs to slow down and take the time to read a place's revealing marks and allow its hidden language to speak to the mind and spirit.

11.5 Planning for Play in Porvoo

Located 50 kilometers (31 miles) east of Helsinki, the capital of Finland, the city of Porvoo, population 49,000, has a mix of old and new buildings. Near the river that runs through the city there is a contemporary housing project made up of painted green, saffron and ochre dwellings. Single-family

Figure 11.9 Trani, a fishing port city in the Puglia region in southern Italy, is one of several Italian cities who formed an association known as *Cittaslow* (slow city).

Planning for Wellbeing

detached units, row housing and apartment buildings stand side by side next to meticulously landscaped paths and public open spaces. The planners of the places paid attention to the outdoor activities of children by placing at the heart of each cluster a play area with a sandbox and swing set (Figure 11.10).

Changing behavioral attitudes, habits and norms takes time for any age group, but it is possible if consistent effort is made for a prolonged period. In the case of outdoor play, schools, media and parents need to lead by example and promote healthy lifestyles. Changes need to be brought to the way we plan communities as well.

11.6 Active Living in Shanghai

In the early morning, seniors gathered in a small park in a Shanghai neighborhood. A man faced the group, played music from a battery-operated cassette player, and demonstrated physical exercises which everyone followed (Tao 2017) (Figure 11.11). The Healthy China 2030 Plan released by the Chinese government in 2016 aims at improving the overall health of the population by promoting healthy lifestyles and physical fitness. The plan is reflected in Shanghai's recent attempt to make sport facilities and recreational space more accessible. Shanghai's aging population is also known to be very physically active. The city's branch of the National Committee on Ageing

Figure 11.10 In the Modern Wooden Town project in Porvoo, Finland, at the heart of each cluster there is a children's play area.

Figure 11.11 A morning gathering of seniors in a small park in a Shanghai neighborhood for physical exercise.

showed that more than 80 percent of Chinese elderly people engage in physical activity at least three times a week (World Health Organization 2016). Furthermore, elderly people in Shanghai tend to use public parks the most, rather than gyms or exercise rooms to engage in physical activity. It is common to find large groups of elderly people dancing, exercising or playing games in parks or other public spaces. Seniors are more inclined to spend their leisure time engaging in tai chi, ballroom dancing and ball games such as football or badminton.

11.7 Final Thoughts

Outdoor public spaces are crucial for the health and wellbeing of all age groups. It is important for urban designers to aid in the promotion of healthy lifestyles, to decrease public health challenges such as obesity, inactivity and poor mental health, and to instead promote physical and mental health. Urban design features, such as the implementation of playground, sports and activity facilities, and outdoor public gyms, represent innovative outdoor "play" areas for individuals ranging from childhood to adulthood. Additionally, urban design features such as outdoor public space, features promoting active transportation and community gardens are methods to engage seniors and help to promote ample physical and mental health within this demographic.

References

Ali, M. J., Rahaman, M. and Hossain, S. I. (2022). Urban green spaces for elderly human health: a planning model for healthy city living. *Land Use Policy* 114: 105970. Retrieved July 1, 2023, from https://doi.org/10.1016/j.landusepol.2021.105970

Alkermes and Otsuka America Pharmaceutical Companies (n.d.). The state of mental health in America. *Mental Health America (MHA)*. Retrieved July 1, 2023, from https://mhanational.org/issues/state-mental-health-america

Brusseau, T. A., Fairclough, S. J. and Lubans, D. R. (eds.) (2020). *The Routledge Handbook of Youth Physical Activity*. Routledge. New York. Retrieved July 1, 2023, from https://doi.org/10.4324/9781003026426

CDC (Centers for Disease Control and Prevention) (2018). *Health-Related Quality of Life (HRQOL): Well-Being Concepts*. Retrieved July 1, 2023, from www.cdc.gov/hrqol/wellbeing.htm

Coleman-Jensen, A., Rabbitt, M. P., Hales, L. and Gregory, C. A. (2022). Food security in the US: key statistics and graphics. USDA Economic Research Service. Retrieved July 1, 2023, from www.ers.usda.gov/topics/food-nutrition-assistance/food-security-in-the-u-s/key-statistics-graphics/#:~:text=In%202021%3A,with%20adults%2C%20were%20food%20insecure

Eigenschenk, B., Thomann, A., McClure, M., Davies, L., Gregory, M., Dettweiler, U. and Inglés, E. (2019). Benefits of outdoor sports for society: a systematic literature review and reflections on evidence. *International Journal of Environmental Research and Public Health* 16(6): 937. Retrieved July 1, 2023, from https://doi.org/10.3390/ijerph16060937

Exercise Equipment in Parks (Outdoor Gyms) (n.d.). *Brisbane City Council*. Retrieved July 1, 2023, from www.brisbane.qld.gov.au/things-to-see-and-do/outdoor-activities/exercise-equipment-in-parks-outdoor-gyms

Friedman, A. (2018). *Neighborhood: Designing a Livable Community*. Véhicule Press. Montréal.

Goethals, L., Barth, N., Hupin, D., Mulvey, M. S., Roche, F., Gallopel-Morvan, K. and Bongue, B. (2020). Social marketing interventions to promote physical activity among 60 years and older: a systematic review of the literature. *BMC Public Health* 20(1). Retrieved July 1, 2023, from https://doi.org/10.1186/s12889-020-09386-x

Jansson, A. K., Lubans, D. R., Smith, J. J., Duncan, M. J., Haslam, R. and Plotnikoff, R. C. (2019). A systematic review of outdoor gym use: current evidence and future directions. *Journal of Science and Medicine in Sport* 22(12): 1335–1343. Retrieved July 1, 2023, from https://doi.org/10.1016/j.jsams.2019.08.003

Kunpeuk, W., Spence, W., Phulkerd, S., Suphanchaimat, R. and Pitayarangsarit, S. (2019). The impact of gardening on nutrition and physical health outcomes: a systematic review and meta-analysis. *Health Promotion International* 35(2): 397–408. Retrieved July 1, 2023, from https://doi.org/10.1093/heapro/daz027

Loke, Y. J., Lim, E. S. and Senadjki, A. (2020). Health promotion and active aging among seniors in Malaysia. *Journal of Health Research* 35(5): 444–456. Retrieved July 1, 2023, from https://doi.org/10.1108/jhr-07-2019-0148

Mental Health Disorder Statistics (n.d.). Health – wellness and prevention. Johns Hopkins Medicine. Retrieved July 1, 2023, from www.hopkinsmedicine.org/health/wellness-and-prevention/mental-health-disorder-statistics

Monteiro, R. and Martins, M. J. (2020). *Understanding Obesity*. Bentham Science. Singapore. Retrieved July 1, 2023, from https://mcgill.on.worldcat.org/search/detail/1154514077?datasource=library_web&search_field=all_fields&search=true&database=all&scope=wz%3A12129&format=&clusterResults=true&func=find-b&q=&topLod=0&queryString=obesity&find=Go&year=2019..2023&groupVariantRecords=false

Reid, C. E., Rieves, E. S. and Carlson, K. (2022). Perceptions of green space usage, abundance, and quality of green space were associated with better mental health during the COVID-19 pandemic among residents of Denver. *Plos One* 17(3). Retrieved July 1, 2023, from https://doi.org/10.1371/journal.pone.0263779

Scott, T. L., Masser, B. M. and Pachana, N. A. (2019). Positive aging benefits of home and community gardening activities: older adults report enhanced self-esteem, productive endeavours, social engagement and exercise. *Sage Open Medicine* 8: 1–13. Retrieved July 1, 2023, from https://doi.org/10.1177/2050312120901732

Slow Movement (2020). Slow cities and the slow movement. *Slow Movement*. Retrieved July 1, 2023, from www.slowmovement.com/slow_cities.php

Tao, N. (2017). It's no game! Shanghai pushes healthy, active life as fitness campaigns flourish. *Shine Beyond a Single Story*. Retrieved July 1, 2023, from www.shine.cn/opinion/chinese-views/1710295603/

Woessner, M. N., Tacey, A., Levinger-Limor, A., Parker, A. G., Levinger, P. and Levinger, I. (2021). The evolution of technology and physical inactivity: the good, the bad, and the way forward. *Frontiers in Public Health* 9. Retrieved July 1, 2023, from https://doi.org/10.3389/fpubh.2021.655491

World Health Organization (n.d.). Obesity. Retrieved July 1, 2023, from www.who.int/health-topics/obesity#tab=tab_1

World Health Organization (2016). Healthy China 2030. Retrieved July 1, 2023, from www.who.int/teams/health-promotion/enhanced-wellbeing/ninth-global-conference/healthy-china

CHAPTER 12
Places for Social Interaction

Dense urban areas can be places of anonymity and isolation. Those same spaces can also provide ample opportunities for interactions, with destinations, attractions and accessible gathering spots. This chapter investigates the relations between places of interaction and social sustainability. It discusses historical development patterns pertaining to social spaces and lists their typologies and their designs. Finally, the potential and importance of Third Places are examined, alongside guidelines on incorporating social gathering spaces into urban design.

12.1 In-person and Media Social Interactions

Social sustainability is defined as the ability of a system to maintain a certain level of wellbeing and to function indefinitely at this level (City of Maple Ridge BC n.d.) (Figure 12.1). Therefore, social sustainability and social interaction relate to one another through mutual support. Additionally, to support and develop social sustainability, actions must be taken to ensure all individuals have equal access to social opportunities (City of Maple Ridge BC n.d.).

Social interaction has been proposed as a fundamental human need, on par with food, sleep and housing due to its significant importance in everyday life, and its multitude of effects on individuals and communities (Orben et al. 2020). Social interaction is believed to be "wired" into human life as an adaptive feature, reflected through studies which found that individuals faced with threats use up more metabolic resources when alone than when in the company of others (Holt-Lunstad 2021). Increased social interaction and mutual support have also been found to be associated with elevated overall social capital, and improved mental and physical health (Twenge et al. 2019) (Figure 12.2). These concerns are increasingly salient, as mental health problems continue to grow, with suicide currently representing the second leading cause of death for Canadian youth, for example (Abi-Jaoude et al. 2020).

There have been many examples throughout history showcasing the negative impacts of the lack of social interactions on physical and mental health. The 1995 Chicago Heat Wave indicated that isolated individuals, especially the elderly and racial minorities, were significantly more likely to suffer and pass away than those with stronger social connections and those of higher socio-economic status (Klinenberg n.d.). Many

Dwelling	Neighbourhood	City
•Type of dwelling •Crowding •Natural light •Indoor air •Sun exposure •Privacy •Views	•Noise •Open spaces •Walkability •Places for interactions •Play area •Activities generators	•Public transit •Bikes & pedestrian lanes •Landscaping & streetscaping •Visual aspects •Gathering places •Natural features •Cultural & public art

Figure 12.1 Social attributes of homes and communities.

DOI: 10.4324/9781003384687-12

Places for Social Interaction

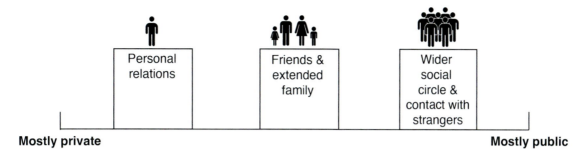

Figure 12.2 Various levels of social interaction from mostly private to mostly public.

of these individuals would not have died if they had not been isolated from others, and if there was not significant socio-economic and racial inequality within the community, highlighting the necessity of social cohesion and increased equality. A more current example is the effects of the COVID-19 pandemic, which increased social isolation for many, and the risk of negative mental and physical health impacts, particularly for marginalized groups (Martin and Nagasawa 2020).

Social interaction is believed to benefit health through many interconnected pathways, such as through psychological, behavioral and biological factors (Holt-Lunstad 2021). Psychologically, social connection can decrease feelings of perceived stress and depression, leading to lower activation of stress pathways such as the sympathetic nervous system and hypothalamus–pituitary–adrenal axis (Holt-Lunstad 2021). Contrastingly, extreme social deprivation has been associated with long-lasting and damaging effects on brain and behavioral development in adolescents (Orben et al. 2020).

With advancements in technology and media, users, especially adolescents, are increasingly using technology as a method of social interaction, through texting and social media applications. This is reflected in the time spent online by adolescents doubling between 2006 and 2016 (Twenge et al. 2019).

A discussion of the effect of social media on in-person social interactions is controversial. Some evidence suggests that social media can facilitate in-person social interactions; stipulating that in-person interactions are at least partially reliant on social media, and that it is the 'modern' and primary way of meeting and connecting with others. Support for this theory stems from the idea that those who are more social in general may have more digital interaction as well as in-person interaction, further maximizing overall interaction (Twenge et al. 2019). However, other evidence suggests the opposite, that social media hinders the prevalence and quality of in-person social interactions and contributes negatively to population health and wellbeing. This is a particular concern during adolescence, where social interaction is crucial for

appropriate development of independence and sense of self (Twenge et al. 2019). This hypothesis, of increased social media usage being detrimental to in-person social interactions, is supported by the fact that individuals have time constraints, and therefore, if increased time is spent on social media, this must result in decreased time dedicated to in-person interactions (Twenge et al. 2019).

Studies have found support for both theories. Particularly, a study conducted by Twenge et al. (2019) found that progressively across different decades, in-person social interaction decreased overall. Specifically, of 12th grade high schoolers in the late 1970s, 52 percent reported seeing friends almost every day, whereas in 2017, only 28 percent of this group reported doing so (Twenge et al. 2019). Additionally, in 1987, students entering college reported spending 13.51 hours a week socializing with friends, which decreased to only 4.37 hours in 2016 (Twenge et al. 2019).

12.2 Typology of Gathering Spaces and Their Design

Social infrastructure refers to the physical conditions and organizations which allow for social capital to develop within a community and shape the ways people interact with each other (Klinenberg 2019). It can be composed of both formal and improvised gathering spaces and will be elaborated below.

12.2.1 Formal Gathering Spaces

Formal gathering spaces refer to spaces with either a direct or indirect purpose of facilitating social interaction and connections (Friedman and Pollock 2022). They can range from temporary organized events, such as festivals, to permanent urban design features.

Town squares have long been included in urban design as instruments of social interaction and engagement. Their integration can be traced back to ancient times, where they

Places for Social Interaction

were created as the central focal point of cities and towns and used as an "outdoor living room" for community members to meet, communicate and develop relationships (Friedman and Pollock 2022). Formal gathering spaces such as town squares may not be possible in every urban setting; however, there are many other formal gathering spaces which can be implemented, on various scales. For example, public parks with ample seating and green space facilitate social interaction. These spaces can also be equipped with outdoor public sports facilities, such as soccer or football fields, outdoor tracks and tennis courts, and with playgrounds for children and outdoor gym equipment for adults.

Community centers and churches are often common indoor formal gathering spaces, where community members can meet and increase their social bond. Not only do these formal spaces attract and promote social interaction, but they also often host group social activities to further promote a sense of community. As shown in Figures 12.3 and 12.4, when proper urban spaces are planned for, they act as "social magnets" in attracting local gathering and hosting events, aiming to promote activity by individuals and fostering community cohesion (Farr 2018) (Figure 12.3 and Figure 12.4).

Figure 12.3 When proper urban spaces are planned for, they act as "magnets" for local gatherings and a backdrop for social activities.

Figure 12.4 Public events draws people to public places.

Places for Social Interaction

Figure 12.5 The High Line in New York City facilitates social interaction and gathering.

A well-known example of a formal gathering space is the High Line in New York City (Klinenberg 2019). This location facilitates serene social interaction and gathering in an otherwise chaotic and sometimes isolating urban center (Klinenberg 2019). The High Line, to be discussed in Chapter 20, is equipped with ample seating, public art, lighting, destinations and attractions such as food stands, and public restrooms, making it an attractive social space for community members (Klinenberg 2019) (Figure 12.5).

In addition to physical permanent spaces, temporary events, such as music festivals, can act as formal gathering spaces. Particularly, Burning Man, an annual temporary event in a Nevada desert, acts as a formal gathering space for over 70,000 individuals (Farr 2018). This festival is specifically focused on developing a sense of community, self-sufficiency and self-expression, through intense, immersive activities and events (Farr 2018).

12.2.2 Informal Gathering Spaces

The COVID-19 pandemic led to a drastic change in the use of public space. This was evident through the significant decrease in use of indoor public gathering spaces, and an increase in the use of outdoor gathering spaces. These human behavior changes have also led to physical changes in urban design, such as the implementation of "sidewalk cafes" and outdoor pubs, many of which did not exist prior to the pandemic, and which have re-envisioned and redefined gathering spaces. Furthermore, throughout the pandemic, people began using spaces such as balconies, porches and driveways as improvised gathering spaces for social interaction (Broudehoux 2021).

These spaces were previously not commonly used as gathering spaces but were turned into improvised spaces due to demand and shifting needs.

The presence of temporary food stands or trucks can also act as official, yet improvised gathering spaces, bringing community members together with a designated purpose (Farr 2018). Adding these attractions into public spaces such as plazas or parks produces an improvised gathering space, providing a focal point and activity within the space, as well as a facet of interaction.

Neighborhood garden produce sharing can be an improvised gathering technique. Food insecurity is an ever-growing problem, with 10.2 percent of the United States, or 33.8 million people, being food insecure in 2021 (Coleman-Jensen et al. 2022). This means that these households were unable to comfortably obtain enough nutrient-dense food to feed all household members (Coleman-Jensen et al. 2022). Additionally, worldwide, one-third of all food ends up going to waste (*Water Wheel* 2017), highlighting a need for food sharing to eliminate this waste. Therefore, not only does backyard garden and produce sharing promote social interaction and cohesion, but it also helps reduce food waste and insecurity issues plaguing our society. Furthermore, there have been examples of spaces being improvised into gathering spaces, such as farmers' markets.

Other informal and improvised gathering spaces include alleys, the sides of buildings, street corners, and areas with seating. These spaces naturally attract people to gather, promoting social interaction. Particularly, outside of office buildings in

Places for Social Interaction

urban areas, there are often groups of people gathering against the sides of buildings, forming an improvised gathering space where they are in close physical and social contact, allowing for opportunities for social interaction. These improvised spaces are enabled by containing edges, paths and nodes, being three of the five urban design elements identified by Kevin Lynch as forming social infrastructure (Lehmann 2020). People naturally travel to and gather at edges, along pathways such as sidewalks or roads, and at nodes or attractions where there is often something of interest. Therefore, spaces with these features have the potential and propensity to become improvised gathering spaces (Figure 12.6).

Urban design can be used as a vehicle to promote social interaction, through its spatial features. Features of spaces including perceived safety, comfort, accessibility and overall enjoyment are crucial to these spaces successfully promoting social interaction and gathering. Available seating, lighting, maintenance and abundance of greenery all influence a space's desirability for use by community members. If a location is isolated, dark, abandoned and poorly maintained, has poor "eyes on the street," and does not have features such as ample lighting or greenery, it is not an enticing space for community members to use, therefore, it will most likely remain isolated and unused, not acting as a successful social gathering space.

A crucial aspect of inclusive design includes making spaces accessible to all, particularly those with physical impairments or reduced mobility (Figure 12.7). This involves incorporating features such as ramps, elevators and other aspects of universal accessibility into urban design (Salman 2018).

Additionally, adding signage in braille and road crossings with audio aids for those with visual impairments help to ensure that all community members feel welcomed and can easily access the space (Salman 2018).

Standard features of space such as water fountains, garbage cans, shaded spaces, and ample seating and lighting are crucial to making spaces welcoming and enticing community members to frequent these spaces and spend time in them (Figure 12.8). However, the placement of these features within the space is important (Farr 2018). Triangulation, being the linkage of people or objects within a space, is a crucial design process to consider in gathering spaces (Farr 2018). For example, designing in terms of triangulation would involve positioning seating, garbage disposal and water fountains in close proximity with one another, forming a spatial and visual connection between them, subsequently increasing their ease of use (Farr 2018).

Furthermore, spaces should be designed in a manner to promote "eyes on the street," in turn promoting perceived safety and comfort within the gathering space. This can be achieved through ensuring the space is amply lit, is open and visible from many locations, has safety features such as public telephones, crosswalks with road crossing lines and long stop times, and does not have dark or hidden areas or features which could promote crime. Ensuring gathering places promote these features to increase perceived safety makes them more desirable for use by community members, thus promoting them as gathering spaces and increasing social interactions.

Figure 12.6 Informal gathering can take place at nodes of attractions or where there is something of interest.

Places for Social Interaction

Figure 12.7 Making spaces accessible to all, particularly those with physical impairments or reduced mobility, is a crucial aspect of inclusive design.

Figure 12.8 Features in gathering places may include elements that make these spaces comfortable and welcoming and entice community members to frequent them and spend time in them.

12.3 The Value of Third Places

A Third Place is a neutral, informal gathering place which provides opportunities to meet, interact and develop a sense of belonging outside a home (being first places), and places of work (being second places) (Bosman and Dolley 2019). The term was initially coined by Ray Oldenburg's influential 1989 book, *The Great Good Place: Cafes, Coffee Shops, Community Centers, Beauty Parlors, General Stores, Bars, Hangouts, and How They Get You Through the Day* (Bosman and Dolley 2019).

Alongside the introduction of this concept, Oldenburg highlighted eight key characteristics of Third Places (Bosman and Dolley 2019; Steinkuehler and Williams 2006). First, these places are neutral meeting grounds, not prioritizing or welcoming certain groups over others, allowing them to be equally accessible to all. This leads to a second characteristic of Third Places, being places which level or encourage social and cultural diversity (Steinkuehler and Williams 2006). Third, they are easily accessible to individuals of all mobilities, accommodating to both sedentary and active activities. Additionally,

Places for Social Interaction

Third Places emphasize conversation as their main activity, particularly expressing playfulness and wit (Steinkuehler and Williams 2006). They are also characterized by a "low-profile" and comfortable atmosphere, described as a "home away from home" (Steinkuehler and Williams 2006). Third Places are characterized as being frequented by "regulars" who attract newcomers to join the spaces.

Third Places include a wide variety of places, falling under the eight defining characteristics. Most commonly, they include neighborhood cafes or restaurants, pubs, outdoor public spaces, gyms, hairdressers and salons, churches, plazas, pedestrian streets, among other locations (Butler and Diaz 2016) (Figure 12.9). Less traditionally, public transportation can be viewed as a Third Place, transforming typical linear and dull commutes into opportunities for social interaction (Bosman and Dolley 2019). Particularly, commuting by private automobile decreases potential for social interaction, in contrast to using public or active transportation, where individuals cross paths with many others from varying demographics, providing ample opportunities for casual social interaction. Features of public and active transportation can also be shaped through urban design to facilitate interactions.

In the absence of urban spaces such as Third Places, individuals end up consumed in a "home-to-work-and-back-again" shuffle, often very mechanistic and depleted of social interaction and vibrancy (Bosman and Dolley 2019). As discussed above, in-person social interactions are crucial for promotion of ample mental and physical health of community members. Oldenburg (1999) states that Third Places act as mediation between the individual and larger society, increasing sense of belonging and sense of community. Overall, Third Places have been found to contribute to decreased anxiety and loneliness, and increased sense of safety, social capital, community health and wellbeing (Bosman and Dolley 2019).

Although Third Places are viewed as inherently "good" and can act as spaces to promote increased equality and opportunity within urban areas, they can still, often unknowingly, act as spaces of exclusion for certain groups or individuals. Therefore, it is crucial to ensure that marginalized groups, women, the elderly and children are equally included into all Third Places, to promote the benefits which they can provide for the community. Despite progressive societal changes over the past several decades, women have often had the majority of their roles confined to the home, limiting opportunities for

Figure 12.9 Third places include neighborhood cafes or restaurants, with indoor or outdoor seating.

Places for Social Interaction

community interaction (Fullagar et al. 2019). Additionally, it has been argued that Third Places, alongside many other spaces, are gendered, perpetuating inequality, patriarchy and complex power relations through the spatial practices they embody, and the everyday interactions which they both promote and inhibit (Fullagar et al. 2019). This may be particularly evident in "private" Third Places, such as restaurants, cafes and bars, which can unintentionally and sometimes unknowingly include and exclude different groups. Additionally, certain public spaces such as large empty public parks may produce a sense of lack of safety for more vulnerable groups such as women, children and the elderly. Despite this, these spaces also represent an opportunity to shift these deeply ingrained influences through urban design, to instead promote greater equality and inclusion, particularly for marginalized and minority groups. A study examining the influence of volunteering at a local community theater on community health and wellbeing found that this space was particularly beneficial to women, leading to a sense of personal growth, and increased sense of freedom and community, as well as the development of performance and production skills (Fullagar et al. 2019).

Additionally, seniors often struggle to develop and maintain social interactions and cohesion, thus Third Places are important methods to help tackle this limitation. A study of an elderly "breakfast group" developed out of a local fast-food restaurant found that this Third Place acted to develop relationships and a sense of community, promoting wellbeing among this group (Fullagar et al. 2019).

There has been abundant research on new ways to implement Third Places into new and existing urban areas. For example, it was found that wet markets in Singapore function as Third Places, being spaces that facilitate casual and regular social interaction between wide demographics of individuals of varying socio-economic status, gender and ethnicities (Bosman and Dolley 2019). Additionally, fast-food outlets often act as Third Places, by their predictability and pervasiveness regularly welcoming diverse groups (Bosman and Dolley 2019). As urbanization rapidly progresses, with UN projections that 75 percent of the world's population will live in urban areas by 2050 (Bosman and Dolley 2019), there is a need to implement spaces such as Third Places to promote social interaction and its subsequent benefits.

12.4 Square Dancing in Mexico City

Dozens of nicely dressed seated and standing elderly men and women were watching others dance in one of Mexico City's neighborhoods (Figure 12.10). On a stage, a DJ played traditional tunes. Many who seem to be singles enjoyed each other company and made acquaintances.

The built environment can offer opportunities to minimize loneliness. This includes public meeting places and organized activities like the one in Mexico City. Robust social infrastructure should be designed to encourage a variety of activities and invite people of all ages and backgrounds to mix and mingle. These spaces should also include spots dedicated to

Figure 12.10 Seniors gather for a dance in Mexico City, Mexico.

Places for Social Interaction

seniors, who disproportionately suffer from loneliness and isolation. When elderly people are surrounded by young people, they draw energy from them. It enables them to have security and a sense of identity to support their life-cycle adjustment. On the other hand, living among seniors allows children and teens to benefit from special attention and mentoring.

12.5 Talent on Front Porches in Montreal

Neighborhoods can harbor citizens' hidden talent. Be it playing a musical instrument, singing or painting, those talents can help bring people together. Making opportunities to display it is essential to communities' life. It makes residents step out of their shell and reach out to one another in a relaxed, enjoyable setting. In Notre-Dame-de-Grâce (NDG) in Montreal, Canada, it happens on Porchfest (Porchfest NDG n.d.) (Figure 12.11).

The concept of the Porchfest can be traced to the Fall Creek and Northside neighborhoods of Ithaca, New York in 2007. Neighbors Gretchen Hildreth and Lesley Greene were inspired by some outdoor ukulele playing and came up with the idea of gathering 20 amateur bands to perform outdoors. Since then, the number of bands grew, and there were 185 bands at the 2016 Porchfest. Porchfest is found today in more than 130 other communities in North America, including Montreal.

Porchfest in NDG usually takes place in the spring and has been going on annually. It is an informal music festival of sorts where amateur and professional musicians perform on front porches throughout the neighborhood. Residents can discover their neighbors' hidden talents in a comfortable and relaxed setting. The music styles range from rock to reggae, and original compositions, cover songs or jam sessions.

Porchfest also helps strengthen relations among residents and celebrate a rich, predominantly invisible artistry. Moreover, it creates a sense of neighborhood pride, a key tenet of social sustainability. During the event, funds are raised to benefit community charities. The 2018 Porchfest event, for example, raised money to support a music program for children at St. Raymond Community Centre, allowing access to musical instruments for young talents.

12.6 The Library of the People

The Little Free Library project began in 2009 when Todd H. Bol from Wisconsin built the first library to honor his late mother who was an avid reader (Little Free Library 2018). It consisted of a simple box, easy to spot and open while remaining protected from the elements. It grew to become a widely successful non-profit organization aimed at encouraging book-sharing and by extension community-building. The organization's philosophy is "take a book, share a book," which seems to work well as millions of books are exchanged each year on an honor system. Thousands of Little Free Libraries have been installed around the world, with more than 80,000 in all 50 American states and 91 other countries. They soon became an improvised meeting place for people (Figure 12.12).

The effect of the libraries was transformative. Three out of four people have reported to have read a book they normally would not have if it had not been found in a Little Free Library.

Figure 12.11 Performing on a porch and in front of a house during Porchfest in Notre-Dame-de-Grâce (NDG), Montreal.

Places for Social Interaction

Figure 12.12 Little Free Libraries have been installed around the world.

Some 73 percent of the residents claim to have expended their circle of acquaintance by stopping at a library, and 92 percent believe their neighborhoods to be a friendlier place thanks to the initiative. Furthermore, in areas where books are scarce, Little Free Libraries offer the Impact Library Program which deposit in them new and old books. More than 1,000 such libraries have been established so far to make reading possible to children who would otherwise not have access to books and improve literacy in communities where books are usually difficult to come by.

12.7 Final Thoughts

The topics discussed in this chapter highlight how both society shapes space, and space shapes society. Spaces are mutable and dynamic, which is particularly evident by the revitalization of lanes in cities, and through the growth of improvised gathering spaces. Spaces are shaped and reshaped over time, being influenced by social dynamics, interactions and needs; however, spaces themselves also influence the prevalence and quality of social interactions and dynamics, due to their presence and features.

Social interaction is crucial to mental and physical health and is important in promoting a sense of community and safety. As social interaction is influenced by urban design, it is crucial to design spaces which facilitate social interaction among diverse groups and avoid design which inhibits or restricts social interaction. Implementing design features which promote in-person social interaction is especially crucial in a time of increasing social media usage and mental health problems. As discussed, formal and improvised gathering spaces, such as the lane and Third Places, are all key urban design features which can be used as vehicles to promote in-person social interactions within cities.

References

Abi-Jaoude, E., Naylor, K. T. and Pignatiello, A. (2020). Smartphones, social media use and youth mental health. *Canadian Medical Association Journal* 192(6). Retrieved July 1, 2023, from https://doi.org/10.1503/cmaj.190434

Bosman, C. and Dolley, J. (2019). Rethinking third places and community building. In *Rethinking Third Places: Informal*

Public Spaces and Community Building, pp. 1–19. Edward Elgar. Cheltenham.

Broudehoux, A.-M. (2021). Post-pandemic cities can permanently reclaim public spaces as gathering places. *The Conversation*. Retrieved July 1, 2023, from https://theconversation.com/post-pandemic-cities-can-permanently-reclaim-public-spaces-as-gathering-places-150729

Butler, S. M. and Diaz, C. (2016). "Third places" as community builders. Brookings. Retrieved July 1, 2023, from www.brookings.edu/blog/up-front/2016/09/14/third-places-as-community-builders/

City of Maple Ridge BC (n.d.). Social sustainability. Maple Ridge, British Columbia. Retrieved July 1, 2023, from www.mapleridge.ca/1779/Social-Sustainability#:~:text=Defining%20Social%20Sustainability&text=Generally%2C%20it%20is%20understood%20as,social%20well%2Dbeing%20should%20be

Coleman-Jensen, A., Rabbitt, M. P., Hales, L. and Gregory, C. A. (2022). Food security in the U.S.: key statistics & graphics. USDA Economic Research Service. Retrieved July 1, 2023, from www.ers.usda.gov/topics/food-nutrition-assistance/food-security-in-the-u-s/key-statistics-graphics/#:~:text=In%202021%3A,with%20adults%2C%20were%20food%20insecure

Farr, D. (2018). *Sustainable Nation: Urban Design Patterns for the Future* (2nd ed.). John Wiley & Sons. Hoboken.

Friedman, A. and Pollock, A. (2022). *Fundamentals of Planning Cities for Healthy Living*. Anthem Press. London.

Fullagar, S., O'Brien, W. and Lloyd, K. (2019). Feminist perspectives on third places. In *Rethinking Third Places: Informal Public Spaces and Community Building*, pp. 20–37. Edward Elgar. Cheltenham.

Holt-Lunstad, J. (2021). The major health implications of social connection. *Current Directions in Psychological Science* 30(3): 251–259. Retrieved July 1, 2023, from https://doi.org/10.1177/0963721421999630

Klinenberg, E. (n.d.). Dying alone: an interview with Eric Klinenberg. Retrieved July 1, 2023, from https://press.uchicago.edu/Misc/Chicago/443213in.html

Klinenberg, E. (2019). *Palaces for the People: How Social Infrastructure Can Help Fight Inequality, Polarization, and the Decline of Civic Life*. Broadway Books. Portland.

Lehmann, S. (2020). The unplanned city: public space and the spatial character of urban informality. *Emerald Open Research* 2. Retrieved July 1, 2023, from https://doi.org/10.35241/emeraldopenres.13580.1

Little Free Library (2018). Little Free Library annual report 2018. Retrieved July 1, 2023, from https://littlefreelibrary.org/wp-content/uploads/2022/07/LFL-AnnualReport-2018_WEBSITE-1-compressed.pdf

Martin, B. and Nagasawa, K. (2020). What Chicago can learn from the 1995 heat wave. *NPR*. Retrieved July 1, 2023, from www.npr.org/local/309/2020/07/14/890758229/what-chicago-can-learn-from-the-1995-heat-wave

Oldenburg, R. (1999). *The Great Good Place: Cafes, Coffee Shops, Bookstores, Bars, Hair Salons, and Other Hangouts at the Heart of a Community*. Da Capo Press. Cambridge.

Orben, A., Tomova, L., and Blakemore, S.-J. (2020). The effects of social deprivation on adolescent development and mental health. *The Lancet Child & Adolescent Health* 4(8): 634–640. Retrieved July 1, 2023, from https://doi.org/10.1016/s2352-4642(20)30186-3

Porchfest NDG (n.d.). About Porchfest. *Porchfest NDG*. Retrieved July 1, 2023, from www.porchfestndg.com/about-agrave-propos.html

Salman, S. (2018). What would a truly disabled-accessible city look like? *The Guardian*. Retrieved July 1, 2023, from www.theguardian.com/cities/2018/feb/14/what-disability-accessible-city-look-like

Steinkuehler, C. A. and Williams, D. (2006). Where everybody knows your (screen) name: online games as "third places". *Journal of Computer-Mediated Communication* 11(4): 885–909. Retrieved July 1, 2023, from https://doi.org/10.1111/j.1083-6101.2006.00300.x

Twenge, J. M., Spitzberg, B. H. and Campbell, W. K. (2019). Less in-person social interaction with peers among U.S. adolescents in the 21st century and links to loneliness. *Journal of Social and Personal Relationships* 36(6): 1892–1913. Retrieved July 1, 2023, from https://doi.org/10.1177/0265407519836170

Water Wheel (2017). Stop food waste in its tracks. *Water Wheel* 16(5): 40–41. Retrieved July 1, 2023, from chrome-extension://efaidnbmnnnibpcajpcglclefindmkaj/; https://www.wrc.org.za/wp-content/uploads/mdocs/WW%20Sept_Oct%202017_web.pdf

CHAPTER 13

Art and the City

This chapter underscores the crucial role that public art installations play in fostering social connectivity and preserving cultural heritage. It delves into guidelines for creative urban design that prioritize the integration of public art, emphasizing the importance of open and flexible public spaces that can accommodate various forms of artistic expression. Additionally, the chapter explores the value of developing place-specific strategies for the integration of art that can enhance the unique character of a community. Furthermore, the chapter highlights the potential of street furnishings as an innovative way to incorporate art into the urban environment. It also explores how art can be leveraged as an educational tool to promote cultural sustainability and awareness of critical issues like climate change. Overall, this chapter serves as a comprehensive guide for urban planners, designers and policymakers to create vibrant, inclusive and sustainable communities through the power of public art.

13.1 The Importance of Public Art to Social and Cultural Sustainability

Unlike the formal confines of a museum display which at times targets a specific audience and can even intimidate some, public art is for all to see. People may go to view public art intentionally, but they mostly come upon it by chance. It can encompass every mode of artistic expression, including, by some accounts, even music. Public art aims to express and affect local culture and fosters a sense of delight in the life of the city. It can stimulate play, creativity and imagination among adults and children. It promotes contact, communication and, at times, debate. It accommodates people by incorporating steps, ledges and benches on which viewers can sit or lean to appreciate and admire. It can bring the various factions of society together by stimulating curiosity and interest in the community's heritage and act as an educator.

Art in the city is also an integral ingredient to many forms of sustainability, among them social by promoting collective identity, culture, cohesion and societal wellbeing. Public art takes many forms, including street lighting, sculpture, building features incorporated into the architectural fabric, land-form artworks and temporary installations (Matthews and Gadaloff 2022) (Figure 13.1). Its value lies in its ability to facilitate placemaking, establishing a unique sense of place and prompting dialogue – occasionally contentious – among community members. Public art stimulates creativity in the community and engages audiences by creating spaces that encourage reflection and identification (Cheung et al. 2021). In this way, art plays a crucial role in promoting community and renewing a sense of place (Sharp et al. 2020).

While some art may be abstract, prompting inquisitive conversations, it can also deliberately reflect a community's ideas, values and unique identity, embodied as a memorial, tribute or prominent landmark. In fact, the French word "monument," from the Latin "monumentum," comes from the word "monere," also Latin, which means to warn, remind and remember. Art is a powerful means to capture a place's past, present and future, providing a shared social legacy and a sense of civic pride for a city. It can document national events and enable people to interact and debate social and political issues, shaping places and communities and composing the relationships between them (Cheung et al. 2021) (Figure 13.2). Furthermore, the ability of art to serve as a tool for diagnosing and addressing social issues is largely dependent on its level of public accessibility and its ability to engage with the public sphere (Smith 2015). Art that is widely available and actively involves the community in its creation and interpretation has the potential to spark important conversations and inspire meaningful change. In this way, the impact of art on society is closely tied to its ability to connect with and reflect the concerns and values of the broader public. It has a unique ability to enhance collective identity by encouraging conversation, sparking questions, and attracting visitors to connect and socialize.

Art and the City

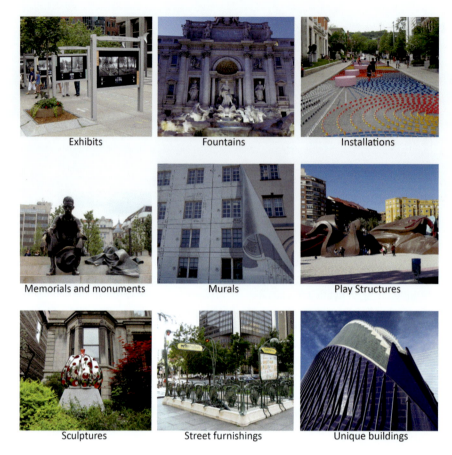

Figure 13.1 Public art can take many forms, including street furnishing, sculptures, buildings, monuments and temporary installations.

Figure 13.2 Memorials and monuments such as the one to the Murdered Jews of Europe in Berlin, Germany (left) and Vietnam Veterans Memorial in Washington, D.C. (right) educate the public about notable events and offer a place to debate social and political issues.

As people encounter public artworks, movement through space is slowed down (Dawoud and Elgizawy 2018). The impact of a single artwork can be significant because, as mentioned, it inspires conversations and sparks debate about the underlying message. In this way, public art serves as a reflection of a city's history and a powerful tool for shaping its future. Equally, many newer communities have recognized that involving public art in planning increases the opportunities to build a creative society and can also humanize cities, promoting people's happiness and improving their mental and physical

Art and the City

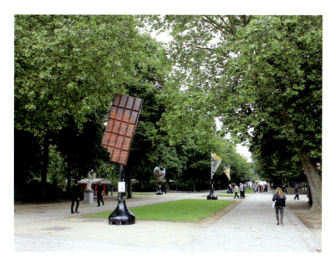

Figure 13.3 Public art can transform spaces into vibrant and unique environments.

health through community building and social connectedness. Bringing color and character to otherwise mundane areas, public art can transform public spaces into vibrant and unique environments (Figure 13.3). Whether it is displayed on buildings, in parklands, along busy roads or in retail settings, it can also have a profound impact on the architectural fabric of a place. By adding a sense of distinctiveness and creating a unique sense of place, public art can help differentiate one location from another and make it stand out from its surroundings. Its impact on built environments is undeniable, providing a visually captivating addition that enhances the beauty and livability of public spaces for residents and visitors alike.

Art can additionally be regarded as a form of branding and marketing for a city. Numerous studies have reported on how public art has become a catalyst for economic and social revival (Kaino 2014; Whybrow 2016), by enhancing a sense of unique identity, drawing in tourists who are interested in exploring the art scene of a city. This can lead to increased spending on local businesses such as restaurants, cafes and shops, as well as increased demand for lodging and transportation services (Figure 13.4). Moreover, public art can breathe new life into neglected or underutilized areas, such as abandoned buildings or vacant lots. By transforming these spaces into vibrant cultural hubs, public art can stimulate economic activity in previously dormant areas.

Copenhagen, Denmark

Lisbon, Portugal

Montreal, Canada

Montreal, Canada

Figure 13.4 Public art can breathe new life into neglected or underutilized areas, such as streets, abandoned buildings or vacant lots.

13.1.1 The Social Message of Graffiti Art

According to Matthews and Gadaloff (2022), graffiti art has become highly popular as public art in many cities and can even attract economic investment in emerging urban areas by positioning a place as creative. Dating back thousands of years, old forms of graffiti were found in the Lascaux cave in France, ancient Roman ruins, Spanish rocks dating to the sixteenth century, the remains of the Mayan city in Central America, as well as in medieval English churches. The term "graffiti" is rooted in the Greek word *graphein*, which means to scratch, draw or write, as well as the Italian word *graffito* which means scratch.

Referring to any form of inscriptions found on walls or floors, graffiti can be regarded as an expressive art form, whether it is done to attract attention or to experience the thrill of engaging in illegal activity by an individual or group. Today graffiti is looked upon as a form of public art, which may contribute to beautifying neighborhoods and cities and known graffiti artist are commonly invited to display their art (Figure 13.5).

Contemporary use of spray-painted graffiti can be traced to the "hip-hop" era of the 1960s and 1970s, which appeared in urban public spaces. The use of bold colors, various types of lettering as well as cartoon-like characters signify that style. At the time, graffiti was mostly associated with gangs in the United States and Europe, who used them to claim territory, to memorialize gang members and to challenge rival gangs. By the late twentieth century, New York was notorious for having a great number of graffiti spray-painted building walls and subway cars. These inspired artists such as Keith Haring and Jean-Michel Basquiat in the 1980s to include graffiti in their artwork. While graffiti artists are mostly concerned with spreading their tags and gaining recognition, street artists do not share this same concern and explore a greater variety of styles and techniques (The Art Story 2020).

Stencils are today a common technique used by street artists who prepare them beforehand out of cardboard or paper and use them on site and spray paint over them. Many artists favor this technique, as it allows them to quickly install their text or image before the authorities catch them. The first artist recorded as having used stencils is John Fekner in 1968. Today, many artists use this technique including British artist Banksy. Banksy is an anonymous British artist who first became known in the 1990s for doing antiauthoritarian art in public areas. Born in Bristol, England, in 1974 he started using stencils in 2000 and developed a unique and recognizable style. Social and political agendas are often targeted by Banksy, who does so through humorous and witty spray-painted illustrations (Artnet 2020).

13.2 Urban Design for Integration of Public Art

Urban designers can incorporate elements into their designs that allow for eventual public art. To achieve this, they need to consider various factors, including creating open and flexible spaces, and planning for accessibility. To create a blank canvas for public art installations, urban designers should strive to create open spaces in their designs, such as plazas, squares and parks. Public space is an essential resource for creating successful communities in modern cities as it offers numerous opportunities for residents to connect with one another and become familiar with their neighbors. This notion is supported by evidence from modern sociologists, who have demonstrated that strong social interactions among residents are integral

Figure 13.5 Graffiti can be regarded as an expressive art form or engagement in illegal activity.

to fostering a healthy community (Dawoud and Elgizawy 2018). These spaces should be designed to be large enough to accommodate different types of installations. For instance, incorporating large walls or facades can provide ample space for murals or other large-scale installations (Figure 13.6). In addition to size, accessibility is also essential. As discussed in this chapter, art that is widely available and actively involves the community in its creation and interpretation can spark important conversations and inspire meaningful change. To ensure accessibility, urban designers should prioritize designing pedestrian-friendly walkways or creating spaces that are easily visible and accessible from public transportation. Finally, urban designers should consider creating adaptable spaces that can be repurposed for different types of public art installations. For example, a space that can be used for a sculpture garden one year could be used for a different temporary installation the next. By incorporating these factors into their designs, urban designers can create spaces that not only serve their intended functions but also provide opportunities for creative expression and engagement with the community through public art.

13.2.1 Grass Roots and Strategic Place-Based Art Integration

As Britt (2014) points out, many designers view integrating art simply as a means to increasing the quality of life, which she describes as "honorable but amorphous." This is because, to fully harness the power of public art, she argues that it must be thoughtfully integrated into specific planning strategies. For instance, in neighborhoods grappling with high rates of obesity and diabetes, interactive and inspiring public art pieces can encourage physical activity. By incorporating public art interventions into a broader health strategy, communities can achieve measurable public health goals.

Spontaneous artistic self-expressions add uniqueness and meaning by humanizing communities to enhance sense of place and local identity. Without them, places can be bland and monotonous. Furthermore, the work can demonstrate cultural values by proposing alternative grassroots perspectives to challenge agreed-upon values and beliefs. They make it part of everyday life, as passers-by may view it at any time of day. The work also promotes placemaking by letting common citizens reflect on and engage socially.

Figure 13.6 Incorporating art on buildings' front plaza or their facades inspires and educates passers-by and beautifies streets.

Art and the City

Unlike galleries or museums, where the display was set for maximum enjoyment with artificial lights, spacing and the relation between the artwork, cities need to be regarded as another kind of museum where people can freely display their skills, which may spark creativity in others and appreciation by all of us.

To ensure the most effective development of artwork in a given space, several factors may be considered. It is important to inquire about the cultural and social practices of the community, such as traditional celebrations and social events, as these can inspire the creation of art that resonates with locals and promotes the existing cultural heritage. Additionally, it may be worthwhile to identify prominent local figures, such as writers, artists, philosophers and community leaders, whose contributions can be celebrated through public art. Another important consideration is the needs of different groups of people who may use the space, such as the elderly, who may require seating, shade and areas for socializing. Understanding the ages and socio-cultural backgrounds of the intended audience can also aid in developing art that is inclusive and engaging for all. By prioritizing ideas and considerations around making spaces functional and livable for people, artists can effectively engage in the art of placemaking. Rather than simply producing a static piece of art, the artist's approach to public art can be more thoughtful and intentional, serving as a means of enhancing the overall experience and functionality of a given space.

Artistic self-expressions add uniqueness and meaning by humanizing communities to enhance sense of place and local identity (Figure 13.7). Without them, places can be bland and

Figure 13.7 Artistic self-expressions by citizens add uniqueness by humanizing communities to enhance their sense of place and local identity.

monotonous. Furthermore, the work can demonstrate cultural values by proposing alternative grassroots perspectives to challenge agreed-upon values and beliefs. They make it part of everyday life, as passers-by may view it at any time of day. The work also promotes placemaking by letting common citizens reflect on and engage socially. Unlike galleries or museums, where the display was set for maximum enjoyment with artificial lights, spacing and the relation between the artwork, cities need to be regarded as another kind of museum where people can freely display their skills, which may spark creativity in others and appreciation by all of us (Hospers 2019).

13.3 Street Furnishings as Art

Cities are transformed into more vibrant and appealing spaces when art is incorporated into everyday features such as street furnishings. Street furniture serves multiple purposes, including beautification, comfort and protection from outside elements (Radwan and Morsy 2017). These elements are specifically designed to positively impact the visual aesthetics of a space and therefore, in addition to functionality, designers must consider aesthetic concerns to ensure that street furniture does not have a negative impact on its surroundings but rather adds to the unique identity of the urban environment. Things like trashcans, benches, bike racks and signage all have the potential to add to a city's creative index (Radwan and Morsy 2017). The beauty of public art is not restricted to grand murals or installations but can also be applied to these ordinary objects that exist within the city. The design of a bench can not only serve a functional purpose but also be aesthetically pleasing, and some ordinary benches can even be transformed into works of art. When artists are involved in their design, they can be an important tool in educating the public about the importance of aesthetics in everyday objects (Figure 13.8).

A prime illustration of the latter is The Bench Warming Project, a collaborative event in the city of Lapeer, United States, featuring multiple artists who were invited to paint on existing benches, thereby converting plain surfaces into vibrant sites bursting with color and creativity (Burkhart 2021). Through this project, benches were elevated from their mundane status to become dynamic and engaging pieces of public art. Additionally, the city of Kamloops, Canada, spearheaded an initiative where local artists were recruited to

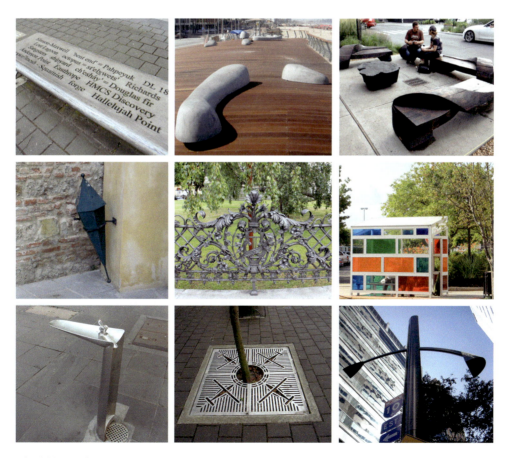

Figure 13.8 Street furnishing can be an important tool in educating the public about the importance of aesthetics in everyday objects.

Art and the City

transform garbage receptacles into canvases, adding an artistic touch to the city's waste management efforts (*Kamloops This Week* 2020). Furthermore, in Vancouver, Canada, one can discover loving tributes, inspiring quotes or beautiful poetry engraved on many of the benches scattered throughout the city.

Color is a crucial element that plays a significant role in shaping our perception of public spaces (Radwan and Morsy 2017). When it comes to street furniture, it is essential that the colors are carefully selected to enhance its visibility and fulfill its intended purpose, while possibly adding a creative touch. In fact, the proper use of color can greatly contribute to the overall quality and ambiance of a public area. Street furnishings provide an unconventional yet perfect site for art to be applied, making cities more attractive and livable. Designers should strive to create tasteful and innovative street furniture that is not only functional but also visually appealing. In the process of designing street furniture, designers may use their own experiences and creativity, while also adhering to general principles of texture, structure, material and color.

13.4 Art as an Educational Tool

Art can also serve as an educational tool to relay a message to community, perhaps about history or ecological issues such as climate change (Figure 13.9). As discussed above, what art does to public space serves to invoke memory, create a site to negotiate conflicting practices and stimulate social encounters between its audiences in shared moments of spectatorship. Furthermore, studies have brought attention to the significant role public art can play to engage the landscape in communicating about climate change (Aragón et al. 2019). By using the landscape as a medium, artists have brought attention to climate change through installations such as "High Tide," a public piece in Boston, United States, designed to bring attention to projected flooding in the area due to sea level rise (Aragón 2022). The complexities surrounding climate change communication, such as the abstract and distant nature of the information, the scientific jargon, and the negative messaging, can make it challenging to engage and motivate people to take action (Boulton 2016). Creative practices in the arts can overcome some of these challenges by providing new forms of

Figure 13.9 Public art can serve an educational tool to relay a message to a community about history or ecological issues.

representation and emotive experiences to an expanded public. In addition, landscape architects, planners and artists can contribute to public engagement by grounding climate change communication in local landscapes and place-based experiences. This approach allows people to connect with climate change issues in a more tangible and meaningful way, fostering a sense of ownership and responsibility for the environment (Aragón et al. 2019).

In addition, artists have the unique ability to bring attention to site-specific historical and cultural motifs, and in doing so, can play a vital role in educating the population about their significance. A prime example of this is the use of plant motifs in street art and design artifacts in India, driven by various historical and cultural factors. Research has indicated that incorporating botanical street art and design can be an effective approach to drawing people's attention to the natural world and combatting "plant blindness" in urban settings (Sachdev 2019). Educators can use this as an opportunity to familiarize the public with the profound historical and cultural connections that exist between people and plants, particularly in India (Sachdev 2019). Additionally, art in public spaces offers a unique platform to stimulate critical thinking. It has the power to challenge people's assumptions, prompt introspection and offer diverse perspectives on a range of issues such as politics, social justice, environmentalism and ethics. By using artistic expression to explore these issues, public art can evoke an emotional response from viewers, creating a more personal and engaging experience that promotes deeper reflection and critical thinking.

13.5 The Monument of Vimy

Vimy Ridge was a strategic point of contention during World War I. Located in northern France, Canadian Army regiments were ordered to seize the area after previous French attacks failed. The French lost a total of 100,000 soldiers by that point, and the Canadians saw 3,500 killed and 7,000 wounded while having successfully taking it. Large efforts were taken in preparation for the assault. New maps were drawn, soldiers went through extensive training, tunnels were dug and investment was made into an artillery unit to prevent German soldiers from fighting back. The achievement was not only important because of its military value, but also because all four Canadian divisions fought as a unified army (Cook 2020) (Figure 13.10).

The monument was built in 1936 on a 100 hectare (247 acres) plot that the French gave to Canada. Made primarily out of limestone shipped from Croatia, the monument consists of 20 sculptures and two 27-meter-tall pylons. It stands near the top of a hill, to make it impressive when viewed from a distance. Designed by Walter Allward, to represent the alliance between Canada and France, the driving idea was to represent the debt that Canada owes to those who gave their lives as the artist stated: "Without the dead we were helpless. So, I have tried to show this in the monument to Canada's fallen, what we owed them and we will forever owe them." Allward created molds and filled them with durable plaster to form the statues, which he then reworked for the final product. The ones on display at Vimy, however, were crafted by French stone carvers, using the original plaster models as a draft, yet doubling their size.

Figure 13.10 The Vimy Ridge World War I commemoration monument was built in 1936 out of limestone and consists of 20 sculptures and two 27-meter-tall pylons.

Art and the City

Seeing the towering Vimy monument from afar against the blue sky is breathtaking. When you approach the site and see the thousands of names of those who gave their lives capturing this ridge carved in stone you comprehend how sacred this place is. An impressive tribute to the young men who gave their lives, the monument also raises thoughts about wars and unnecessary life lost.

13.6 The Laneways of Melbourne

The laneways of many cities are places to avoid. Also known as *dark alleys*, they are unattended, smelly, poorly lit places where rubbish is dumped, cars are parked and goods are delivered. An unfortunate necessity of city planning and function.

The Laneways in Melbourne's Central Business District are part of the place's culture and history that can be traced back to 1837 when Europeans first started to parcel the land. The subdivision resulted in narrower streets at the back of properties, which fronted wider streets. The rectangular grid, in which the land was organized, designed by surveyor Robert Hodde, soon lost its sense of order, as lanes and alleys appeared throughout city blocks to serve as access points for servants and carts carrying merchandise (Poulton 2011).

Since the 2000s the city went on to commission graffiti artwork and organize festivals in the Laneways (Figure 13.11). Selected every year by the Love Your Laneway program, some lanes see improvement of infrastructure in addition to beautification and cultural activities. Since 2008 the program has transformed 24 of Melbourne's Laneways to make them known internationally. In 2016, the city also launched the Green Your Laneway program, with the objective of including vegetation and seating in Laneways to further enhance their attraction.

Melbourne is known today as a place where the presence of street art is strong and greatly valued. Furthermore, the creation of new lane art is encouraged and sponsored by funding from the Laneway Commissions. The Laneway Music Festival, which was created in 2004, draws young artists to inspire creative endeavors (Melbourne Heritage Action n.d.).

13.7 Public Art as a Dark Narrative

Some places have a narrative to tell. Rooted in their distant or recent past, some places cast a dark shadow on their community for a long time and serve as a reminder of an unfortunate past. The Radegast train station in Lodz, Poland, is an example of a place with a narrative of horror. It was the place from which Jews were sent to the Chelmno and Auschwitz-Birkenau death camps. In addition to preservation and a museum, the station is also a memorial site. The displays show life in the ghettos and depict the lives of some 145,000 victims. The station also includes railroad cars similar to those used for the deportations and original transport lists.

In Vienna's Judenplatz, a giant square of stone is found which reveals itself as a sort of inverted library. The monument was designed by Rachel Whiteread to challenge and provoke thought and unveiled in 2000. It is dedicated to the 65,000 Austrian Jews who were deported and murdered during the Holocaust. The names of the concentration camps where the victims died, as well as a dedication to them, are found on the monument's wide plinth (Visiting Vienna 2020).

Figure 13.11 Since the 2000s the city of Melbourne has commissioned graffiti artwork and organized festivals in laneways.

Art and the City

At the center of Zgody Square in Krakow, Poland, lies an artistic installation featuring up to 33 oversized chairs which are scattered around the square, where each chair represents a thousand lives (MacFarlane 2019). The empty chairs symbolize the absence of Jews which followed the war, as the Jewish population of Krakow went from 60,000 to 5,000 after the fall of the Nazi regime. Zgody Square used to be a marketplace, but during the Third Reich it became a ghetto where Jews were kept prior to their killing.

Another moving Holocaust memorial are the more than 70,000 metal plates known as *Solpersteine* or "stumbling stones" in more than 1,200 towns and cities across Europe and Russia. The plates commemorate victims and are placed outside their last-known place of residence. They were conceived by German artist Gunter Demnig in Cologne in 1992 who has since then overseen and coordinated their installation in other places.

The *Solpersteine* are just under 10 centimeter-square (1.55 square inch) and are made of brass and are embedded into the street's pavement. Inscribed in each plate are the victim's name, date of birth, place of deportation and date of death when known (Whiting 2017).

Inaugurated in 2005 and initiated by film director Can Togay and sculptor Gyula Pauer on the banks of the Danube in Budapest, Hungary is a memorial composed of 60 pairs of human-sized iron shoes of different sizes and styles pointing towards the river. During the war Jews in Budapest were rounded, lined-up and shot into the Danube River after they were forced to remove their shoes, which would be sold or used, as these were valuable items. It was estimated that 20,000 local Jews were shot by Arrow Cross militiamen from December 1944 to January 1945. The uniqueness of each shoe also echoes the personalities of those who were shot (Figure 13.12).

Krakow, Poland

Lodz, Poland

Rome, Italy

Vienna, Austria

Budapest, Hungary

Figure 13.12 Rooted in their distant or recent past some places' public art can serve as a reminder of an unfortunate or tragic past.

13.8 Final Thoughts

Public art plays a vital role in promoting social and cultural sustainability, offering a unique sense of place, sparking dialogue and nurturing creativity within communities. It has the power to capture a location's history, present and future, creating a shared social legacy and fostering civic pride within cities. The impact of public art on society is closely linked to its ability to connect with and reflect the broader public's concerns and values, promoting conversation, generating questions and drawing visitors to connect and socialize. Integrating public art into planning can provide communities with an opportunity to build a creative society, humanize cities, promote happiness, improve mental and physical health through community building and social connectedness. Public art can transform public spaces, breathing life and character into otherwise mundane areas. Urban designers have a critical role to play in integrating public art into their designs by creating open and adaptable public spaces that can accommodate future art installations. This involves considering various factors, such as accessibility, size and adaptability. Urban designers should prioritize designing pedestrian-friendly walkways, creating spaces that are visible and easily accessible from public transportation, and providing ample space for large-scale installations, such as murals on large walls or facades. By creating adaptable spaces, urban designers can ensure their designs remain open to new ideas, promoting creativity and innovation. It also ensures public art remains an integral part of their designs, providing opportunities for ongoing community engagement, sparking important conversations and inspiring meaningful change. Overall, public art is a critical component of creating vibrant and unique environments that enrich the lives of individuals and communities alike.

References

Aragón, C. (2022). High tide. *CODAworx*. Retrieved July 1, 2023, from www.codaworx.com/projects/high-tide/

Aragón, C., Buxton, J. and Infield, E. H. (2019). The role of landscape installations in climate change communication. *Landscape and Urban Planning* 189: 11–14. Retrieved July 1, 2023, from https://doi.org/10.1016/j.landurbplan.2019.03.014

Artnet (2020). Banksy. *Artnet*. Retrieved July 1, 2023, from http://www.artnet.com/artists/banksy/

Boulton, E. (2016). Climate change as a "hyperobject": a critical review of Timothy Morton's reframing narrative. *WIREs Climate Change* 7(5): 772–785. Retrieved July 1, 2023, from https://doi.org/10.1002/wcc.410

Britt, M. F. (2014). The intersection of public art and city planning. *ARTS Blog*. Retrieved April 29, 2023, from https://blog.americansforthearts.org/2019/05/15/the-intersection-of-public-art-and-city-planning

Burkhart, E. (2021). Revitalizing a city: the bench warming project adds colour and life to downtown Lapeer. *Arts Help*. Retrieved July 1, 2023, from www.artshelp.com/the-bench-warming-project/

Cheung, M., Smith, N. and Craven, O. (2021). The impacts of public art on cities, places and people's lives. *The Journal of Arts Management, Law, and Society* 52(1): 37–50. Retrieved July 1, 2023, from https://doi.org/10.1080/10632921.2021.1942361

Cook, T. (2020). The Battle of Vimy Ridge, 9–12 April 1917. War Museum. Retrieved July 1, 2023, from www.warmuseum.ca/the-battle-of-vimy-ridge/

Dawoud, M. M. and Elgizawy, E. M. (2018). The correlation between art and architecture to promote social interaction in public space. *Cities' Identity Through Architecture and Arts*, 99–105. Retrieved July 1, 2023, from https://doi.org/10.1201/9781315166551-9

Hospers, J. (2019). Art as expression. *Encyclopedia Britannica*. Retrieved July 1, 2023, from www.britannica.com/topic/philosophy-of-art/Art-as-expression

Kaino, L. (2014). "There's something special about this little town": cultural identity and the legacy of Hundertwasser in Kawakawa, New Zealand. *Continuum – Journal of Media and Cultural Studies*, 28(1): 65–76. doi: 10.1080/10304312.2013.854864

Kamloops This Week (2020). Turning garbage bins in Kamloops into works of art. Retrieved July 1, 2023, from www.kamloopsthisweek.com/community/turning-garbage-bins-in-kamloops-into-works-of-art-4445689

MacFarlane, K. (2019). The empty chairs of Krakow. *Hasta*. Retrieved July 1, 2023, from www.hasta-standrews.com/features/2019/2/18/the-empty-chairs-of-krakow

Matthews, T. and Gadaloff, S. (2022). Public art for placemaking and urban renewal: insights from three regional Australian cities. *Cities* 127: 103747. Retrieved July 1, 2023, from https://doi.org/10.1016/j.cities.2022.103747

Melbourne Heritage Action (n.d.). Melbourne laneways. Retrieved July 1, 2023, from https://melbourneheritageaction.wordpress.com/current-campaigns/laneways/

Poulton, F. (2011). Little Latrobe Street and the historical significance of Melbourne's laneways. *The Journal of Public Record Office Victoria* 10: 95–104. Retrieved July 1, 2023, from https://prov.vic.gov.au/sites/default/files/files/media/provenance2011_poulton.pdf

Radwan, A. H. and Morsy, A. A. G. (2017). The importance of integrating street furniture in the visual image of the city. *International Journal of Modern Engineering Research (IJMER)*

9(2). Retrieved July 1, 2023, from https://papers.ssrn.com/sol3/papers.cfm?abstract_id=3264621

Sachdev, G. (2019). Engaging with plants in an urban environment through street art and design. *Plants, People, Planet* 1(3): 271–289. Retrieved July 1, 2023, from https://doi.org/10.1002/ppp3.10055

Sharp, J., Pollock, V. and Paddison, R. (2020). Just art for a just city: public art and social inclusion in urban regeneration. *Culture-Led Urban Regeneration*, 156–178. Retrieved July 1, 2023, from https://doi.org/10.4324/9781315878768-9

Smith, C. (2015). Art as a diagnostic: assessing social and political transformation through public art in Cairo, Egypt. *Social & Cultural Geography* 16(1): 22–42. Retrieved July 1, 2023, from https://doi.org/10.1080/14649365.2014.936894

The Art Story (2020). Street and graffiti art. *The Art History*. Retrieved July 1, 2023, from www.theartstory.org/movement/street-art/history-and-concepts/

Visiting Vienna (2020). The Holocaust Memorial. *Visiting Vienna*. Retrieved July 1, 2023, from www.visitingvienna.com/sights/museums/holocaust-memorial/

Whiting, A. F. (2017). Berlin: how my street tells the tragedy of the Holocaust. *AlexFW.com*. Retrieved July 1, 2023, from https://alexfw.com/2017/04/24/berlin-how-my-street-tells-the-tragedy-of-the-holocaust/

Whybrow, N. (2016). Folkestone perennial: the enduring work of art in the re-constitution of place. *Cultural Geographies* 23(4): 671–692. doi: 10.1177/1474474016638047

CHAPTER 14
Streets and Sidewalks for Living

The accommodation of motor vehicles has dominated road planning since automobiles was introduced in the early twentieth century. This chapter explores the double role that streets and sidewalks play as both arteries of movement and generators of social activities. The chapter begins by highlighting of how automobiles "took over" cities, with attention to infrastructure changes that resulted from and further facilitated use of cars. Next, developments encapsulating a new mind-set toward streets and sidewalks are discussed. Additionally, urban design features including mixed-use development and accommodating safe walking are investigated in relation to mobility.

14.1 The Rise of Car Dominance in Planning

Car use has been a topic of investigation by planners and active mobility supporters for decades (Reversing car dependency 2021; Walsh 2017). The increased demand for and use of private automobiles has contributed to accommodating its ease of use. In the early years of the twentieth century, activities occurring at streets and sidewalks were markedly different than they are today (Sleiman 2019). Streets were pedestrian-centric, "belonging" to the people and places of social activities. With the invention of the automobile, the focus of city planners shifted to instead cater to cars, to which car companies' lobbying contributed (Lewis 2014; Norton 2007; Shill 2019; Sleiman 2019). Additionally, advancements in automobile technology led to their increased efficiency, comfort and affordability, further encouraging their ownership (Ostermeijer et al. 2022). This rising demand subsequently led to increasing road widths, construction of newer and higher-speed roadways, and the introduction of parking quotas (Norton 2007; Ostermeijer et al. 2022; Shoup 1997; Doheim et al. 2020).

Roads were expanded, and new ones constructed, in attempts to relieve traffic congestion and foster more efficient car travel (Chen and Klaiber 2020). Known as the *Downs-Thomson Paradox*, this widening of roads produces a vicious cycle, where congestion may be temporarily relieved, but it subsequently leads to increased car use and congestion due to induced demand (Zhang et al. 2016) (Figure 14.1). Alternatively, despite seeming counter-intuitive, reducing the capacity of a roadway has been found to instead lead to decreased congestion (Reducing roads can cause traffic to "evaporate" 2019). Additionally, narrower road width is known to be associated with slower driving, therefore decreasing risk and severity of crashes for vehicles and pedestrian fatalities (Lane width 2015).

An example of expansive road widths contributing to decreased walkability is evident in Salt Lake City, United States, which was planned with many six-lane-wide roadways and with intersections the length of two football fields (Friedman and Pollock 2022). Not only does this enlarged scale

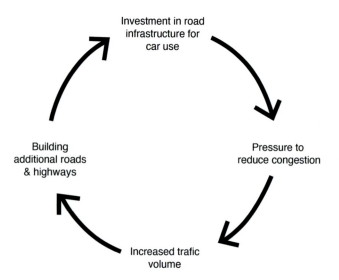

Figure 14.1 Known as the Downs-Thomson Paradox, the widening of roads produces a vicious cycle where congestion may be temporarily relieved, but it subsequently leads to increased car use and congestion due to induced demand.

makes the street more intimidating to pedestrians, and void of human-scale, but also more dangerous. This is due to the six-lane-wide crosswalks which may not provide enough time for all pedestrians to cross, as well as the high volume of high-speed car traffic, increasing the risk of incidents between vehicles, or between pedestrians and vehicles.

Parking quotas, being the legally mandated minimum parking requirements imposed on developments, are intended to ensure that there are adequate parking spaces available for cars, which according to Shill is often vastly overestimated (2019). Large quantities of parking spaces take up valuable land which could instead be used for housing or green space (Shill 2019) (Figure 14.2). This notion is supported by a variety of studies, including one by Rogers et al. (2016) who found that overbuilding residential parking contributes to increased car ownership, rising traffic congestion and longer travel distances, and subsequently decreases the use of active and public transit (Rogers et al. 2016).

The increased criminalization of pedestrians, and the decreased restrictions placed on cars, has also contributed to the societal dominance of cars (Lewis 2014; Ostermeijer et al. 2022; Shill 2019). This restriction of pedestrians, often through legislation, was initially framed to protect them from vehicles; however, this was not necessarily the intention, and instead was facilitated by the automobile industry to further gain dominance (Norton 2008). For example, "jaywalking," being the act of crossing a street where there is no crosswalk, became criminalized as a result of lobbying by the motor industry in the 1920s. This law acted as a tool of socially reconstructing how streets are used, and who they are intended for, by restricting pedestrians and benefiting cars (Lewis 2014).

14.2 A New Mindset for Streets and Sidewalk Design

There are methods of decreasing the use of cars and alerting transportation patterns and our mind-sets to instead focus on active mobility and public transit. A key approach is to design urban spaces, particularly streets and sidewalks, to cater to varying shared uses (Sharifi 2019). This for example can be accomplished through the implementation of *woonerf*-type streets and car-free communities.

The *woonerf*, meaning "street for living" in Dutch, which was discussed in Chapter 5, contributes to the shared uses of streets (Sharifi 2019; Leereveld 2023). Introduced in the mid-1970s in the Netherlands, they are intended to be a lower-cost alternative to conventional streets (Dudek 2019; Leereveld 2023). The streets have no distinction between sidewalks and car lanes, and are intended to be shared among pedestrians, cyclists, public transit and motorists (den Boer 2021). Within *woonerfs*, safety for pedestrians and cyclists is prioritized, by setting car speed limits of 15km per hour (9.3 miles per hour) and not allowing cars to park at some locations (den Boer 2021) (Figure 14.3).

The *woonerf* is based on five key design principles: the presence of a recognizable gateway, incorporation of multi-functional features, absence of continuous curbs, meandering of the road, and adequate parking facilities (Leereveld 2023).

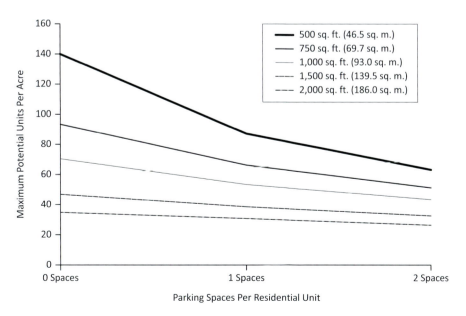

Figure 14.2 Parking spaces take up valuable land which could be used for housing or green areas.

Streets and Sidewalks for Living

Figure 14.3 Introduced originally in the mid-1970s in the Netherlands, the *woonerf* is a lower cost alternative to conventional streets by combining the street and the sidewalk and slowing traffic.

First, entrances to a *woonerf* must be clearly marked to ensure all pedestrians and drivers are aware they are accessing the space from typical roadways. Second, features have multiple purposes, such as street furniture and playgrounds being used by pedestrians for social activities, yet also acting as traffic-calming devices (Leereveld 2023). Additionally, the absence of continuous curbs allows the street to be unified and shared among all transportation modes without hindrance. The road is also designed in a curved design, which acts to calm traffic and create an organic feel, as opposed to a typical straight street (Leereveld 2023). Finally, although parking spaces are limited on *woonerfs*, the few that are implemented must be incorporated into the design in an organic, nondisruptive way, where there is open space, as opposed to being in a continuous line on the edge of the street (Leereveld 2023).

Car-free communities refer to places with either no cars or shared streets, and are still relatively new, with the first opening in Germany in 1992 (Oost 2022) (Figure 14.4). Some cities have gradually introduced this concept to various degrees. For example, Mexico City's "car-free Sundays," where motorists are discouraged from driving on this day, and instead citizens are encouraged to engage in active transportation and social activities, such as to "dance, jog and cycle on the streets" and partake in salsa classes held on the streets (Mendez 2014). Simultaneously, Mexico City has invested in

Figure 14.4 Car-free communities refer to places with either no car access or by having shared streets as seen here in the German cities Stuttgart (left) and Esslingen am Neckar (right).

140

Streets and Sidewalks for Living

extensive cycling infrastructure to support these decreases in car use, which has successfully culminated in a 40 percent decrease in car use for short distance trips (Mendez 2014).

Some factors identified as contributing to a car-free community's success include the presence of greenery, reduced parking, ample and efficient alternative transportation methods, clear agreements among residents and authorities on the features of the community, and mixed-use development with high-density of walkability attractions and services (Oost 2022). A key factor to successfully creating car-free communities is the inclusion of infrastructure that effectively supports alternative modes of transportation, such as walking, cycling or public transportation. Buses are often the most cost-effective mode of public transport to implement in smaller communities, where there may not be high enough ridership to justify comprehensive subway or light rail systems (Avenali et al. 2020; Zhang 2009).

14.3 Streets and Sidewalks for Social Engagements

The accessibility and desirability of using urban space for social activities is often closely dependent on its design. Small changes to the built environment can induce significant changes in how it is used, encourage active mobility, decrease car use and increase social engagement. Key aspects include mixed-use higher-density development, and the creation and maintenance of safe walking environments in a comfortable human-scale.

Mixed-use development refers to incorporation of a variety of land uses into a single space, such as blending residential, commercial, institutional and industrial uses, and has been found to provide a variety of environmental, economic, social and health benefits for the community (Institute for Public Administration at the University of Delaware n.d.; Peña n.d.). Mixed-use streets increase street vibrancy and contribute to the promotion of social capital by helping to foster social interactions and activities between community members (Sharifi 2019). Mixed-use streets are also perceived as safer due to a higher degree of social control resulting from the increased concentration of people (Sharifi 2019). The diversity of uses associated with mixed-use development also promote activities on sidewalks (Figure 14.5). Specifically, transit-oriented development is a feature of mixed-use development centered around walkability and a variety of active and public transportation modes within a single space (Transit Oriented Development Institute n.d.). This involves having abundant, "mixed" and well-connected routes of active and public transportation within an area, incentivizing their use as opposed to cars through their abundance and efficiencies (Transit Oriented Development Institute n.d.). If these public and active transportation systems are disconnected, this makes their use seem undesirable, by decreasing efficiency and ease of use (Transit Oriented Development Institute n.d.).

As discussed in Chapter 12, social interaction is crucial to maintaining wellbeing and positive mental and physical health. It has also been found to increase social engagement and interaction among citizens, leading to a stronger sense of community (Field 2016). Furthermore, as discussed in Chapter 11,

Figure 14.5 The diversity of uses associated with mixed-use developments promotes vibrant sidewalk activities.

Streets and Sidewalks for Living

active transportation is associated with increased physical activity and mental health (Brusseau et al. 2020). Therefore, incorporating mixed-use development, which maximizes the diversity and density of destinations and attractions within an area, and increasing the number of individuals using the space, is key to promoting increased social interactions and activities. This not only promotes a more vibrant and dynamic street life, but also promotes enhanced health and wellbeing.

14.4 Streets for Safe Walking

Car crashes are a significant cause of severe injury and death, both for drivers and pedestrians, posing a serious barrier to safe walking (Doheim et al. 2020). Vehicle crash prevalence has increased over time, reaching 1.35 million deaths worldwide in 2016 alone (Doheim et al. 2020). Furthermore, as car speeds increase, risk of death and serious injury to pedestrians in a collision increases exponentially, particularly for more vulnerable road users, such as the elderly and children (Shill 2019). Additionally, the infrastructure of many urban areas is built so that higher-speed roadways are more prevalent in lower-income and higher-minority areas, further increasing safety risks for these demographics (Adams 2021). This demands streets to be made safer for pedestrians, cyclists and others, to make individuals feel safe and comfortable in their use.

A key method to increase pedestrian safety from cars is to decrease car speed and volume (Friedman 2007; Lane width 2015). This can be accomplished through urban design strategies, such as reducing the number of car lanes, narrowing street widths, incorporating speed bumps and changing road surface material from asphalt to a highly textured surface. Installing speed bumps is a strategy to help slow traffic and increase pedestrian and cyclist safety, slowing traffic by 24 to 32 kilometers per hour (15 to 20 miles per hour) when multiple speed bumps are implemented synchronously (Speed hump 2015). Another strategy is to narrow road widths, which naturally causes cars to decrease in speed (Lane width 2015). The excess roadway resulting from the narrowed lanes can be used to widen sidewalks or create separate bike lanes, helping promote active transportation as opposed to driving.

Furthermore, ensuring that all streets have sidewalks is crucial to ensuring safe walking (Kweon et al. 2021). This may seem fairly intuitive, however less than 20 percent of collector and arterial roads in urban areas in the US have sidewalks, preventing many pedestrians and cyclists from feeling safe (Kweon et al. 2021). It has also been found that installing sidewalks decreased the risk of pedestrian–car collisions by 50 percent (Kweon et al. 2021).

To promote safe walking, streets and sidewalks must be adequately maintained. This involves ensuring that they are smooth and do not pose a hazard for pedestrians to trip and fall, and that they are de-iced and cleared of snow in winter (Friedman and Pollock 2022). A study by Bärwolff et al. (2021), studying pedestrian and cyclist behavior in the winter, found that for three-quarters of pedestrians, and two-thirds of cyclists investigated, snow or ice conditions on streets and sidewalks led to falls and physical injury (Bärwolff et al. 2021). This is particularly important for those with mobility restrictions, or the elderly, who may be more vulnerable to falling and the physical repercussions which can result (Pulvirenti et al. 2020). Ensuring safe walking conditions for the elderly, particularly in the winter, is also crucial to preventing feelings of social isolation, as utilizing streets and sidewalks to walk outdoors is often one of their primary sources of transportation, as well as physical and social activity (Bergen et al. 2022). Additionally, although de-icing and snowplowing on public streets is under the jurisdiction of the municipality, crowdsourcing of data by community members or others can be used to highlight areas in need of snow or ice removal, to make these services more efficient and comprehensive.

Greenery along streets and on sidewalks is beneficial not only to increase their aesthetic appeal and safety for pedestrians and cyclists, but also to help reduce traffic noise and instead amplify more peaceful, natural sounds (Leereveld 2023). This is important as it is estimated that traffic noise, in Europe alone, reduces disability-free life expectancy by over one million years annually (Fritschi et al. 2011). Studies have also found urban greenery is strongly linked to positive health and decreased mortality of residents, specifically by lowering stress and anxiety (van den Berg et al. 2015).

The presence of curb cuts between sidewalk curbs and roads at crosswalks allows for increased accessibility for those with mobility issues or individuals with wheelchairs or strollers, and decreases risks of pedestrians tripping or falling over regular curbs (Sheridan 2021). Implementation of universal accessibility features such as curb cuts contributes to the phenomenon of "the curb cut effect," stating that when urban design caters to those with disabilities, it creates a design which is better for the entire population (Sheridan 2021). These urban design features promote safe walking for all in the community, helping to promote community cohesion and social activities.

Furthermore, the presence of sidewalk buffers, ample lighting and open, visible public areas promotes perceived safety and encourages social activities in streets and sidewalks (Figure 14.6). Sidewalk buffers are trees or greenery, street furniture or other forms of barriers which separate sidewalks from the

Streets and Sidewalks for Living

Figure 14.6 The presence of green buffers, trees, ample lighting and visible public areas ensure pedestrians' safety.

roadway and have been found to increase perceived safety by pedestrians and improve the overall aesthetic of the street and sidewalk, increasing the enjoyability of walking for pedestrians and cyclists (Kweon et al. 2021). Ample lighting increases pedestrian safety by allowing visibility between vehicles, cyclists and pedestrians, as well as increasing perceived safety of the area by commuters, particularly at night (Office of Safety and Cheung n.d.). This is a salient design feature to promote safe walking, as in 2020, 76 percent of all pedestrian fatalities from vehicle collisions occurred during the dark (Office of Safety and Cheung n.d.). Open, visible areas have a similar effect as they allow commuters to see surroundings ahead of them, identify hazards, and feel safer in terms of there being a greater presence of "eyes on the street" as discussed in Chapter 12.

As noted in Chapter 13, including public art in urban design is known to increase the visual appeal and vibrancy of streets and sidewalks and attract more pedestrians to partake in active mobility (Jeffrey 2021). Furthermore, implementing engaging features along the streets and sidewalks, such as interactive art or public games, such as sidewalk chess or chalk painting, can promote social activities and community cohesion on the sidewalk (Farr 2018). Furthermore, ensuring there is adequate signage and maps of the area promotes active transportation, navigation and the use of the space, and contributes to a pedestrian-focused streetscape (Shashank 2017). This may include signage along sidewalks directing people to key landmarks or features, such as public parks,

museums or other attractions (Shashank 2017). Additionally, implementing signage in braille and road crossings with audio aids, are features at the human-scale which increase accessibility of and social activities within the space to all, particularly to individuals with visual impairments (Salman 2018) (Figure 14.7).

14.5 Shared Streets in Malmö

With the decline of shipbuilding in the 1970s and the abandonment of the area's industrial heartland and port known as Västra Hamnen, near Malmö, Sweden, the local government decided to convert the 30-hectare (74.1 acre) site into a residential area in which some 1,100 dwellings were planned (Figure 14.8). Many environmental initiatives introduced in this architecturally colorful and diverse place. Developers had to respect guidelines set by planners that included ample public spaces along with energy-efficient construction and exterior building materials. They also had to rethink the traditional place of cars in neighborhoods (Foletta and Field 2014).

Making walking and cycling pleasant was the designers' greatest achievement. It began by considering the whole. Central parking was limited to 0.7 spots per dwelling, and a pool of electric vehicles was made available for residents who didn't own a car. Vehicle speed on local streets was set at 15 kilometers (9.3 miles) per hour, and pedestrians, cyclists and buses were given priority.

Streets and Sidewalks for Living

Figure 14.7 Having adequate signage and public art contributes to a pedestrian-focused streetscape.

Then there were local interventions to enhance walking. Tall buildings were sited along the seashore to block incoming winter winds. All streets are paved with a yellowish brick, permeable surfaces and lined with trees and public benches for rest. Rock and water comprise the public art theme of the place; along the humanly scaled streets you can spot granite stone carvings from which water springs. Rainwater is collected from all roofs and balconies to run in open canals where plants grow. The shops and cafes on the ground floors of many of the taller buildings also make getting around pleasant.

As we rethink planning future communities and fix existing ones, we may want to take a hard look at our streets and reclaim them.

Figure 14.8 Making walking safe and pleasant in Västra Hamnen, near Malmö, Sweden was achieved by changing the streets' texture, incorporating public art and greenery.

Streets and Sidewalks for Living

Figure 14.8 (Continued)

14.6 Pathway in Kfar Sava

In the Israeli city Kfar Sava, population 26,000, a paved 5-meter (16.5 foot) wide pedestrian passageway ran between tall buildings. Orange trees are growing on the path's one side and streetlights installed intermittently along the other. The path crosses a street and enters a square park, framed by apartment buildings, with a small play structure and tall broadleaf trees (Figure 14.9).

The path crosses a road into the next cluster where tall trees and a man-made grassy hill formed its heart. It reaches a pedestrian mall where people sit around tables under arched colonnades. A beautifully landscaped civic square with a performing arts center and a library lie in the distance. The path ends at the city's main open-air shopping mall where the fashionable stores on various levels are crowded, and people were also sitting at the ground floor cafes.

It takes fifteen minutes to traverse the six-block stretch, a pleasant stroll in a town of neighborhoods. The path connected edges, offered opportunities to turn a stranger into an acquaintance, and to get a bit of exercise. But even more important was the way it enabled a pedestrian to see a place and get to know its culture. Walking there offered an opportunity to experience intimacy with other people and proximity to objects one could not have while driving. A person could view details and read expressions because of the slow rhythm in which the information revealed itself.

Walking is a necessary instrument for a place appreciation. We, unfortunately, are not doing much of it nowadays, and, as a result, compromise our ability to connect, know and have a better sense of place.

14.7 Final Thoughts

Streets and sidewalks can have a double role, as both arteries of movement and spaces for social activities. Despite the dominance of cars, urban design of streets and sidewalks present an opportunity to reclaim the streets for people, parallel to promoting active mobility and social activities. This can be exemplified through implementations of shared streets and car-free communities. Additionally, urban design features, such as mixed-use development, design for safe walking and adequate human-scale can be used to promote social activity and walkability.

Figure 14.9 Spots along the pedestrian path in Kfar Sava, Israel.

References

Adams, C. (2021). Black people are more likely to die in traffic accidents. covid made it worse. *NBC News*. Retrieved July 1, 2023, from www.nbcnews.com/news/nbcblk/black-people-are-more-likely-die-traffic-accidents-covid-made-n1271716

Avenali, A., Catalano, G., Gregori, M. and Matteucci, G. (2020). Rail versus bus local public transport services: a social cost comparison methodology. *Transportation Research Interdisciplinary Perspectives* 7: 100200. Retrieved July 1, 2023, from https://doi.org/10.1016/j.trip.2020.100200

Bärwolff, M., Reinartz, A. and Gerike, R. (2021). Correlates of pedestrian and cyclist falls in snowy and icy conditions. *Transactions on Transport Sciences* 12(3): 67–77. Retrieved July 1, 2023, from https://doi.org/10.5507/tots.2021.007

Bergen, K., Jubenvill, M., Shaw, K., Steen, E., Loewen, H., Mbabaali, S. and Barclay, R. (2022). Factors associated with outdoor winter walking in older adults: a scoping review. *Canadian Journal on Aging / La Revue Canadienne Du Vieillissement*, 1–12. Retrieved July 1, 2023, from https://doi.org/10.1017/s0714980822000460

Brusseau, T. A., Fairclough, S. J. and Lubans, D. R. (eds.) (2020). *The Routledge Handbook of Youth Physical Activity*. Routledge. New York. Retrieved July 1, 2023, from https://doi.org/10.4324/9781003026426

Chen, W. and Klaiber, H. A. (2020). Does road expansion induce traffic? an evaluation of vehicle-kilometers traveled in China. *Journal of Environmental Economics and Management* 104: 102387. Retrieved July 1, 2023, from https://doi.org/10.1016/j.jeem.2020.102387

den Boer, R. (2021). *Happy Living on a Woonerf*. Thesis. Retrieved July 1, 2023, from https://frw.studenttheses.ub.rug.nl/3744/

Doheim, R. M., Farag, A. A. and Badawi, S. (2020). Success measures for transforming into car-free cities. *Humanizing Cities Through Car-Free City Development and Transformation*, 231–267. Retrieved July 1, 2023, from https://doi.org/10.4018/978-1-7998-3507-3.ch010

Dudek, J. (2019). Design guidelines for creating a vital Woonerf Street. *SGEM International Multidisciplinary Scientific GeoConference EXPO Proceedings*, 19(6). Retrieved July 1, 2023, from www.sgem.org/index.php/component/jresearch/?view=publication&task=show&id=6542

Farr, D. (2018). *Sustainable Nation: Urban Design Patterns for the Future* (2nd ed.). John Wiley & Sons. Hoboken.

Field, J. (2016). *Social Capital* (3rd ed.). Routledge. London.

Foletta, N. and Field, S. (2014). *Europe's New Low Car(bon) Communities*. Retrieved July 1, 2023, from https://www.itdp.org/publication/europes-vibrant-new-low-carbon-communities-2/

Friedman, A. (2007). *Sustainable Residential Developments: Design Principles for Green Neighborhoods*. McGraw-Hill. New York.

Friedman, A. and Pollock, A. (2022). *Fundamentals of Planning Cities for Healthy Living*. Anthem Press. London.

Fritschi, L., Brown, A. L., Kim, R., Schwela, D. and Kephalopoulos, S. (eds.) (2011). Burden of disease from environmental noise: quantification of healthy life years lost in Europe. World Health Organization (WHO) – Regional Office for Europe. Retrieved July 1, 2023, from https://publications.jrc.ec.europa.eu/repository/handle/JRC64428

Institute for Public Administration at the University of Delaware. (n.d.). Mixed-use development. Planning for Complete Communities in Delaware. Retrieved July 1, 2023, from www.completecommunitiesde.org/planning/landuse/mixed-use-development/#:~:text=Use%20in%20Delaware-,What%20Is%20Mixed%2DUse%20Development%3F,%2C%20and%2For%20industrial%20uses

Jeffrey, E. (2021). *Public Art and Reshaping Public Space*. Thesis. University of Detroit Mercy – School of Architecture & Community Development.

Kweon, B.-S., Rosenblatt-Naderi, J., Ellis, C. D., Shin, W.-H. and Danies, B. H. (2021). The effects of pedestrian environments on walking behaviors and perception of pedestrian safety. *Sustainability* 13(16): 8728. Retrieved July 1, 2023, from https://doi.org/10.3390/su13168728

Lane width (2015). National Association of City Transportation Officials. Retrieved July 1, 2023, from https://nacto.org/publication/urban-street-design-guide/street-design-elements/lane-width/

Leereveld, T. (2023). Comparison of predicted and actual tranquility in Woonerf streets: "An assessment of streetscape greenery and sound levels using a Green View Index and mobile sound measurements". Thesis. Retrieved July 1, 2023, from https://frw.studenttheses.ub.rug.nl/4107/

Lewis, A. (2014). Jaywalking: how the car industry outlawed crossing the road. *BBC News*. Retrieved July 1, 2023, from www.bbc.com/news/magazine-26073797

Mendez, G. (2014). Beyond move in Mexico City: integrating sustainable mobility into the everyday. *TheCityFix*. Retrieved July 1, 2023, from https://thecityfix.com/blog/beyond-move-mexico-city-integrating-sustainable-mobility-ecobici-biking-gisela-mendez/

Norton, P. D. (2007). Street rivals: jaywalking and the invention of the motor age street. *Technology and Culture* 48(2): 331–359. Retrieved July 1, 2023, from https://doi.org/10.1353/tech.2007.0085

Norton, P. D. (2008). Fighting traffic: the dawn of the motor age in the American city. Oxford Academic MIT Press Scholarship Online. Retrieved July 1, 2023, from https://doi.org/10.7551/mitpress/9780262141000.001.0001

Office of Safety and Cheung, J. (n.d.). Lighting for pedestrian safety. US Department of Transportation. Retrieved July 1, 2023, from https://safety.fhwa.dot.gov/roadway_dept/night_visib/docs/Lighting_for_Pedestrian_Safety_2pager.pdf

Oost, T. (2022). How to make car-free neighbourhoods work. Retrieved July 1, 2023, from https://frw.studenttheses.ub.rug.nl/4022/1/S3223779_Thijs%20Oost_Master%20Thesis_FINAL.pdf

Ostermeijer, F., Koster, H. R., van Ommeren, J. and Nielsen, V. M. (2022). Automobiles and urban density. *Journal of Economic Geography* 22(5): 1073–1095. Retrieved July 1, 2023, from https://doi.org/10.1093/jeg/lbab047

Peña, J. (n.d.). Supporting active living through mixed-use developments. American Planning Association. Retrieved March 20, 2023, from www.planning.org/blog/9227408/supporting-active-living-through-mixed-use-developments/

Pulvirenti, G., Distefano, N. and Leonardi, S. (2020). Elderly perception of critical issues of pedestrian paths. *Civil Engineering and Architecture* 8(1): 26–37. Retrieved July 1, 2023, from https://doi.org/10.13189/cea.2020.080104

Reducing roads can cause traffic to "evaporate" (2019). Rapid Transition Alliance. Retrieved July 1, 2023, from www.rapidtransition.org/stories/reducing-roads-can-cause-traffic-to-evaporate/

Reversing car dependency (2021). ITF. Retrieved July 1, 2023, from www.itf-oecd.org/reversing-car-dependency

Rogers, J., Emerine, D., Haas, P., Jackson, D., Kauffmann, P., Rybeck, R. and Westrom, R. (2016). Estimating parking utilization in multifamily residential buildings in Washington, D.C. *Transportation Research Record: Journal of the Transportation Research Board* 2568(1): 72–82. Retrieved July 1, 2023, from https://doi.org/10.3141/2568-11

Salman, S. (2018). What would a truly disabled-accessible city look like? *The Guardian*. Retrieved July 1, 2023, from www.theguardian.com/cities/2018/feb/14/what-disability-accessible-city-look-like

Sharifi, A. (2019). Resilient urban forms: a review of literature on streets and street networks. *Building and Environment* 147: 171–187. Retrieved July 1, 2023, from https://doi.org/10.1016/j.buildenv.2018.09.040

Shashank, A. (2017). Walkability and wayfinding. *Applied*. Retrieved July 1, 2023, from www.appliedinformation.group/insight/walkability-and-wayfinding

Sheridan, E. (2021). The curb cut effect: how universal design makes things better for everyone. *Medium*. Retrieved July 1, 2023, from https://uxdesign.cc/the-curb-cut-effect-universal-design-b4e3d7da73f5

Shill, G. H. (2019). Should law subsidize driving? *SSRN Electronic Journal*. Retrieved July 1, 2023, from https://doi.org/10.2139/ssrn.3345366

Shoup, D. C. (1997). The high cost of free parking. *Journal of Planning Education and Research* 17(1): 3–20. Retrieved July 1, 2023, from https://doi.org/10.1177/0739456x9701700102

Sleiman, J. (2019). How cars took over our cities, and how some are fighting back. *WHYY PBS*. Retrieved July 1, 2023, from www.wbur.org/hereandnow/2019/07/03/cars-streets-cities-congestion

Speed hump (2015). National Association of City Transportation Officials. Retrieved July 1, 2023, from https://nacto.org/publication/urban-street-design-guide/street-design-elements/vertical-speed-control-elements/speed-hump/

Transit Oriented Development Institute (n.d.). *Transit Oriented Development*. Retrieved July 1, 2023, from www.tod.org/

van den Berg, M., Wendel-Vos, W., van Poppel, M., Kemper, H., van Mechelen, W. and Maas, J. (2015). Health benefits of green spaces in the living environment: a systematic review of epidemiological studies. *Urban Forestry & Urban Greening* 14(4): 806–816. Retrieved July 1, 2023, from https://doi.org/10.1016/j.ufug.2015.07.008

Walsh, D. (2017, December 13). Reducing our reliance on cars: the shifting future of urban transportation. *MIT Sloan*. Retrieved July 1, 2023, from https://mitsloan.mit.edu/ideas-made-to-matter/reducing-our-reliance-cars-shifting-future-urban-transportation

Zhang, F., Lindsey, R. and Yang, H. (2016). The Downs–Thomson paradox with imperfect mode substitutes and alternative transit administration regimes. *Transportation Research Part B: Methodological* 86: 104–127. Retrieved July 1, 2023, from https://doi.org/10.1016/j.trb.2016.01.013

Zhang, M. (2009). Bus versus rail. *Transportation Research Record: Journal of the Transportation Research Board* 2110(1): 87–95. Retrieved July 1, 2023, from https://doi.org/10.3141/2110-11

CHAPTER 15
Slowing Down Vehicular Traffic

This chapter joins the previous one in discussing ways cities can promote safe walking and biking. The chapter begins by highlighting the value of cycling and walking for public health, promoting social interaction and reducing the negative environmental impacts of driving. Next, measures for slowing car speed are introduced, including narrowing roadways, having shorter blocks, adding traffic lights and changing streets' surface texture. This is followed by urban design methods to enhance the safety of pedestrians and cyclists.

15.1 The Social Value of Cycling and Walking

Public health is the collective effort of society to promote wellbeing and prevent illness and injury (What is public health? n.d.). This is particularly relevant for children, as active mobility is found to contribute to their physical and mental development (Tranter and Tolley 2020). Neighborhoods centered around active transportation are not only more financially and environmentally sustainable, but they also positively contribute to public health (Anciaes 2022). In contrast, excessive car use is linked to obesity, stress, collisions and injuries, poor air quality, and noise (Anciaes 2022). Studies have shown that walking and biking to school by children has significantly decreased, with 47.7 percent commuting by active transport in 1969, but only 9.6 percent doing so in 2017 (Kontou et al. 2020). Some cities took steps to encourage organized walking to school by children (Figure 15.1). The value of cycling and walking is also highlighted by the World Health Organization (WHO) in its *2018 to 2030 Global Action Plan for Physical Activity*. It suggests that improving road safety, promoting compact urban design, and prioritizing active and public transportation is crucial to society's health (Brusseau et al. 2020).

As discussed in Chapter 11, obesity and poor mental health are increasingly prevalent societal problems, perpetuating a public health challenge. Obesity is a health problem caused by lifestyle choices, including poor diet and inactivity, and it has worsened since cars began to dominate the commute (Monteiro and Martins 2020; Alessio et al. 2021). It is associated with serious health outcomes, such as diabetes and cardiovascular disease. Therefore, it is important to decrease the prevalence of obesity through increasing activity (Monteiro and Martins 2020).

Figure 15.1 Cities such as Rome, Italy (left) and Saint-Bruno-de-Montarville, Canada (right) organized supervised daily walks to school.

Slowing Down Vehicular Traffic

A study by Giles-Corti and Donovan (2002) found that streetscapes can act to promote physical activity, and specifically contribute to obesity prevention (Giles-Corti and Donovan 2002). Streets are particularly important to promote active mobility, as it has been found that they are used significantly more for physical activity than public open spaces (Kweon et al. 2021). Poor mental health is often also exacerbated by inactivity and limited social interactions (Reid et al. 2022). Specifically, a study by Woessner et al. (2021) correlated physical activity with increased cognitive and mental health benefits. It has also been found that regular moderate-intensity physical activity contributes to a significantly decreased risk of developing over twenty chronic health conditions, thereby improving public health (Martin et al. 2014).

It is particularly important that neighborhoods have equal access to safe, active transportation routes, so that all citizens can benefit from the health impacts of walking and cycling. More privileged neighborhoods are often equipped with superior active transportation infrastructure, partially due to their inequitably greater access to decision-making processes (Mohith 2019). It has also been found that residential areas with reduced car speeds are associated with more social use of the street by adults and play by children (Tranter and Tolley 2020).

As discussed above, social interaction is crucial to promoting mental and physical health and is often viewed as a fundamental human need (Orben et al. 2020). When people are commuting in their own vehicles, there is little opportunity for any form of social interaction. On the other hand, while walking or cycling, there are abundant opportunities for activities where people can meet others. Encouraging social interactions by pedestrians calls for wider sidewalks and comfortable environments, with slow car traffic, aesthetic streetscapes with ample street furniture, greenery and lighting (Figure 15.2).

15.2 Measures of Slowing Vehicle Traffic Locally

Car manufacturing and marketing has often focused on speeds to entice buyers. In fact, many vehicles are even advertised as being able to reach a speed of 322 kilometers per hour (200 miles per hour), which is significantly faster than any roadways allow (Tranter and Tolley 2020). This resulted in a cultural obsession with speed and timesaving, with dangerous consequences for drivers and pedestrians (Tranter and Tolley 2020; Lubbe et al. 2022). Specifically, car speeding was the cause of 29 percent of traffic-related fatalities in 2020 (United States Department of Transportation n.d.-b). Slowing traffic can be accomplished through narrowing roadways, shortening block lengths, changing street surface texture to a highly textured surface, and having more traffic lights. These measures will be outlined below.

15.2.1 Narrowing Roadways

Motorists drive faster on wider, open roadways, and slower on narrower ones (Friedman 2018). Narrowing roadways decreases car speeds, promoting safety for pedestrians and cyclists, as well as providing excess space for social uses (Figure 15.3). If it is not possible to physically narrow roadways, it has also been found that giving a visual illusion that the roadway is narrower works to slow vehicle speeds (Anderson 2018). This can be accomplished by lining sidewalks with trees or benches, which requires drivers to visually and mentally process these objects, leading to slower driving speeds (Anderson 2018). Open, wider

Figure 15.2 Wider sidewalks facilitate social interactions and activities such as exhibits and dining.

Slowing Down Vehicular Traffic

Figure 15.3 Narrow roadways decrease car speed, promoting safety for pedestrians and cyclists.

roads intuitively make drivers feel more comfortable, leading to faster driving at or above the speed limit (Anderson 2018). It has been found that a one-meter (3.2 feet) reduction in the width of a street lane is associated with a 5.6 kilometers per hour (3.5 miles per hour) decrease in vehicle speed (Nogueira and Mennis 2019). Narrower roadways also allow for shorter crosswalks for pedestrians, especially important for those with walking impairments. A study in the UK found that most older adults cannot walk fast enough to cross the street within the time allotted, posing a significant risk to their safety and making walking less enjoyable (Asher et al. 2012).

15.2.2 Shorter Blocks and Traffic Lights

Having shorter blocks slows vehicle traffic by requiring them to stop frequently at intersections (Figure 15.4). Studies have found that longer block lengths, such as those 183 meters (600 feet) or longer, are associated with drivers surpassing the designated speed limit (Oregon Sustainable Transportation Initiative n.d.). Additionally, shorter block lengths increase the connectivity of urban areas, providing easier, safer and greater access for pedestrians and cyclists to different amenities and services along the street (Oregon Sustainable Transportation Initiative n.d.; Tranter and Tolley 2020). Short block lengths, around 61 to 91 meters (200 to 300 feet) in length, help reduce walking times between destinations, and allow for a greater number of intersections and preventing illegal jaywalking (Oregon Sustainable Transportation Initiative n.d.). Furthermore, shorter block lengths increase the quantity of street corners, which in turn increases the density and number of commercial spaces that are highly visible, promoting economic growth for these businesses and greater access to use them (Oregon Sustainable Transportation Initiative n.d.; Tranter and Tolley 2020). These street corners also provide space for social gathering, specifically on the often-calmer side streets to which they adjoin (Oregon Sustainable Transportation Initiative n.d.). These slightly larger corner spaces allow for street furniture and greenery to be implemented, acting as spaces of interaction and spaces for those commuting by active transportation to rest.

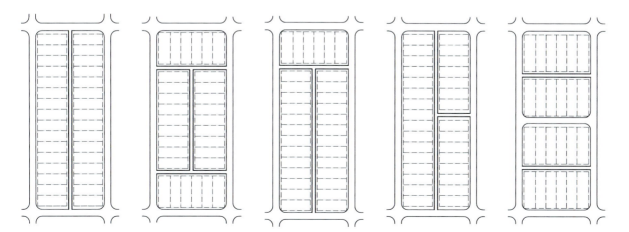

Figure 15.4 Having shorter blocks slows cars by requiring them to stop frequently at intersections.

15.2.3 Changing Street Surface Texture

Changing street surface to a highly textured one slows vehicle speeds, by increasing friction between the roadway and vehicle tires, leading drivers to slow down (Roshani and Kouchaki 2021; Nogueira and Mennis 2019; Yu and Lu 2013).

There is large variance in the type of road surface texture which can be used, which varies based on the materials employed and application technique (Roshani and Kouchaki 2021). As for pavements, there are three categories of texture: micro-texture, macro-texture and mega-texture (Roshani and Kouchaki 2021). Micro-texture is the smoothest surface and produces the least amount of friction between the vehicle tires and the roadway, whereas mega-texture is the most highly textured of the three and produces the highest degree of friction (Roshani and Kouchaki 2021). However, different road materials such as brick or cobblestone can also be used to alter street surface to slow traffic (Figure 15.5). Specifically, it has been found that with every 0.0004233 meter per kilometer (one inch per mile) increase in 'roughness' of a roadway, vehicle speed decreased by 0.01336 kilometers per hour (0.0083 miles per hour) (Yu and Lu 2013).

A study by Nogueira and Mennis (2019) found that compared to traditional asphalt streets, streets composed of granite blocks reduced vehicle speeds by approximately 11.7 kilometers per hour (7 miles per hour), and brick streets reduced speeds by approximately 4.8 kilometers per hour (3 miles per hour) (Nogueira and Mennis 2019). The study found that drivers intentionally slowed due to the higher textures which these paving materials produced, compared to asphalt (Nogueira and Mennis 2019). Granite and brick paving was commonly used on roadways, prior to the introduction of asphalt paving in the nineteenth century, which has become the dominant street surface (Nogueira and Mennis 2019). Additionally, another study found that following roadway repaving, vehicle speeds increased by 2.5 kilometers per hour (1.6 miles per hour) (Nogueira and Mennis 2019). It has also been found that vehicles reduce their speeds by 5 percent when roadways transition from smooth to rough surfaces (Nogueira and Mennis 2019). Varying road texture can also be used to signify usage of roadways. For example, shared streets with pedestrians often have a more highly textured surface, such as brick, compared to freeways and larger roadways where there are fewer pedestrians, which may have a smoother asphalt texture.

15.3 Enhancing Safety

It has been found that every year, pedestrians and cyclists account for approximately 19 percent of all traffic fatalities in collisions with vehicles (United States Department of Transportation n.d.-a). Additionally, accidents and potential collisions between pedestrians and cyclists on shared pathways are also quite frequent (Mesimäki and Luoma 2021). Introducing features such as street lighting or surveillance cameras can increase safety. Adequate lighting improves the perception of safety in terms of crime, but it also makes pedestrians and cyclists more visible to oncoming vehicles at night. Furthermore, a study found that when there are greater numbers of pedestrians and cyclists using a space, there is a lower risk of collision with vehicles (Jacobsen 2015). Although this may seem counter-intuitive, it has been found that motorists drive more cautiously when there is a greater presence of people engaging in active transportation, reflecting that increased active transportation itself enhances safety (Jacobsen 2015). Some additional safety measures will be outlined below.

Figure 15.5 Paving materials such as brick or cobblestone can be used as street surface to slow traffic.

Slowing Down Vehicular Traffic

Figure 15.6 Designated bike paths for cyclists are separated from the sidewalk and the roadway.

15.3.1 Designated Bike Paths

Designated bike paths for cyclists are separated from the sidewalk and the roadway (Figure 15.6). This increases safety for pedestrians from faster speed cyclists and protects cyclists from altercations with vehicles on the roadways. Specifically, many surveys have found that pedestrians, particularly the elderly, express fear of bicycles traveling along the same pathway as them, therefore it is important to have separate paths (Tranter and Tolley 2020).

There are multiple types of bike paths, some being paths shared with automobiles, and others separated from the roadway, either by a line or physical barrier, and solely designated for cyclists (*Safe Cycling Guide 9th Edition* n.d.) (Figure 15.7). Barriers not only increase safety for cyclists, but

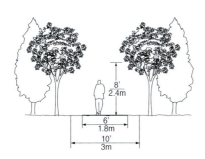

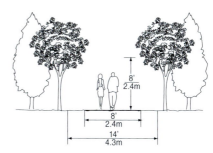

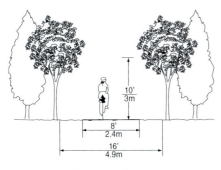

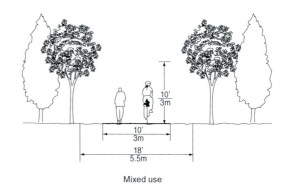

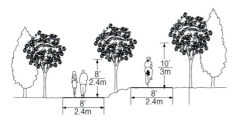

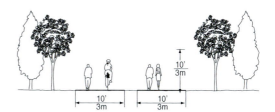

Figure 15.7 Dimensions and arrangements of bike and pedestrian paths.

Slowing Down Vehicular Traffic

they also add aesthetic appeal to the streetscape, particularly if the barrier is composed of greenery or a form of public art. There are five main design criteria for bike paths to promote cycling, these being safety, coherence, directness, attractiveness and comfort (Tranter and Tolley 2020). The criterion for safety stipulates that bike paths be separated from the roadway for vehicles, promoting safe cycling for cyclists of all ages and abilities (Tranter and Tolley 2020). Coherence and directness refer to the ease of navigation and use of the bike paths (Tranter and Tolley 2020). Attractiveness refers to the bike paths being aesthetically pleasing, encouraging their use, as well as having adequate street lighting and natural surveillance (Tranter and Tolley 2020). Lastly, comfort refers to the bike paths being designed and maintained to optimize use, safety and comfort for cyclists (Tranter and Tolley 2020).

15.4 Global Pedalling for a Greener Planet

Among the challenges that occupy the minds of policymakers and planners in cities around the world are an urgent need for a local response to climate change and easing traffic congestion. The problem is more acute in big cities where more cars are driven, and larger amounts of carbon dioxide are emitted.

A solution embraced by many cities was the introduction of bikeshare systems. Whether conventional or e-bikes, they joined other means of "green" transportation such as the electric carshare and scooters. The bikeshare bicycles on their street stations stand out as a global phenomenon, an overnight success of sorts and a product of the digital age. An estimated 1 million bikeshare bicycles were on the road worldwide at the end of 2015, with China home to three-quarters of them. In 2017, some 35 million e-bikes were sold worldwide. Not surprisingly, Copenhagen, where bike riding is embedded in the social and urban cultures, was where e-bikes were introduced first (Thompson 2018) (Figure 15.8).

More than a new type of mobility, bikeshares offer a lesson to public official and citizens. Combatting environmental challenges must be a win-win situation for all the parties involved. Using bikeshares, which as far as municipal bureaucracy goes, was relatively easy to introduce since it was offered as a hardware and software package, is relatively inexpensive compared to building new roads as it uncouples peoples from buying and maintaining cars, is simple to use and pay for, created jobs, let its users avoid traffic congestion, and makes one feel that they do their civic part fighting global warming. And then there are the health benefits. It was demonstrated that in countries where bike riding is common, the rates of obesity are also low. In addition, bikeshare users were found to be avid users of other modes of public transit, which explains why agencies are collaborating with cities and private companies to introduce urban mobility as an integrated system.

Bikeshare seems to have become a permanent fixture of the world's urban landscape. Its instant popularity serves as a model for the introduction of future ideas that make the planet greener and citizens healthy.

Figure 15.8 A solution embraced globally is the bikeshare system.

Slowing Down Vehicular Traffic

Melbourne, Australia

Montreal, Canada

Stuttgart, Germany

Tel Aviv, Israel

Valencia, Spain

Vienna, Austria

Figure 15.8 (Continued)

15.5 Cycling Priority in the Netherlands

With population of roughly 17 million it is estimated that the Netherlands has 22.5 million bicycles. That's on average 1.3 bicycles per person. There are between 33,000 to 35,000 kilometers (20,505 to 21,748 miles) of dedicated bicycle paths on top of those that share the roads with motorized vehicles, which amounts to an additional 55,000 kilometers (34,175 miles) (Pucher and Buehler 2008) (Figure 15.9).

The popularity of cycling in the Netherlands is anchored in the 1970s government's determination to invest in cycling infrastructure and shift away from car-centric road-building policies. With an official National Bicycling Master Plan, the Dutch went on to build a large network of wide cycling paths with clear signaling that resulted in the lowest non-fatal injuries and fatality rate among cyclists, confirming the network's safety.

Since then, cycling levels and bikeshare went up to 27 percent, while for example, the levels in Australia, the UK and the United States increased by only 1 percent. Daily cycling per capita is also highest in the Netherlands, with a value of 2.5 kilometers (1.5 miles). Cycling is also promoted through extensive rights of way, a wide range of bike parking options, proper integration with public transit, comprehensive traffic education and training, and promotional events (Pucher and Buehler 2008).

Land-use policies also play a part by promoting compact and mixed-use developments which makes trips shorter and more

Slowing Down Vehicular Traffic

Figure 15.9 The popularity of cycling in the Netherlands is anchored in the 1970s government's determination to invest in cycling infrastructure and shift away from car-centric roadbuilding policies.

favourable to cycling by default. It is indeed a set of mutually reinforcing policies which makes promotion of cycling so successful in cities across the Netherlands. Promotional cycling programs also tend to be organized locally even if funding comes from the central government.

The many benefits associated with safe biking include positive economic impacts, an improved quality of life, less roadway congestion and better public health. The lesson the Dutch taught the world is that when a nation makes it a priority to invest in infrastructure and promotion, cycling will become a reality shared by many.

15.6 A Walkable Green Suburb in Vienna

The first thing one notices when walking in the Grüne Welle (Green Wave), a suburban housing project in Vienna, Austria, is the absence of cars. Designed by the firm Superblock and built by developer WBV GÖD, it has 46 apartments, 87 terraced homes and 14 two-stacked dwellings on top of one another, all with a focus on the integration of green features. According to the architects the higher density of this subsidised community strengthens neighborly ties, and its diversity promotes cross-generational and social mix (Singhal 2015) (Figure 15.10).

Figure 15.10 Grüne Welle (Green Wave), a suburban housing project in Vienna, Austria, is a car-free community.

With deep roots in innovative Viennese social housing such as the Karl Marks Hof, which was built between 1927 and 1930 by city planner Karl Ehn, the Grüne Welle neighborhood has a linear street layout, with patches of greenery at the rear and no parking spaces. With the compact nature of the place, all the public outdoor areas are shared and connected.

The "village green" area, a busy common space, stands in contrast with the private quiet backyards behind the homes. By creating public spaces rather than building roads, and a private backyard where there is local food production, residents have a choice to spend time with either their neighbors or their families. Residents who drive, park in an underground common parking garage and bike or walk to their homes, thereby indirectly forcing chance encounters and friendly neighborhood relations.

Noticeable, and different from typical suburbs, was the close proximity between the homes and the main pathways. Yet, even in this narrow space people had room to place a table and chairs. The width of the terraced homes varied, which contributed to having units of different sizes and therefore a demographic mix.

Among the green features there are solar panels and green roofs that are uncommon in the vocabulary of social housing in many nations. There was also an indoor meeting room for community gatherings. On the community's edge there was a large flower patch for people to help themselves when they wish to adorn their homes.

Grüne Welle stands for the principles that need to guide the planning of every suburban community let alone social housing. Its notable attributes, such as car free, green features and mixed type of dwellings, make it a model for others to follow.

15.7 Final Thoughts

Safe conditions for walking and cycling are crucial to their encouragement as a mode of transportation for their many public health, environmental and societal benefits. These benefits include public health, decreased societal impacts on environmental degradation, and promoting social interaction. Key strategies to accomplish this include slowing vehicle traffic through narrowing roadways, implementing shorter block lengths and more traffic lights, and changing street surface textures. Additionally, implementing features to promote safer walking and cycling are also crucial, including implementing sidewalk buffers, separated bike paths and car-free streets.

References

Alessio, H. M., Bassett, D. R., Bopp, M. J., Parr, B. B., Patch, G. S., Rankin, J. W., Rojas-Rueda, D., Roti, M. W. and Wojcik, J. R. (2021). Climate change, air pollution, and physical inactivity: is active transportation part of the solution? *Medicine and Science in Sports AndExercise* 53(6): 1170–1178. Retrieved June 28, 2023, from https://doi.org/10.1249/mss.0000000000002569

Anciaes, P. (2022). Book review: slow cities – conquering our speed addiction for health and sustainability. *Urban Studies* 59(12): 2601–2604. Retrieved June 28, 2023, from https://doi.org/10.1177/00420980221086418

Anderson, D. (2018). How to design a road that shouts, "slow 'er down!". *CBCnews*. Retrieved June 28, 2023, from www.cbc.ca/news/canada/calgary/road-design-calgary-psychology-of-speed-1.4850684

Asher, L., Aresu, M., Falaschetti, E. and Mindell, J. (2012). Most older pedestrians are unable to cross the road in time: a cross-sectional study. *Age and Ageing* 41(5): 690–694. Retrieved June 28, 2023, from https://doi.org/10.1093/ageing/afs076

Brusseau, T. A., Fairclough, S. J. and Lubans, D. R. (eds.) (2020). *The Routledge Handbook of Youth Physical Activity*. Routledge. New York. Retrieved June 28, 2023, from https://doi.org/10.4324/9781003026426

Friedman, A. (2018). *Neighborhood: Designing a Livable Community*. Véhicule Press. Montréal.

Giles-Corti, B. and Donovan, R. J. (2002). The relative influence of individual, social and physical environment determinants of physical activity. *Social Science & Medicine* 54(12): 1793–1812. Retrieved June 28, 2023, from https://doi.org/10.1016/s0277-9536(01)00150-2

Jacobsen, P. (2015). Safety in numbers: more walkers and bicyclists, safer walking and bicycling. *Injury Prevention* 21(4): 271–275. Retrieved June 28, 2023, from https://doi.org/10.1136/ip.9.3.205rep

Kontou, E., McDonald, N. C., Brookshire, K., Pullen-Seufert, N. C. and LaJeunesse, S. (2020). U.S. active school travel in 2017: prevalence and correlates. *Preventive Medicine Reports* 17: 101024. Retrieved June 28, 2023, from https://doi.org/10.1016/j.pmedr.2019.101024

Kweon, B.-S., Rosenblatt-Naderi, J., Ellis, C. D., Shin, W.-H. and Danies, B. H. (2021). The effects of pedestrian environments on walking behaviors and perception of pedestrian safety. *Sustainability* 13(16): 8728. Retrieved June 28, 2023, from https://doi.org/10.3390/su13168728

Lubbe, N., Wu, Y. and Jeppsson, H. (2022). Safe speeds: fatality and injury risks of pedestrians, cyclists, motorcyclists, and car drivers impacting the front of another passenger car as a function of closing speed and age. *Traffic Safety Research* 2: 000006. Retrieved June 28, 2023, from https://doi.org/10.55329/vfma7555

Martin, A., Goryakin, Y. and Suhrcke, M. (2014). Does active commuting improve psychological wellbeing? Longitudinal evidence from eighteen waves of the British Household Panel Survey. *Preventive Medicine* 69: 296–303. Retrieved June 28, 2023, from https://doi.org/10.1016/j.ypmed.2014.08.023

Mesimäki, J. and Luoma, J. (2021). Near accidents and collisions between pedestrians and cyclists. *European Transport Research Review* 13(1). Retrieved June 28, 2023, from https://doi.org/10.1186/s12544-021-00497-z

Mohith, M. (2019). *(In)Equity in Active Transportation Planning: Toronto's Overlooked Inner Suburbs*. Thesis. Master of Environmental Studies, Faculty of Environmental Studies, York University. Retrieved June 28, 2023, from https://yorkspace.library.yorku.ca/xmlui/handle/10315/38617

Monteiro, R. and Martins, M. J. (2020). *Understanding Obesity*. Bentham Science. Singapore. Retrieved June 28, 2023 from https://mcgill.on.worldcat.org/search/detail/1154514077?datasource=library_web&search_field=all_fields&search=true&database=all&scope=wz%3A12129&format=&clusterResults=true&func=find-b&q=&topLod=0&queryString=obesity&find=Go&year=2019..2023&groupVariantRecords=false

Nogueira, X. R. and Mennis, J. (2019). The effect of brick and granite block paving materials on traffic speed. *International Journal of Environmental Research and Public Health* 16(19): 3704. Retrieved June 28, 2023, from https://doi.org/10.3390/ijerph16193704

Orben, A., Tomova, L. and Blakemore, S.-J. (2020). The effects of social deprivation on adolescent development and mental health. *The Lancet Child & Adolescent Health* 4(8): 634–640. Retrieved June 28, 2023, from https://doi.org/10.1016/s2352-4642(20)30186-3

Oregon Sustainable Transportation Initiative (n.d.). Strategy report: increased connectivity & shorter block lengths. Oregon Department of Transportation. Retrieved June 28, 2023, from www.oregon.gov/odot/Planning/Documents/SR-Increased-Connectivity-Shorter-Block-Lengths.pdf

Pucher, J. and Buehler, R. (2008). Making cycling irresistible: lessons from the Netherlands, Denmark and Germany. *Transport Reviews* 28(4): 495–528. DOI 10.1080/01441640701806612

Reid, C. E., Rieves, E. S. and Carlson, K. (2022). Perceptions of green space usage, abundance, and quality of green space were associated with better mental health during the COVID-19 pandemic among residents of Denver. *Plos One* 17(3).

Retrieved June 28, 2023, from https://doi.org/10.1371/journal.pone.0263779

Roshani, H. and Kouchaki, S. (2021). How the texture of a pavement surface contributes to the tire-pavement friction. *Roads & Bridges*. Retrieved June 28, 2023, from https://www.roadsbridges.com/pavement-maintenance/article/10654346/how-the-texture-of-a-pavement-surface-contributes-to-the-tire-pavement-friction

Safe Cycling Guide 9th Edition (n.d.). Government of Quebec, Road Safety. Retrieved June 28, 2023, from https://saaq.gouv.qc.ca/fileadmin/documents/publications/safe-cycling-guide.pdf

Singhal, S. (2015). Grüne Welle in Vienne, Austria by SUPERBLOCK. *AECCafé*. Retrieved June 28, 2023, from https://www10.aeccafe.com/blogs/arch-showcase/2015/03/13/grune-welle-in-vienna-austria-by-superblock/

Thompson, H. (2018). Combining e-bikes and bikeshares is urban alchemy: a winning transit solution. *Forbes, For Cities*. Retrieved June 28, 2023, from www.forbes.com/sites/energyinnovation/2018/01/08/combining-e-bikes-and-bikeshares-is-urban-alchemy-a-winning-transit-solution-for-cities/#2cc18353e092

Tranter, P. and Tolley, R. (2020). *Slow Cities*. Elsevier. Amsterdam.

United States Department of Transportation (n.d.-a). Pedestrian & bicycle safety. Federal Highway Administration (FHWA). Retrieved June 28, 2023, from https://highways.dot.gov/safety/pedestrian-bicyclist

United States Department of Transportation (n.d.-b). Speeding and aggressive driving. National Highway Traffic Safety Administration (NHTSA). Retrieved June 28, 2023, from www.nhtsa.gov/risky-driving/speeding

What is public health? (n.d.). Canadian Public Health Association | Association Canadienne de Santé Publique. Retrieved June 28, 2023, from www.cpha.ca/what-public-health

Woessner, M. N., Tacey, A., Levinger-Limor, A., Parker, A. G., Levinger, P. and Levinger, I. (2021). The evolution of technology and physical inactivity: the good, the bad, and the way forward. *Frontiers in Public Health*, 9. Retrieved June 28, 2023, from https://doi.org/10.3389/fpubh.2021.655491

Yu, B. and Lu, Q. (2013). Empirical model of roughness effect on vehicle speed. *International Journal of Pavement Engineering* 15(4): 345–351. Retrieved June 28, 2023, from www.researchgate.net/publication/263760293_Empirical_model_of_roughness_effect_on_vehicle_speed

CHAPTER 16
Urban Preservation

As planners seek to meet the needs of the population in rapidly urbanized cities and foster a parallel economic growth, the importance of preserving existing urban environments cannot be overstated. The preservation of cultural heritage sites is an important economic and social strategy to achieve sustainable and vibrant spaces for people to live, work and play. Urban preservation and sustainability are interconnected principles that help build livable and efficient communities. This chapter explores the merit and practices of preserving urban environments and the associated dangers of gentrification by investigating large-scale preservations in residential, commercial and mixed-use areas.

16.1 The Value of the Past

Urban preservation provides communities with an appreciation of and connection with the spaces they interact with daily. Dating back to the early twentieth century, the practice of urban preservation was established to care for singular monuments (Langdalen 2016). Since then, conservation strategies have evolved to encompass the dynamic process of conserving historical, cultural and architecturally significant parts of cities. Preservation holds social value by fostering a sense of place and a link to their past and a vehicle for economic growth. Scholars note that urban heritage sites contribute to tourism that contribute to local wealth (Farhan et al. 2020; Lee 1996; Loach et al. 2017). On a global scale, monuments such as the Eiffel Tower, Taj Mahal and Parthenon are common examples of culturally significant edifices that pay homage to the rich history of cities while also serving as a major tourist attraction and source of wealth generation (Figure 16.1).

This section discusses the relationship between preservation and cultural sustainability along with the value of urban preservation as a tool for social and economic growth.

16.1.1 The Relation Between Preservation and Cultural Sustainability

There is high value in looking at the past, not only from an architectural point of view but from a cultural sustainability perspective that underscores the practices and ideas that reflect the spaces, people and understandings of the past.

Figure 16.1 The Parthenon is a culturally significant ancient edifice that pays homage to the rich history of Rome while also serving as a major tourist attraction.

Urban Preservation

Cultural heritage is a vital source of identity and a valuable factor for empowering communities and enabling vulnerable groups to participate fully in social and cultural life (UNESCO 2023).

There is an intrinsic value in preserving culture as a way of expressing the collective interests of people through aesthetics, historical sites, heritage and artistic manifestations (Figure 16.2). Indeed, there is a growing body of scholarship that seeks to understand this relationship between heritage preservation and cultural sustainability through the construction of conceptual frameworks. For example, Soini and Dessein adopt a multi-layered framework that acknowledges how culture acts *as*, *for* and *in* sustainability. Under this framework, Soini and Dessein argue that a heritage site possesses aesthetic and historical, and therefore intrinsic value, in part due to how long the site has lasted, but also because it possesses an instrumental value for creating a sense of identity for people living close to that site or for raising economic wellbeing through tourism (Soini and Joost 2016). Therefore, preservation should be conceptualized as part of achieving cultural sustainability through the built environment, that is, understanding how conservation is connected to enhancing and uplifting the history and culture of a community.

16.1.2 Preservation as Economic and Social Tools

Thinking of urban preservation as a mechanism of achieving cultural sustainability is critical to creating vibrant social spaces and stimulating economic growth. The physical conservation of significant buildings such as museums and libraries are integral to preserving the cultural assets of communities. Furthermore, it is argued that preserving important buildings that honor past knowledge allows for the passage of information to future generations and provides strong links to the community (Loach et al. 2017). In that sense, preservation should be seen as a mechanism that not only allows for the conservation of urban environments but also a way to preserve the ideas and understandings of the past (Figure 16.3).

Often perceived as being antithetical to economic development, preservation serves as an integral economic and social strategy to bolster tourism, reduce unnecessary environmental destruction and cut costs. As noted by Ryberg-Webster, the role of historic preservation has not received significant discussion and is even outright dismissed within scholarship about urban sustainability (Ryberg-Webster 2016). Preservation, however, can and should play a positive role in bolstering the economies and social settings of places. The preservation of properties and community areas of cultural significance should be seen as a way to meet the needs of a community's development and growth objectives (Goddard-Bowman 2014). Although the COVID-19 pandemic almost universally halted tourism, prior to the pandemic, tourism was a key factor in international commerce and is steadily recovering. According to UNESCO, in 2019, tourism injected US$8.9 trillion into the global economy, or 10.3 percent of the world's gross domestic product, 40 percent of which was solely attributed to cultural tourism (UNESCO 2023). The preservation and conversion of notable historic buildings is paramount to sustaining cultural heritage, but intersects with job creation, the conservation of natural environments by preventing urban sprawl, and contributes to the overall revitalization of local and urban areas (Figure 16.4). The reuse of portions of a building is a profitable investment as it reduces the materials needed to construct buildings, reduces construction expenses, and has the potential to bring vacant and underused buildings back to life. Furthermore, they offer diverse spaces for new businesses and small retailers, therefore creating a new tax

Figure 16.2 There is an intrinsic value in preserving culture as a way of expressing the collective interests of people through historical sites, heritage and traditional celebrations, as seen here in Barcelona, Spain (left) and Valetta, Malta (right).

Urban Preservation

Figure 16.3 Preservation should be regarded as a mechanism to record past events. It was the case in the markings of the World War II ghetto walls in Warsaw, Poland (left), Budapest, Hungary (top right), and a wall made up of broken Jewish tombstones in Krakow, Poland (bottom right).

Figure 16.4 The extensive preservation of gardens and buildings in Vienna, Austria is paramount to sustaining cultural heritage which also contributes to a vibrant tourism activity.

Urban Preservation

base and employment opportunities for a new class of workers. Even businesses and buildings that are not directly affected by urban preservation benefit from this conservation process. By boosting tourism within the area, preserved built environments offer attractive experiences for tourists that allow for increased foot traffic and revenue for nearby food, retail, entertainment and cultural production sectors (Hobeika 2021). For these reasons, the past serves as a valuable feature that should be accentuated and integrated into urban planning, not destroyed.

Additionally, with heightened interest in and transition to sustainability, cities are closely examining models of the circular economy and their potential application to urban planning and preservation. The circular economy is a reconceptualization of the current economic system, with the goal of minimizing disposal of construction material and building components as much as possible. The current economic model that underpins contemporary architectural design and construction is linear, meaning that it relies on a "take-make-waste" model. Extracted raw materials are used for a period of time and then disposed of. In a circular economy, however, the end-of-life idea that defines the linear economy is replaced with revitalization, through the use of renewable resources and impeccable design of products to maintain their quality for as long as possible, and the eventual reuse at the end of a product's useful life (Figure 16.5).

16.2 Preservation Strategies

There is no singular universal standard for achieving preservation. Whether one seeks to preserve the built environment at a macro-scale such as a whole neighborhood, or preserve a singular feature on the micro-scale, the needs of community stakeholders must be taken into consideration at all parts of the planning and building process.

16.2.1 What is Worth Preserving?

The debate about what areas to preserve and what to demolish raged between conservationists and the development industry for a long time. Places with buildings from past centuries seem to get in the way of progress. The discussion often centered around what constitutes a heritage building. The question of what will become tomorrow's historic buildings is even more relevant and challenging.

Those arguing for conservation voiced louder concerns after World War II. Early modernists such as Le Corbusier, Mies van der Rohe or Walter Gropius introduced beautifully expressed simplicity and cleanliness of forms to make it a truly refreshing style when it was first introduced (Figure 16.6). Yet, many builders of later structures took advantage of the newly introduced simplicity by altering sense of place. The introduction of repetition, sameness and ignoring historic harmony

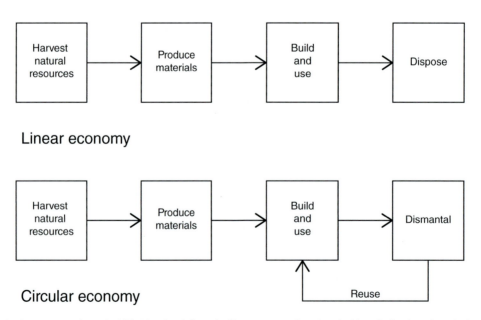

Figure 16.5 In a circular economy, the end-of-life idea that defines the linear economy is replaced with revitalization, through the use of renewable quality products that maintain the building's useful life for as long as possible.

Urban Preservation

Figure 16.6 Early modernists like architect Mies van der Rohe's work embodied cleanliness of forms and a refreshing style when it was introduced in this apartment building in Stuttgart's Weissenhof Estate.

became known as the International Style. Designers failed to take advantage of the richness that the surrounding old buildings provided, in favor of a fresh start. A wakeup call was sounded by thinkers like Jean Jacobs who argued that clearing entire districts causes irreparable damage to a city, its social fabric and sense of place (Jacobs 1961).

There are principles that must be remembered. Buildings from centuries past are reflections of the care and craftsmanship that their architects, builders and craftsmen took in designing and erecting them. Upscale or modest residences, institutional buildings or factories all seem to have cherished and admired features. Stained glass windows, intricate facade brickwork, unique ironwork on a guardrail or elevator doors, exquisite stone arrangement, and imaginative woodwork are hallmarks of past eras (Figure 16.7). Paying attention to and investing in meticulous details was possible in a time of low labor and material costs, and few building booms. Simple, modest structures were built, yet even in them there was an attempt to fit the structure in with its surroundings and to respect an urban context. Well-crafted old buildings from centuries past need to be appreciated not only as *objets d'art*, but as place-creating tools and continuing manifestations of who we are.

The decisions regarding which urban areas worth preserving are dependent on the unique cultural context of what one is attempting to preserve. For preservation to foster social benefits, the conservation project must be widely accepted by

Figure 16.7 Small artifacts such as unique ironwork and exquisite stone items are hallmarks of past eras and therefore must be preserved.

Urban Preservation

Figure 16.8 Infill structures, like the ones seen here in Bruges, Belgium and Amsterdam, the Netherlands, can pay a homage to the general character of the adjacent buildings.

the community. In some instances, buildings such as schools or churches cannot be maintained to function for their intended purpose. From a micro-perspective, infill housing, that is, repurposing vacant or run-down land and property, is a key strategy to achieving sustainability. It provides new functions to unused housing, densifies housing so as to avoid urban sprawl, and revitalizes derelict neighborhoods. From a broader macro-perspective, however, using the past as a model is an innovative way to develop a new purpose for buildings (Figure 16.8).

The inner-city Toronto neighborhood known as The Junction is a prime example of using urban preservation to promote successful commercial heritage development. To enhance the neighborhood's economic development, particularly its digital and media economy businesses, local building owners began transforming the historic commercial Dundas Street into a center for new media business (Goddard-Bowman 2014). The aesthetically pleasing brick-stone residential homes, restored vacant apartments and revamped industrial-finished lofts have since fostered significant media attention, with The Junction being labeled one of the "50 coolest" neighborhoods in the world (Osojnik 2019). Neighborhood associations also continue to serve as important forces to ensure the physical environment stays true to the history of the neighborhood.

Yet, at times, it is not the physical features of the built environment we are solely seeking to preserve, but more importantly, the messages and collective experiences that are symbolized and reflected in the built environment. For example, in the 1970s, the local preservation movement of the Art Deco District in Miami Beach opened spaces for members of the LGBTQ community to participate in the art deco scene (Figure 16.9). Since then, built features such as rainbow signage, murals and artwork now line the neighborhood. These

Figure 16.9 Preserved Art Deco buildings in Miami Beach, Florida.

features continue to be preserved not only because of their aesthetic and economic value but because of how these physical features reflect the shared experiences of the queer community. The history of the HIV/AIDS crisis, gentrification-led displacements, and the ongoing fight for queer acceptance and empowerment within the community is embedded within the urban environment – this is what makes the art worth preserving (Zebracki 2018). The collective experiences, ideas and understandings of a community of people are therefore central toward understanding not only what can be physically preserved, but why a feature must be preserved in the first place. For preservation efforts to be successful, sustainable and accepted by the community of interest, it is key that planners understand the cultural significance and symbolism of the urban environments they seek to develop.

16.3 Avoiding Gentrification

While there is little doubt about the merits to urban preservation, there is no denying that there lies a danger in revitalizing neighborhoods without considering who will be affected by preservation strategies. Low-income and marginalized populations often bear the burden of so-called "revitalization" projects that end up displacing communities. Enter the growing phenomenon of gentrification.

Coined during the 1960s to describe the transformation of working-class areas in London, gentrification refers to the process by which central urban neighborhoods that have undergone disinvestments and economic decline experience a reversal, reinvestment and the in-migration of a well-off middle- and upper-middle-class populations at the expense of displacing lower-income racialized households (Schnake-Mahl et al. 2020). In essence, gentrification is a process in which marginalized communities are often displaced in favor of wealthy, college-educated individuals. Terms such as "neighborhood revitalization" and "regeneration" are often substituted as more neutral and friendly terms for masking the racial and socio-economic implications of gentrification. As higher-income households purchase and renovate their homes, and participate in economic activity within local neighborhoods, this slowly begins to increase housing prices, thereby pushing out lower-income people who can no longer afford to live in the neighborhood (Lees et al. 2010). Overall, evidence points to gentrification having a negative impact on low-income residents in the form of physical and/or cultural displacement, segregation and the erasure of local cultures.

To combat and ultimately avoid gentrification requires collaborative efforts from both community and government stakeholders.

Preventing gentrification requires significant changes to zoning ordinances by adopting more inclusionary zoning and housing laws, building genuine affordable mixed-income housing for all incomes, providing tax breaks for planners and local governments to control displacement, and ensuring community input is part of all aspects of the redevelopment of neighborhoods (Lees et al. 2010). On a community level, scholars cite creative community organizing as an important mechanism to ensure stakeholders are informed and educated about the harms and processes of gentrification (Thurber and Christiano 2019). From a planning perspective, while urban planners are encouraged to consider creating more efficient, productive and inclusive environments, planners must ensure that the preservation of urban spaces meets the needs and demographics of the current community and not restrict their focus to the future insofar as negating the voices of those who understand and know the community from living there for years.

16.4 Venice of China

Zhouzhuang, population 138,000 near Shanghai, referred to as the *Venice of China* and the *Number 1 Water Town*, is a tourist draw. Dating back to the year 1086 and the Ming Qing dynasty, it is stretched along a river delta where the inhabitants have fished for generations. Homes clad with stone and roofed with red tiles edge the canals and rows of small boats are tied to the banks (Figure 16.10).

Nowadays, the residents of Zhouzhuang are harvesting another resource: tourism. Foreigners flock to the place to stroll on the narrow sidewalks that line the water, buy souvenirs in the many craft shops, take photographs on one of the famous stone bridges that arch over the canals, and eat Wansan pork, the sweet fried meat, a local delicacy.

Walking in the place's side streets and back alleys and seeing the impoverished homes, it is easy to notice that, more than a tourist attraction, the place is a ladder. It is a way for craft makers, boat rowers, waitresses and shopkeepers to improve their lives. The people of Zhouzhuang realized that their place of living is of interest to others and a source of wealth. They are invested in preservation and urban renewal, making their town welcoming and publicizing it.

Some of the tourist revenues are being invested in restoring old structures to their former state under a strict government guidance. In this regard, architecture won. Zhouzhuang's intricate stonework, unique ironwork and imaginative woodwork are hallmarks of the place's past which turned places into an urban museum (Zhouzhuang 2023).

Urban Preservation

Figure 16.10 Dating back to the year 1086 and the Ming Qing dynasty, Zhouzhuang is stretched along a river delta where the inhabitants fished for generations and is now a tourist attraction.

16.5 Learning from Tuscany

The view from Pina and Felice's kitchen is breathtaking. The Tuscan hills, some covered with freshly cut light yellow hay, rolled on gently into the horizon. Rows of green grapevines hanging from wires, and patches of sunflowers and olive groves dotting the natural quilt. On distant hilltops, there are homes with red terracotta roof-tiles.

Pina and Felice moved here from the island of Sardinia in southern Italy about twenty years ago. Unable to find land in their own birthplace, they purchased this farm in which they invested the better years of their lives. Noticing heavy tourist traffic en route to the nearby town of Volterra, they wanted to supplement their income by joining the hospitality business

known here as *agriturismo*. In addition to farming, they now had five rental suites.

In Tuscany, new construction in the countryside is strictly forbidden. Locals are only permitted to renovate or add to existing structures. The provincial authority had recognized that the beauty of the countryside would not last if rapid development took place. To obtain a permit, one needs to engage a certified restoration expert, who measures and draws meticulous drawings of the building (Figure 6.11).

The authorities realized that if the strict laws were to be lifted, the old buildings would be demolished, and the land use rapidly changed from agricultural to commercial or residential. The landscape would be paved over. Low-density gated

Figure 16.11 The restored building of Pina and Felice near Volterra, Italy which now serves as *agriturismo*.

condominium estates for wealthy overseas investors would likely follow. Roads would be expanded to accommodate increased traffic, and commercial land use. Ignoring preservation, the Tuscans have realized, would not only erase architectural heritage, and alter the landscape, but would uproot a way of life that has lasted centuries.

Tuscany's cultural past embeds winemaking, olive and sunflower harvesting that contributed to the sense of place. It also contributed to the livelihood of generations of past farmers and future ones. By preserving their countryside, the Tuscans also attracted visitors from afar to support the local hospitality economy. They selected the route of self-imposed discipline that is appreciated now and will be valued in years to come.

16.6 Rebuilding L'Aquila

On April 6, 2009, a magnitude 6.3 earthquake rocked L'Aquila in central Italy, about 96.5 kilometers (60 miles) northeast of Rome. This powerful earthquake left over 300 people dead and an estimated 60,000 others homeless, while leaving most of the historic thirteenth-century city greatly damaged. Between 3,000 to 11,000 buildings were damaged, some beyond repair. Most citizens had to abandon their homes or the city altogether (Ray 2020).

I visited L'Aquila twice. The first visit, to witness the widespread damage the quake had caused, and the second to attend a workshop about the rebuilding of the city's old center. I was impressed by the rebuild and the commitment of central and local governments to revive the place while preserving its urban and architectural heritage. Multidisciplinary teams of experts not only join forces to consult on the rebuilding but to develop methods to prevent damage in case another earthquake strikes. It was done while considering new challenges that buildings and modern cities face, such as energy efficiency and the use of sustainable materials.

On my second visit, I saw signs of new life. Although many of the buildings are being restored, others are already occupied. People occupied some of the restored apartments, stores welcomed patrons and people crowded into cafes and restaurants.

The desire to live and thrive in L'Aquila while making preservation of heritage a priority is an inspiring lesson to other places that have experienced natural disasters (Figure 16.12).

16.7 Final Thoughts

There is great potential for urban preservation to be used as a sustainable strategy to cut costs, preserve natural environments and protect the unique cultural heritage of communities. There are vacant areas in urban pockets throughout the world where preservation strategies can be harnessed to revitalize derelict neighborhoods. Simply put, for urban preservation to be successful, developers and government bodies, as well as the needs of community stakeholders, must be part of the preservation process. Of course, this is easier said than done. As the rise of gentrification in urban areas continues to segregate and erase local cultures, there is a growing need for significant housing and zoning policy reform at all levels of government. Using existing templates, structures and features are important guiding principles to create meaningful, productive and effective neighborhoods. There is beauty in preserving the history and culture of neighborhoods. Thus, for cities to achieve sustainability, urban preservation must be employed carefully whenever possible.

Urban Preservation

Figure 16.12 Abandoned structures (top left), buildings under restoration (top right) and a restored one (bottom left and right) in L'Aquila, Italy.

References

Farhan, S., Akef, V. and Nasar, Z. (2020). The transformation of the inherited historical urban and architectural characteristics of Al-Najaf's old city and possible preservation insights. *Frontiers of Architectural Research* 9(4): 820–836. Retrieved July 4, 2023, from https://doi.org/10.1016/j.foar.2020.07.005

Goddard-Bowman, R. (2014). Something old is something new: the role of heritage preservation in economic development. *Papers in Canadian Economic Development* 9: 96–109. Retrieved July 4, 2023, https://openjournals.uwaterloo.ca/index.php/pced/article/view/4002/4957

Hobeika, R. (2021). Heritage preservation can enhance urban development. *MEED*. Retrieved July 4, 2023, from www.meed.com/heritage-preservation-can-enhance-urban-development

Jacobs, J. (1961). *The Death and Life of Great American Cities*. Vintage Books. New York.

Langdalen, E. (2016). Urban preservation. *Columbia GSAPP*. 2016. Retrieved July 4, 2023, from www.arch.columbia.edu/courses/20905-1212-urban-preservation

Lee, S.L. (1996). Urban conservation policy and the preservation of historical and cultural heritage: the case of Singapore. *Cities, Issues In Urban Conservation* 13(6): 399–409. Retrieved July 4, 2023, from https://doi.org/10.1016/0264-2751(96)00027-3

Lees, L., Slater, T. and Wyly, E. (2010). *The Gentrification Reader* (1st ed.). Routledge. New York.

Loach, K., Rowley, J. and Griffiths, J. (2017). Cultural sustainability as a strategy for the survival of museums and libraries. *International Journal of Cultural Policy* 23(2): 186–198. Retrieved July 4, 2023, from https://doi.org/10.1080/10286632.2016.1184657

Osojnik, S. (2019). The Junction: Toronto's coolest neighborhood right now. *Time Out Toronto*. Retrieved July 4, 2023, from www.timeout.com/toronto/things-to-do/junction-toronto-guide

Ray, M. (2020). L'Aquila earthquake of 2009. *Encyclopaedia Britannica*. Retrieved July 4, 2023, from www.britannica.com/event/LAquila-earthquake-of-2009

Ryberg-Webster, S. (2016). Heritage amid an urban crisis: historic preservation in Cleveland, Ohio's Slavic village neighborhood. *Cities* 58(October): 10–25. Retrieved July 4, 2023, from https://doi.org/10.1016/j.cities.2016.05.005

Schnake-Mahl, A. S., Jahn, J. L., Subramanian, S., Waters, M. C. and Arcaya, M. (2020). Gentrification, neighborhood change, and population health: a systematic review. *Journal of Urban*

Health: Bulletin of the New York Academy of Medicine 97(1): 1–25. Retrieved July 4, 2023, from https://doi.org/10.1007/s11524-019-00400-1

Soini, K. and Joost, D. (2016). Culture-sustainability relation: towards a conceptual framework. *Sustainability* 8(2): 167. Retrieved July 4, 2023, from https://doi.org/10.3390/su8020167

Thurber, A. and Christiano, J. (2019). Confronting gentrification: can creative interventions help people keep more than just their homes? *Engaged Scholar Journal: Community-Engaged Research, Teaching, and Learning* 5(2): 95. Retrieved July 4, 2023, from https://doi.org/10.15402/esj.v5i2.68338

UNESCO (2023). Cutting edge: bringing cultural tourism back in the game. Retrieved July 4, 2023, from www.unesco.org/en/articles/cutting-edge-bringing-cultural-tourism-back-game

Zebracki, M. (2018). Urban preservation and the queerying spaces of (un)remembering: memorial landscapes of the Miami Beach art deco historic district. *Urban Studies Journal* 55(10): 2261–2285. Retrieved July 4, 2023, from https://doi.org/10.1177/0042098017709197

Zhouzhuang (2023). *In Wikipedia*. Retrieved July 4, 2023, from https://en.wikipedia.org/wiki/Zhouzhuang

CHAPTER 17
Planning for Urban Evolution

As urbanization soars worldwide, there is a growing need to ensure that cities are well-suited to meet the demands of future generations. Given the vast array of changes in population make-up, technology, lifestyle and workplace preferences, it is paramount that resiliency and flexibility are made central to conceptualizing tomorrow's built environments. This chapter explores urban design methods that regard cities and buildings as places of ongoing change and investigates strategies and models to create resilient and dynamic environments.

17.1 Evolving Cities and Buildings

The evolution of cities and buildings refers to the physical and social transformations regarding their structure and function. Ensuring that communities and buildings are designed with flexibility in mind is therefore paramount to any changes they may face. When designing a building, architects commonly seek to ensure that the place meets the short-term needs of the occupants at the time of design. However, there is a need to consider whether the design will be economically, culturally and environmentally viable in the long term (Ellen MacArthur Foundation 2022).

Given the rapidly changing nature of people's preferences, often shaped by local and global issues, this rigid conceptualization of land-use planning makes buildings irrelevant and unusable to emerging conditions. There is a particular incentive to consider the impact of long-term changes when designing cities, such as climate change, natural resource depletions, population aging but also the imminent possibility of unprecedented challenges such as a worldwide pandemic. In addition, the twentieth century introduced new technologies that have permitted more efficient, safer and faster urban and building practices. Planning for future conversion of rundown ports or industrial areas into new land uses should be part of resilient and sustainable design, as was the case in La

Confluence, Lyon, France and Hafen City, Hamburg, Germany (Figure 17.1).

The concept of transformation can best be demonstrated in suburban communities. Once lauded as an efficient way of mass-producing housing, the traditional suburban paradigms of detached single-family homes are being reconsidered. After World War II, suburban sprawl became common, particularly in North America. Yet, little attention was paid to the consequences of vehicle use on carbon emissions. In fact, the width of roads, the area of parking lots and the location of commerce were all planned to accommodate automobiles. At present, urban planners are seeking to dethrone the automobile's grip on urban planning in favor of promoting denser, walkable and public-transit-oriented neighborhoods.

Fueled by tax and mortgage incentives paired with the comfort of the single detached house drew families to the suburbs. Today, there is a change in how newer generations seek to live. The allure of a domestic, traditional and secluded way of life is no longer so attractive to some (Kelly 1993). Cities are growing rapidly and the demand for housing in them is subsequently increasing. Building denser mixed-use communities is a common planning strategy to accommodate growing urban populations. Planners need to consider how cities will accommodate growing and changing populations in a way that affords citizens meaningful, accessible and diverse spaces to live, work and play.

The city of Montreal, Canada, is an example of how cities can accommodate growing populations while continuing to serve as a dynamic place for growth, change, innovation and creativity. In the core, skyscrapers exist near old, styled buildings. Vibrant districts such as Old Montreal provide a unique window into the history of Montreal's transformation from a fur-trading hub to one of Canada's most culturally and economically diverse cities (Figure 17.2).

DOI: 10.4324/9781003384687-17

Planning for Urban Evolution

Figure 17.1 Planning for the future evolution of areas should be part of a resilient and sustainable design strategy as was the case in Hafen City, Hamburg, Germany (top images) and La Confluence, Lyon, France (bottom images).

Figure 17.2 The Old Montreal district provide a unique window into the history of the city's transformation from a trading hub to one of Canada's most culturally diverse and visited cities.

Similarly, in Istanbul, Turkey, markets and teahouses express the unique culture and history of the city. The buildings and cultural heritage sites of Istanbul illustrate the city's connections with medieval Occident and Islamic civilizations (Figure 17.3). Montreal and Istanbul are two cities that have evolved with time to accommodate new needs.

Planning for Urban Evolution

Figure 17.3 The buildings and cultural heritage sites of Istanbul illustrate the city's connections with Medieval Occident and Islamic civilizations.

17.2 Planning Strategies for Renewal and Resiliency

Adaptability to emerging realities is key to human survival and a vital aspect of sustainable design. Flexible urban planning practices are a way to rise to the challenges presented by the ever-changing technological, social and economic realities of today's urban environments. For dynamic urban spaces to be created, planners need to consider the role of renewal and resiliency. There is no single strategy or rigid set of guidelines on how to plan for resilient cities. There is great difficulty in accurately predicting how spaces will be used in the next decade, let alone the next century. Gradual trends such as demographic transformations provide planners with ideas of who to plan for. For example, the global rise of the non-traditional family, made up of single, elderly and single-parent households, call for a change of philosophy and form in the design of dwellings.

On the micro-scale, one of the keys to designing sustainable and resilient buildings is through *flexible zoning*. For example, during the COVID-19 pandemic, many workplaces saw a shift from in-person to online work; some of it became permanent (Figure 17.4). For many people, this meant transforming homes into workplaces, and turning living rooms into a school space for children. Also, businesses worldwide needed to change how they used their spaces which detached them from a particular location and moved them online. As health recommendations and requirements change, it has become apparent that not everybody is keen on returning to their former workplace. In June 2021, a Leger survey found that around 80 percent of employees prefer a hybrid model of working and do not want to return to work daily (The Canadian Press 2021). Similarly, the Angus Reid Institute in March 2022 found that more than half of Canadian respondents reported that they would look for another job if asked to return in-person to work, with almost a quarter reporting that they would quit immediately (Korzinski 2022). Although employers continue to ask their employees to return to work in person, there is a consensus that workplaces have fundamentally shifted and so have people's lifestyles to a certain extent. Therefore, physical spaces such as city buildings will have to adapt as well.

In some cases, office spaces have been turned into residences and even derelict industrial places have been transformed into residential and commercial spaces to house people and amenities. Indeed, having a flexible mind-set regarding flexible zoning will allow planners to easily alter places to fit the function and needs of people once the appropriate circumstances arise.

Government policies that allow for more flexibility regarding shifting land use on both the macro- and micro-level scale are essential to keep up with urban changes. For example, when the COVID-19 pandemic disrupted many aspects of human social life including limiting recreational opportunities and managing one's own physical and mental health, public parks and outdoor green spaces served as key places to allow for safe enjoyment, especially for low-income and immigrant communities (Volenec et al. 2021). Parks experienced high visitation rates and many people sought to use outdoor recreational spaces to work during the summer, and meet with friends and family at a safe distance. Municipal and commercial services also took advantage of this trend by allowing for more outdoor seating in restaurants and creating outdoor workspaces with

Planning for Urban Evolution

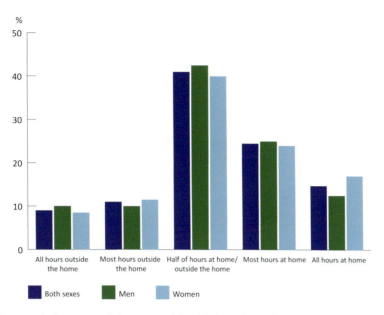

Figure 17.4 During the COVID-19 pandemic, many workplaces saw a shift of their employees from in-person to online work, which for some workers became permanent.

Figure 17.5 During the COVID-19 pandemic restaurants introduced more outdoor seating and municipalities set up outdoor workspaces with WiFi as was the case in Montreal, Canada.

WiFi (Figure 17.5). Recreational spaces increasingly functioned as mixed-use zones that allowed for greater flexibility while still preserving the identity and character of communities.

17.3 The Art of Renewal in North Adams

Some cities plan for change while others improvise when adversity strikes or when they fall into despair. When it comes to small and mid-sized cities some lacked the resources necessary to reverse their downward spiral. A city that reinvented itself innovatively following decline is North Adams in the commonwealth of Massachusetts, United States. Linked by a tunnel to Boston in the east and to the Great Lakes in the west, for years the place was known for its sprawling cotton dyeing mill that was established in 1872. The mill drew thousands of workers where they resided for generations. Unable to obtain orders during World War II, the mill closed in 1942. The plant was taken over by another corporation that decades later also closed, leading to an economic decline.

Planning for Urban Evolution

Figure 17.6 Using public art and invited international artists, North Adams in the commonwealth of Massachusetts, US, reinvented its downtown innovatively following a decline.

When contemplating renewal, the city decided to center its redevelopment around art. It began in 1999 with the conversion of the old mill buildings into the MASS MoCA (Massachusetts Museum of Contemporary Art) to be discussed in Chapter 20. The city became a hub for around 100,000 art-loving tourists who visit the museum each year. Art display flowed to other parts of the center. The core feels like being in a giant museum with murals on walls, painted crosswalks and sculptures in empty lots. Signage and markings on the ground direct visitors to artworks to make it a pleasant walk (Figure 17.6).

The city also saw the conversion of a neglected row houses across from the mill into an inn called Porches to house visiting tourists. Jack Wasdworth, a business student alumnus from a nearby college, revitalized the run-down buildings (The Porches Inn 2020). Located in front of MASS MoCA, the architecture is distinctively Victorian, yet it has a modern twist thanks to the color choice that gives it a homey and playful aesthetic (Figure 17.7).

Global and local economic shifts, future commercial and buying trends, and the nation's demographic make-up are all unknown factors which are bound to affect the future of small cities.

North Adams demonstrated that foresight, innovation and some resources can turn the fortune of places around to offer them another chance.

17.4 Innovative Reclamation in Manhattan

In the mid-1800s, freight trains delivering food to lower Manhattan operated at street level, which put pedestrians at risk. In 1934, after many fatalities, the West Side Elevated Line was opened. By the 1980s the trains had been replaced by trucks carrying goods, which led to the abandonment of the line in the elevated structure. In the ensuing years, a garden of wild plants grew to populate the platform.

In 1999, New York Mayor Rudi Giuliani had authorised the demolition of the structure. Local activists who recognized the space's potential argued that it should be saved and began a dialogue that focused on conservation. In 2003, a competition to redevelop the High Line was held, and by 2009, the upper park was ready to welcome the public. Owing its popularity to

Designing Sustainable Buildings

Figure 18.8 An old textile factory in Lodz, Poland was converted to a textile museum. In the same location one can also visit heritage homes to create a vibrant cultural spot and a tourist attraction for the city.

can sell local goods and services (Cole and Lorch 2005). Consequently, city architecture can serve as a "cultural ingredient" that can revitalize existing neighborhoods without displacing existing inhabitants from their communities (Mihaila 2014).

Old buildings can serve a place and its citizens when they portray what the city looked like in the past. Often, preserving buildings creates cultural and architectural cohesion while also stimulating the local economies (Dessein et al. 2015). For instance, an old fabric factory in Lodz, Poland was converted to a textile museum. On the same place's grounds one can also visit vintage homes from the same era, creating a vibrant cultural spot and a tourist attraction (Figure 18.8).

18.3 The Green on the Sixth Floor in Toronto

The COVID-19 pandemic cast new light on the challenges of apartment living. The need to quarantine for a long period indoors was particularly hard for families with young children. Many wondered if the interior of their apartment was the only place children could play in.

60 Richmond Cooperative Housing is an 11-storey apartment building with above ground outdoor green spaces. Designed by Teeple Architects, the structure contains 85 units and integrated leisure spaces (Friedman 2017). The program sought to incorporate social spaces for food production. As a result, the architects designed a dynamic space known as an *urban permaculture*. For example, the resident-owned and operated restaurant, as well as a training kitchen on the ground floor, are supplied by the vegetables and other produce grown on the sixth-floor terrace (Figure 18.9).

By extension, this notion of urban permaculture is multi-faceted and affects more than one level of functions. The garden is irrigated via storm water runoff from the roof. More importantly, the organic waste produced by the restaurant and training kitchen is collected and used as compost to nourish the roof garden, making the building self-sufficient. When referring to its design, unlike the myriad of condominiums visible in the downtown landscape, 60 Richmond was conceived as a solid mass that was carved into to create openings and terraces at various levels. The deconstruction of its mass results in open spaces stepping out and back from the street level. More importantly, the visually appealing and fluent gestures employed by the architects is integral in achieving

Designing Sustainable Buildings

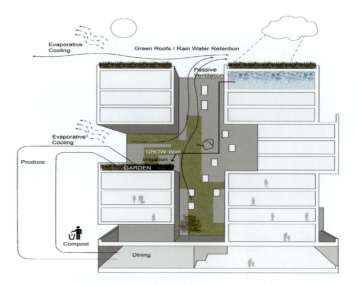

Figure 18.9 60 Richmond Cooperative Housing is an 11-story apartment building with above-ground outdoor green space.

certain goals. These include but are not limited to creating the kitchen garden, drawing light into the building's interior, and providing green outdoor space. In addition, the garden terraces created while deconstructing the facades help cool and cleanse the air, which ultimately limits the heat island effect in the urban core.

18.4 A Pathway to the 10th Floor in Copenhagen

Designed by the Danish firm BIG, the 10-story 8 House complex, with 476 dwelling units and 10,000 square meters (107,639 square foot) of commercial space and a spectacular view of the Copenhagen Canal, provides food for thought to builders and architects alike (Friedman 2018).

Its designers justly dubbed it a "3-dimensional neighborhood" because it feels like one. Shaped like the number 8, hence the name, it has declining edges that, from a distance, makes it look like a pyramid. Similar to a bowtie, it is squeezed in the middle to enclose two courtyards. The structure is a mix of several ingredients not commonly found in an apartment building. The dwellings include 150 townhouses, conventional apartments and small units, as well as stores, a cafe and amenities such as a daycare center. Those who wish to work near home can rent office space on the ground floor (Figure 18.10).

But perhaps the most unusual feature of 8 House is an open-air path that loops around the building all the way to the 10th floor. Walking along the sloping ramp, one passes the "front yards" of units where lawn chairs, toys, flowerpots and, of course, bikes are visible.

To enhance community spirit, the developer included a 500-square meter (5,382 square feet) gathering room where common issues are discussed, and residents get to know their neighbors better. To help foster a healthy lifestyle, children can play in the two beautifully landscaped courts while their parents look down from balconies. There are also outdoor exercise machines, and this being Copenhagen, lots of places to park bicycles.

As is commonly the case in all Scandinavian countries, and often decreed by governments, Copenhagen's 8 House is an environmental masterpiece. With harvested and recycled water,

Designing Sustainable Buildings

Figure 18.10 An unusual feature of 8 House is a combination bicycle and pedestrian open-air path that loops around the building.

Designing Sustainable Buildings

a green roof and a highly energy-efficient design, the project set high national and international standards for others to follow.

18.5 Celebrating Local History in Oudeschild

Many cities record and display local history and culture. When these undertakings are initiated by small towns, it is even more appreciative given the resources it took to make it happen and keep it going. It is the case in the Kaap Skil Maritime and Beachcombers Museum in Oudeschild, population 1,200, on the island of Texel, in the Northwestern Wadden Sea of the Netherlands (Discover 2020) (Figure 18.11).

Due to limited natural resources, the sea was an important part of Texel Island's livelihood. It was used as a starting point for expeditions to the far east by the Dutch East India Company in the seventeenth and eighteenth centuries. The ships docked there until the winds were favorable, and the island was equipped for maintenance, trade and housing waiting sailors.

Once the Golden Age passed, Oudeschild became a fishing village.

Designed by the Dutch firm Mecanoo and opened in 2011, the museum depicts the Golden Age with lower-level exhibit dedicated to Reede van Texel (which was located off the island's east side). Visitors watch projections and animations that recreate past maritime scenes. The first floor is dedicated to underwater archaeology where one gets to see numerous artifacts such as parts of boats and salvaged tools.

The museum's four-ridged roof design mimic the rooftops of the surrounding homes which are uneven and were meant to be seen from the sea to resemble waves rising. Intrinsically, not having forested areas, for centuries the islanders have been using driftwood for construction. As an homage to the past, the facade uses these driftwood planks. By spacing the planks apart, the glass facade leaves sufficient gaps for sunlight, essentially turning the front and back elevations to a large window open to a distant view. The museum and the island draw nearly a million tourists yearly thanks to the history and beautiful landscape.

Figure 18.11 The Kaap Skil Maritime and Beachcombers Museum in Oudeschild, on the island of Texel, in the Netherlands is an example of recording local history in a small town.

As noted above, a key pillar of sustainability is enhancement of local culture. It contributes to a place's identity, pride and forms a much-needed foundation for other future endeavors. No matter how big or small a community is, recording and displaying the past is a rudimentary part of what society is.

18.6 Final Thoughts

Sustainable building design is essential to reaching communal wellbeing. Reducing carbon emissions and promoting efficient and renewable energy sources is paramount to reducing urban impacts on climate change. These environmental solutions must be considered by planners in relation to social, cultural and economic strategies. As global issues such as climate change, rapid urbanization, and the provision of basic services and amenities continue to stress natural landscapes and social environments, sustainable building design will be crucial to adapt to the changing needs of populations. Designing buildings that do not heavily tax the environment while also being affordable and culturally appropriate is an immense challenge providing planners with a flexible and dynamic way to create innovative, practical and equitable designs.

References

Altman, I. and Zube, E. (1989). *Public Places and Spaces*. Springer. New York. Retrieved July 5, 2023, from https://doi.org/10.1007/978-1-4684-5601-1

Berardi, U. (2013). Clarifying the new interpretations of the concept of sustainable building. *Sustainable Cities and Society* 8: 72–78. Retrieved July 5, 2023, from https://doi.org/10.1016/j.scs.2013.01.008

Boström, M. (2012). A missing pillar? Challenges in theorizing and practicing social sustainability: introduction to the special issue. *Sustainability: Science, Practice and Policy* 8(1): 3–14. Retrieved July 5, 2023, from https://doi.org/10.1080/15487733.2012.11908080

Cole, R.J. and Lorch, R. (2005). Buildings, culture and environment: informing local and global practices. *International Journal of Sustainability in Higher Education*, 6(1). Retrieved July 5, 2023, from https://doi.org/10.1108/ijshe.2005.24906aae.006

Dave, S. (2011). Neighbourhood density and social sustainability in cities of developing countries. *Sustainable Development* 19(3): 189–205. Retrieved July 5, 2023, from https://doi.org/10.1002/sd.433

Dessein, J., Battaglini, E. and Horlings, L. (eds.). (2015). *Cultural Sustainability and Regional Development: Theories and Practices of Territorialisation*. Routledge. London. Retrieved July 5, 2023, from https://doi.org/10.4324/9781315737430

Discover (2020). Museum Kaap Skil. Retrieved July 5, 2023, from www.kaapskil.nl/en/discover/400-years-skil/new-entrance-building-new-name/

Friedman, A. (2017). *Innovative Apartment Buildings; New Direction in Sustainable Design*. Edition Axel Menges GmbH. Fellbach.

Friedman, A. (2018). *Smart Homes and Communities: Fostering Sustainable Architecture*. Images Publishing. Victoria.

Gieryn, T. F. (2002). What buildings do. *Theory and Society* 31(1): 35–74.

Gifford, R. (n.d.). Environmental psychology matters. *Annual Review of Psychology*. Retrieved July 5, 2023, from www.annualreviews.org/doi/10.1146/annurev-psych-010213-115048

Lacroix, R. and Stamatiou, E. (2007). *Architecture, Green Design & Sustainability: Concepts and Practices*. Retrieved July 5, 2023, from www.researchgate.net/publication/326773991_Architecture_Green_Design_Sustainability-Concepts_and_Practices

Lee, J. L. C. and Ho, R. T. H. (2022). Creating exercise spaces in parks for older adults with fitness, rehabilitation, and play elements: a review and perspective. *Gerontology and Geriatric Medicine*. Retrieved July 5, 2023, from https://doi.org/10.1177/23337214221083404

Lewis, C. and Buffel, T. (2020). Aging in place and the places of aging: a longitudinal study. *Journal of Aging Studies*, 54: 100870. Retrieved July 5, 2023, from https://doi.org/10.1016/j.jaging.2020.100870

Maywald, C. and Riesser, F. (2016). Sustainability – the art of modern architecture. *Procedia Engineering* 155: 238–248. Retrieved July 5, 2023, from https://doi.org/10.1016/j.proeng.2016.08.025

Mihaila, M. (2014). City architecture as cultural ingredient. *Procedia – Social and Behavioral Sciences* 149: 565–569. Retrieved July 5, 2023, from https://doi.org/10.1016/j.sbspro.2014.08.211

Mulliner, E., Riley, M. and Maliene, V. (2020). Older people's preferences for housing and environment characteristics. *Sustainability* 12(14): Article 14. Retrieved July 5, 2023, from https://doi.org/10.3390/su12145723

Nenadović, A. and Milošević, J. (2022). Creating sustainable buildings: structural design based on the criterion of social benefits for building users. *Sustainability* 14(4): Article 4. Retrieved July 5, 2023, from https://doi.org/10.3390/su14042133

Purvis, B., Mao, Y. and Robinson, D. (2019). Three pillars of sustainability: In search of conceptual origins. *Sustainability Science* 14(3): 681–695. Retrieved July 5, 2023, from https://doi.org/10.1007/s11625-018-0627-5

Qian, Q. K., Ho, W. K. O., Jayantha, W. M., Chan, E. H. W. and Xu, Y. (2022). Aging-in-place and home modifications for urban regeneration. *Land*, 11(11): Article 11. Retrieved July 5, 2023, from https://doi.org/10.3390/land11111956

United Nations (2023). *Sustainability*. Retrieved July 5, 2023, from www.un.org/en/academic-impact/sustainability

United States General Services Administration (2023). *Climate Action and Sustainability*. Retrieved July 5, 2023, from www.gsa.gov/governmentwide-initiatives/climate-action-and-sustainability

Vivintel (2021). New study by Vividata sheds light on our desire to age-in-place. *Vividata*. Retrieved July 5, 2023, from https://vividata.ca/press_release/new-study-by-vividata-sheds-light-on-our-desire-to-age-in-place/

Wang, N. and Adeli, H. (2014). Sustainable building design. *Journal of Civil Engineering and Management*, 20(1). Retrieved July 5, 2023, from https://doi.org/10.3846/13923730.2013.871330

Wu, S. R., Fan, P. and Chen, J. (2015). Incorporating culture into sustainable development: a cultural sustainability index framework for green buildings. *Sustainable Development* 24(1): 64–76. Retrieved July 5, 2023, from https://doi.org/10.1002/sd.1608

Yang, E., Kim, Y. and Hong, S. (2021). Does working from home work? Experience of working from home and the value of hybrid workplace post-COVID-19. *Journal of Corporate Real Estate* 25(1): 50–76. Retrieved July 5, 2023, from https://doi.org/10.1108/JCRE-04-2021-0015

Zhang, J. (2012). Delivering environmentally sustainable economic growth: the case of China made possible with support from the Bertelsmann Foundation. Asia Society. Retrieved July 5, 2023, from https://asiasociety.org/files/pdf/Delivering_Environmentally_Sustainable_Economic_Growth_Case_China.pdf

CHAPTER 19

Powering Cities
Net Zero and District Heating

Net-zero communities that produce their own power and district heating systems that use a single communal source are important mechanisms for powering cities in a sustainable, affordable and efficient manner. As global energy consumption is expected to rise sharply, decarbonizing cities will take center stage. Adopting "net-zero" design principles to achieve sustainable and greenhouse gas (GHG) emission-free buildings might be some of the options considered. It also makes the need to transition to sustainable renewable energy sources such as wind, solar and geothermal energy crucial. This chapter focuses on the current energy challenges associated with the climate emergency and the need to power cities with alternative energy sources and efficient methods.

19.1 The Energy Challenge

The International Energy Agency (IEA) (n.d.) stresses the importance of ensuring adequate energy security, that is, the uninterrupted and reliable availability of energy sources at an affordable price. The major challenge to achieving energy security, however, is not only about ensuring people have access to energy but about having access to clean sources. Smith (2012) notes that roughly 78 percent of the world's primary energy is currently generated by burning fossil fuels. Therefore, even when people have access to various forms of energy, the use of non-renewable sources requires environmentally detrimental methods of extraction, burning and processing. Scholarship on climate change warns how the resulting release of carbon emissions into the atmosphere from fossil fuels is causing catastrophic and irreversible changes to the world's ecosystems. The extinction of vital species in the food chain, sea-level rise, and hazardous air and water conditions are just a few examples of how global warming is destroying both the environment and socio-economic livelihoods of people worldwide (Filho et al. 2021; Perera 2018; Krane 2017; Barbir et al. 1990). Moreover, as urbanization and population rates continue to soar, particularly in the Global South, there

is additional pressure for energy systems to accommodate the basic economic and social needs of populations. Consequently, cities must respond to the energy crisis by re-evaluating and reconfiguring urban areas and systems to shift away from fossil fuels and develop clean and sustainable ways to power cities for future generations to learn, work and grow.

A growing consensus of climate research illustrates that significant amounts of GHG emissions in the atmosphere are becoming an increasing environmental concern. As temperatures currently hover between 1.1°C and 1.3°C (33.98°F and 34.34°F) above pre-industrial levels, the world is witnessing more frequent weather events and a significant loss of agricultural land and ecosystems (Rae et al. 2021). Crop failures, water shortages, poverty and hunger, mass migration, and conflict represent just a couple of short-term climate change consequences (Masson-Delmotte et al. 2018).

Climate change is especially a concern for coastal communities. In 2019, the Intergovernmental Panel on Climate Change projected that 680 million people worldwide currently live in low-lying coastal zones, and this number is expected to reach more than one billion by 2050 (IPCC 2022; McMichael et al. 2020). NASA satellite observations indicate that global warming will increase sea levels by up to 30 centimetres (12 inches) by 2050 (Younger 2022). Consequently, some cities and countries are at risk of being flooded.

However, the impacts of climate change are noticeably unequal. At the global scale, countries north of the equator in the "Global North" are responsible for over half of the world's emissions since the Industrial Revolution and produce a carbon footprint 100 times greater than countries south of the equator in the "Global South" (Strazzante et al. 2021). Similarly, in 2019, the World Inequality Lab found that the top 10 percent of global emitters, or around 771 million individuals, were responsible for about 48 percent of global CO_2 emissions, while the bottom 50 percent of the population,

191 DOI: 10.4324/9781003384687-19

Powering Cities

United States	Argentina	Uganda
American emissions are about **16 tons** per capita	Argentina emissions are about **4 tons** per capita	Uganda emissions are about **0.1 tons** per capita

Figure 19.1 The World Inequality Lab found that the top 10 percent of global emitters, or around 771 million people, were responsible for about 48 percent of global CO_2 emissions, while the bottom 50 percent of the population, around 3.8 billion individuals, were responsible for only 12 percent of all emissions.

around 3.8 billion people, were responsible for only 12 percent of all emissions (Chancel 2022) (Figure 19.1). Despite contributing the least to carbon emissions, countries in the Global South are more susceptible to the consequences of climate change. On a nation-level scale, Black, Indigenous, and people of colour (BIPOC) are more vulnerable to the impacts of climate change (Smith 2021). For instance, the Joint Center for Political and Economic Studies found that 30 percent of Black residents in New Orleans did not own a car before Hurricane Katrina, weakening their ability to leave prior to the catastrophic storm (Morse 2008). Climate change is not independent of socio-economic inequalities. Rather, the persistent inequality in global, national and local political and economic systems makes responding to climate change an increasingly challenging task. Consequently, there is a growing need to shift away from fossil fuels toward alternative energy sources to power cities in a safe, efficient and environmentally sustainable way that will drastically reduce carbon emissions.

19.2 Types of Renewable Energy

Energy sources can be divided into two categories: renewable and non-renewable (Figure 19.2). As opposed to non-renewable resources, renewable resources can be replenished naturally in a short time and converted into heat and electricity (Zohuri and McDaniel 2021; Owusu and Asumadu-Sarkodie 2016). Certain types of renewable energy can be more effective than others depending on the specific context and needs of a community.

19.2.1 Wind

In wind energy electricity is produced via rotation of a turbine's blades, thereby turning a rotor connected to a generator. Wind turbines help nations achieve their emission reduction goals for several reasons. They do not directly generate emissions, rely on universal natural forces, and are less expensive to build and maintain compared to nuclear power (Solarin and Bello 2022; Kuşkaya and Bilgili 2020). Wind energy does not produce as much electricity compared to its non-renewable fossil fuel counterparts and may not be suitable for all cities given the amount of space needed to build and maintain its structures. Yet, the wind energy sector is growing significantly (Figure 19.3). The Global Wind Energy Council suggests that at the current rate of implementation and investment, wind energy systems have the potential to provide 20 percent of the global demand for electricity by 2030 (Darwish and Al-Dabbagh 2020).

19.2.2 Solar

Solar energy is a more adaptable and city-friendly renewable source of energy that can be implemented on existing buildings. A key benefit of solar energy is that the photovoltaic panels can be conveniently integrated into all types of land use including residential, commercial and industrial buildings (Thadani and Go 2021) (Figure 19.4). Furthermore, solar panels can adapt to different types of climates from humid tropical areas in Indonesia to mixed-use residential buildings in colder climates found in Canada (Hachem-Vermette et al. 2016). In the city of Calgary, Canada, solar panels were installed on the

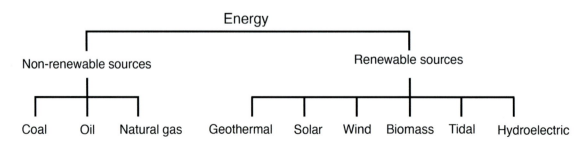

Figure 19.2 Energy sources are commonly organized into two categories: renewable and non-renewable.

Powering Cities

Figure 19.3 Wind turbines, seen here on a building top, do not produce as much electricity compared to their non-renewable fossil fuel counterparts and may not be suitable for all locations.

roofs of supermarkets, office buildings and houses. Despite cold and snowy weather conditions, solar panels generated varied amounts of electricity (Thadani and Go 2021). Yet, the effectiveness of solar energy varies given its dependence on unstable weather conditions. However, at the household level, solar energy can reduce electricity costs, and having solar panels is associated with higher property values and opportunities for households to receive "green energy" subsidies (El-Azab 2021).

19.2.3 Hydro

Hydropower is another widely discussed renewable source of energy. Moran et al. (2018) note that hydropower is the leading source of electricity generation accounting for up to 71 percent of renewable energy supply as of 2016 in (Figure 19.5). For instance, in Ontario, the Hydro One corporation provides electricity to roughly 1.4 million people with over 66 stations and 241 dams (OPG 2023). However, hydroelectric dams are also scrutinized for their environmental and social impact in disrupting river ecology, displacing residents and endangering sacred wildlife (Moran et al. 2018).

While the Earth's climate has changed over the course of its existence, there is no doubt that humans have accelerated this natural warming process at an unprecedented and unsustainable rate. Even if fossil fuel extraction halted worldwide immediately, Buis notes that current carbon dioxide emissions already released into the atmosphere can linger anywhere from 300 to 1,000 years, leaving future generations to bear the potential risks of food insecurity, displacement and poverty (Buis 2019). Consequently, there is a need to transition away from fossil fuels toward more renewable sources of energy that will mitigate the amount of CO_2 and greenhouse gas emissions entering the atmosphere. Enter the concept of net-zero communities and buildings.

19.3 Net-Zero Communities and Buildings

A *net-zero*-energy building is defined as an energy-efficient structure where the onsite production of energy offsets the output of energy from a building. That is, the building

Powering Cities

Figure 19.4 A key benefit of solar energy is that photovoltaic panels can be conveniently integrated into all types of land use including institutional as seen here on the grounds of Middlebury College in Vermont, United States.

Figure 19.5 Hydropower is the leading source of electricity generation.

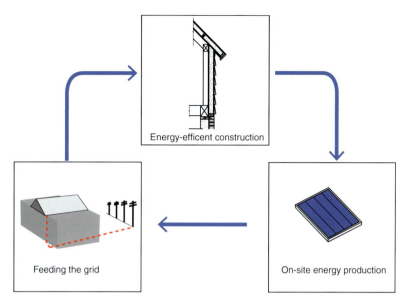

Figure 19.6 The three principles of net-zero buildings are energy-efficient construction, onsite energy production and the feeding of excess power back into the grid.

possesses reduced energy needs whereby the amount of energy generated by a building is equal to or greater than the total amount of energy consumed (Carlisle et al. 2009; Massachusetts Department of Energy Resources n.d.). A net-zero-energy community applies the same principles but on a larger scale. In essence, both net-zero buildings and communities are often powered by renewable energy sources and equipped with sustainable technological amenities that help households and communities avoid reliance on grid electricity.

A major challenge associated with net-zero buildings and communities is that they require significant time and cost. According to the World Bank, cities account for over 70 percent of global carbon emissions and are physically structured in such a way that buildings are structurally reliant on mainly fossil-fuel-powered grids (Dasgupta et al. 2022). Decarbonizing cities by transitioning infrastructure, transportation and services away from using fossil-fuel-powered energy sources is a challenging task that varies across climates, income levels and political regulations. For instance, many older and more populous cities have inherited carbon-intensive infrastructure and produce significant emissions to power their populations.

Carlisle et al. (2009) conceptualize achieving net-zero communities by considering four different types of considerations: buildings, transportation, community infrastructure, and behaviour. The three principles of Net-Zero buildings are energy-efficient construction, onsite energy production and the feeding of power back to the grid (Moghaddasi et al. 2021) (Figure 19.6). Implementing solar panels and natural ventilation is effective for buildings that have access to stable amounts of sunlight and healthy air. Similarly, installing ground-source heat pumps in areas with geothermal potential are effective ways to reduce costs and increase the efficiency of energy production (Carlisle et al. 2009). Maximizing unshaded rooftop surface area in existing and newly created buildings is another consideration to allow for the flexible implementation and cost-effective adaptation of renewable energy systems.

Reducing transportation times is another important consideration. Including diverse land uses and densities along with promoting walkable urban designs can drastically reduce the need for fossil-fuel-reliant transportation methods and promote active transportation methods such as walking and cycling (Brown et al. 2009). Ensuring community infrastructure is sustainable by implementing LED traffic lights and "smart-grid" technology that provides users with feedback on their energy consumption is key to also changing the behavior of energy consumers. Feedback is an important learning tool that allows energy users to regulate and reduce their energy consumption (Darby 2006). Therefore, net-zero energy is not only about ensuring the physical features of buildings limit energy loss and carbon emissions but also about developing an urban form that incentivizes people to take active individual measures to reduce their carbon footprint, generate their own energy, and not rely on the grid.

Powering Cities

19.4 District Heating

A vital yet overlooked part of powering cities is *district heating*, a key component of achieving net-zero communities. In contemporary arrangements, each home contains a boiler or form of heating system that is controlled by the occupants. However, these heating systems are criticized for their lack of efficiency and wasted energy which is especially concerning given buildings already consume about 40 percent of the world's global energy consumption (Ozdemir and Ozdemir 2019). Approximately 85 percent of the energy consumed within buildings is used for heating and cooling purposes, and almost half of the heat losses are from the roof, windows and ventilation elements alone (Ozdemir and Ozdemir 2019). Consequently, there is a growing need to reduce the wasteful consumption of heating and cooling while also increasing the efficiency of heating designs to ensure residents, particularly in northern latitudes, can stay warm during cold seasons and cool during warm seasons.

District energy is undergoing rapid changes in form and function toward more efficient and flexible means of distributing energy to residents. Ravelli (2022) argues that dense urban areas are ideal for district heating and cooling systems as they can easily provide heat to multiple buildings in an efficient and timely manner that reduces primary energy consumption and local greenhouse gas emissions. District heating is a centralized underground infrastructure system often found in major cities where thermal energy, or heat, is generated and then distributed to various buildings via pipelines from a centralized energy facility (Slorach and Stamford 2021) (Figure 19.7). District heating can be powered through renewable energy sources such as geothermal energy, which draws thermal energy from the earth's surface, and central solar heating plants which can significantly reduce environmental impacts by up to 86.5 percent compared to natural gas heating plants (Kim et al. 2019). Previous heating systems faced significant heat loss problems and high installation costs. However, these heating systems have evolved. The goal with current fourth- and future fifth-generation district heating systems is to pursue low-temperature heat sources and use these heat sources to provide more efficient heat to buildings while simultaneously reducing installation costs (Slorach and Stamford 2021). District heating systems are integral for residential space heating and domestic hot water which account for the largest share of energy consumption in buildings (Talebi et al. 2016).

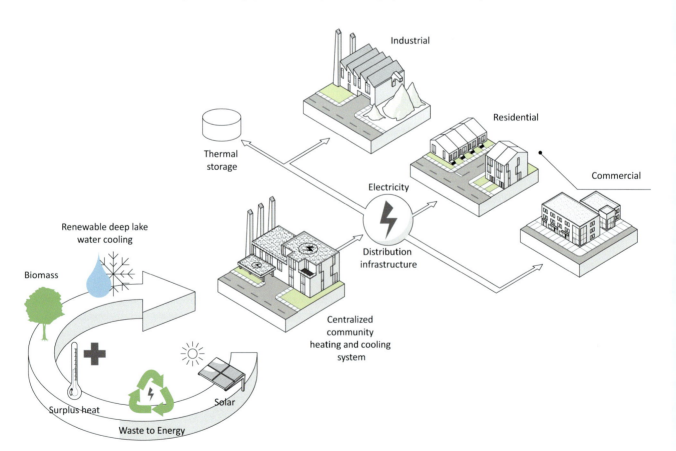

Figure 19.7 District heating is a centralized underground infrastructure system often found in major cities where thermal energy, or heat, is generated and then distributed to various buildings via pipelines from a centralized energy facility.

District heating systems work hand-in-hand with achieving local and national net-zero carbon emission goals. In Denmark, a large proportion of buildings are connected to electricity grids, and around half of the buildings are connected to district heating systems. Connolly et al. (2014) found that excess heat produced from net-zero buildings can help benefit district heating systems. The excess heat can be stored in the building, decreasing the heat needed to supply net-zero buildings. Therefore, net-zero buildings and district heating are complementary systems that can allow for sustainable and efficient energy use. There is great potential to tap into district heating, however, heating systems must also consider the importance of achieving net-zero buildings and communities and work with existing urban infrastructure to supply heat and hot water.

19.5 Winds of Change in Glasgow

White-painted wind turbines stood tall as far as the eye could see in the Whitelee Windfarm in Scotland near Glasgow. The light breeze made their blades swing gently. Inside the visitors' center, school children encircled a guide who walked them through the science of renewable wind energy production method and its contribution to the environment (Figure 19.8).

Whitelee is the UK's largest onshore windfarm. It includes 215 turbines able to generate up to 539 megawatts of electricity which is enough energy to power almost 300,000 homes. This estimate is based on an expected capacity factor of 27 percent, and an average annual domestic electricity usage of 4,266-kilowatt hour. It has shown great promise in terms of providing enough energy to power up to 4.47 million homes in just six months, roughly twice the number of homes in Scotland with leftover sent to other parts of the UK (ScottishPower Renewables 2020).

The International Renewable Energy Agency (IRENA) states that renewable sources of energy would represent up to 86 percent of global energy by 2050. The UK, Sweden and Germany rank as the top three countries to have invested in wind, solar, hydropower and bioenergy as renewable energy sources. Germany, for example, has pledged to transform its electricity supply to 100 percent renewable energy by 2050 and reduce greenhouse gas emissions by 40 percent below 1990 levels by 2020 and by 80–85 percent by 2050 from 1990 levels.

While many countries are turning to renewable sources to meet high energy demands, others cannot rely on renewable sources due to lack of economic means or the lay of their land to support such infrastructure. The overall direction of the world's energy production, however, gives rise to optimism and the lessening of the damaging effects of GHG emissions. If sustainability, by definition, calls to live within the Earth's available means, not tapping into non-renewable resources will leave some for future generations as well.

Figure 19.8 Whitelee is the UK's largest onshore windfarm. It includes 215 turbines able to generate up to 539 megawatts of electricity which is enough energy to power almost 300,000 homes.

19.6 A Gift from the Sun in Almere

Solar panels on rooftops catch your eyes when you enter. Planned by Dutch architect Rem Koolhaus, the Noordplassen district of Almere in the Netherlands showcases renewable energy. On the outskirts of the community there is a massive solar farm comprised of 520 panels, spanning an area of 7,000 m² (64,600 sq. ft.) – the equivalent of 1.5 football fields. It is the world's third-largest solar energy center that supplies most of the development's electricity and heating needs (Bellini 2020).

The process of utilizing solar energy for district heating is relatively simple. Water is heated using the energy collected by the panels to pump it into the system which provides 2,700 homes with hot water and central heating. Annually, the plant provides 9,750 gigajoules of renewable energy, enough to supply one-third of all the electricity needs of the community. By using district heating system and solar energy, carbon dioxide emissions in Almere have been lowered by 50 percent, the equivalent of every household driving 12,000 kilometers (7,456 miles) less each year.

The community's success also lies in the design of its dwellings. There are 550 solar homes and 600 low-energy homes, and more solar homes are planned, all of which will have a minimum of 10 m² (108 sq. ft.) of solar panels installed on each roof or facade. Typical housing in Almere is built to be 10 percent more energy efficient than conventionally constructed homes (Figure 19.9).

A transfer to generating power from renewable energy sources required intervention by national and local authorities. The central Dutch government has implemented a series of policies aimed at incentivizing the use of solar panels in the built environment. For instance, an energy tax rebate is awarded for people who generate their own sustainable power by using solar panels. Homes that generate surplus power have the option to send it back to the grid in exchange for credit.

19.7 Harvesting Energy from Waste

Domestic recycling programs have, it seems, become a natural way out of a difficult situation. They have helped reduce mounting loads in landfills and are regarded as the politically correct thing to do. Moreover, they represent the single most

Figure 19.9 In Almere, the Netherlands, there are 550 solar homes and 600 low-energy homes, all which have a minimum of 10 m² (108 sq. ft.) of solar panels installed on each roof or façade.

Powering Cities

Figure 19.9 (Continued)

successful form of mass education about the environment. Waste can also help reduce or even eliminate our energy bills.

It seems to work in Hammarby Sjöstad near Stockholm, Sweden. Home to 20,000 people, the place is a refreshing approach to sustainable design (Future Communities 2014). Mixed-use buildings, cyclist/pedestrian priority, carbon neutrality and net-zero energy consumption are some of the principles that the district was modeled on. As for waste, an ENVAC Waste Smart system uses pressurized air to force it to central collection points from which it is transported to incineration plants. This eliminates the need for pick-up services and, as a result, significantly reduces the carbon produced by trucks. Yet only one-third of the waste plant is devoted to incineration. The remaining two-thirds are for emission management – that is, these sectors ensure that 94 percent of emissions are released as water vapor. In addition, the residents' liquid sewage is converted into heat and biogas, which in turn is used to power municipal buses, and solid sewage is used as compost for forested areas (Figure 19.10). The results are impressive. Some 47 percent of Hammarby's energy needs come from household waste, 34 from purified wastewater and the rest from biofuel and solar power.

The success of Hammarby lies not only in its incredible infrastructure, but also in the commitment of its citizens to sustainability. Seeking to improve on these already impressive commitments to environmental living, Hammarby's developers set up an education center to encourage pro-environmental behavior on a micro level. These initiatives have been highly successful in encouraging a variety of green behaviors.

19.8 Final Thoughts

The impending consequences of climate change on urban environments are not to be understated. Cities are vast contributors to global anthropogenic climate change by emitting a vast amount of greenhouse gases. Yet, cities are simultaneously vulnerable to the effects of climate change-induced sea-level rise and extreme weather events. The world is at the beginning phase of changing how communities consume energy at both the national and local scale, thus the goal of net-zero communities and district heating systems requires significant attention. Analyzing the price and accessibility of renewable energy sources is a key consideration as planners, municipalities and nations seek to adapt to the impacts of global warming. It will

Powering Cities

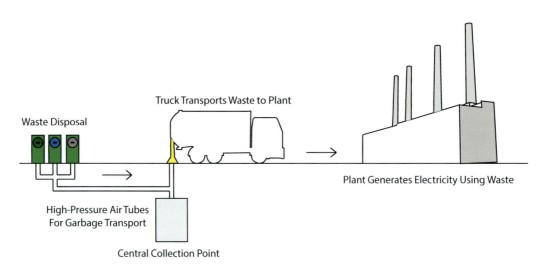

Figure 19.10 In Hammarby Sjöstad near Stockholm, Sweden an ENVAC Waste Smart system uses pressurized air to force it to central collection points from which it is transported to an energy producing incineration plant.

be essential for planners to also consider how climate resiliency measures will fall along unequal lines and find ways to address these inequalities in access to sustainable and climate change-resilient technologies.

References

Barbir, F., Veziroğlu, T. N. and Plass, H. J. (1990). Environmental damage due to fossil fuels use. *International Journal of Hydrogen Energy* 15(10): 739–749. Retrieved July 6, 2023, from https://doi.org/10.1016/0360-3199(90)90005-J

Bellini, E. (2020). More than 100 GW of solar in the Netherlands? Possible by 2050. *PV Magazine*. Retrieved July 6, 2023, from www.pv-magazine.com/2020/04/22/more-than-100-gw-of-solar-in-the-netherlands-possible-by-2050/

Brown, B. B., Yamada, I., Smith, K. R., Zick, C. D., Kowaleski-Jones, L. and Fan, J. X. (2009). Mixed land use and walkability: variations in land use measures and relationships with BMI, overweight, and obesity. *Health & Place* 15(4): 1130–1141. Retrieved July 6, 2023, from https://doi.org/10.1016/j.healthplace.2009.06.008

Buis, A. (2019). The atmosphere: getting a handle on carbon dioxide. Global climate change: vital signs of the planet. *NASA*. Retrieved July 6, 2023, from https://climate.nasa.gov/news/2915/the-atmosphere-getting-a-handle-on-carbon-dioxide

Carlisle, N., Van Geet, O. and Pless, S. (2009). *Definition of a 'Zero Net Energy' Community*. Retrieved July 6, 2023, from https://doi.org/10.2172/969716

Chancel, L. (2022). Global carbon inequality over 1990–2019. *Nature Sustainability* 5(11): 931–938. Retrieved July 6, 2023, from https://doi.org/10.1038/s41893-022-00955-z

Connolly, D., Lund, H., Mathiesen, B. V., Werner, S., Möller, B., Persson, U., Boermans, T., Trier, D., Østergaard, P. A. and Nielsen, S. (2014). Heat roadmap Europe: combining district heating with heat savings to decarbonise the EU energy system. *Energy Policy* 65: 475–489.

Darby, S. (2006). *The Effectiveness of Feedback on Energy Consumption: A Review for Defra of the Literature on Metering, Billing and Direct Displays*. Environmental Change Insititute, University of Oxford. Retrieved July 6, 2023, from www.eci.ox.ac.uk/research/energy/downloads/smart-metering-report.pdf

Darwish, A. S. and Al-Dabbagh, R. (2020). Wind energy state of the art: present and future technology advancements. *Renewable Energy and Environmental Sustainability* 5: 7. Retrieved July 6, 2023, from https://doi.org/10.1051/rees/2020003

Dasgupta, S., Lall, S. and Wheeler, D. (2022). Cutting global carbon emissions: where do cities stand? *Sustainable Cities*. Retrieved July 6, 2023, from https://blogs.worldbank.org/sustainablecities/cutting-global-carbon-emissions-where-do-cities-stand

El-Azab, R. (2021). Smart homes: potentials and challenges. *Clean Energy* 5(2): 302–315. Retrieved July 6, 2023, from https://doi.org/10.1093/ce/zkab010

Filho, W. L., Matandirotya, N. R., Lütz, J. M., Alemu, E. A., Brearley, F. Q., Baidoo, A. A., Kateka, A., Ogendi, G. M., Adane, G. B., Emiru, N. and Mbih, R. A. (2021). Impacts of climate change to African indigenous communities and examples of adaptation responses. *Nature Communications* 12(1): Article 1. Retrieved July 6, 2023, from https://doi.org/10.1038/s41467-021-26540-0

Future Communities (2014). "Building a 'green' city extension." Retrieved July 6, 2023, from www.ghd.com/en/expertise/future-communities.aspx

Hachem-Vermette, C., Cubi, E. and Bergerson, J. (2016). Energy performance of a solar mixed-use community. *Sustainable Cities and Society* 27: 145–151. Retrieved July 6, 2023, from https://doi.org/10.1016/j.scs.2015.08.002

IEA (n.d.). Energy security – topics. Retrieved July 6, 2023, from www.iea.org/topics/energy-security

Intergovernmental Panel on Climate Change (IPCC) (2022). *The Ocean and Cryosphere in a Changing Climate: Special Report of the Intergovernmental Panel on Climate Change* (1st ed.). Cambridge University Press. Cambridge. Retrieved July 6, 2023, from https://doi.org/10.1017/9781009157964

Kim, M.-H., Kim, D., Heo, J, and Lee, D.-W. (2019). Techno-economic analysis of hybrid renewable energy system with solar district heating for net zero energy community. *Energy*, 187: 115916. Retrieved July 6, 2023, from https://doi.org/10.1016/j.energy.2019.115916

Krane, J. (2017). Climate change and fossil fuel: an examination of risks for the energy industry and producer states. *MRS Energy & Sustainability* 4: E2. Retrieved July 6, 2023, from https://doi.org/10.1557/mre.2017.3

Kuşkaya, S. and Bilgili, F. (2020). The wind energy-greenhouse gas nexus: the wavelet-partial wavelet coherence model approach. *Journal of Cleaner Production* 245: 118872. Retrieved July 6, 2023, from https://doi.org/10.1016/j.jclepro.2019.118872

Massachusetts Department of Energy Resources (n.d.). What is a zero net energy building? *Mass.gov*. Retrieved July 6, 2023, from www.mass.gov/service-details/what-is-a-zero-net-energy-building

Masson-Delmotte, V., Zhai, P., Pörtner, H.-O., Roberts, D., Skea, J., Shukla, P., Pirani, A., Moufouma-Okia, W., Péan, C., Pidcock, R., Connors, S., Matthews, J., Chen, Y., Zhou, X., Gomis, M., Lonnoy, E., Maycock, T., Tignor, M. and Waterfield, T. (2018). Global warming of 1.5°C: an IPCC special report on the impacts of global warming of 1.5°C above pre-industrial levels and related global greenhouse gas emission pathways, in the context of strengthening the global response to the threat of climate change, sustainable development, and efforts to eradicate poverty. Retrieved July 6, 2023, from www.ipcc.ch/site/assets/uploads/sites/2/2019/06/SR15_Full_Report_Low_Res.pdf

McMichael, C., Dasgupta, S., Ayeb-Karlsson, S. and Kelman, I. (2020). A review of estimating population exposure to sea-level rise and the relevance for migration. *Environmental Research Letters* 15(12): 123005. Retrieved July 6, 2023, from https://doi.org/10.1088/1748-9326/abb398

Moghaddasi, H., Culp, C. and Vanegas, J. (2021). Net zero energy communities: integrated power system, building and transport sectors. *Energies* 14(21): Article 21. Retrieved July 6, 2023, from https://doi.org/10.3390/en14217065

Moran, E. F., Lopez, M. C., Moore, N., Müller, N. and Hyndman, D. W. (2018). Sustainable hydropower in the 21st century. *Proceedings of the National Academy of Sciences* 115(47): 11891–11898. Retrieved July 6, 2023, from https://doi.org/10.1073/pnas.1809426115

Morse, R. (2008). *Environmental Justice Through the Eye of Hurricane Katrina*. Joint Center For Political and Economic Studies Health Policy Institute. Washington, D.C. Retrieved July 6, 2023, from https://inequality.stanford.edu/sites/default/files/media/_media/pdf/key_issues/Environment_policy.pdf

OPG (2023). Powering Ontario > Hydroelectric power. *OPG*. Retrieved July 6, 2023, from www.opg.com/powering-ontario/our-generation/hydro/

Owusu, P. A. and Asumadu-Sarkodie, S. (2016). A review of renewable energy sources, sustainability issues and climate change mitigation. *Cogent Engineering* 3(1): 1167990. Retrieved December 6, 2023, from https://doi.org/10.1080/23311916.2016.1167990

Ozdemir, Y. and Ozdemir, S. (2019). Residential heating system selection using the generalized Choquet integral method with the perspective of energy. *Energy & Environment* 30(1): 121–140. Retrieved July 6, 2023, from https://doi.org/10.1177/0958305X18787298

Perera, F. (2018). Pollution from fossil-fuel combustion is the leading environmental threat to global pediatric health and equity: solutions exist. *International Journal of Environmental Research and Public Health*, 15(1). https://doi.org/10.3390/ijerph15010016

Rae, J. W. B., Zhang, Y. G., Liu, X., Foster, G. L., Stoll, H. M. and Whiteford, R. D. M. (2021). Atmospheric CO2 over the past 66 million years from marine archives. *Annual Review of Earth and Planetary Sciences* 49(1): 609–641. Retrieved July 6, 2023, from https://doi.org/10.1146/annurev-earth-082420-063026

Ravelli, S. (2022). District heating and cooling towards net zero. *Energies* 15(16): Article 16. Retrieved July 6, 2023, from https://doi.org/10.3390/en15166033

ScottishPower Renewables (2020). Whitelee windfarm. *ScottishPower Renewables*. Retrieved July 6, 2023, from www.whiteleewindfarm.co.uk/whitelee-windfarm-about-us

Slorach, P. C. and Stamford, L. (2021). Net zero in the heating sector: technological options and environmental sustainability from now to 2050. *Energy Conversion and Management* 230: 113838. Retrieved July 6, 2023, from https://doi.org/10.1016/j.enconman.2021.113838

Smith, C. L. (2012). The energy challenge. *Applied Petrochemical Research* 2(1): 3–6. Retrieved July 6, 2023, from https://doi.org/10.1007/s13203-012-0010-x

Smith, K. A. (2021, June 7). How communities of color are hurt most by climate change. *Forbes Advisor*. Retrieved July 6, 2023, from www.forbes.com/advisor/personal-finance/communities-of-color-and-climate-change/

Solarin, S. A. and Bello, M. O. (2022). Wind energy and sustainable electricity generation: evidence from Germany. *Environment, Development and Sustainability* 24(7): 9185–9198. Retrieved July 6, 2023, from https://doi.org/10.1007/s10668-021-01818-x

Strazzante, E., Rycken, S. and Winkler, V. (2021). Global north and global south: how climate change uncovers global inequalities – Generation Climate Europe. *Generation Climate Europe*. Retrieved July 6, 2023, from https://gceurope.org/global-north-and-global-south-how-climate-change-uncovers-global-inequalities/

Talebi, B., Mirzaei, P. A., Bastani, A. and Haghighat, F. (2016). A review of district heating systems: modeling and optimization. *Frontiers in Built Environment* 2. Retrieved July 6, 2023, from www.frontiersin.org/articles/10.3389/fbuil.2016.00022

Thadani, H. L. and Go, Y. I. (2021). Integration of solar energy into low-cost housing for sustainable development: case study in developing countries. *Heliyon* 7(12): e08513. Retrieved July 6, 2023, from https://doi.org/10.1016/j.heliyon.2021.e08513

Younger, S. (2022). NASA study: rising sea level could exceed estimates for U.S. coasts. Global climate change: vital signs of the planet. *NASA*. Retrieved July 6, 2023, from https://climate.nasa.gov/news/3232/nasa-study-rising-sea-level-could-exceed-estimates-for-us-coasts

Zohuri, B. and McDaniel, P. (2021). Energy insight: an energy essential guide. In B. Zohuri and P. McDaniel (eds.), *Introduction to Energy Essentials*, pp. 321–370. Academic Press. Cambridge, MA. Retrieved July 6, 2023, from https://doi.org/10.1016/B978-0-323-90152-9.00009-8

CHAPTER 20
Old Buildings, New Life

Buildings can be regarded as historic windows to the past and as monuments to events or people. Appreciating the value of historic buildings and methods of their preservation at the micro scale can provide insight into how designers can maintain the character and identity of cities. This chapter outlines the various strategies for retooling old buildings while keeping their original architectural character by analyzing the transformation of buildings from technological and functional points of view.

20.1 The Value of the Past of Buildings

Some old buildings are embedded with a rich history worth preserving. Preservation of buildings and monuments dates back to the Roman Empire. Theodoric the Great, king of the Ostrogoths and ruler of the independent Ostrogothic Kingdom of Italy (493 AD to 526 AD), was known for his desire to conserve and restore culturally significant works of art and buildings, including the Aurelian Walls, aqueducts and even the Colosseum which remains a focal piece of Rome's contemporary cultural urban landscape (Jokhileto 1986) (Figure 20.1). Yet, this appreciation of the past has not remained stable throughout history. In the latter half of the twentieth century, demolition was perceived as pivotal to launch nations into a new era of progress and modernity. In the United Kingdom, the demolition of historic small houses and castles accelerated as property owners began to see large estates as not only inefficient to maintain, but also as relics of an old way of life antithetical to socio-economic modernization shifts occurring at the time (Waugh 2023). In the United States, 7.5 million homes were destroyed between 1950 and 1980 to make way for suburban single-family detached homes

Figure 20.1 Theodoric, king of the Ostrogoths and ruler of the independent Ostrogothic Kingdom of Italy (493 AD to 526 AD) was known for the restoration of culturally significant works of art and buildings including the Coliseum, which remains a focal piece of Rome's cultural heritage.

Old Buildings, New Life

with state-of-the-art amenities (Ammon 2016). The large-scale clearance of buildings was a common practice in making way for a new socio-political national vision of modernity and progress in which the past was perceived as a burden, not a way forward.

In contrast, according to Yazdani Mehr (2019), preserving buildings is key to maintaining the character of cities for present and future generations to learn from and appreciate. Yazdani Mehr (2019) also note that during the Renaissance, extending the life of a heritage building to ensure it was functional was paramount for cultural progress. Furthermore, in today's contemporary setting, creative industries view old buildings and cultural heritage sites as intangible assets for sustainable and productive workplaces to produce new innovations (Arcos-Pumarola et al. 2023). Therefore, rather than live and work in banal buildings, people, and nowadays companies, appreciate the value of the "old" for both cultural and economic reasons.

20.2 Circular Economy and Adaptability

Circular economy refers to a sustainable framework that aims to change human production and consumption patterns along with rethinking business models to ensure world issues such as climate change, waste and pollution are tackled. The circular economy is based on three principles: eliminating waste and pollution, circulating products and materials at their highest value, and regenerating nature (Ellen MacArthur Foundation 2023) (Figure 20.2). Embedded in the circular economy model is the goal of minimizing the negative consequences of human activity such as urban sprawl, wasted materials and greenhouse gas emissions through the application of reducing, reusing and recycling material (Rahla et al. 2021; Scarpellini et al. 2020).

The circular economy model is growing in acceptance. In the past, for a building to be transformed, workers had to demolish

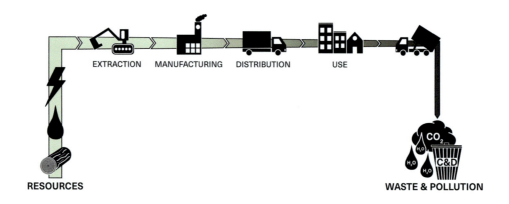

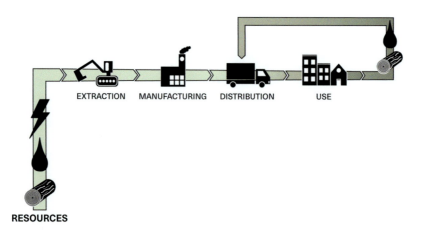

Figure 20.2 In a circular economy, the end-of-life idea that defines the linear economy is replaced with revitalization, through the use of renewable resources and impeccable design of products to maintain their quality for as long as possible and eventual reuse.

Figure 20.3 Buildings on their spaces and components can be designed for adaptive reuse or/and to be added to like this old warehouse in Hafen City, Hamburg, Germany (left), and a hotel in Montreal, Canada to which a residential wing was added.

some of it, thereby creating waste. Demolition is not an entirely wasteful procedure if a building is too unsafe or in critical need of repair or if the structural integrity of the building is too weak to function in any form of land use. However, the increased shortage of resources and the growing understanding of the environmental and economic toll of the complete destruction merits the re-evaluation of current building practices.

Designing buildings that operate in a closed-loop system is an effective way of conserving energy, cutting down costs and helping create environmentally sustainable cities. Buildings and spaces and components can be designed to be reused or added to, like the buildings shown here in Hafen City, Hamburg, Germany, and Montreal, Canada, for different purposes and therefore help contribute to reduce waste (Figure 20.3). If materials cannot be reused for different purposes, they can be recycled to make different products and building materials to avoid landfill buildup. On a micro-scale, when thinking of individual rooms in a home, ensuring that there is room for flexibility in how one may reconfigure their living spaces to meet a resident's changing lifestyle is important, and being able to reuse and recycle material from different spaces can help reduce waste and conserve energy. For the circular economy model to effectively work, one must reflect on all aspects of a building, such as the circulation, main utilities, windows and stairs, which are just a few aspects of a building that can be designed for flexibility and conservation.

Demolishing buildings is an expensive process that produces an excessive amount of waste that can be detrimental to public health and displace low-income families (Elshaboury et al. 2022; Bristol 2015; Hansman 2017). Indeed, buildings take a great deal of energy to make. From steel girders and concrete to the appliances and furnishings, buildings rely on energy-intensive extraction, manufacturing, transportation and construction techniques that pose significant environmental strain on the world's depleting finite supply of natural resources. Research shows that 50 percent of all construction worldwide is for end-of-life activities in which buildings are demolished and not reused, particularly in the United States which produces 534 million tons of construction and demolition waste (Akanbi et al. 2018; Kibert 2016).

Rather than demolishing and disposing of building materials, there is a need to invest in the circular economy, which involves transitioning from an environmentally and economically wasteful "take, make, dispose" mind-set to a more sustainable "reuse, reduce, recycle" paradigm of consumption (Patwa et al. 2021). Foster (2020) argues for an adaptive reuse circular nexus specific to old heritage buildings that focuses on refurbishing, repurposing and refusing or adding new elements to buildings. In other words, heritage buildings can be refurbished to take on new purposes, or planners can choose to refuse to compromise with certain elements of the building.

20.3 Strategies for a Building's Renewal

Appreciating its contribution to the past is an important foundation of a building's renewal process. Preservation experts must decide which strategies to incorporate in their plans. There are three major schools of thought in the preservation movement: a conservationist view, a functionalist view, and a view of adding onto existing old structures.

20.3.1 Conservationist View: Absolute Preservation

The conservationist school of thought is one of absolute preservation. When there is an old building deemed worth preserving, all its parts must be respected. Very little about the interior and exterior should be altered, changed or repurposed so as to provide a unique sense of place and accurate window of the past (Markham et al. 2016). The rationale behind this perspective comes from the view of local heritage at risk. According to the 2020 Heritage at Risk World Report, approximately 65 percent of sites with artistic or cultural significance are at danger of physical deterioration due to a lack of proper maintenance and a poor conservation state (Machat and Ziesemer 2020). Building conservation heritage refers to buildings as a legacy of tangible items with intangible attributes that must be conserved for their socio-cultural and historic value (ICOMOS 2011). Heritage conservation therefore emphasizes delaying the natural deterioration processes of buildings (Otero 2021). This conservationist framework therefore argues that a building's physical structures and social purpose will remain the same throughout its lifespan.

Enia and Martella (2019) propose a "do nothing" strategy where, simply put, planners do nothing to change a building. Under certain circumstances, this strategy can work as a flexible approach to protect a place and even reclaim its cultural importance in communities such as the Léon Aucocsquare in Bordeaux, France. In Bordeaux, the city council asked two urban planners to redesign a small square outside the city center. After careful consideration of the logical use of the site, the planners responded that the place needed no modifications – not due to a lack of desire to change anything – but because the optimal way to preserve the social character of the square was leaving it alone (Enia and Martella 2019).

The conservation of buildings, however, is a complex task. Conservation is about the physical and cultural preservation of a building's appearance, structure and identity, while also negotiating these qualities with the various actors (Taher Tolou Del et al. 2020; Yarrow 2018). Except for the frequent cleaning and maintenance of the building's exterior and interior, nothing has changed from the doorknobs, the woodwork, to the windows of the building. Maintenance procedures involve assessing and cleaning spaces to prolong the longevity of artefacts, and retrofitting intervention is only employed if damage has already occurred to a part of a building (Figure 20.4). Support of this thorough conservation process, however, is not limited to a select group of urban planners, organizations and admirers, but also political bodies.

In 1940, the UK passed the Town and Country Planning Act which legislatively protected buildings individual properties and "conservation areas" as a way to guard the exterior appearance of buildings (Yarrow 2018). At the micro-scale, some buildings deemed worth preserving are protected by preservation and conservation laws to ensure both the interior and exterior of buildings remain intact. These top-down regulations include preventative actions such as zoning laws that prevent buildings from being renovated and laws that control the surrounding environmental conditions of a building (Otero 2021). Consequently, these laws ensure a building's function and purpose remain preserved for public audiences to appreciate. Therefore, the conservationist view prioritizes preservation, historical integrity, and very few, if any, changes to a building.

Figure 20.4 Maintenance of heritage buildings involve assessing and cleaning spaces to prolong the longevity of artefacts is shown here in Hamburg's City Hall.

20.3.2 Functionalist View: Keeping the Exterior, Changing the Interior

The functionalist view strikes a balance between restoring or repurposing a historic building. Functionalists agree with conservationists insofar as ensuring the exterior of the building is maintained to provide a visual depiction of the past. Where the two streams diverge is that the functionalist view aims at performing extensive adaptations for new users. That is, a building can be both functional and historically respectful, whereby one keeps the exterior of the building the same but can make needed changes to the interior (Austin et al. 1988). Remedial and restoration processes can bring items to their former condition, however, as the components of a building continue to age, it becomes more challenging to find the resources and appropriate techniques to bring the interior of a building back to its period of origin (Mekonnen et al. 2022). Furthermore, ensuring the building serves a functional purpose that takes advantage of modern trends and patterns of urban planning can also serve to improve access, tourism and cultural appreciation (Figure 20.5). Importantly, the functionalist view conceptualizes adaptions and alterations to buildings as complementary to cultural heritage, and changes should be respectful of the historical character of the building.

The Intergovernmental Panel on Climate Change (IPCC) Report views adaptation as a nexus of structural, institutional, ecological and behavioral strategies to adjust human systems in response to harmful processes or beneficial processes to the natural and human environment (IPCC 2021). Indeed, frameworks such as Foster's multi-prong adaptive reuse model take an environmental emphasis on the value of converting a building into a new use or change the purpose of the building by reducing as much waste as possible (Foster 2020). Indeed, the benefits of altering spaces can be extended to the preservation of cultural heritage sites and old buildings. Scholars emphasize that urban planners must shift heritage conservation from a view of "heritage through conservation" to "conservation through transformation" in which alterations to a building prolong the life of a building, enhancing access to a rich understanding and education about the past (Arfa et al. 2022).

The Museum of Fine Arts in Montreal, Canada, serves as a prime example of this adaptation. Architects Edward Maxwell and William Sutherland Maxwell's Beaux-Arts pavilion was inspired by the prevalence of French culture in the city through implementing "sober and majestic" motifs to the facade (Germain 2007) (Figure 20.6). The stone facade and pillars position the museum as an important institution for learning and exploring the past. The building itself is home to important cultural artifacts and the architectural motifs that line the building are an homage to ancient civilizations, but nowadays serve as a reminder of Montreal's growth as an artistic hub for history and culture (Montreal Museum of Fine Arts 2023; Germain 2007).

Even as the building's interior changed with a nearby modernized pavilion and a more contemporary-designed building across the street, the facade of the original building remains the same. The exterior serves as a reminder of Montreal's history and a symbol of the city's cultural roots. Changing the interior of the historic museum to fit the needs of current and future generations, however, does not compromise the cultural value of the building. As the loss of cultural heritage and artifacts continues to endanger the lifespan of buildings, interior adaptations are a valuable tool to enhance tourism and access to educate visitors about these unique spaces (Seekamp and Jo 2020).

Figure 20.5 The functionalist view of conservation aims at performing extensive adaptations for new users while keeping the building's exterior, as was done in this ice-making factory in Valencia, Spain, which was turned into a social hub (left) and a bank in Montreal, Canada turned into a cafe (right).

Old Buildings, New Life

Figure 20.6 Over the years the Museum of Fine Arts in Montreal, Canada underwent extensive adaptation and additions, yet its original facade was kept intact.

20.3.3 Addition View: New Parts with "Old Character"

The third viewpoint is preserving the original layout of the building but adding components that respect its historic and cultural character. This view of "adding" onto buildings combines the idea that buildings are worth preserving in their physical and social use (Enia and Martella 2019; ICOMOS 2011) but can also be functional in their purpose. For example, designing parts for buildings that focus on disassembly, such as making mechanical joint solutions more flexible for dismantling, can prolong the service life of heritage buildings (Eberhardt et al. 2019). The inherent value of an old building can serve as an opportunity for the creation of a new building. By building a new room or constructing an extension the lifespan of heritage structures can be extended, leading to new uses, economic opportunities and jobs (Rudan 2023). Farjami and Türker (2019) argue that the preservation and repurposing of old buildings with additional features can foster a sustainable form of conservation whereby tourism serves as a financial support tool for preservation.

There are various strategies for introducing additions to buildings. Robert (1989) argues additions can be categorized into seven strategies of building: within, over, around, alongside buildings, and built in the same or completely new style compared to the original building using new or recycled material (Figure 20.7). For example, suppose a homeowner wants to add a new wing to an older building to allow for more

On top

Over

Figure 20.7 Types of additions to buildings.

208

Figure 20.7 (Continued)

space. The new wing can be added as an extension that preserves the original building where the wing can be built with recycled material in a style that respects the cultural aesthetic and character of the building while cutting environmental and economic costs (Arfa et al. 2022). Therefore, a building can be financed and repurposed in an economically and environmentally sustainable way. However, it is equally important to ensure that preservation and tourism do not come at a social cost that threatens the heritage value of the site (Farjami and Türker 2019; Rudan 2023). Therefore, when adding to a building, there is a balance that must be maintained between ensuring a closed-loop, environmentally sustainable heritage site while also ensuring the quality of heritage materials and values are maintained.

20.4 Creative Hub in Amsterdam

The history of "Netherland Shipbuilding Company," known as NDSM (Nederlandse Do ken Scheepsbouq Maatschappij), after the shipyard that operated here, dates to the seventeenth century and ship building for the then powerful East India Company (I amsterdam 2020; Smart Cities Dive 2017). Over the centuries, a succession of companies built some of the world's largest vessels on this site. Failing to compete with other ship building nations, since the 1990s the Dutch gradually stopped operations here, leaving these enormous buildings empty.

In the following decade, squatting artists began to use the space as a large communal studio, resisting eviction attempts. They campaigned for the refurbishing of the space as a creative co-working space, eventually generating enough support to sway the city government to join. The space was retooled by Max van Aerschot architects, who sought to mix existing elements with new ones to create a dynamic and stimulating environment to work in (Figure 20.8).

Today, the NDSM still retains the features that made it a shipyard such as old work sheds, slipways and cranes which are now national monuments, and includes a lot of space of creative experimentation. Artists, designers, architects and other entrepreneurs have used abandoned industrial hangars to establish their workshops and ateliers. Companies in the creative industries such as MTV Networks have established themselves there, turning the place into a springboard of novel artistic ideas and expression. The entire area can be thought of as being to Amsterdam what Brooklyn is to New York: out of the box creative hub and a field of experimentation for spontaneous urban enterprises.

It took the stubbornness and persistence of artists to bring life to and make this location special. To fuel creativity and generate new ideas, cities need such places and the people who create in them.

20.5 Buildings' Rebirth in North Adams

Notable in North Adams in northwestern Massachusetts's Berkshire County is an area with sprawling complex of large industrial brick buildings of various sizes. Starting in the colonial period, from the late 1770s to the mid-1800s, manufacturing took place in the area, as it was located at the junction of two branches of the Hoosic river, which supported small-scale industries due to the river's waterpower. Businesses found on and near the site included wholesale shoe manufacturers, a sawmill, cabinetmakers, hat manufacturers and ironworks to name a few.

Old Buildings, New Life

Figure 20.8 The old Netherland Shipbuilding Company (NDSM) building now houses space for artists, architects and entrepreneurs in creative fields.

In 1860, the print works O. Arnold and Company set up shop on part of the site, with the most modern equipment for printing cloths. The company became a major supplier of fabric for the Union Army and the largest employer in North Adams during the Civil War. However, due to competition, the print work had to close part of its facility in 1942. Sprague Electric Company then bought the site that same year. While it left most building exteriors intact, the company made many changes to the interiors to turn the previous textile mills into an electronics plant. Sprague became especially important during World War II to design and manufacture high-tech weapon systems. The complex was a major research and development center focusing on semi-conducting materials. In 1985, once more due to competition from lower-waged producing nations, Sprague had to close its operations.

A year later, the city of North Adams began seeking a way to use the vacant Sprague plant. When the William College Museum of Art was looking for an economic space where large works of contemporary art could be exhibited, the mayor of North Adams, John Barrett III, suggested the former Sprague site, and the idea of creating a contemporary arts center came about. Architect David Childs was appointed lead architect of the newly named Massachusetts Museum of Contemporary Art (MASS MoCA) project in 1992, and with the help of architects Simeon Bruner, Frank Gehry and Robert Venturi, the design was completed, and the museum opened to the public in 1999, to continue the site's long history of innovation and experimentation in a new endeavor (MASS MoCA n.d.).

Originally, the center was to serve as a place for the permanent display of contemporary art, but its purpose evolved to become a place for changing exhibitions and a venue for other artistic events as well as supporting the creation of new art. Today MASS MoCA is one of the world's most dynamic centres for creating and enjoying current art which attracts local and international visitors. The museum engages in a variety of art such as music, film, photography and theater. Most of the work

Old Buildings, New Life

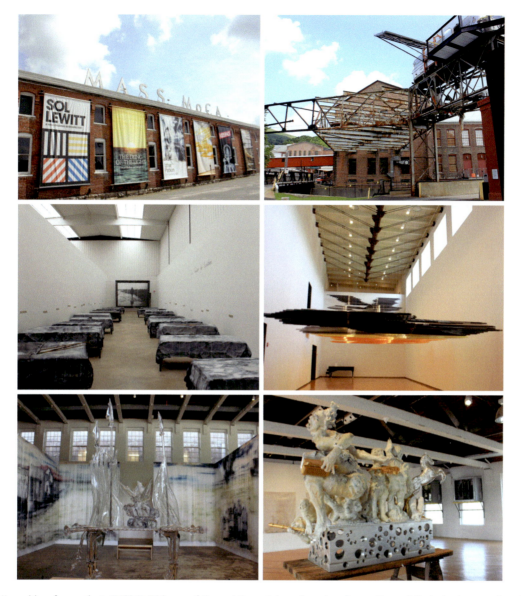

Figure 20.9 Housed in a former plant, MASS MoCA is one of the world's most dynamic centers for creating and displaying large- and small-scale contemporary art that attracts local and international visitors.

exhibited is created at the museum by artists who are brought to North Adams throughout the year as visiting residence (Figure 20.9).

20.6 Bergen's Colourful Structures

The ten wooden four-story buildings about 10 meters (30 feet) wide each, stand out along the wharf of Bergen's old port in Norway for their architecture and striking colours. Painted ochre and saffron they belong to a distant past. The shops that occupied the ground floor told that they assume a new use. More buildings are at the heart of the block. It seems that the place was frozen in time and one can imagine fishermen stepping out of lower floor warehouses and parents calling children from upper balconies. At one place workers were restoring the foundation of a structure while paying meticulous attention to details (Figure 20.10).

Bryggen, as the place is known locally, is recognized as one of the oldest port cities of Norway dating back to the twelfth century. The city served as an important center of trade for the Hanseatic League from the fourteenth to sixteenth century, a trade federation between northern European cities, mostly German. They established an office in the port and the harbor served as the hub to control the trade of cod.

Old Buildings, New Life

Figure 20.10 The overall preservation of Bryggen's wooden structures in Bergen, Norway, is a fine example of how a nation and a city pays tribute to the past.

Several fires have ravaged Bryggen but each time the town was rebuilt. The port's current unique architecture originated after the fire of 1702. Vernacular wood laying method distinguishes its design, coupled with the houses' medieval aesthetic and use of colors. Only sixty-two of the town's original structures remain, typically two to three stories tall. Construction methods, materials and use of urban space in Bryggen reflect the fourteenth-century German culture that colonized the area, with long parallel rows of buildings facing the ocean, wooden houses for the merchants to stay the winter and storerooms (UNESCO World Heritage Centre n.d.).

In April 1944 the Dutch vessel Voorbode, loaded with 123,831 kg (273,000 lb) of explosives caught fire and exploded in Bergen's port, levelling many buildings, heavily damaging the row's exterior and foundation. It stood vacant until the decision to restore them was made. The preservation began in the 1960s and accelerated when in 1979 it was placed on the World Heritage List, recognized as perfect example of the culture and history of Hanseatic merchants. According to UNESCO, rebuilding has traditionally followed old patterns and methods, therefore leaving its main structure preserved, which is a relic of an ancient wooden urban structure once common in northern Europe.

The overall preservation of Bryggen and the row is a fine example of how a nation and a city pays tribute to the past.

Though there were many circumstances and reasons to demolish the place, the voices that recognized its importance as a link to the past won. Centuries-long commitments are necessary to preserve buildings, create architectural heritage and unique places. The Norwegians selected the route of self-imposed discipline that is appreciated now and will be valued in years to come.

20.7 Retooling the Past in Lodz

What draw newcomers to Lodz, Poland's third largest city, in the early nineteenth century was robust textile manufacturing that was introduced in 1838 by Ludwik Geyer, who went on to build a sprawling plant powered by steam. Seizing on the opportunity, other entrepreneurs soon followed. One of them, Izrael Kalmanowicz Poznanski, went on to expand a modest warehouse and a shop into a thriving fabrication place of an immense scale called Manufaktura. Hundreds of looms filled floors of multi-story brick buildings.

After World War II, the plant grew back to its former production levels, creating thousands of jobs. The economic crises of the 1990s caused the re-established company to fail, and the factory was abandoned. Manufaktura had to be repurposed for a different demand and use. The city no longer needed a textile factory, but a center that would display the country's

Old Buildings, New Life

Figure 20.11 Manufaktura's structures in Lodz, Poland, was converted from a textile fabrication factory into a hotel and conference center, the ms2 modern art museum, a theater, cinema, scores of restaurants and fashionable stores.

new capitalist face. In 1992, a proposal was put forward to transform the buildings into a commercial hub. Centrally located, the place offered an opportunity to stimulate the city's declining economy. Construction began in 2003 and was completed in 2006 (Cudny 2016) (Figure 20.11).

One of Manufaktura's structures was converted into a hotel and conference center. Another to the ms² modern art museum. There is a theater, cinema, scores of restaurants and fashionable stores. A newly built shopping mall draws crowds of visitors from the city and beyond. Poznanski's own residence, a lavish baroque style building, was turn into the City of Lodz's Museum. The refurbishment of the buildings was done while respecting the old red-brick industrial architecture and a small museum was dedicated to telling the story of the past (Figure 20.11).

Manufaktura offer a lesson about the future of the past. Buildings whose architecture stood the test of time need not be demolished and new contemporary uses can usher their transition to a new era while respecting and paying homage to the past.

20.8 Final Thoughts

Buildings are some of the most visible symbols of cultural heritage and value. As the world continues to build at a rapid pace and scale, there remain many questions about what will happen to old buildings. As cities seek to modernize their images through implementing infrastructure embedded with the latest technology and architectural designs, there is a dire need to preserve old structures and to maintain the character and identity of cities. Often the debate about building preservation lies in how to do so. Whether it be absolute preservation, functional or an addition, these methods spark a new and necessary life into urbanity.

References

Akanbi, L. A., Oyedele, L. O., Akinade, O. O., Ajayi, A. O., Davila Delgado, M., Bilal, M. and Bello, S. A. (2018). Salvaging building materials in a circular economy: a BIM-based whole-life performance estimator. *Resources, Conservation and Recycling* 129: 175–186. Retrieved July 6, 2023, from https://doi.org/10.1016/j.resconrec.2017.10.026

Ammon, F. R. (2016). *Bulldozer*. Yale University Press. London. Retrieved July 6, 2023, from https://yalebooks.yale.edu/9780300200683/bulldozer

Arcos-Pumarola, J., Paquin, A. G. and Sitges, M. H. (2023). The use of intangible heritage and creative industries as a tourism asset in the UNESCO creative cities network. *Heliyon* 9(1): e13106. Retrieved July 6, 2023, from https://doi.org/10.1016/j.heliyon.2023.e13106

Arfa, F. H., Zijlstra, H., Lubelli, B. and Quist, W. (2022). Adaptive reuse of heritage buildings: from a literature review to a model of practice. *The Historic Environment: Policy & Practice*, 13(2): 148–170. Retrieved July 6, 2023, from https://doi.org/10.1080/17567505.2022.2058551

Austin, R. L., Woodcock, D. G., Steward, W. C. and Forrester, R. A. (1988). *Adaptive Reuse: Issues and Case Studies in Building Preservation*. Van Nostrand Reinhold. Washington, D.C.

Bristol, K. G. (2015). The Pruitt-Igoe myth. *Journal of Architectural Education* 44(3): 163–171. Retrieved July 6, 2023, from https://doi.org/10.1080/10464883.1991.11102687

Cudny, W. (2016). Manufaktura in Łódź, Poland: an example of a festival marketplace. *Norsk Geografisk Tidsskrift* [*Norwegian Journal of Geography*] 70(5): 276–291. Retrieved July 6, 2023, from https://doi.org/10.1080/00291951.2016.1239654

Eberhardt, L. C. M., Birgisdottir, H. and Birkved, M. (2019). Potential of circular economy in sustainable buildings. *IOP Conference Series: Materials Science and Engineering* 471(9): 092051. Retrieved July 6, 2023, from https://doi.org/10.1088/1757-899X/471/9/092051

Ellen MacArthur Foundation (2023). What is a circular economy? *Ellen MacArthur Foundation*. Retrieved July 6, 2023, from https://ellenmacarthurfoundation.org/topics/circular-economy-introduction/overview

Elshaboury, N., Al-Sakkaf, A., Mohammed Abdelkader, E. and Alfalah, G. (2022). Construction and demolition waste management research: a science mapping analysis. *International Journal of Environmental Research and Public Health* 19(8): 4496. Retrieved July 6, 2023, from https://doi.org/10.3390/ijerph19084496

Enia, M. and Martella, F. (2019). Reducing architecture: doing almost nothing as a city-making strategy in 21st century architecture. *Frontiers of Architectural Research* 8(2): 154–163. Retrieved July 6, 2023, from https://doi.org/10.1016/j.foar.2019.01.006

Farjami, E. and Türker, Ö. (2019). *Integrating Adaptive Reuse of Heritage Buildings with Environmental Rating Systems*. University of Leuven. Retrieved July 6, 2023, from https://ees.kuleuven.be/eng/unitwin2019/proceedings/Proceedings UNITWIN2019-Farjami.pdf

Foster, G. (2020). Circular economy strategies for adaptive reuse of cultural heritage buildings to reduce environmental impacts. *Resources, Conservation and Recycling* 152: 104507. Retrieved July 6, 2023, from https://doi.org/10.1016/j.resconrec.2019.104507

Germain, G.-H. (2007). *Un musée dans la ville. Une histoire du Musée des Beaux-arts de Montréal*. Musée des Beaux-arts de Montréal. Montreal.

Hansman, B. (2017). *Pruitt-Igoe*. Arcadia Publishing. Mount Pleasant, South Carolina.

I amsterdam (2020). NDSM werf. *I amsterdam*. Retrieved July 6, 2023, from www.iamsterdam.com/en/amsterdam-qr/north/ndsm-werf

ICOMOS (2011). *The Athens Charter for the Restoration of Historic Monuments—1931—International Council on Monuments and Sites*. Retrieved July 6, 2023, from www.icomos.org/en/167-the-athens-charter-for-the-restoration-of-historic-monuments

IPCC (2021). *Climate Change 2021: The Physical Science Basis*. Retrieved July 6, 2023, from www.ipcc.ch/report/ar6/wg1/

Jokhileto, J. (1986). A history of architectural conservation. *ICCROM*. Retrieved July 6, 2023, from www.iccrom.org/publication/history-architectural-conservation

Kibert, C. J. (2016). *Sustainable Construction: Green Building Design and Delivery*. John Wiley & Sons. Hoboken.

Machat, C. and Ziesemer, J. (eds.) (2020). *Heritage at Risk. World Report 2016–2019 on Monuments and Sites in Danger*. hendrik Bäßler verlag. Berlin. Retrieved July 6, 2023, from www.icomos.de/icomos/pdf/hr20_2016_2019.pdf

Markham, A., Osipova, E., Lafrenz Samuels, K. and Caldas, A. (2016). *World Heritage and Tourism in a Changing Climate*. UNESCO Publishing. Paris.

MASS MoCA (n.d.). History. *MASS MoCA*. Retrieved July 6, 2023, from https://massmoca.org/about/history/

Mekonnen, H., Bires, Z. and Berhanu, K. (2022). Practices and challenges of cultural heritage conservation in historical and religious heritage sites: evidence from North Shoa Zone, Amhara Region, Ethiopia. *Heritage Science* 10(1): 172. Retrieved July 6, 2023, from https://doi.org/10.1186/s40494-022-00802-6

Montreal Museum of Fine Arts (2023). Jean-Noël Desmarais pavilion. *MMFA*. Retrieved July 6, 2023, from www.mbam.qc.ca/en/the-museum/jean-noel-desmarais-pavilion/

Otero, J. (2021). Heritage conservation future: where we stand, challenges ahead, and a paradigm shift. *Global Challenges* 6(1): 2100084. Retrieved July 6, 2023, from https://doi.org/10.1002/gch2.202100084

Patwa, N., Sivarajah, U., Seetharaman, A., Sarkar, S., Maiti, K. and Hingorani, K. (2021). Towards a circular economy: an emerging economies context. *Journal of Business Research* 122: 725–735. Retrieved July 6, 2023, from https://doi.org/10.1016/j.jbusres.2020.05.015

Rahla, K. M., Mateus, R. and Bragança, L. (2021). Implementing circular economy strategies in buildings: from theory to practice. *Applied System Innovation* 4(2): 26. Retrieved July 6, 2023, from https://doi.org/10.3390/asi4020026

Robert, P. (1989). *Adaptations: New Uses for Old Buildings*. Princeton Architectural Press. Princeton.

Rudan, E. (2023). Circular economy of cultural heritage: possibility to create a new tourism product through adaptive reuse. *Journal of Risk and Financial Management* 16(3): Article 3. Retrieved July 6, 2023, from https://doi.org/10.3390/jrfm16030196

Scarpellini, S., Valero-Gil, J., Moneva, J. M. and Andreaus, M. (2020). Environmental management capabilities for a "circular eco-innovation". *Business Strategy and the Environment* 29(5): 1850–1864. Retrieved July 6, 2023, from https://doi.org/10.1002/bse.2472

Seekamp, E. and Jo, E. (2020). Resilience and transformation of heritage sites to accommodate for loss and learning in a changing climate. *Climatic Change* 162(1): 41–55. Retrieved July 6, 2023, from https://doi.org/10.1007/s10584-020-02812-4

Smart Cities Dive (2017). Amsterdam-Noord: from abandoned shipyard to Amsterdam's creative district. *Smart Cities Dive*. Retrieved July 6, 2023, from www.smartcitiesdive.com/ex/sustainablecitiescollective/amsterdam-noord-abandoned-shipyard-amsterdam-s-creative-district/191391/

Taher Tolou Del, M. S., Saleh Sedghpour, B. and Kamali Tabrizi, S. (2020). The semantic conservation of architectural heritage: the missing values. *Heritage Science* 8(1): 70. Retrieved July 6, 2023, from https://doi.org/10.1186/s40494-020-00416-w

UNESCO World Heritage Centre (n.d.). Bryggen. UNESCO World Heritage Centre. Retrieved July 6, 2023, from https://whc.unesco.org/en/list/59/

Waugh, E. (2023). *Brideshead Revisited*. Back Bay Books. New York.

Yarrow, T. (2018). How conservation matters: ethnographic explorations of historic building renovation. *Journal of Material Culture* 24(1): 3–21. Retrieved July 6, 2023, from https://doi.org/10.1177/1359183518769111

Yazdani Mehr, S. (2019). Analysis of 19th and 20th century conservation key theories in relation to contemporary adaptive reuse of heritage buildings. *Heritage* 2(1): Article 1. Retrieved July 6, 2023, from https://doi.org/10.3390/heritage2010061

Illustration Credits

Figures not listed below are in the public domain or have been conceived, drawn or photographed by the author and members of his research and design teams who are listed in the acknowledgments. Every effort has been made to list all contributors and sources. In case of omission, the author and the publisher will include appropriate acknowledgment or correction in any subsequent edition of this book.

Figure 1.4: Based on data from Statistics Canada (2006b). *CYB Overview 2006: Population and Demography*. Ottawa.

Figure 1.5: After Hodges, T. (2010). *Public Transportations Role in Responding to Climate Change*. The Federal Transit Administration, U.S. Department of Transportation, Washington, DC.

Figure 1.6: After Food and Agriculture Organization of the United Nations (via World Bank). Retrieved July 27, 2023, from https://datacatalog.worldbank.org/search/dataset/0037712/world-development-indicators.

Figure 1.9: Source: United Nations Sustainable Development Goals, retrieved July 27, 2023, from https://sdgs.un.org/goals.

Figure 2.10: After Dimond, J. (1976). Residential density and housing form. *Journal of Architectural Education*, 3, February.

Figure 3.10: After data from the International Obesity Taskforce, World Health Organization (2010).

Figure 8.1: Based on data from United Nations, Population Division (2018).

Figure 8.3: Based on data from Kourik, R. (2004). *Designing and Maintaining your Edible Landscape Naturally*. Permanent Publications. Hampshire.

Figure 8.4: After De la Salle, J., Holland, M. et al. (2010). Agricultural Urbanism: Handbook for Building Sustainable Food and Agriculture Systems in 21st Century Cities. Green Frigate Books. Winnipeg.

Figure 8.6: After De la Salle, J., Holland, M. et al. (2010). Agricultural Urbanism: Handbook for Building Sustainable Food and Agriculture Systems in 21st Century Cities. Green Frigate Books. Winnipeg.

Figure 11.1: After Canadian Community Health Survey (2018). Statistics Canada. Ottawa. Retrieved July 27, 2023, from www.150.statcan.gc.ca/n1/daily-quotidien/190625/dq190625b-eng.htm

Figure 17.4: After Statistics Canada Labour Force Survey and Labour Force Supplement February 2021, Ottawa. Retrieved July 27, 2023, from www.150.statcan.gc.ca/n1/daily-quotidien/210312/dq210312a-eng.htm

Figure 19.1: Based on data from WorldOmeter (2016). Retrieved July 27, 2023, from www.worldometers.info/co2-emissions/co2-emissions-per-capita/

References

Abi-Jaoude, E., Naylor, K. T. and Pignatiello, A. (2020). Smartphones, social media use and youth mental health. *Canadian Medical Association Journal* 192(6). Retrieved July 1, 2023, from https://doi.org/10.1503/cmaj.190434

Aboutorabi, M. (2018). Culture, space, and place: an inquiry into the urban landscape of multicultural cities. *Journal of Engineering and Architecture* 6(2). 10.15640/jea.v6n2a2. Retrieved June 23, 2023, from www.researchgate.net/publication/330510624_Culture_Space_and_Place_An_Inquiry_into_the_Urban_Landscape_of_Multicultural_Cities

Adams, C. (2021). Black people are more likely to die in traffic accidents. covid made it worse. *NBC News*. Retrieved July 1, 2023, from www.nbcnews.com/news/nbcblk/black-people-are-more-likely-die-traffic-accidents-covid-made-n1271716

Aguilar, C. (2014). Markthal Rotterdam / MVRDV. *ArchDaily*. Retrieved June 24, 2023, from www.archdaily.com/553933/markthal-rotterdam-mvrdv

Akanbi, L. A., Oyedele, L. O., Akinade, O. O., Ajayi, A. O., Davila Delgado, M., Bilal, M. and Bello, S. A. (2018). Salvaging building materials in a circular economy: a BIM-based whole-life performance estimator. *Resources, Conservation and Recycling* 129: 175–186. Retrieved July 6, 2023, from https://doi.org/10.1016/j.resconrec.2017.10.026

Alessio, H. M., Bassett, D. R., Bopp, M. J., Parr, B. B., Patch, G. S., Rankin, J. W., Rojas-Rueda, D., Roti, M. W. and Wojcik, J. R. (2021). Climate change, air pollution, and physical inactivity: is active transportation part of the solution? *Medicine and Science in Sports And Exercise* 53(6): 1170–1178. Retrieved June 28, 2023, from https://doi.org/10.1249/mss.0000000000002569

Ali, M. J., Rahaman, M. and Hossain, S. I. (2022). Urban green spaces for elderly human health: a planning model for healthy city living. *Land Use Policy* 114: 105970. Retrieved July 1, 2023, from https://doi.org/10.1016/j.landusepol.2021.105970

Alkermes and Otsuka America Pharmaceutical Companies (n.d.). The state of mental health in America. *Mental Health America (MHA)*. Retrieved July 1, 2023, from https://mhanational.org/issues/state-mental-health-america

Altman, I. and Zube, E. (1989). *Public Places and Spaces*. Springer. New York. Retrieved July 5, 2023, from https://doi.org/10.1007/978-1-4684-5601-1

Amadeo, K. (2020). Hurricane Katrina facts, damage, and costs. *The Balance*. Retrieved July 5, 2023, from www.thebalance.com/hurricane-katrina-facts-damage-and-economic-effects-3306023

American Museum of Natural History (n.d.). What is biodiversity? Retrieved June 24, 2023, from www.amnh.org/research/center-for-biodiversity-conservation/what-is-biodiversity

Ammon, F. R. (2016). *Bulldozer*. Yale University Press. London. Retrieved July 6, 2023, from https://yalebooks.yale.edu/9780300200683/bulldozer

Anciaes, P. (2022). Book review: slow cities – conquering our speed addiction for health and sustainability. *Urban Studies* 59(12): 2601–2604. Retrieved June 28, 2023, from https://doi.org/10.1177/00420980221086418

Anderson, D. (2018). How to design a road that shouts, "slow 'er down!". *CBCnews*. Retrieved June 28, 2023, from www.cbc.ca/news/canada/calgary/road-design-calgary-psychology-of-speed-1.4850684

Apfelbeck, B., Snep, R. P., Hauck, T. E., Ferguson, J., Holy, M., Jakoby, C., Scott MacIvor, J., Schär, L., Taylor, M. and Weisser, W. W. (2020). Designing wildlife-inclusive cities that support human-animal co-existence. *Landscape and Urban Planning* 200: 1–11. doi:10.1016/j.landurbplan.2020.103817

Aragón, C. (2022). High tide. *CODAworx*. Retrieved July 1, 2023, from www.codaworx.com/projects/high-tide/

Aragón, C., Buxton, J. and Infield, E. H. (2019). The role of landscape installations in climate change communication. *Landscape and Urban Planning* 189: 11–14. Retrieved July 1, 2023, from https://doi.org/10.1016/j.landurbplan.2019.03.014

Arcos-Pumarola, J., Paquin, A. G. and Sitges, M. H. (2023). The use of intangible heritage and creative industries as a tourism asset in the UNESCO creative cities network. *Heliyon* 9(1): e13106. Retrieved July 6, 2023, from https://doi.org/10.1016/j.heliyon.2023.e13106

References

Arfa, F. H., Zijlstra, H., Lubelli, B. and Quist, W. (2022). Adaptive reuse of heritage buildings: from a literature review to a model of practice. *The Historic Environment: Policy & Practice*, 13(2): 148–170. Retrieved July 6, 2023, from https://doi.org/10.1080/17567505.2022.2058551

The Art Story (2020). Street and graffiti art. *The Art History*. Retrieved July 1, 2023, from www.theartstory.org/movement/street-art/history-and-concepts/

Artnet (2020). Banksy. *Artnet*. Retrieved July 1, 2023, from http://www.artnet.com/artists/banksy/

Asher, L., Aresu, M., Falaschetti, E. and Mindell, J. (2012). Most older pedestrians are unable to cross the road in time: a cross-sectional study. *Age and Ageing* 41(5): 690–694. Retrieved June 28, 2023, from https://doi.org/10.1093/ageing/afs076

Ashik, F. R., Rahman, M. H. and Kamruzzaman, M. (2022). Investigating the impacts of transit-oriented development on transport-related CO2 emissions. *Transportation Research Part D: Transport and Environment* 105: 103227. Retrieved June 22, 2023, from www.sciencedirect.com/science/article/abs/pii/S1361920922000578

Aurand, A. (2010). Density, housing types and mixed land use: smart tools for affordable housing? *Urban Studies* 47(5): 1015–1036. Retrieved June 23, 2023, from https://journals.sagepub.com/doi/pdf/10.1177/0042098009353076

Austin, R. L., Woodcock, D. G., Steward, W. C. and Forrester, R. A. (1988). *Adaptive Reuse: Issues and Case Studies in Building Preservation*. Van Nostrand Reinhold. Washington, D.C.

Avenali, A., Catalano, G., Gregori, M. and Matteucci, G. (2020). Rail versus bus local public transport services: a social cost comparison methodology. *Transportation Research Interdisciplinary Perspectives* 7: 100200. Retrieved July 1, 2023, from https://doi.org/10.1016/j.trip.2020.100200

Baobeid, A., Koç, M. and Al-Ghamdi, S. G. (2021). Walkability and its relationships with health, sustainability, and livability: elements of physical environment and evaluation frameworks. *Frontiers in Built Environment* 7(721218): 1–17. Retrieved June 23, 2023, from www.frontiersin.org/articles/10.3389/fbuil.2021.721218/full

Barbir, F., Veziroğlu, T. N. and Plass, H. J. (1990). Environmental damage due to fossil fuels use. *International Journal of Hydrogen Energy* 15(10): 739–749. Retrieved July 6, 2023, from https://doi.org/10.1016/0360-3199(90)90005-J

Bärwolff, M., Reinartz, A. and Gerike, R. (2021). Correlates of pedestrian and cyclist falls in snowy and icy conditions. *Transactions on Transport Sciences* 12(3): 67–77. Retrieved July 1, 2023, from https://doi.org/10.5507/tots.2021.007

Bellini, E. (2020). More than 100 GW of solar in the Netherlands? Possible by 2050. *PV Magazine*. Retrieved July 6, 2023, from www.pv-magazine.com/2020/04/22/more-than-100-gw-of-solar-in-the-netherlands-possible-by-2050/

Berardi, U. (2013). Clarifying the new interpretations of the concept of sustainable building. *Sustainable Cities and Society* 8: 72–78. Retrieved July 5, 2023, from https://doi.org/10.1016/j.scs.2013.01.008

Bergen, K., Jubenvill, M., Shaw, K., Steen, E., Loewen, H., Mbabaali, S. and Barclay, R. (2022). Factors associated with outdoor winter walking in older adults: a scoping review. *Canadian Journal on Aging / La Revue Canadienne Du Vieillissement*, 1–12. Retrieved July 1, 2023, from https://doi.org/10.1017/s0714980822000460

Bertelsmann Stiftung (2019). Norway. *Sustainable Governance Indicators*. Retrieved June 22, 2023, from www.sgi-network.org/2017/Norway/Environmental_Policies

Bonesio, L. (1997). *Geofilosofia del paesaggio*. Mimesis. Milan.

Borunda, A. (2018). See how a warmer world primed California for large fires. *National Geographic*. Retrieved June 22, 2023, from www.nationalgeographic.com/environment/2018/11/climate-change-california-wildfire/

Bosman, C. and Dolley, J. (2019). Rethinking third places and community building. In *Rethinking Third Places: Informal Public Spaces and Community Building*, pp. 1–19. Edward Elgar. Cheltenham.

Boström, M. (2012). A missing pillar? Challenges in theorizing and practicing social sustainability: introduction to the special issue. *Sustainability: Science, Practice and Policy* 8(1): 3–14. Retrieved July 5, 2023, from https://doi.org/10.1080/15487733.2012.11908080

Boulton, E. (2016). Climate change as a "hyperobject": a critical review of Timothy Morton's reframing narrative. *WIREs Climate Change* 7(5): 772–785. Retrieved July 1, 2023, from https://doi.org/10.1002/wcc.410

Bratman, G. N., Anderson, C. B., Berman, M. G., Cochran, B., de Vries, S., Flanders, J., Folke, C., Frumkin, H., Gross, J. J., Hartig, T., Kahn, P. H., Kuo, M., Lawler, J. J., Levin, P. S., Lindahl, T., Meyer-Lindenberg, A., Mitchell, R., Ouyang, Z., Roe, J., Scarlett, L., Smith, J. R., van den Bosch, M., Wheeler, B. W., White, M. P., Zheng, H. and Daily, G. C. (2019). Nature and mental health: an ecosystem service perspective. *Science Advances* 5(7). Retrieved June 24, 2023, from https://doi.org/10.1126/sciadv.aax0903

Breukers, C. P. M. (2001). Creating water management strategies for the northern part of Holland using a collaborative planning process. In *Integrated Water Resources Management*, pp. 427–452. IAHS. Wallingford.

Bricas, N. (2019). Urbanization issues affecting food system sustainability. In *Designing Urban Food Policies*. Springer. Cham. Retrieved June 24, 2023, from https://doi.org/10.1007/978-3-030-13958-2_1

Bridgewater, P. and Rotherham, I. D. (2019). A critical perspective on the concept of biocultural diversity and its emerging role in nature and heritage conservation. *People and Nature* 1(3): 291–304. doi:10.1002/pan3.10040

Bristol, K. G. (2015). The Pruitt-Igoe myth. *Journal of Architectural Education* 44(3): 163–171. Retrieved July 6, 2023, from https://doi.org/10.1080/10464883.1991.11102687

Britt, M. F. (2014). The intersection of public art and city planning. *ARTS Blog*. Retrieved April 29, 2023, from https://blog.americansforthearts.org/2019/05/15/the-intersection-of-public-art-and-city-planning

Brittion, T., Billings, L., Beunderman, J., Alexander, M., Johar, I., Specht, M., Oliver, M., Owczarek, M., Walding, E. and Bowen, R. (2015). Designed to scale mass participation to build resilient neighbourhoods. academia.edu. *Open Works*. Retrieved June 23, 2023, from www.academia.edu/26403441/Designed_to_Scale_Mass_participation_to_build_resilient_neighbourhoods

Broudehoux, A.-M. (2021). Post-pandemic cities can permanently reclaim public spaces as gathering places. *The Conversation*. Retrieved July 1, 2023, from https://theconversation.com/post-pandemic-cities-can-permanently-reclaim-public-spaces-as-gathering-places-150729

Brown, B. B., Yamada, I., Smith, K. R., Zick, C. D., Kowaleski-Jones, L. and Fan, J. X. (2009). Mixed land use and walkability: variations in land use measures and relationships with BMI, overweight, and obesity. *Health & Place* 15(4): 1130–1141. Retrieved July 6, 2023, from https://doi.org/10.1016/j.healthplace.2009.06.008

Brusseau, T. A., Fairclough, S. J. and Lubans, D. R. (eds.) (2020). *The Routledge Handbook of Youth Physical Activity*. Routledge. New York. Retrieved July 1, 2023, from https://doi.org/10.4324/9781003026426

Buchan, R., Cloutier, D. S. and Friedman, A. (2019). Transformative incrementalism: planning for transformative change in local food systems. *Progress in Planning* 134: 100424. Retrieved June 24, 2023, from https://doi.org/10.1016/j.progress.2018.07.002

Buis, A. (2019). The atmosphere: getting a handle on carbon dioxide. Global climate change: vital signs of the planet. *NASA*. Retrieved July 6, 2023, from https://climate.nasa.gov/news/2915/the-atmosphere-getting-a-handle-on-carbon-dioxide

Burden, D. (2001). Building communities with transportation. *Transportation Research Project*, 1773(1). Retrieved June 23, 2023, from https://journals.sagepub.com/doi/abs/10.3141/1773-02

Burke, S. (2016). Placemaking and the human scale city. *RSS*. Retrieved June 23, 2023, from www.pps.org/article/placemaking-and-the-human-scale-city

Burkhart, E. (2021). Revitalizing a city: the bench warming project adds colour and life to downtown Lapeer. *Arts Help*. Retrieved July 1, 2023, from www.artshelp.com/the-bench-warming-project/

Burton, E. and Mitchell, L. (2006). *Inclusive Urban Design: Streets for Life* (1st ed.). Elsevier. Amsterdam.

Butler, S. M. and Diaz, C. (2016). "Third places" as community builders. Brookings. Retrieved July 1, 2023, from www.brookings.edu/blog/up-front/2016/09/14/third-places-as-community-builders/

Campbell, B. M., Beare, D. J., Bennett, E. M., Hall-Spencer, J. M., Ingram, J. S., Jaramillo, F., Ortiz, R., Ramankutty, N., Sayer, J. A. and Shindell, D. (2017). Agriculture production as a major driver of the Earth system exceeding planetary boundaries. *Ecology and Society* 22(4). Retrieved June 24, 2023, from https://doi.org/10.5751/es-09595-220408

The Canadian Press (2021). 80% of employees don't want to return to office daily post-pandemic: survey. *Benefits Canada.Com*. Retrieved July 4, 2023, from www.benefitscanada.com/human-resources/hr-other/survey-says-20-of-employees-want-to-return-to-office-daily-after-coronavirus-crisis/

Carlisle, N., Van Geet, O. and Pless, S. (2009). *Definition of a 'Zero Net Energy' Community*. Retrieved July 6, 2023, from https://doi.org/10.2172/969716

Carneiro, F., Sergio, M., Corban, C., Ehrlich, D., Florczyk, A., Kemper, T., Maffenini, L., Melchiorri, M., Pesaresi, M., Schiavina, M. and Tommasi, P. (2019). *Atlas of the Human Planet 2019*. Publications Office of the European Union. Luxembourg.

Cascone, S. (2019). Green roof design: state of the art on technology and materials. *Sustainability* 11(11): 3020. Retrieved June 24, 2023, from https://doi.org/10.3390/su11113020

CDC (Centers for Disease Control and Prevention) (2018). *Health-Related Quality of Life (HRQOL): Well-Being Concepts*. Retrieved July 1, 2023, from www.cdc.gov/hrqol/wellbeing.htm

Çetin, N., Mansuroğlu, S. and Önaç, A. (2018). Xeriscaping feasibility as an urban adaptation method for global warming: a case study from Turkey. *Polish Journal of Environmental Studies* 27(3): 1009–1018. Retrieved June 24, 2023, from https://doi.org/10.15244/pjoes/76678

Chakraborty, R. and Demsas, J. (2021). How the US made affordable homes illegal. *Vox*. Retrieved June 23, 2023, from www.vox.com/videos/2021/8/17/22628750/how-the-us-made-affordable-homes-illegal

Chancel, L. (2022). Global carbon inequality over 1990–2019. *Nature Sustainability* 5(11): 931–938. Retrieved July 6, 2023, from https://doi.org/10.1038/s41893-022-00955-z

Charles, R. W. (2011). Lessons from Italy's Matera, the sustainable city of stone. *The Atlantic*. Retrieved June 22, 2023, from www.theatlantic.com/international/archive/2011/09/lessons-from-italys-matera-the-sustainable-city-of-stone/244622/

Chekol, C. (2021). The health effects of genetically modified foods: a brief review. *International Journal of Nutritional Sciences* 6(1). Retrieved June 24, 2023, from https://doi.org/10.26420/intjnutrsci.2021.1047

References

Chen, W. and Klaiber, H. A. (2020). Does road expansion induce traffic? an evaluation of vehicle-kilometers traveled in China. *Journal of Environmental Economics and Management* 104: 102387. Retrieved July 1, 2023, from https://doi.org/10.1016/j.jeem.2020.102387

Cheung, M., Smith, N. and Craven, O. (2021). The impacts of public art on cities, places and people's lives. *The Journal of Arts Management, Law, and Society* 52(1): 37–50. Retrieved July 1, 2023, from https://doi.org/10.1080/10632921.2021.1942361

City of Maple Ridge BC (n.d.). Social sustainability. Maple Ridge, British Columbia. Retrieved July 1, 2023, from www.mapleridge.ca/1779/Social-Sustainability#:~:text=Defining%20Social%20Sustainability&text=Generally%2C%20it%20is%20understood%20as,social%20well%2Dbeing%20should%20be

Cole, R. J. and Lorch, R. (2005). Buildings, culture and environment: informing local and global practices. *International Journal of Sustainability in Higher Education*, 6(1). Retrieved July 5, 2023, from https://doi.org/10.1108/ijshe.2005.24906aae.006

Coleman-Jensen, A., Rabbitt, M. P., Hales, L. and Gregory, C. A. (2022). Food security in the US: key statistics and graphics. USDA Economic Research Service. Retrieved July 1, 2023, from www.ers.usda.gov/topics/food-nutrition-assistance/food-security-in-the-u-s/key-statistics-graphics/#:~:text=In%202021%3A,with%20adults%2C%20were%20food%20insecure

Connolly, C., Keil, R. and Ali, S. H. (2020). Extended urbanisation and the spatialities of infectious disease: demographic change, infrastructure and governance. *Urban Studies* 58(2): 245–263. Retrieved June 23, 2023, from https://doi.org/10.1177/0042098020910873

Connolly, D., Lund, H., Mathiesen, B. V., Werner, S., Möller, B., Persson, U., Boermans, T., Trier, D., Østergaard, P. A. and Nielsen, S. (2014). Heat roadmap Europe: combining district heating with heat savings to decarbonise the EU energy system. *Energy Policy* 65: 475–489.

Connolly, R., Bogue, J. and Repar, L. (2022). Farmers' markets as resilient alternative market structures in a sustainable global food system: A small firm growth perspective. *Sustainability* 14(18): 11626. Retrieved June 24, 2023, from https://doi.org/10.3390/su141811626

Cook, T. (2020). The Battle of Vimy Ridge, 9–12 April 1917. War Museum. Retrieved July 1, 2023, from www.warmuseum.ca/the-battle-of-vimy-ridge/

Crespi-Vallbona, M. and Dimitrovski, D. (2017). Food markets from a local dimension: La Boqueria (Barcelona, Spain). *Cities* 70: 32–39. Retrieved June 24, 2023, from https://doi.org/10.1016/j.cities.2017.06.011

Cudny, W. (2016). Manufaktura in Łódź, Poland: an example of a festival marketplace. *Norsk Geografisk Tidsskrift* [*Norwegian Journal of Geography*] 70(5): 276–291. Retrieved July 6, 2023, from https://doi.org/10.1080/00291951.2016.1239654

Curnow, P. (2010). Story of the Amalfi coast lemon. *Delicious Italy*. Retrieved June 24, 2023, from www.deliciousitaly.com/campania-naples-food/story-of-the-amalfi-coast-lemon

Darby, S. (2006). *The Effectiveness of Feedback on Energy Consumption: A Review for Defra of the Literature on Metering, Billing and Direct Displays*. Environmental Change Insititute, University of Oxford. Retrieved July 6, 2023, from www.eci.ox.ac.uk/research/energy/downloads/smart-metering-report.pdf

Darwish, A. S. and Al-Dabbagh, R. (2020). Wind energy state of the art: present and future technology advancements. *Renewable Energy and Environmental Sustainability* 5: 7. Retrieved July 6, 2023, from https://doi.org/10.1051/rees/2020003

Dasgupta, S., Lall, S. and Wheeler, D. (2022). Cutting global carbon emissions: where do cities stand? *Sustainable Cities*. Retrieved July 6, 2023, from https://blogs.worldbank.org/sustainablecities/cutting-global-carbon-emissions-where-do-cities-stand

Dave, S. (2011). Neighbourhood density and social sustainability in cities of developing countries. *Sustainable Development* 19(3): 189–205. Retrieved July 5, 2023, from https://doi.org/10.1002/sd.433

Dawoud, M. M. and Elgizawy, E. M. (2018). The correlation between art and architecture to promote social interaction in public space. *Cities' Identity Through Architecture and Arts*, 99–105. Retrieved July 1, 2023, from https://doi.org/10.1201/9781315166551-9

den Boer, R. (2021). *Happy Living on a Woonerf*. Thesis. Retrieved July 1, 2023, from https://frw.studenttheses.ub.rug.nl/3744/

Dessein, J., Battaglini, E. and Horlings, L. (eds.). (2015). *Cultural Sustainability and Regional Development: Theories and Practices of Territorialisation*. Routledge. London. Retrieved July 5, 2023, from https://doi.org/10.4324/9781315737430

Diao, J. and Lu, S. (2022). The culture-oriented urban regeneration: place narrative in the case of the inner city of Haiyan (Zhejiang, China). *Sustainability* 14(13): 7992. Retrieved June 23, 2023, from https://doi.org/10.3390/su14137992

Dick, L. (2004). Butchart Gardens. *The Public Historian* 26(4): 88–90. DOI: 10.1525/tph.2004.26.4.88

Discover (2020). Museum Kaap Skil. Retrieved July 5, 2023, from www.kaapskil.nl/en/discover/400-years-skil/new-entrance-building-new-name/

Doheim, R. M., Farag, A. A. and Badawi, S. (2020). Success measures for transforming into car-free cities. *Humanizing Cities Through Car-Free City Development and Transformation*, 231–267. Retrieved July 1, 2023, from https://doi.org/10.4018/978-1-7998-3507-3.ch010

Dona, C. G. W., Mohan, G. and Fukushi, K. (2021). Promoting urban agriculture and its opportunities and challenges: a global review. *Sustainability* 13(17): 9609. Retrieved June 24, 2023, from https://doi.org/10.3390/su13179609

References

Dudek, J. (2019). Design guidelines for creating a vital Woonerf Street. *SGEM International Multidisciplinary Scientific GeoConference EXPO Proceedings*, 19(6). Retrieved July 1, 2023, from www.sgem.org/index.php/component/jresearch/?view=publication&task=show&id=6542

Duhamel, G. (n.d.). Historique. Les Jardins Henri le Sidaner. Retrieved June 24, 2023, from www.lesjardinshenrilesidaner.com/

Eberhardt, L. C. M., Birgisdottir, H. and Birkved, M. (2019). Potential of circular economy in sustainable buildings. *IOP Conference Series: Materials Science and Engineering* 471(9): 092051. Retrieved July 6, 2023, from https://doi.org/10.1088/1757-899X/471/9/092051

Eigenschenk, B., Thomann, A., McClure, M., Davies, L., Gregory, M., Dettweiler, U. and Inglés, E. (2019). Benefits of outdoor sports for society: a systematic literature review and reflections on evidence. *International Journal of Environmental Research and Public Health* 16(6): 937. Retrieved July 1, 2023, from https://doi.org/10.3390/ijerph16060937

El-Azab, R. (2021). Smart homes: potentials and challenges. *Clean Energy* 5(2): 302–315. Retrieved July 6, 2023, from https://doi.org/10.1093/ce/zkab010

Elghamry, R. and Neveen Youssef Azmy, N.Y. (2017). Buildings orientation and its impact on the energy consumption. *Al Azhar 14th International Conference (AEIC) on Engineering, Architecture & Technology*. Retrieved December 4, 2023, from www.researchgate.net/publication/327623184

Ellen MacArthur Foundation (2022). Reimagining our buildings and spaces for a circular economy. *Built Environment*. Retrieved July 4, 2023, from https://ellenmacarthurfoundation.org/topics/built-environment/overview

Ellen MacArthur Foundation (2023). What is a circular economy? *Ellen MacArthur Foundation*. Retrieved July 6, 2023, from https://ellenmacarthurfoundation.org/topics/circular-economy-introduction/overview

Elshaboury, N., Al-Sakkaf, A., Mohammed Abdelkader, E. and Alfalah, G. (2022). Construction and demolition waste management research: a science mapping analysis. *International Journal of Environmental Research and Public Health* 19(8): 4496. Retrieved July 6, 2023, from https://doi.org/10.3390/ijerph19084496

Encyclopedia Britannica (2020). Amalfi. *Encyclopedia Britannica*. Retrieved June 24, 2023, from www.britannica.com/place/Amalfi

Enia, M. and Martella, F. (2019). Reducing architecture: doing almost nothing as a city-making strategy in 21st century architecture. *Frontiers of Architectural Research* 8(2): 154–163. Retrieved July 6, 2023, from https://doi.org/10.1016/j.foar.2019.01.006

Euclid v. Ambler, 272 U.S. 365 (1926). *Justia Law*. Retrieved June 23, 2023, from https://supreme.justia.com/cases/federal/us/272/365/

Ewing, R. and Handy, S. (2009). Measuring the unmeasurable: urban design qualities related to walkability. *Journal of Urban Design* 14(1): 65–84. Retrieved June 23, 2023, from www.tandfonline.com/doi/full/10.1080/13574800802451155

Exercise Equipment in Parks (Outdoor Gyms) (n.d.). *Brisbane City Council*. Retrieved July 1, 2023, from www.brisbane.qld.gov.au/things-to-see-and-do/outdoor-activities/exercise-equipment-in-parks-outdoor-gyms

Farhan, S., Akef, V. and Nasar, Z. (2020). The transformation of the inherited historical urban and architectural characteristics of Al-Najaf's old city and possible preservation insights. *Frontiers of Architectural Research* 9(4): 820–836. Retrieved July 4, 2023, from https://doi.org/10.1016/j.foar.2020.07.005

Farjami, E. and Türker, Ö. (2019). *Integrating Adaptive Reuse of Heritage Buildings with Environmental Rating Systems*. University of Leuven. Retrieved July 6, 2023, from https://ees.kuleuven.be/eng/unitwin2019/proceedings/ProceedingsUNITWIN2019-Farjami.pdf

Farr, D. (2018). *Sustainable Nation: Urban Design Patterns for the Future* (2nd ed.). John Wiley & Sons. Hoboken.

Fedler, J. (2011). Agriculture in Israel: coping with population growth. *Jewish Virtual Library*. Retrieved June 24, 2023, from https://www.jewishvirtuallibrary.org/agriculturally-coping-with-population-growth

FEMA (2015). Hurricane Katrina overview. Retrieved June 22, 2023, from www.fema.gov/hurricane-katrina-overview

Field, J. (2016). *Social Capital* (3rd ed.). Routledge. London.

Filali, H., Barsan, N., Souguir, D., Nedeff, V., Tomozei, C. and Hachicha, M. (2022). Greywater as an alternative solution for a sustainable management of water resources—a review. *Sustainability* 14(2): 665. Retrieved June 24, 2023, from https://doi.org/10.3390/su14020665

Filho, W. L., Matandirotya, N. R., Lütz, J. M., Alemu, E. A., Brearley, F. Q., Baidoo, A. A., Kateka, A., Ogendi, G. M., Adane, G. B., Emiru, N. and Mbih, R. A. (2021). Impacts of climate change to African indigenous communities and examples of adaptation responses. *Nature Communications* 12(1): Article 1. Retrieved July 6, 2023, from https://doi.org/10.1038/s41467-021-26540-0

Foletta, N. and Field, S. (2014). *Europe's New Low Car(bon) Communities*. Retrieved July 1, 2023, from https://www.itdp.org/publication/europes-vibrant-new-low-carbon-communities-2/

Foster, G. (2020). Circular economy strategies for adaptive reuse of cultural heritage buildings to reduce environmental impacts. *Resources, Conservation and Recycling* 152: 104507. Retrieved July 6, 2023, from https://doi.org/10.1016/j.resconrec.2019.104507

Francis, L. F. and Jensen, M. B. (2017). Benefits of green roofs: a systematic review of the evidence for three ecosystem services. *Urban Forestry & Urban Greening* 28: 167–176. Retrieved June 24, 2023, from https://doi.org/10.1016/j.ufug.2017.10.015

References

Francis, M. and Griffith, L. (2011). The meaning and design of farmers' markets as public space: an issue-based case study. *Landscape Journal* 30(2): 261–279. Retrieved June 24, 2023, from https://doi.org/10.3368/lj.30.2.261

Frenchman, D. (2021). Narrative places and the new practice of urban design. In *Imaging the City*, pp. 257–282. Routledge. London.

Friedman, A. (2002). *The Adaptable House: Designing for Choice and Change*. McGraw-Hill, New York.

Friedman, A. (2007). *Sustainable Residential Developments: Design Principles for Green Neighborhoods*. McGraw-Hill. New York.

Friedman, A. (2010). *Narrow Houses: New Directions in Efficient Design*. Princeton Architectural Press. New York.

Friedman, A. (2014). *Planning Small and Mid-Sized Towns: Designing and Retrofitting for Sustainability*. Routledge. London.

Friedman, A. (2015). Design strategies for integration of green roofs in sustainable housing. *Vitruvio – International Journal of Architectural Technology and Sustainability* 1: 57. Retrieved June 24, 2023, from https://doi.org/10.4995/vitruvio-ijats.2015.4475

Friedman, A. (2016). *A Place in Mind: The Search for Authenticity*. Véhicule Press. Montreal.

Friedman, A. (2017a). *Designing Sustainable Communities*. Bloomsbury Academic. London.

Friedman, A. (2017b). *Innovative Apartment Buildings; New Direction in Sustainable Design*. Edition Axel Menges GmbH. Fellbach.

Friedman, A. (2018a). *Neighborhood: Designing a Livable Community*. Véhicule Press. Montréal.

Friedman, A. (2018b). *Smart Homes and Communities: Fostering Sustainable Architecture*. Images Publishing. Victoria.

Friedman, A. and Pollock, A. (2022). *Fundamentals of Planning Cities for Healthy Living*. Anthem Press. London.

Frisch, M. (2002). Planning as a heterosexist project. *Journal of Planning Education and Research* 21(3): 254–266. Retrieved June 23, 2023, from www.researchgate.net/publication/238430139

Fritschi, L., Brown, A. L., Kim, R., Schwela, D. and Kephalopoulos, S. (eds.) (2011). Burden of disease from environmental noise: quantification of healthy life years lost in Europe. World Health Organization (WHO) – Regional Office for Europe. Retrieved July 1, 2023, from https://publications.jrc.ec.europa.eu/repository/handle/JRC64428

Fullagar, S., O'Brien, W. and Lloyd, K. (2019). Feminist perspectives on third places. In *Rethinking Third Places: Informal Public Spaces and Community Building*, pp. 20–37. Edward Elgar. Cheltenham.

Furness, W. W. and Gallaher, C. M. (2018). Food access, food security and community gardens in Rockford, IL. *Local Environment* 23(4): 414–430. Retrieved June 24, 2023, from https://doi.org/10.1080/13549839.2018.1426561

Future Communities (2014). "Building a 'green' city extension." Retrieved July 6, 2023, from www.ghd.com/en/expertise/future-communities.aspx

Gehl, J. (2010). *Cities for People*. Island Press. Washington, D.C.

Germain, G.-H. (2007). *Un musée dans la ville. Une histoire du Musée des Beaux-arts de Montréal*. Musée des Beaux-arts de Montréal. Montreal.

Gibbens, S. (2019). Hurricane Katrina, explained. *National Geographic*. Retrieved June 22, 2023, from www.nationalgeographic.com/environment/natural-disasters/reference/hurricane-katrina/

Gieryn, T. F. (2002). What buildings do. *Theory and Society* 31(1): 35–74.

Gieseking, J., Mangold, W., Katz, C., Low, S. and Saegert, S. (2014). Section 3: place and identity. In *The People, Place, and Space Reader*, pp. 68–77. Routledge. London.

Gifford, R. (n.d.). Environmental psychology matters. *Annual Review of Psychology*. Retrieved July 5, 2023, from www.annualreviews.org/doi/10.1146/annurev-psych-010213-115048

Giles-Corti, B. and Donovan, R. J. (2002). The relative influence of individual, social and physical environment determinants of physical activity. *Social Science & Medicine* 54(12): 1793–1812. Retrieved June 28, 2023, from https://doi.org/10.1016/s0277-9536(01)00150-2

Global Designing Cities Initiative (2016). *Global Street Design Guide*. Island Press. Washington, D.C. Retrieved June 23, 2023, from https://globaldesigningcities.org/publication/global-street-design-guide/

Goddard-Bowman, R. (2014). Something old is something new: the role of heritage preservation in economic development. *Papers in Canadian Economic Development* 9: 96–109. Retrieved July 4, 2023, https://openjournals.uwaterloo.ca/index.php/pced/article/view/4002/4957

Goethals, L., Barth, N., Hupin, D., Mulvey, M. S., Roche, F., Gallopel-Morvan, K. and Bongue, B. (2020). Social marketing interventions to promote physical activity among 60 years and older: a systematic review of the literature. *BMC Public Health* 20(1). Retrieved July 1, 2023, from https://doi.org/10.1186/s12889-020-09386-x

Goldie, J. (2017). Benny farm redevelopment: maintaining community while greening affordable housing. *Sustainable Heritage Case Studies*. Retrieved June 24, 2023, from https://sustainableheritagecasestudies.ca/2017/12/08/renewing-social-housing/

Granchamp, L. (2019). Adjusting food practices to climate prescriptions: vegetable gardening as a way to reduce food-related greenhouse gas emissions. *Review of Agricultural, Food and Environmental Studies* 100(1–4): 1–25. Retrieved June 24, 2023, from https://doi.org/10.1007/s41130-019-00087-7

Greytak, N., Bartholow, M., Dryke, J., Powell, M., Olson, M., Davis, E., Prendergast, C., Schlegel, C., Kalenberg, C., Lindner, C.,

McQuillan, K., Servais, M., Wege, A., Berg, H., Khan, N., Jung, S., Lee, V., Gallahue, S., Yentzer, B., Bascom, M., Druziako, S. and Monnens, A. (2019). Creating an edible landscape: policy & ordinances, best practices, sustainability, budget, and plant data. Resilient Communities Project (RCP), University of Minnesota. Retrieved June 24, 2023, from https://hdl.handle.net/11299/206729

Hachem-Vermette, C., Cubi, E. and Bergerson, J. (2016). Energy performance of a solar mixed-use community. *Sustainable Cities and Society* 27: 145–151. Retrieved July 6, 2023, from https://doi.org/10.1016/j.scs.2015.08.002

Hansman, B. (2017). *Pruitt-Igoe*. Arcadia Publishing. Mount Pleasant, South Carolina.

Harada, Y. and Whitlow, T. (2020). Urban rooftop agriculture: challenges to science. *Frontiers in Sustainable Food Systems* 4(76): 1–8.

Hashemnezhad, H., Heidari, A. A. and Hoseini, P. M. (2013). "Sense of place" and "place attachment". *International Journal of Architecture and Urban Development* 3(1): 5–12. Retrieved June 23, 2023, from https://ijaud.srbiau.ac.ir/article_581_a90b5ac919ddc57e6743d8ce32d19741.pdf

Hatala, A. R., Njeze, C., Morton, D., Pearl, T. and Bird-Naytowhow, K. (2020). Land and nature as sources of health and resilience among indigenous youth in an urban Canadian context: a photovoice exploration. *BMC Public Health* 20(1): 1–14. doi:10.1186/s12889-020-08647-z

Hergül, Ö. C. and Göker, P. (2021). Determining the suitability level of urban markets to the urban planning and design criteria: case of Bilecik, Turkey. *Environment, Development and Sustainability* 23(12): 18443–18470. Retrieved June 24, 2023, from https://ideas.repec.org/a/spr/endesu/v23y2021i12d10.1007_s10668-021-01454-5.html

Hobeika, R. (2021). Heritage preservation can enhance urban development. *MEED*. Retrieved July 4, 2023, from www.meed.com/heritage-preservation-can-enhance-urban-development

Hohenberg, P. M. (2004). The historical geography of European cities: and interpretive essay. In J. V. Henderson and J. F. Thisse (eds.), *Handbook of Regional and Urban Economics*, pp. 3021–3052. Retrieved June 23, 2023, from http://citeseerx.ist.psu.edu/viewdoc/download?doi=10.1.1.112.3064&rep=rep1&type=pdf

Holt-Lunstad, J. (2021). The major health implications of social connection. *Current Directions in Psychological Science* 30(3): 251–259. Retrieved July 1, 2023, from https://doi.org/10.1177/0963721421999630

Hospers, J. (2019). Art as expression. *Encyclopedia Britannica*. Retrieved July 1, 2023, from www.britannica.com/topic/philosophy-of-art/Art-as-expression

Howard, E. (1902). *Garden Cities of Tomorrow* [original 1898 title: *Tomorrow: A Peaceful Path to Real Reform*]. Swan Sonnenschein & Co. London.

Hung, K.-L. J., Kingston, J. M., Albrecht, M., Holway, D. A. and Kohn, J. R. (2018). The worldwide importance of honey bees as pollinators in natural habitats. *Proceedings of the Royal Society B: Biological Sciences* 285(1870): 20172140. Retrieved June 24, 2023, from https://doi.org/10.1098/rspb.2017.2140

Hwang, Y. H., Lum, Q. J. and Chan, Y. K. (2015). Micro-scale thermal performance of tropical urban parks in Singapore. *Building and Environment* 94: 467–476. Retrieved June 24, 2023, from https://doi.org/10.1016/j.buildenv.2015.10.003

I amsterdam (2020). NDSM werf. *I amsterdam*. Retrieved July 6, 2023, from www.iamsterdam.com/en/amsterdam-qr/north/ndsm-werf

ICOMOS (2011). *The Athens Charter for the Restoration of Historic Monuments—1931—International Council on Monuments and Sites*. Retrieved July 6, 2023, from www.icomos.org/en/167-the-athens-charter-for-the-restoration-of-historic-monuments

IEA (n.d.). Energy security – topics. Retrieved July 6, 2023, from www.iea.org/topics/energy-security

Institute for Public Administration at the University of Delaware. (n.d.). Mixed-use development. Planning for Complete Communities in Delaware. Retrieved July 1, 2023, from www.completecommunitiesde.org/planning/landuse/mixed-use-development/#:~:text=Use%20in%20Delaware-,What%20Is%20Mixed%2DUse%20Development%3F,%2C%20and%2For%20industrial%20uses

Intergovernmental Panel on Climate Change (IPCC) (2022). *The Ocean and Cryosphere in a Changing Climate: Special Report of the Intergovernmental Panel on Climate Change* (1st ed.). Cambridge University Press. Cambridge. Retrieved July 6, 2023, from https://doi.org/10.1017/9781009157964

IPCC (2021). *Climate Change 2021: The Physical Science Basis*. Retrieved July 6, 2023, from www.ipcc.ch/report/ar6/wg1/

Jacobs, J. (1961). *The Death and Life of Great American Cities*. Vintage Books. New York.

Jacobs, J. (1969). *The Economy of Cities*. Random House. New York.

Jacobsen, P. (2015). Safety in numbers: more walkers and bicyclists, safer walking and bicycling. *Injury Prevention* 21(4): 271–275. Retrieved June 28, 2023, from https://doi.org/10.1136/ip.9.3.205rep

Janssens, F. and Sezer, C. (2013). 'Flying markets' activating public spaces in Amsterdam. *Built Environment* 39(2): 245–260. Retrieved June 24, 2023, from https://doi.org/10.2148/benv.39.2.245

Jansson, A. K., Lubans, D. R., Smith, J. J., Duncan, M. J., Haslam, R. and Plotnikoff, R. C. (2019). A systematic review of outdoor gym use: current evidence and future directions. *Journal of Science and Medicine in Sport* 22(12): 1335–1343. Retrieved July 1, 2023, from https://doi.org/10.1016/j.jsams.2019.08.003

References

Jeffrey, E. (2021). *Public Art and Reshaping Public Space*. Thesis. University of Detroit Mercy – School of Architecture & Community Development.

Jennings, V. and Bamkole, O. (2019). The relationship between social cohesion and urban green space: an avenue for health promotion. *International Journal of Environmental Research and Public Health* 16(3): 452. doi:10.3390/ijerph16030452

Jokhileto, J. (1986). A history of architectural conservation. *ICCROM*. Retrieved July 6, 2023, from www.iccrom.org/publication/history-architectural-conservation

Kaino, L. (2014). "There's something special about this little town": cultural identity and the legacy of Hundertwasser in Kawakawa, New Zealand. *Continuum – Journal of Media and Cultural Studies*, 28(1): 65–76. doi: 10.1080/10304312.2013.854864

Kamloops This Week (2020). Turning garbage bins in Kamloops into works of art. Retrieved July 1, 2023, from www.kamloopsthisweek.com/community/turning-garbage-bins-in-kamloops-into-works-of-art-4445689

Kelley, V. (2015). The streets for the people: London's street markets 1850–1939. *Urban History* 43(3): 391–411. Retrieved June 24, 2023, from https://doi.org/10.1017/s0963926815000231

Kelly, B. M. (1993). Little boxes, big ideas. *Design Quarterly* 158: 26–31. Retrieved July 4, 2023, from https://doi.org/10.2307/4091292

Kibert, C. J. (2016). *Sustainable Construction: Green Building Design and Delivery*. John Wiley & Sons. Hoboken.

Kim, M.-H., Kim, D., Heo, J, and Lee, D.-W. (2019). Techno-economic analysis of hybrid renewable energy system with solar district heating for net zero energy community. *Energy*, 187: 115916. Retrieved July 6, 2023, from https://doi.org/10.1016/j.energy.2019.115916

Kirk, H., Garrard, G. E., Croeser, T., Backstrom, A., Berthon, K., Furlong, C., Hurley, J., Thomas, F., Webb, A. and Bekessy, S. A. (2021). Building biodiversity into the urban fabric: a case study in applying Biodiversity Sensitive Urban Design (BSUD). *Urban Forestry & Urban Greening* 62: 127176. Retrieved June 24, 2023, from https://doi.org/10.1016/j.ufug.2021.127176

Klinenberg, E. (2019). *Palaces for the People: How Social Infrastructure Can Help Fight Inequality, Polarization, and the Decline of Civic Life*. Broadway Books. Portland.

Klinenberg, E. (n.d.). Dying alone: an interview with Eric Klinenberg. Retrieved July 1, 2023, from https://press.uchicago.edu/Misc/Chicago/443213in.html

Kontou, E., McDonald, N. C., Brookshire, K., Pullen-Seufert, N. C. and LaJeunesse, S. (2020). U.S. active school travel in 2017: prevalence and correlates. *Preventive Medicine Reports* 17: 101024. Retrieved June 28, 2023, from https://doi.org/10.1016/j.pmedr.2019.101024

Korzinski, D. (2022). Back to work(place): as employers beckon, telecommuters grow more entrenched at home. Angus Reid Institute. Retrieved July 4, 2023, from https://angusreid.org/covid-19-pandemic-work-from-home-return-to-work/

Kostof, S. (1991). *The City Shaped: Urban Patterns and Meaning Throughout History*. Thames & Hudson. London.

Krane, J. (2017). Climate change and fossil fuel: an examination of risks for the energy industry and producer states. *MRS Energy & Sustainability* 4: E2. Retrieved July 6, 2023, from https://doi.org/10.1557/mre.2017.3

Kumar, P. (2021). Climate change and cities: challenges ahead. *Frontiers in Sustainable Cities* 3(645613): 1–8.

Kunpeuk, W., Spence, W., Phulkerd, S., Suphanchaimat, R. and Pitayarangsarit, S. (2019). The impact of gardening on nutrition and physical health outcomes: a systematic review and meta-analysis. *Health Promotion International* 35(2): 397–408. Retrieved July 1, 2023, from https://doi.org/10.1093/heapro/daz027

Kuşkaya, S. and Bilgili, F. (2020). The wind energy-greenhouse gas nexus: the wavelet-partial wavelet coherence model approach. *Journal of Cleaner Production* 245: 118872. Retrieved July 6, 2023, from https://doi.org/10.1016/j.jclepro.2019.118872

Kweon, B.-S., Rosenblatt-Naderi, J., Ellis, C. D., Shin, W.-H. and Danies, B. H. (2021). The effects of pedestrian environments on walking behaviors and perception of pedestrian safety. *Sustainability* 13(16): 8728. Retrieved July 1, 2023, from https://doi.org/10.3390/su13168728

Lacroix, R. and Stamatiou, E. (2007). *Architecture, Green Design & Sustainability: Concepts and Practices*. Retrieved July 5, 2023, from www.researchgate.net/publication/326773991_Architecture_Green_Design_Sustainability-Concepts_and_Practices

Landi, S., Tordoni, E., Amici, V., Bacaro, G., Carboni, M., Filibeck, G., Scoppola, A. and Bagella, S. (2020). Contrasting patterns of native and non-native plants in a network of protected areas across spatial scales. *Biodiversity and Conservation* 29(6): 2035–2053. doi:10.1007/s10531-020-01958-y

Lane width (2015). National Association of City Transportation Officials. Retrieved July 1, 2023, from https://nacto.org/publication/urban-street-design-guide/street-design-elements/lane-width/

Langdalen, E. (2016). Urban preservation. *Columbia GSAPP*. 2016. Retrieved July 4, 2023, from www.arch.columbia.edu/courses/20905-1212-urban-preservation

Langemeyer, J., Madrid-Lopez, C., Mendoza Beltran, A. and Villalba Mendez, G. (2021). Urban agriculture: a necessary pathway towards urban resilience and global sustainability? *Landscape and Urban Planning* 210: 104055. Retrieved June 24, 2023, from https://doi.org/10.1016/j.landurbplan.2021.104055

Lee, J. L. C. and Ho, R. T. H. (2022). Creating exercise spaces in parks for older adults with fitness, rehabilitation, and play elements: a review and perspective. *Gerontology and Geriatric Medicine*. Retrieved July 5, 2023, from https://doi.org/10.1177/23337214221083404

Lee, S.L. (1996). Urban conservation policy and the preservation of historical and cultural heritage: the case of Singapore. *Cities*,

Issues In Urban Conservation 13(6): 399–409. Retrieved July 4, 2023, from https://doi.org/10.1016/0264-2751(96)00027-3

Leereveld, T. (2023). Comparison of predicted and actual tranquility in Woonerf streets: "An assessment of streetscape greenery and sound levels using a Green View Index and mobile sound measurements". Thesis. Retrieved July 1, 2023, from https://frw.studenttheses.ub.rug.nl/4107/

Lees, L., Slater, T. and Wyly, E. (2010). *The Gentrification Reader* (1st ed.). Routledge. New York.

Lehmann, S. (2020). The unplanned city: public space and the spatial character of urban informality. *Emerald Open Research* 2. Retrieved July 1, 2023, from https://doi.org/10.35241/emeraldopenres.13580.1

Leichman, A. K. (2020). Why the future of agriculture lies in Israel's desert. *Israel21c*. Retrieved June 24, 2023, from www.israel21c.org/why-the-future-of-agriculture-lies-in-israels-desert/

Lewis, A. (2014). Jaywalking: how the car industry outlawed crossing the road. *BBC News*. Retrieved July 1, 2023, from www.bbc.com/news/magazine-26073797

Lewis, C. and Buffel, T. (2020). Aging in place and the places of aging: a longitudinal study. *Journal of Aging Studies*, 54: 100870. Retrieved July 5, 2023, from https://doi.org/10.1016/j.jaging.2020.100870

Li, M., Jia, N., Lenzen, M., Malik, A., Wei, L., Jin, Y. and Raubenheimer, D. (2022). Global food-miles account for nearly 20% of total food-systems emissions. *Nature Food* 3(6): 445–453. Retrieved June 24, 2023, from www.researchgate.net/publication/361432691_Global_food-miles_account_for_nearly_20_of_total_food-systems_emissions

Li, Y. (2011). The impact of China housing reform on residents' living conditions. University of Oregon. Retrieved June 23, 2023, from https://scholarsbank.uoregon.edu/xmlui/bitstream/handle/1794/11498/Li_Yao_mpa2011sp.pdf?isAllowed=y&sequence=1

Little Free Library (2018). Little Free Library annual report 2018. Retrieved July 1, 2023, from https://littlefreelibrary.org/wp-content/uploads/2022/07/LFL-AnnualReport-2018_WEBSITE-1-compressed.pdf

Loach, K., Rowley, J. and Griffiths, J. (2017). Cultural sustainability as a strategy for the survival of museums and libraries. *International Journal of Cultural Policy* 23(2): 186–198. Retrieved July 4, 2023, from https://doi.org/10.1080/10286632.2016.1184657

Logan, T. (1976). The Americanization of German zoning. *Journal of the American Institute of Planners* 42(4): 377–385.

Lohrberg, F., Lička, Lilli, Scazzosi, L. and Timpe, A. (2016). *Urban Agriculture Europe*. Jovis. Berlin.

Loke, Y. J., Lim, E. S. and Senadjki, A. (2020). Health promotion and active aging among seniors in Malaysia. *Journal of Health Research* 35(5): 444–456. Retrieved July 1, 2023, from https://doi.org/10.1108/jhr-07-2019-0148

Lotfi, Y., Refaat, M., El Attar, M. and Salam, A. (2020). Vertical gardens as a restorative tool in urban spaces of New Cairo. *Ain Shams Engineering Journal* 11(3): 839–848. Retrieved June 24, 2023, from www.sciencedirect.com/science/article/pii/S2090447919301856

Lubbe, N., Wu, Y. and Jeppsson, H. (2022). Safe speeds: fatality and injury risks of pedestrians, cyclists, motorcyclists, and car drivers impacting the front of another passenger car as a function of closing speed and age. *Traffic Safety Research* 2: 000006. Retrieved June 28, 2023, from https://doi.org/10.55329/vfma7555

MacFarlane, K. (2019). The empty chairs of Krakow. *Hasta*. Retrieved July 1, 2023, from www.hasta-standrews.com/features/2019/2/18/the-empty-chairs-of-krakow

Machat, C. and Ziesemer, J. (eds.) (2020). *Heritage at Risk. World Report 2016–2019 on Monuments and Sites in Danger*. hendrik Bäßler verlag. Berlin. Retrieved July 6, 2023, from www.icomos.de/icomos/pdf/hr20_2016_2019.pdf

Mammen, G. and Iancovich, V. (2015). Why walking to school is better than driving for your kids. University of Toronto. Retrieved June 23, 2023, from www.utoronto.ca/news/why-walking-school-better-driving-your-kids#:~:text=walking%20to%20school%3F-,Children%20who%20walk%20to%20school%20have%20been%20found%20to%20have,on%20the%20journey%20to%20school

Markham, A., Osipova, E., Lafrenz Samuels, K. and Caldas, A. (2016). *World Heritage and Tourism in a Changing Climate*. UNESCO Publishing. Paris.

Marselle, M. R., Lindley, S. J., Cook, P. A. and Bonn, A. (2021). Biodiversity and health in the urban environment. *Current Environmental Health Reports* 8(2): 146–156. Retrieved June 24, 2023, from https://doi.org/10.1007/s40572-021-00313-9

Martin, A., Goryakin, Y. and Suhrcke, M. (2014). Does active commuting improve psychological wellbeing? Longitudinal evidence from eighteen waves of the British Household Panel Survey. *Preventive Medicine* 69: 296–303. Retrieved June 28, 2023, from https://doi.org/10.1016/j.ypmed.2014.08.023

Martin, B. and Nagasawa, K. (2020). What Chicago can learn from the 1995 heat wave. *NPR*. Retrieved July 1, 2023, from www.npr.org/local/309/2020/07/14/890758229/what-chicago-can-learn-from-the-1995-heat-wave

MASS MoCA (n.d.). History. *MASS MoCA*. Retrieved July 6, 2023, from https://massmoca.org/about/history/

Massachusetts Department of Energy Resources (n.d.). What is a zero net energy building? *Mass.gov*. Retrieved July 6, 2023, from www.mass.gov/service-details/what-is-a-zero-net-energy-building

Masson-Delmotte, V., Zhai, P., Pörtner, H.-O., Roberts, D., Skea, J., Shukla, P., Pirani, A., Moufouma-Okia, W., Péan, C., Pidcock, R., Connors, S., Matthews, J., Chen, Y., Zhou, X., Gomis, M., Lonnoy, E., Maycock, T., Tignor, M. and Waterfield, T. (2018).

References

Global warming of 1.5°C: an IPCC special report on the impacts of global warming of 1.5°C above pre-industrial levels and related global greenhouse gas emission pathways, in the context of strengthening the global response to the threat of climate change, sustainable development, and efforts to eradicate poverty. Retrieved July 6, 2023, from www.ipcc.ch/site/assets/uploads/sites/2/2019/06/SR15_Full_Report_Low_Res.pdf

Matthews, T. and Gadaloff, S. (2022). Public art for placemaking and urban renewal: insights from three regional Australian cities. *Cities* 127: 103747. Retrieved July 1, 2023, from https://doi.org/10.1016/j.cities.2022.103747

Mayrand, F. and Clergeau, P. (2018). Green roofs and green walls for biodiversity conservation: a contribution to urban connectivity? *Sustainability* 10(4): 985. Retrieved June 24, 2023, from https://doi.org/10.3390/su10040985

Maywald, C. and Riesser, F. (2016). Sustainability – the art of modern architecture. *Procedia Engineering* 155: 238–248. Retrieved July 5, 2023, from https://doi.org/10.1016/j.proeng.2016.08.025

McMichael, C., Dasgupta, S., Ayeb-Karlsson, S. and Kelman, I. (2020). A review of estimating population exposure to sea-level rise and the relevance for migration. *Environmental Research Letters* 15(12): 123005. Retrieved July 6, 2023, from https://doi.org/10.1088/1748-9326/abb398

Mead, D., Ransom, K., Reed, S. and Sager, S. (2020). The impact of the COVID-19 pandemic on food price indexes and data collection. Retrieved June 24, 2023, from www.bls.gov/opub/mlr/2020/article/the-impact-of-the-covid-19-pandemic-on-food-price-indexes-and-data-collection.htm

Mead, N. (2008). Benefits of sunlight: A bright spot for human health. *Environment Health Perspectives* 116(4): 160–167.

Mekonnen, H., Bires, Z. and Berhanu, K. (2022). Practices and challenges of cultural heritage conservation in historical and religious heritage sites: evidence from North Shoa Zone, Amhara Region, Ethiopia. *Heritage Science* 10(1): 172. Retrieved July 6, 2023, from https://doi.org/10.1186/s40494-022-00802-6

Melbourne Heritage Action (n.d.). Melbourne laneways. Retrieved July 1, 2023, from https://melbourneheritageaction.wordpress.com/current-campaigns/laneways/

Mellano, P. (2017). Regaining the culture of cities. *City, Territory and Architecture* 4(1). Retrieved June 23, 2023, from https://doi.org/10.1186/s40410-017-0063-3

Mendez, G. (2014). Beyond move in Mexico City: integrating sustainable mobility into the everyday. *TheCityFix*. Retrieved July 1, 2023, from https://thecityfix.com/blog/beyond-move-mexico-city-integrating-sustainable-mobility-ecobici-biking-gisela-mendez/

Mental Health Disorder Statistics (n.d.). Health – wellness and prevention. Johns Hopkins Medicine. Retrieved July 1, 2023, from www.hopkinsmedicine.org/health/wellness-and-prevention/mental-health-disorder-statistics

Mesimäki, J. and Luoma, J. (2021). Near accidents and collisions between pedestrians and cyclists. *European Transport Research Review* 13(1). Retrieved June 28, 2023, from https://doi.org/10.1186/s12544-021-00497-z

Mihaila, M. (2014). City architecture as cultural ingredient. *Procedia – Social and Behavioral Sciences* 149: 565–569. Retrieved July 5, 2023, from https://doi.org/10.1016/j.sbspro.2014.08.211

Moghaddasi, H., Culp, C. and Vanegas, J. (2021). Net zero energy communities: integrated power system, building and transport sectors. *Energies* 14(21): Article 21. Retrieved July 6, 2023, from https://doi.org/10.3390/en14217065

Mohith, M. (2019). *(In)Equity in Active Transportation Planning: Toronto's Overlooked Inner Suburbs*. Thesis. Master of Environmental Studies, Faculty of Environmental Studies, York University. Retrieved June 28, 2023, from https://yorkspace.library.yorku.ca/xmlui/handle/10315/38617

Monteiro, R. and Martins, M. J. (2020). *Understanding Obesity*. Bentham Science. Singapore. Retrieved June 28, 2023 from https://mcgill.on.worldcat.org/search/detail/1154514077?datasource=library_web&search_field=all_fields&search=true&database=all&scope=wz%3A12129&format=&clusterResults=true&func=find-b&q=&topLod=0&queryString=obesity&find=Go&year=2019..2023&groupVariantRecords=false

Montreal Museum of Fine Arts (2023). Jean-Noël Desmarais pavilion. *MMFA*. Retrieved July 6, 2023, from www.mbam.qc.ca/en/the-museum/jean-noel-desmarais-pavilion/

Moran, E. F., Lopez, M. C., Moore, N., Müller, N. and Hyndman, D. W. (2018). Sustainable hydropower in the 21st century. *Proceedings of the National Academy of Sciences* 115(47): 11891–11898. Retrieved July 6, 2023, from https://doi.org/10.1073/pnas.1809426115

Morano, P., Tajani, F. and Anelli, D. (2020). Urban planning decisions: an evaluation support model for natural soil surface saving policies and the enhancement of properties in disuse. *Property Management* 38(5): 699–723. doi:10.1108/pm-04-2020-0025

Morse, R. (2008). *Environmental Justice Through the Eye of Hurricane Katrina*. Joint Center For Political and Economic Studies Health Policy Institute. Washington, D.C. Retrieved July 6, 2023, from https://inequality.stanford.edu/sites/default/files/media/_media/pdf/key_issues/Environment_policy.pdf

Moseman, A. (2022). How many new trees would we need to offset our carbon emissions? Retrieved June 24, 2023, from https://climate.mit.edu/ask-mit/how-many-new-trees-would-we-need-offset-our-carbon-emissions

Mulliner, E., Riley, M. and Maliene, V. (2020). Older people's preferences for housing and environment characteristics. *Sustainability* 12(14): Article 14. Retrieved July 5, 2023, from https://doi.org/10.3390/su12145723

Mumford, L. (1961). *The City in History: Its Origins, Its Transformations, and its Prospects*. Harcourt. New York.

Myers, S. S. and Frumkin, H. (eds.) (2020). *Planetary Health: Protecting Nature to Protect Ourselves*. Island Press. Washington, D.C. Retrieved June 24, 2023, from www.researchgate.net/publication/343426449_Planetary_Health_Protecting_Nature_to_Protect_Ourselves

Navapan, N. and Charoenkit, S. (2022). Local markets: how the ordinary public places can support urban sustainable development. *GMSARN International Journal* 16(3): 308–313. Retrieved June 24, 2023, from http://gmsarnjournal.com/home/wp-content/uploads/2021/10/vol16no3-12.pdf

Navarro, M. (1989). The personal is political: Las Madres de Plaza de Mayo. In *Power and Protest: Latin American Social Movements*, pp. 241–258. University of California Press. Berkeley and Los Angeles.

Nenadović, A. and Milošević, J. (2022). Creating sustainable buildings: structural design based on the criterion of social benefits for building users. *Sustainability* 14(4): Article 4. Retrieved July 5, 2023, from https://doi.org/10.3390/su14042133

Nogueira, X. R. and Mennis, J. (2019). The effect of brick and granite block paving materials on traffic speed. *International Journal of Environmental Research and Public Health* 16(19): 3704. Retrieved June 28, 2023, from https://doi.org/10.3390/ijerph16193704

Norton, P. D. (2007). Street rivals: jaywalking and the invention of the motor age street. *Technology and Culture* 48(2): 331–359. Retrieved July 1, 2023, from https://doi.org/10.1353/tech.2007.0085

Norton, P. D. (2008). Fighting traffic: the dawn of the motor age in the American city. Oxford Academic MIT Press Scholarship Online. Retrieved July 1, 2023, from https://doi.org/10.7551/mitpress/9780262141000.001.0001

NY Facts (2020). The high line. *NY Facts You Ought to Know*. Retrieved July 4, 2023, from https://nyfacts.com/the-high-line/

Office of Safety and Cheung, J. (n.d.). Lighting for pedestrian safety. US Department of Transportation. Retrieved July 1, 2023, from https://safety.fhwa.dot.gov/roadway_dept/night_visib/docs/Lighting_for_Pedestrian_Safety_2pager.pdf

Oldenburg, R. (1999). *The Great Good Place: Cafes, Coffee Shops, Bookstores, Bars, Hair Salons, and Other Hangouts at the Heart of a Community*. Da Capo Press. Cambridge.

Oost, T. (2022). How to make car-free neighbourhoods work. Retrieved July 1, 2023, from https://frw.studenttheses.ub.rug.nl/4022/1/S3223779_Thijs%20Oost_Master%20Thesis_FINAL.pdf

OPG (2023). Powering Ontario > Hydroelectric power. *OPG*. Retrieved July 6, 2023, from www.opg.com/powering-ontario/our-generation/hydro/

Oppla (2019). Oslo biodivercity: maintaining ecosystem services in a rapidly developing but biodiversity rich city. Retrieved June 22, 2023, from https://oppla.eu/casestudy/19231

Orben, A., Tomova, L. and Blakemore, S.-J. (2020). The effects of social deprivation on adolescent development and mental health. *The Lancet Child & Adolescent Health* 4(8): 634–640. Retrieved June 28, 2023, from https://doi.org/10.1016/s2352-4642(20)30186-3

Oregon Sustainable Transportation Initiative (n.d.). Strategy report: increased connectivity & shorter block lengths. Oregon Department of Transportation. Retrieved June 28, 2023, from www.oregon.gov/odot/Planning/Documents/SR-Increased-Connectivity-Shorter-Block-Lengths.pdf

Osojnik, S. (2019). The Junction: Toronto's coolest neighborhood right now. *Time Out Toronto*. Retrieved July 4, 2023, from www.timeout.com/toronto/things-to-do/junction-toronto-guide

Ostermeijer, F., Koster, H. R., van Ommeren, J. and Nielsen, V. M. (2022). Automobiles and urban density. *Journal of Economic Geography* 22(5): 1073–1095. Retrieved July 1, 2023, from https://doi.org/10.1093/jeg/lbab047

Otero, J. (2021). Heritage conservation future: where we stand, challenges ahead, and a paradigm shift. *Global Challenges* 6(1): 2100084. Retrieved July 6, 2023, from https://doi.org/10.1002/gch2.202100084

Ow, L. F. and Ghosh, S. (2017). Urban cities and road traffic noise: reduction through vegetation. *Applied Acoustics* 120: 15–20. Retrieved June 24, 2023, from https://doi.org/10.1016/j.apacoust.2017.01.007

Owusu, P. A. and Asumadu-Sarkodie, S. (2016). A review of renewable energy sources, sustainability issues and climate change mitigation. *Cogent Engineering* 3(1): 1167990. Retrieved December 6, 2023, from https://doi.org/10.1080/23311916.2016.1167990

Oxford Languages (2023). Definition of market. *Oxford Learners Dictionaries*. Retrieved June 24, 2023, from www.oxfordlearnersdictionaries.com/definition/english/market_1

Ozdemir, Y. and Ozdemir, S. (2019). Residential heating system selection using the generalized Choquet integral method with the perspective of energy. *Energy & Environment* 30(1): 121–140. Retrieved July 6, 2023, from https://doi.org/10.1177/0958305X18787298

Palanivel, T. (2017). Rapid urbanisation: opportunities and challenges to improve the well-being of societies. United Nations Development Programme. Retrieved June 22, 2023, from https://hdr.undp.org/content/rapid-urbanisation-opportunities-and-challenges-improve-well-being-societies

Patwa, N., Sivarajah, U., Seetharaman, A., Sarkar, S., Maiti, K. and Hingorani, K. (2021). Towards a circular economy: an emerging economies context. *Journal of Business Research* 122: 725–735. Retrieved July 6, 2023, from https://doi.org/10.1016/j.jbusres.2020.05.015

Peña, J. (n.d.). Supporting active living through mixed-use developments. American Planning Association. Retrieved March 20, 2023, from www.planning.org/blog/9227408/supporting-active-living-through-mixed-use-developments/

References

Perera, F. (2018). Pollution from fossil-fuel combustion is the leading environmental threat to global pediatric health and equity: solutions exist. *International Journal of Environmental Research and Public Health*, 15(1). https://doi.org/10.3390/ijerph15010016

The Porches Inn (2020). Hotel near MASS MoCA. Porches in at MASS MoCA. Retrieved July 4, 2023, from www.porches.com/

Porchfest NDG (n.d.). About Porchfest. *Porchfest NDG*. Retrieved July 1, 2023, from www.porchfestndg.com/about-agrave-propos.html

Poulton, F. (2011). Little Latrobe Street and the historical significance of Melbourne's laneways. *The Journal of Public Record Office Victoria* 10: 95–104. Retrieved July 1, 2023, from https://prov.vic.gov.au/sites/default/files/files/media/provenance2011_poulton.pdf

Project for Public Space (2009). 10 benefits of creating good public spaces. Retrieved June 23, 2023, from www.pps.org/article/10benefits

Pucher, J. and Buehler, R. (2008). Making cycling irresistible: lessons from the Netherlands, Denmark and Germany. *Transport Reviews* 28(4): 495–528. DOI 10.1080/01441640701806612

Pucher, J., Buehler, R., Geller, R. and Marqués, R. (2021). Implementation of pro-bike policies in Portland and Seville. In *Cycling for Sustainable Cities*, pp. 371–399. MIT Press. Cambridge, MA.

Pulvirenti, G., Distefano, N. and Leonardi, S. (2020). Elderly perception of critical issues of pedestrian paths. *Civil Engineering and Architecture* 8(1): 26–37. Retrieved July 1, 2023, from https://doi.org/10.13189/cea.2020.080104

Purvis, B., Mao, Y. and Robinson, D. (2019). Three pillars of sustainability: In search of conceptual origins. *Sustainability Science* 14(3): 681–695. Retrieved July 5, 2023, from https://doi.org/10.1007/s11625-018-0627-5

Qian, Q. K., Ho, W. K. O., Jayantha, W. M., Chan, E. H. W. and Xu, Y. (2022). Aging-in-place and home modifications for urban regeneration. *Land*, 11(11): Article 11. Retrieved July 5, 2023, from https://doi.org/10.3390/land11111956

Radwan, A. H. and Morsy, A. A. G. (2017). The importance of integrating street furniture in the visual image of the city. *International Journal of Modern Engineering Research (IJMER)* 9(2). Retrieved July 1, 2023, from https://papers.ssrn.com/sol3/papers.cfm?abstract_id=3264621

Rae, J. W. B., Zhang, Y. G., Liu, X., Foster, G. L., Stoll, H. M. and Whiteford, R. D. M. (2021). Atmospheric CO2 over the past 66 million years from marine archives. *Annual Review of Earth and Planetary Sciences* 49(1): 609–641. Retrieved July 6, 2023, from https://doi.org/10.1146/annurev-earth-082420-063026

Rahla, K. M., Mateus, R. and Bragança, L. (2021). Implementing circular economy strategies in buildings: from theory to practice. *Applied System Innovation* 4(2): 26. Retrieved July 6, 2023, from https://doi.org/10.3390/asi4020026

Ravelli, S. (2022). District heating and cooling towards net zero. *Energies* 15(16): Article 16. Retrieved July 6, 2023, from https://doi.org/10.3390/en15166033

Ray, M. (2020). L'Aquila earthquake of 2009. *Encyclopaedia Britannica*. Retrieved July 4, 2023, from www.britannica.com/event/LAquila-earthquake-of-2009

Recio, A., Linares, C., Banegas, J. R. and Díaz, J. (2016). Road traffic noise effects on cardiovascular, respiratory, and metabolic health: an integrative model of biological mechanisms. *Environmental Research*. Retrieved June 24, 2023, from https://pubmed.ncbi.nlm.nih.gov/26803214/

Reducing roads can cause traffic to "evaporate" (2019). Rapid Transition Alliance. Retrieved July 1, 2023, from www.rapidtransition.org/stories/reducing-roads-can-cause-traffic-to-evaporate/

Regeneration International (n.d.). What is no-till farming? Retrieved June 24, 2023, from https://regeneration international.org/2018/06/24/no-till-farming/

Reid, C. E., Rieves, E. S. and Carlson, K. (2022). Perceptions of green space usage, abundance, and quality of green space were associated with better mental health during the COVID-19 pandemic among residents of Denver. *Plos One* 17(3). Retrieved July 1, 2023, from https://doi.org/10.1371/journal.pone.0263779

Relph, E. (1987). The invention of modern town planning: 1890–1940. In *The Modern Urban Landscape*, pp. 49–75. The Johns Hopkins University Press. Baltimore.

Ren, P., Zhu, H., Sun, Z. and Wang, C. (2020). Effects of artificial islands construction on the spatial distribution and risk assessment of heavy metals in the surface sediments from a semi-closed bay (Longkou Bay), China. *Bulletin of Environmental Contamination and Toxicology* 106(1): 44–50. doi:10.1007/s00128-020-03032-3

Reversing car dependency (2021). ITF. Retrieved July 1, 2023, from www.itf-oecd.org/reversing-car-dependency

Ripoll González, L., Belén Yanotti, M. and Lehman, K. (2022). Local focus: farmers' markets as an approach to sustainable tourism. *Tourism, Hospitality & Event Management*, 95–113. Retrieved June 24, 2023, from https://doi.org/10.1007/978-3-030-92208-5_7

The Rise (n.d.). Integral Group. Retrieved June 23, 2023, from www.integralgroup.com/projects/the-rise/

Robert, P. (1989). *Adaptations: New Uses for Old Buildings*. Princeton Architectural Press. Princeton.

Rogers, J., Emerine, D., Haas, P., Jackson, D., Kauffmann, P., Rybeck, R. and Westrom, R. (2016). Estimating parking utilization in multifamily residential buildings in Washington, D.C. *Transportation Research Record: Journal of the Transportation Research Board* 2568(1): 72–82. Retrieved July 1, 2023, from https://doi.org/10.3141/2568-11

Rogers, R. and Urban Task Force (1999). *Towards an Urban Renaissance: Final Report of the Urban Task Force Chaired by Lord Rogers of Riverside*. Department of the Environment, Transport and the Regions. London.

Rondeau, D., Perry, B. and Grimard, F. (2020). The consequences of covid-19 and other disasters for wildlife and biodiversity. *Environmental and Resource Economics* 76(4): 945–961. doi:10.1007/s10640-020-00480-7

Roshani, H. and Kouchaki, S. (2021). How the texture of a pavement surface contributes to the tire-pavement friction. *Roads & Bridges*. Retrieved June 28, 2023, from https://www.roadsbridges.com/pavement-maintenance/article/10654346/how-the-texture-of-a-pavement-surface-contributes-to-the-tire-pavement-friction

Rudan, E. (2023). Circular economy of cultural heritage: possibility to create a new tourism product through adaptive reuse. *Journal of Risk and Financial Management* 16(3): Article 3. Retrieved July 6, 2023, from https://doi.org/10.3390/jrfm16030196

Rudofsky, B. (1965). *Architecture without Architects*. Doubleday & Company, Inc. New York.

Ruel, M. (2020). Growing cities, growing food insecurity: how to protect the poor during rapid urbanization. Center for Strategic and International Studies. Retrieved June 22, 2023, from www.csis.org/analysis/growing-cities-growing-food-insecurity-how-protect-poor-during-rapid-urbanization

Ruff, J. (2007). For sale: the American dream. *American History*, 29–42. Retrieved July 3, 2023, from www.bartleby.com/essay/For-Sale-The-American-Dream-Analysis-FJAJJ5WGUFV

Ryberg-Webster, S. (2016). Heritage amid an urban crisis: historic preservation in Cleveland, Ohio's Slavic village neighborhood. *Cities* 58(October): 10–25. Retrieved July 4, 2023, from https://doi.org/10.1016/j.cities.2016.05.005

Sachdev, G. (2019). Engaging with plants in an urban environment through street art and design. *Plants, People, Planet* 1(3): 271–289. Retrieved July 1, 2023, from https://doi.org/10.1002/ppp3.10055

Saddington, D. B. (1972). The city in classical antiquity. *Akroterion* 17: 14–22. Retrieved June 22, 2023, from https://hdl.handle.net/10520/AJA03031896_147

Safe Cycling Guide 9th Edition (n.d.). Government of Quebec, Road Safety. Retrieved June 28, 2023, from https://saaq.gouv.qc.ca/fileadmin/documents/publications/safe-cycling-guide.pdf

Sage, A. (2011). Kinya Ishikawa, potter-1001 pots founder. *Kickass Canadians*. Retrieved June 23, 2023, from https://kickasscanadians.ca/kinya-ishikawa/

Sagredo, A. M. (2013). The "madonnelle" in Rome. *Italian Ways*. Retrieved June 23, 2023, from www.pinterest.fr/pin/532058143482675717/

Salman, M. (2019). Sustainability and vernacular architecture: rethinking what identity is. *Urban and Architectural Heritage Conservation within Sustainability*. Retrieved June 23, 2023, from https://doi.org/10.5772/intechopen.82025

Salman, S. (2018). What would a truly disabled-accessible city look like? *The Guardian*. Retrieved July 1, 2023, from www.theguardian.com/cities/2018/feb/14/what-disability-accessible-city-look-like

Sanford, C., Sabapathy, D., Morrison, H. and Gaudreau, K. (2015). *Pesticides and Human Health*. Retrieved June 24, 2023, from www.princeedwardisland.ca/sites/default/files/publications/cpho_pesticide_part_1.pdf

Scarpellini, S., Valero-Gil, J., Moneva, J. M. and Andreaus, M. (2020). Environmental management capabilities for a "circular eco-innovation". *Business Strategy and the Environment* 29(5): 1850–1864. Retrieved July 6, 2023, from https://doi.org/10.1002/bse.2472

Schmitt, P. J. (1990). *Back to Nature: The Arcadian Myth in Urban America*. The Johns Hopkins University Press. Baltimore.

Schnake-Mahl, A. S., Jahn, J. L., Subramanian, S., Waters, M. C. and Arcaya, M. (2020). Gentrification, neighborhood change, and population health: a systematic review. *Journal of Urban Health: Bulletin of the New York Academy of Medicine* 97(1): 1–25. Retrieved July 4, 2023, from https://doi.org/10.1007/s11524-019-00400-1

Schoenauer, N. (2000). *6,000 Years of Housing*. W. W. Norton. New York.

Schoennagel, T., Balch, J. K., Dennison, P. E., Harvey, B. J., Krawchuk, M. A., Mietkiewicz, N., Morgan, P., Moritz, M. A., Rasker, R., Turner, M. G. and Whitlock, C. (2017). Adapt to more wildfire in western North American forests as climate changes. *Proceedings of the National Academy of Sciences of the United States of America* 114(18): 4582–4590. Retrieved June 22, 2023, from https://doi.org/10.1073/pnas.1617464114

Scott, J. C. (2020). The high modernist city: an experiment and a critique. In *Seeing Like a State*, pp. 103–146. Yale University Press. London.

Scott, T. L., Masser, B. M. and Pachana, N. A. (2019). Positive aging benefits of home and community gardening activities: older adults report enhanced self-esteem, productive endeavours, social engagement and exercise. *Sage Open Medicine* 8: 1–13. Retrieved July 1, 2023, from https://doi.org/10.1177/2050312120901732

ScottishPower Renewables (2020). Whitelee windfarm. *ScottishPower Renewables*. Retrieved July 6, 2023, from www.whiteleewindfarm.co.uk/whitelee-windfarm-about-us

Seekamp, E. and Jo, E. (2020). Resilience and transformation of heritage sites to accommodate for loss and learning in a changing climate. *Climatic Change* 162(1): 41–55. Retrieved July 6, 2023, from https://doi.org/10.1007/s10584-020-02812-4

Sharifi, A. (2019). Resilient urban forms: a review of literature on streets and street networks. *Building and Environment* 147: 171–187. Retrieved July 1, 2023, from https://doi.org/10.1016/j.buildenv.2018.09.040

References

Sharp, J., Pollock, V. and Paddison, R. (2020). Just art for a just city: public art and social inclusion in urban regeneration. *Culture-Led Urban Regeneration*, 156–178. Retrieved July 1, 2023, from https://doi.org/10.4324/9781315878768-9

Shashank, A. (2017). Walkability and wayfinding. *Applied*. Retrieved July 1, 2023, from www.appliedinformation.group/insight/walkability-and-wayfinding

Sheridan, E. (2021). The curb cut effect: how universal design makes things better for everyone. *Medium*. Retrieved July 1, 2023, from https://uxdesign.cc/the-curb-cut-effect-universal-design-b4e3d7da73f5

Shill, G. H. (2019). Should law subsidize driving? *SSRN Electronic Journal*. Retrieved July 1, 2023, from https://doi.org/10.2139/ssrn.3345366

Shoup, D. C. (1997). The high cost of free parking. *Journal of Planning Education and Research* 17(1): 3–20. Retrieved July 1, 2023, from https://doi.org/10.1177/0739456x9701700102

Singhal, S. (2015). Grüne Welle in Vienne, Austria by SUPERBLOCK. *AECCafé*. Retrieved June 28, 2023, from www10.aeccafe.com/blogs/arch-showcase/2015/03/13/grune-welle-in-vienna-austria-by-superblock/

Sleiman, J. (2019). How cars took over our cities, and how some are fighting back. *WHYY PBS*. Retrieved July 1, 2023, from www.wbur.org/hereandnow/2019/07/03/cars-streets-cities-congestion

Slorach, P. C. and Stamford, L. (2021). Net zero in the heating sector: technological options and environmental sustainability from now to 2050. *Energy Conversion and Management* 230: 113838. Retrieved July 6, 2023, from https://doi.org/10.1016/j.enconman.2021.113838

Slow Movement (2020). Slow cities and the slow movement. *Slow Movement*. Retrieved July 1, 2023, from www.slowmovement.com/slow_cities.php

Smart Cities Dive (2017). Amsterdam-Noord: from abandoned shipyard to Amsterdam's creative district. *Smart Cities Dive*. Retrieved July 6, 2023, from www.smartcitiesdive.com/ex/sustainablecitiescollective/amsterdam-noord-abandoned-shipyard-amsterdam-s-creative-district/191391/

Smith, C. (2015). Art as a diagnostic: assessing social and political transformation through public art in Cairo, Egypt. *Social & Cultural Geography* 16(1): 22–42. Retrieved July 1, 2023, from https://doi.org/10.1080/14649365.2014.936894

Smith, C. L. (2012). The energy challenge. *Applied Petrochemical Research* 2(1): 3–6. Retrieved July 6, 2023, from https://doi.org/10.1007/s13203-012-0010-x

Smith, K. A. (2021, June 7). How communities of color are hurt most by climate change. *Forbes Advisor*. Retrieved July 6, 2023, from www.forbes.com/advisor/personal-finance/communities-of-color-and-climate-change/

Soini, K. and Joost, D. (2016). Culture-sustainability relation: towards a conceptual framework. *Sustainability* 8(2): 167. Retrieved July 4, 2023, from https://doi.org/10.3390/su8020167

Solarin, S. A. and Bello, M. O. (2022). Wind energy and sustainable electricity generation: evidence from Germany. *Environment, Development and Sustainability* 24(7): 9185–9198. Retrieved July 6, 2023, from https://doi.org/10.1007/s10668-021-01818-x

Sonko, S., Maksymenko, N., Vasylenko, O., Chornomorets, V. and Koval, I. (2021). Biodiversity and landscape diversity as indicators of sustainable development. *E3S Web of Conferences* 255: 01046. doi:10.1051/e3sconf/202125501046

Specht, K., Siebert, R., Hartmann, I., Freisinger, U. B., Sawicka, M., Werner, A., Thomaier, S., Henckel, D., Walk, H. and Dierich, A. (2013). Urban agriculture of the future: an overview of sustainability aspects of food production in and on buildings. *Agriculture and Human Values* 31(1): 33–51. Retrieved June 24, 2023, from https://doi.org/10.1007/s10460-013-9448-4

Speed hump (2015). National Association of City Transportation Officials. Retrieved July 1, 2023, from https://nacto.org/publication/urban-street-design-guide/street-design-elements/vertical-speed-control-elements/speed-hump/

Steinkuehler, C. A. and Williams, D. (2006). Where everybody knows your (screen) name: online games as "third places". *Journal of Computer-Mediated Communication* 11(4): 885–909. Retrieved July 1, 2023, from https://doi.org/10.1111/j.1083-6101.2006.00300.x

Stobart, J. and Van Damme, I. (2015). Introduction: markets in modernization: transformations in urban market space and practice, c. 1800–c. 1970. *Urban History* 43(3): 358–371. Retrieved June 24, 2023, from https://doi.org/10.1017/s0963926815000206

Stoevska, V. (2020). COVID 19 is driving up food prices all over the world. *ILOSTAT*. Retrieved June 24, 2023, from https://ilostat.ilo.org/covid-19-is-driving-up-food-prices-all-over-the-world/

Strazzante, E., Rycken, S. and Winkler, V. (2021). Global north and global south: how climate change uncovers global inequalities – Generation Climate Europe. *Generation Climate Europe*. Retrieved July 6, 2023, from https://gceurope.org/global-north-and-global-south-how-climate-change-uncovers-global-inequalities/

Taher Tolou Del, M. S., Saleh Sedghpour, B. and Kamali Tabrizi, S. (2020). The semantic conservation of architectural heritage: the missing values. *Heritage Science* 8(1): 70. Retrieved July 6, 2023, from https://doi.org/10.1186/s40494-020-00416-w

Talebi, B., Mirzaei, P. A., Bastani, A. and Haghighat, F. (2016). A review of district heating systems: modeling and optimization. *Frontiers in Built Environment* 2. Retrieved July 6, 2023, from www.frontiersin.org/articles/10.3389/fbuil.2016.00022

Tan, J. K. N., Belcher, R. N., Tan, H. T. W., Menz, S. and Schroepfer, T. (2021). The urban heat island mitigation potential of vegetation depends on local surface type and shade. *Urban Forestry*

References

& Urban Greening 62: 127128. Retrieved June 24, 2023, from https://doi.org/10.1016/j.ufug.2021.127128

Tao, N. (2017). It's no game! Shanghai pushes healthy, active life as fitness campaigns flourish. *Shine Beyond a Single Story*. Retrieved July 1, 2023, from www.shine.cn/opinion/chinese-views/1710295603/

Tapia, C., Randall, L., Wang, S. and Aguiar Borges, L. (2021). Monitoring the contribution of urban agriculture to urban sustainability: an indicator-based framework. *Sustainable Cities and Society* 74: 103130. Retrieved June 24, 2023, from https://doi.org/10.1016/j.scs.2021.103130

Thadani, H. L. and Go, Y. I. (2021). Integration of solar energy into low-cost housing for sustainable development: case study in developing countries. *Heliyon* 7(12): e08513. Retrieved July 6, 2023, from https://doi.org/10.1016/j.heliyon.2021.e08513

Thompson, C. W. (2002). Urban open space in the 21st century. *Landscape and Urban Planning* 60(2): 59–72. Retrieved June 23, 2023, from www.sciencedirect.com/science/article/pii/S0169204602000592

Thompson, H. (2018). Combining e-bikes and bikeshares is urban alchemy: a winning transit solution. *Forbes, For Cities*. Retrieved June 28, 2023, from www.forbes.com/sites/energyinnovation/2018/01/08/combining-e-bikes-and-bikeshares-is-urban-alchemy-a-winning-transit-solution-for-cities/#2cc18353e092

Thurber, A. and Christiano, J. (2019). Confronting gentrification: can creative interventions help people keep more than just their homes? *Engaged Scholar Journal: Community-Engaged Research, Teaching, and Learning* 5(2): 95. Retrieved July 4, 2023, from https://doi.org/10.15402/esj.v5i2.68338

Transit Oriented Development Institute (n.d.). *Transit Oriented Development*. Retrieved July 1, 2023, from www.tod.org/

Tranter, P. and Tolley, R. (2020). *Slow Cities*. Elsevier. Amsterdam.

Twenge, J. M., Spitzberg, B. H. and Campbell, W. K. (2019). Less in-person social interaction with peers among U.S. adolescents in the 21st century and links to loneliness. *Journal of Social and Personal Relationships* 36(6): 1892–1913. Retrieved July 1, 2023, from https://doi.org/10.1177/0265407519836170

U.S. Department of Transportation (n.d.). *The Walking Environment*. Retrieved June 23, 2023, from https://safety.fhwa.dot.gov/saferjourney1/library/countermeasures/01.htm

U.S. Environmental Protection Agency (2022a). Soak up the rain: trees help reduce runoff. Retrieved June 24, 2023, from https://www.epa.gov/soakuptherain/soak-rain-trees-help-reduce-runoff

U.S. Environmental Protection Agency (2022b). Reduce urban heat island effect. Retrieved June 24, 2023, from https://www.epa.gov/green-infrastructure/reduce-urban-heat-island-effect

Ullah, A., Tlak Gajger, I., Majoros, A., Dar, S. A., Khan, S., Kalimullah, Haleem Shah A., Nasir Khabir, M., Hussain, R.,

Khan, H. U., Hameed, M. and Anjum, S. I. (2021). Viral impacts on honey bee populations: a review. *Saudi Journal of Biological Sciences* 28(1): 523–530. Retrieved June 24, 2023, from https://doi.org/10.1016/j.sjbs.2020.10.037

UN (United Nations) (2016). Specifications for the application of the United Nations framework classification for fossil energy and mineral reserves and resources 2009 to renewable energy resources, pp. 1–21.

UN (United Nations) (2022). United Nations Conference on the Environment, Stockholm 1972. Retrieved June 22, 2023, from www.un.org/en/conferences/environment/stockholm1972

UNESCO (2019). The Trulli of Alberobello. Retrieved June 24, 2023, from https://whc.unesco.org/en/list/787/

UNESCO (2023). Cutting edge: bringing cultural tourism back in the game. Retrieved July 4, 2023, from www.unesco.org/en/articles/cutting-edge-bringing-cultural-tourism-back-game

UNESCO World Heritage Centre (n.d.). *Bryggen*. UNESCO World Heritage Centre. Retrieved July 6, 2023, from https://whc.unesco.org/en/list/59/

United Nations (2023). *Sustainability*. Retrieved July 5, 2023, from www.un.org/en/academic-impact/sustainability

United Nations Department of Economic and Social Affairs (2018). 68% of the world population projected to live in urban areas by 2050, says UN. United Nations Department of Economic and Social Affairs. Retrieved June 24, 2023, from https://www.un.org/development/desa/en/news/population/2018-revision-of-world-urbanization-prospects.html

United Nations Department of Economic and Social Affairs (2022). *The Sustainable Development Goals: Report 2022*. UN. Retrieved June 24, 2023, from https://unstats.un.org/sdgs/report/2022/The-Sustainable-Development-Goals-Report-2022.pdf

United States Department of Transportation (n.d.-a). Pedestrian & bicycle safety. Federal Highway Administration (FHWA). Retrieved June 28, 2023, from https://highways.dot.gov/safety/pedestrian-bicyclist

United States Department of Transportation (n.d.-b). Speeding and aggressive driving. National Highway Traffic Safety Administration (NHTSA). Retrieved June 28, 2023, from www.nhtsa.gov/risky-driving/speeding

United States Environmental Protection Agency (2022). Reduce urban heat island effect. Retrieved June 22, 2023, from www.epa.gov/green-infrastructure/reduce-urban-heat-island-effect#:~:text=%22Urbanheatislands%22occurwhen,heat-relatedillnessandmortality

United States General Services Administration (2023). *Climate Action and Sustainability*. Retrieved July 5, 2023, from www.gsa.gov/governmentwide-initiatives/climate-action-and-sustainability

University of Rochester (2010). Spending time in nature makes people feel more alive, study shows. Retrieved June 23, 2023, from www.sciencedaily.com/releases/2010/06/100603172219.htm

References

Urb Cultural Planning (2020). Urban cultural planning as a method. *Urbcultural*. Retrieved June 23, 2023, from https://urbcultural.eu/urban-cultural-planning-as-a-method/

Urbano Gutiérrez, R. and de la Plaza Hidalgo, L. (2019). *Elements of Sustainable Architecture*. Routledge. London. Retrieved June 24, 2023, from https://doi.org/10.4324/9781351256445

van den Berg, M., Wendel-Vos, W., van Poppel, M., Kemper, H., van Mechelen, W. and Maas, J. (2015). Health benefits of green spaces in the living environment: a systematic review of epidemiological studies. *Urban Forestry & Urban Greening* 14(4): 806–816. Retrieved July 1, 2023, from https://doi.org/10.1016/j.ufug.2015.07.008

Verma, A. K., Rout, P. R., Lee, E., Bhunia, P., Bae, J., Surampalli, R. Y., Zhang, T. C., Tyagi, R. D., Lin, P. and Chen, Y. (2020). Biodiversity and sustainability. In *Sustainability*, pp. 255–275. Wiley. Basel. Retrieved June 24, 2023, from https://doi.org/10.1002/9781119434016.ch12

Visiting Vienna (2020). The Holocaust Memorial. *Visiting Vienna*. Retrieved July 1, 2023, from www.visitingvienna.com/sights/museums/holocaust-memorial/

Vivintel (2021). New study by Vividata sheds light on our desire to age-in-place. *Vividata*. Retrieved July 5, 2023, from https://vividata.ca/press_release/new-study-by-vividata-sheds-light-on-our-desire-to-age-in-place/

Volenec, Z. M., Abraham, J. O., Becker, A. D. and Dobson, A. P. (2021). Public parks and the pandemic: how park usage has been affected by COVID-19 policies. *Plos One* 16(5): e0251799. Retrieved July 4, 2023, from https://doi.org/10.1371/journal.pone.0251799

Walsh, D. (2017, December 13). Reducing our reliance on cars: the shifting future of urban transportation. *MIT Sloan*. Retrieved July 1, 2023, from https://mitsloan.mit.edu/ideas-made-to-matter/reducing-our-reliance-cars-shifting-future-urban-transportation

Wang, N. and Adeli, H. (2014). Sustainable building design. *Journal of Civil Engineering and Management*, 20(1). Retrieved July 5, 2023, from https://doi.org/10.3846/13923730.2013.871330

Water Wheel (2017). Stop food waste in its tracks. *Water Wheel* 16(5): 40–41. Retrieved July 1, 2023, from chrome-extension://efaidnbmnnnibpcajpcglclefindmkaj/; https://www.wrc.org.za/wp-content/uploads/mdocs/WW%20Sept_Oct%202017_web.pdf

Waugh, E. (2023). *Brideshead Revisited*. Back Bay Books. New York.

WCED (World Commission on Environment and Development) (1987). *Our Common Future*. Oxford University Press. Geneva.

What is public health? (n.d.). Canadian Public Health Association | Association Canadienne de Santé Publique. Retrieved June 28, 2023, from www.cpha.ca/what-public-health

Whiting, A. F. (2017). Berlin: how my street tells the tragedy of the Holocaust. *AlexFW.com*. Retrieved July 1, 2023, from https://alexfw.com/2017/04/24/berlin-how-my-street-tells-the-tragedy-of-the-holocaust/

WHO (World Health Organization) (2022). Ageing and health. Retrieved June 22, 2023, from www.who.int/news-room/fact-sheets/detail/ageing-and-health#:~:text=By2050%2Cthe world'spopulation,2050toreach426million

Whybrow, N. (2016). Folkestone perennial: the enduring work of art in the re-constitution of place. *Cultural Geographies* 23(4): 671–692. doi: 10.1177/1474474016638047

Woessner, M. N., Tacey, A., Levinger-Limor, A., Parker, A. G., Levinger, P. and Levinger, I. (2021). The evolution of technology and physical inactivity: the good, the bad, and the way forward. *Frontiers in Public Health* 9. Retrieved July 1, 2023, from https://doi.org/10.3389/fpubh.2021.655491

World Health Organization (2016). Healthy China 2030. Retrieved July 1, 2023, from www.who.int/teams/health-promotion/enhanced-wellbeing/ninth-global-conference/healthy-china

World Health Organization (n.d.). Obesity. Retrieved July 1, 2023, from www.who.int/health-topics/obesity#tab=tab_1

Wu, S. R., Fan, P. and Chen, J. (2015). Incorporating culture into sustainable development: a cultural sustainability index framework for green buildings. *Sustainable Development* 24(1): 64–76. Retrieved July 5, 2023, from https://doi.org/10.1002/sd.1608

Yang, E., Kim, Y. and Hong, S. (2021). Does working from home work? Experience of working from home and the value of hybrid workplace post-COVID-19. *Journal of Corporate Real Estate* 25(1): 50–76. Retrieved July 5, 2023, from https://doi.org/10.1108/JCRE-04-2021-0015

Yari, A., Eslamian, S. and Eslamian, F. (2020). *Urban and Industrial Water Conservation Methods*. CRC Press. Boca Raton. Retrieved June 24, 2023, from https://doi.org/10.1201/9781003081531

Yarrow, T. (2018). How conservation matters: ethnographic explorations of historic building renovation. *Journal of Material Culture* 24(1): 3–21. Retrieved July 6, 2023, from https://doi.org/10.1177/1359183518769111

Yazdani Mehr, S. (2019). Analysis of 19th and 20th century conservation key theories in relation to contemporary adaptive reuse of heritage buildings. *Heritage* 2(1): Article 1. Retrieved July 6, 2023, from https://doi.org/10.3390/heritage2010061

Yogerst, J. (2019). Everything to know about Yellowstone National Park. *National Geographic*. Retrieved June 22, 2023, from www.nationalgeographic.com/travel/national-parks/yellowstone-national-park/

Younger, S. (2022). NASA study: rising sea level could exceed estimates for U.S. coasts. Global climate change: vital signs of the planet. *NASA*. Retrieved July 6, 2023, from https://climate.nasa.gov/news/3232/nasa-study-rising-sea-level-could-exceed-estimates-for-us-coasts

Yu, B. and Lu, Q. (2013). Empirical model of roughness effect on vehicle speed. *International Journal of Pavement Engineering* 15(4): 345–351. Retrieved June 28, 2023, from www.

researchgate.net/publication/263760293_Empirical_model_of_roughness_effect_on_vehicle_speed

Zebracki, M. (2018). Urban preservation and the queerying spaces of (un)remembering: memorial landscapes of the Miami Beach art deco historic district. *Urban Studies Journal* 55(10): 2261–2285. Retrieved July 4, 2023, from https://doi.org/10.1177/0042098017709197

Zhang, F., Lindsey, R. and Yang, H. (2016). The Downs–Thomson paradox with imperfect mode substitutes and alternative transit administration regimes. *Transportation Research Part B: Methodological* 86: 104–127. Retrieved July 1, 2023, from https://doi.org/10.1016/j.trb.2016.01.013

Zhang, J. (2012). Delivering environmentallSy sustainable economic growth: the case of China made possible with support from the Bertelsmann Foundation. Asia Society. Retrieved July 5, 2023, from https://asiasociety.org/files/pdf/Delivering_Environmentally_Sustainable_Economic_Growth_Case_China.pdf

Zhang, M. (2009). Bus versus rail. *Transportation Research Record: Journal of the Transportation Research Board* 2110(1): 87–95. Retrieved July 1, 2023, from https://doi.org/10.3141/2110-11

Zhouzhuang (2023). *In Wikipedia*. Retrieved July 4, 2023, from https://en.wikipedia.org/wiki/Zhouzhuang

Zohuri, B. and McDaniel, P. (2021). Energy insight: an energy essential guide. In B. Zohuri and P. McDaniel (eds.), *Introduction to Energy Essentials*, pp. 321–370. Academic Press. Cambridge, MA. Retrieved July 6, 2023, from https://doi.org/10.1016/B978-0-323-90152-9.00009-8

Zucker, P. (1970). *Town and Square: From the Agora to the Village Green*. MIT Press. Cambridge, MA.

Index

Note: Pages in *italics* refer to figures.

accessibilty 118, *119*, 142
addition view of building renewal 208–209
aging *see* seniors
agora 33, 35, 39
Agricultural Urbanism (AU) vs production agriculture (PA) 74–75
Alberobella, Italy: local stone use 59
Almere, Netherlands: solar energy 198, *199*
amorphous squares 36
Amsterdam: creative hub 209; infill structure *164*
art *see* Amsterdam: creative hub, culture of places, North Adams, Massachusetts (MASS MoCA), public art
Art Deco District, Miami Beach 164–165
artifacts, historical and cultural *96*, 133, *163*, 207
artisan food production 77
asphalt surfaces, alternatives to 152
Australia *62*, 134, 180–181, *182*
Austria *see* Vienna

Banksy 128
barrios 36
Belgium *see* Bruges, Belgium
The Bench Warming Project, Lapeer, US 131
Bergen's old port (Bryggen), Norway 211–212
Berlin, Germany: Holocaust memorial *126*
bike paths 153–154
'bike-ability' 45, *46*
bikeshare systems 154, *155*
biking *see* cycling
biodiversity: fundamentals and importance of 61–62; Norway 9–10; Singapore 8–9, 63–64; Yellowstone Park, US 10; *see also* landscape creation; natural settings and natural features
blocks, shorter 151
bluegrass turf 65, *66*
brick, cobblestone and granite surfaces 152
Bruges, Belgium: infill structure *164*; markets *34*, *85*; narrow living 21

Brundtland Commission and report 5, 179
Budapest, Hungary: Holocaust memorial art 135, *161*
buffer zones 45, *46*, 142–143
building materials and circular economy 162, 204–205
Burano, Venice 94–95
Butchart, J. 68–69

Canada 30, 101–102, 131–132, 182–184; *see also* Montreal; Toronto
Canadian–French alliance: Vimy monument 133–134
car crashes/traffic-related incidents 142, 143, 150
car speeds and speeding 150
car-free cities 47
car-free communities 140–141
carbon emissions 191–192, 193, *194*; per passenger mile *4*; and trees 54
carbon footprint measurement 7, 8
chemical fertilizers and pesticides 72
children: cycling *29*; and third places 120–121; *see also* play areas
Childs, D. 210
China 30–31, 91, 111–112, 165, *166*
churches 116
circular economy 162, 204–205
Cittaslow, Trani, Italy 110
climate change 1–2; art as education tool 132–133; impacts of 191–192; IPCC 191, 207; and vegetable gardening 76
closed squares 35
cobblestone, granite and brick surfaces 152
Cologne, Germany: Holocaust memorial art 135
color: Bergen's old port (Bryggen) 211–212; street furnishings 132; Superkilen, Copenhagen 98–101
commercial spaces and services 151, 160–*161*, 164, 184–185; *see also* markets
community centers 116
community infrastructure 195

Index

community/neighborhood gardens: and domestic agriculture 75–77; health benefits 107, *109*; as informal gathering places 117; Montreal 77–78, *79*

conservationist view of building renewal 206

Copenhagen: e-bikes 154; pathway to 10th floor 186–188; Superkilen 98–101

COVID-19 pandemic: and flexible zoning 172–173; and food insecurity 71, 74; and mental health 104; and social interaction 115, 117, 172; and social sustainability 180; and tourism 160

cultural sustainability: and design 179–180; importance of art to social and 125–127; and preservation, relation between 159–160

culture: and biodiversity 51; SDG 6, *7*

culture of places 94; design for 95–97; and economy 97; Edam, Netherlands 98, *100*; elements of 94–95; and faith, Italy 98; and narrative of 97–98; Val-David, Quebec 101–102

curb cuts 142

cycling: European children *29*; priority in Netherlands 155–156; safety enhancement for walking and 142–143, 152–154; social value of walking and 149–150; *see also entries beginning* bike

Dalian market, China 91

Declaration of Belem (1988) 51

Delta Works project, Netherlands 58

Demnig, G. 135

Denmark *see* Copenhagen

denser mixed use communities 23, *23*–32; contemporary history of zoning 23–25; historical *see* Bruges, Belgium, Matera, Italy; key density indexes 25–26; Saint-Valery-sur-Somme: living above the store 28–30; Shanghai 30–31; Smart Growth planning 18, *19*, *20*; sustainable and mixed land uses 26–28; Vancouver: upper neighborhood 30

disability: accessibility 118, *119*, 142; social model of 43, *44*; visual impairments 118, 143; *see also* seniors

district heating 196–197

domestic recycling 198–199, *200*

domestic water-saving measures 65, *66*

Downs-Thomson Paradox 138

e-bikes 154, *155*

early modernist architecture 162–163

ecological footprint measurement 7–8

economic and social tools, preservation as 160–162

economic sustainability 180, *181*, 184

economy: circular 162, 204–205; and culture of places 97, 101–102; SDG 6

Edam, Netherlands: homage to the past 98, *100*

edible landscape creation 74–75

education tool, art as 132–133

8 House, Copenhagen 186–188

elderly population *see* seniors

emissions *see* carbon emissions, greenhouse gas (GHG) emissions

energy: challenge 191–192; district heating 196–197; harvesting from waste 198–199, *200*; hydropower 193, *194*; net-zero communities and buildings 193–196; solar 192–193, *194*, 198, *199*; sources *192*; types of renewable 192–193; wind 192, 197

environment: SDG 5

environmental sustainability 180–181, 184

Euclid v. Ambler case 23

Euclidean zoning 16–17, 23

Ewing, R. and Handy, S. 41

'eyes on the street' 95–96, 118

fairs 97

farmers markets 86–87

farms 71; artisan food production 77; challenges of current urban food system 71–74; edible landscape creation 74–75; Matera roof pots, Italy 78, *80*; Negev Desert, Israel 78–80, *81*; *see also* community/neighborhood gardens

feedback and energy efficiency 195

Finland, Porvoo play areas 110–111

flexible zoning 172–173

flooding risk 58, 191

floor-area ratio, density index 26

flora and fauna, preserving 55, *56*

Food and Agriculture Organization, undernourished global population *4*

food deserts 72–74

food production *see* community/neighborhood gardens, farms

food security/insecurity 4, 51, 107, *109*, 117

food swamps 72–74

formal gathering places 115–117

forum, Roman 33, *34*

fourth places, concept of 97

France 28–30, 57, *85*, 133–134, *171*

Frenchman, D. 97–98

functionalist view of building renewal 207, *208*

Garden by the Bay, Singapore 8–9

garden city and emergence of suburbia 15–17, *18*

gardens: rooftop 67–68, 76, 78, *80*; *see also* community/neighborhood gardens; landscape creation

genesis of urban development 12–14, *15*

gentrification, avoiding 165

Gerberoy, France: rose bushes 57

Germany *36*, *78*, *126*, 135, *140*, *171*, 197, *205*; and Bryggen, Norway 211–212

Glasgow, Scotland: wind turbines 197

Global North/Global South 191–192

governance: SDG 7

government land use measures *24*

Index

graffiti, social message of 128, 134

granite, cobblestone and brick surfaces 152

Greek settlements 14; public squares 33, *34*, 39, *40*

green roofs 67–68

green on the sixth floor, Toronto 185–186

green spaces *see* landscape creation, natural settings and natural features, public parks

greenery along streets and sidewalks 142–143

greenhouse gas (GHG) emissions 71, 191, 193

greenhouses: Negev Desert, Israel 80; rooftop 76

gross and net density indexes 26

grouped squares 35–36

Grüne Welle (Green Wave) suburb, Vienna 156–157

gyms 105, *107*

Haarlem, Netherlands: human scale 48, *49*

Hammarby Sjöstad, Sweden: ENVAC Waste Smart system 199, *200*

health and wellbeing 103; challenges 103–104; Cittaslow, Trani, Italy 110; and diets 51, 72–74; and green spaces 38, 62–63; and greenery along streets and sidewalks 142; and social interaction 114–115; value of cycling and walking 149–150; *see also* play areas; seniors

heat islands *see* urban heat islands (UHI)

heat-absorbing pavements 61, *62*

heating, district 196–197

height to width ratio 42–43

high density index 25, *26*

historical/heritage sites *see* culture of places, old buildings, planning for urban evolution, preservation

history and planning for future 12; adaptable narrow living, Bruges 21; garden city and emergence of suburbia 15–17, *18*; genesis of urban development 12–14, *15*; Smart Growth 18, *19*, *20*; stone dwellings of Matera, Italy 18–21

Holocaust memorial art *126*, 134–135, *161*

Howard, E. 15–16

human practices and impacts 51

human scale 42–43, *44*

Hurricane Katrina 1–2, *3*, 192

hybrid model of working 172–173, 180

hydropower 193, *194*

in-person and media social interactions 114–115

inactivity: challlenge of 104; *see also* health and wellbeing; play areas; seniors; walking and cycling

India 133, 182

industrial buildings: transformation to mixed-use 184–185, 212–213; *see also* North Adams, Massachusetts (MASS MoCA)

Industrial Revolution 15, 36, 101

industrialization of agriculture 71–74; and supermarkets 86

infill housing 164

informal gathering places 117–118

Intergovernmental Panel on Climate Change (IPCC) 191, 207

International Energy Agency (IEA) 191

International Renewable Energy Agency (IRENA) 197

International style 162–163

irrigation 65

Israel 78–80, *81*, 145, *146*

Istanbul, Turkey 171, *172*

Italy 18–21, 59, 68, 78, *80*, 94–95, *96*, 98, *99*, 110, 167, *168*; *see also* Rome; *entries beginning* Roman

Jacobs, J. 163

"jaywalking" 139

The Junction, Toronto 164

K2 apartment buildings, Windsor, Australia 180–181, *182*

Kameiros, Rhodes 39, *40*

Kfar Sava pathway, Israel 145, *146*

Kostof, S. 12–14, 35

Krakow, Poland: Holocaust memorial art 135, *161*

landscape creation: fundamentals and importance of biodiversity 61–62; green roofs 67–68; Positano, Italy: lemon orchards 68; strategies and methods 62–64; Victoria quarry garden, Canada 68–69; water conservation 65–67

L'Aquila, Italy: post-earthquake rebuilding 167, *168*

Le Corbusier 162, 182

LED lights: traffic 195; urban agriculture 76

lemon orchards of Positano, Italy 68

Levittown, US 16–17

lighting 143, 152; *see also* LED lights

linear vs circular economy 162

Little Free Library project 122–123

local food systems (LFS) 74–75

local history: Oudeschild, Netherlands 188–189

local stone use, Italy 18–21, 59

local traffic slowing measures 150–152

Lodz, Poland: Holocaust memorial art 134, *135*; textile factory conversion 185, 212–213

low density index 25, *26*

low-rise residences 28

Ludi Xiangianaqino Chang, Shianghai 30–31

Malmö, Sweden: shared streets in 143–144, *145*; Västra Hamnen: social sustainability 180, *181*

marketing/branding and public art 127

markets 84; Bruges, Belgium *34*; Dalian, China 91; and fairs 97; genesis and evolution of 84–86; Rotterdam: mixing market and housing 91–93; social and economic functions of 86–88, 97; typologies and design 88–91

Matera, Italy: roof pots 78, *80*; stone dwellings 18–21

Melbourne: hear-absorbing construction *62*; Laneways of 134

236

memorials and monuments *126*; Holocaust *126*, 134–135, *161*; Vimy, France 133–134

mental health 104, 115, 150

Mexico *36*

Mexico City: car-free strategy 140–141; square dancing 121–122

Mies van der Rohe, L. 162, *163*

mixed-use development 26–28, 141–142; industrial buildings 184–185, 212–213; market and housing, Rotterdam 91–93; *see also* denser mixed use communities

Montreal: adaptive reuse *205*; community farm 77–78, *79*; Museum of Fine Arts 207, *208*; Old 170, *171*; response to COVID-19 pandemic *173*; talent on front porches 122; timeless design in 176, *177*

monuments *see* memorials and monuments

Morgan's Rock, Nicaragua 58–59

multi-family housing and zoning policies 23, 25

narrative: and culture of places 97–98; Holocaust memorials 134–135

narrow living: Bruges, Belgium 21

narrowing roadways 150–151

native species: green spaces 63; vegetable gardening 77

natural settings and natural features 50–51; Alberobella, Italy: local stone use 59; alternative design process 56–57; Gerberoy, France: rose bushes 57; human practices and impacts 51; integration 54–55, *56*; Netherlands: weaving development and water 58; Nicaragua: Morgan's Rock 58–59; typology of natural features 51–54

Negev Desert, Israel 78–80, *81*

neighborhood density index 26

neighborhood gardens *see* community/neighborhood gardens

neighborhood squares 37–38

net and gross density indexes 26

net-zero communities and buildings 193–196

Netherlands 48, *49*, 58, 91–93, 98, *100*, *105*, 188–189, 198, *199*; cycling priority in 155–156; "streets for living" (woonerf) 44–45, 139–140; *see also* Amsterdam

New York: Central Park 63, *64*; graffiti 128; Heights of Buildings Commission 23, *25*; Manhattan High Line 117, 174–176; Times Square *36*

Nicaragua *see* Sun Juan del Zur, Nicaragua

"no-till agriculture" 57

non-traditional family 172

North Adams, Massachusetts (MASS MoCA) 173–174, *175*, 209–211

Norway 9–10, 211–212

nuclear squares 35

obesity 103–104, 149–150; elderly population 105

old buildings 203; Amersterdam 209; Bergen's old port (Bryggen) 211–212; circular economy and adaptability 204–205; industrial buildings as mixed-use spaces 184–185, 212–213;

North Adams, Massachusetts (MASS MoCA) 173–174, *175*, 209–211; strategies for renewal 205–209; value of past 203–204; *see also* planning for urban evolution; preservation

Oldenburg, R. 119, 120

Oudeschild, Netherlands: celebrating local history 188–189

outdoor play areas *see* play areas

parking quotas/spaces 139

Pauer, G. 135

pedestrian friendly environment 45

pedestrian-focused landscape and art 143, *144*

pedestrians: criminalization of 139; safety enhancement for cyclists and 142–143, 152–154; traffic-related deaths and injuries 142, 143, 150

permaculture 186–*187*

pesticides 72

physical activity *see* health and wellbeing, play areas, seniors, walking and cycling

placemaking 43, *44*, 62, *63*, 125, 130, 131

planning for urban evolution 170; evolving cities and buildings 170–171, *172*; Manhattan: innovative reclamation 174–176; Montreal: timeless design 176, *177*; North Adams, Massachusetts: art of renewal 173–174, *175*, 209–211; strategies for renewal and resiliency 172–173; *see also* old buildings; preservation

plant mofits: art as education tool 133

play areas 104–105, *106*; Porvoo, Finland 110–111

plaza 36

Plex, Montreal 176, *177*

Poland 134, 135, *161*, 185, 212–213

Pompeii 14, *15*

population statistics and projections 1, *72*, 121; aging/senior 2, *3*, 107; impacts of climate change 191–192; undernourished *4*

porches 95–96; Porchfest, Montreal 122

Porvoo, Finland: play areas 110–111

Positano, Italy: lemon orchards 68

powering cities *see* energy

"precision agriculture" 57

preservation 159; avoiding gentrification 165; L'Aquila: post-earthquake restoration 167, *168*; strategies 162–165; Tuscany 166–167; value of past 159–162; Venice of China 165, *166*

Projcct for Public Space (2009) 37–38

public art 125; as dark narrative 134–135; as education tool 132–133; importance to social and cultural sustainability 125–127; integration 128–131; Laneways of Melbourne 134; pedestrian-focused landscape 143, *144*; social message of graffiti 128, 134; street furnishings as 131–132; Vimy monument, France 133–134; *see also* culture of places

public parks/spaces: COVID-19 pandemic 172; as formal gathering places 116; gym equipment 105, *107*; physical activity among seniors 107, *108*; Superkilen, Copenhagen 98–101

Index

public squares 33; civic functions of 38–39; evolution and functions of 33, *34*; as formal gathering places 115–116; importance in high-density settings 37–38; Kameiros, Rhodes 39, *40*; typology of 35–37

public transport as Third Place 120

race and class: avoiding gentrification 165; food deserts and food swamps 72–74; impacts of climate change 192; social interaction 114–115; zoning 23–25

Radburn, New Jersey 16, *17–18*

religious imagery, Italy 98, *99*

renewable energy, types of 192–193

renewal and restoration *see* old buildings, planning for urban evolution, preservation

Rhodes: Kameiros 39, *40*

Rogers, R. and Urban Task Force (1999) 38

Roman public squares 33, *34*, 35, 36, 39

Roman settlements 14, *15*

Rome: heritage sites *96*, 159, 203; Holocaust memorial art *135*

rooftops 67–68, 76, 78, *80*

rose bushes of Gerberoy, France 57

Rotterdam: mixing market and housing 91–93

Rudofsky, B. 18–19

safety enhancement for pedestrians and cyclists 142–143, 152–154

Saint-Valery-sur-Somme, France 28–30

seniors 105–107, *108*, *109*; active living, Shanghai 111–112; home modifications 179–180, 182–184; population statistics and projections 2, *3*, 107; square dancing, Mexico City 121–122; and third places 120–121

sense of place 51, 125, 130–131; destruction of 162–163; establishing 41–44; Sun Juan del Zur, Nicaragua 47–48

Shanghai: high-density communities 30–31; seniors, active living 111–112

shared pathways 152

shared streets in Malmö 143–144, *145*

signage 143, *144*

Singapore 63–64; Garden by the Bay 8–9

single-family zoning policies 23

Sitte, C. 42–43

60 Richmond Cooperative Housing, Toronto 185–186

slow cities, Italy 110

Smart Growth planning 18, *19*, *20*

social class *see* race and class

social and economic tools, preservation as 160–162

social interaction 95–97, 114; and COVID-19 pandemic 115, 117, 172; in-person and media 114–115; Little Free Library project 122–123; Mexico City: square dancing 121–122; Montreal: porches 122; street corners 151; streets and sidewalks 141–142; typology and design of gathering places 115–118, *119*; value of third places 119–121; walking and cycling 150

social media 115

social message of graffiti 128, 134

social model of disability 43, *44*

social sustainability 180; definition of 114; importance of art to cultural and 125–127

social value of cycling and walking 149–150

society: SDG 6

soil conservation 56–57

solar energy 192–193, *194*, 198, *199*

Spanish colonial design 36

speed bumps 142

sports 105

square dancing, Mexico City 121–122

squares *see* public squares

Stein, C. and Wright, H. 16

stencils 128

stone buildings, Italy 18–21, 59

street furnishings as art 131–132

street shrines (Madonnelle), Italy 98, *99*

"streets for living" (woonerf) 44–45, 139–140

streets and sidewalks 138; new mindset for 139–141; pathway in Kfar Sava 145, *146*; shared streets in Malmö 143–144, *145*; for social engagements 141–142; surface texture 152; *see also* traffic

suburbia: concept of transformation 170; garden city and emergence of 15–17, *18*; and joining units 27; and supermarkets 86; Vienna 156–157; zoning 23

Sun Juan del Zur, Nicaragua: Morgan's Rock 58–59; sense of place 47–48

sun path and wind direction 53

Superkilen, Copenhagen 98–101

supermarkets 86

sustainability: contemporary challenges 1–4; measurement 7–8; mind-set 4–8; Norway 9–10; principles and typology 5–7, 179–181; Singapore 8–9; Yellowstone Park, US 10

sustainable buildings 179; Copenhagen: pathway to 10th floor 186–188; creating urban spaces with 182–185; defining 179–181, *182*; Oudeschild: celebrating local history 188–189; Toronto: green on the sixth floor 185–186

Sustainable Development Goals (SDGs) 5–7

Sweden 143–144, *145*, 180, *181*, 197, 199, *200*

taller buildings 28

third places, value of 119–121

Thompson, C. W. 37–38

Togay, C. 135

topography, natural 51, *52*

Toronto: green on the sixth floor 185–186; The Junction 164

tourism 97, 127, 159, 160–162, 185; markets 87, *88*; North Adams, Massachusetts (MASS MoCA) 174, *175*; Venice of China 165, *166*

Town and Country Planning Act (1940), UK 206

traffic: congestion 2–3; reducing and eliminating 45–47; rise of car dominance in planning 138–139; safety enhancement 142–143, 152–154; slowing measures 150–152; tailpipe emissions per passenger mile *4*; *see also entries beginning car*

traffic lights 151, 195

Trani, Italy: Cittaslow 110

transformation, concept of 170

transportation times, reduction of 195

trees 53–54, *55*

triangulation of informal gathering places 118

Tuscany, Italy: preservation 166–167

UK 36, *37*, 128, 197, 206; Glasgow, Scotland: wind turbines 197

UN: sustainable development principles 5–7

UNDESA 71

UNESCO 59, 160, 212

urban heat islands (UHI) 1, *2*, 61–62; and trees 54

urban permaculture 186–*187*

Urban Task Force report (1999) 38

US 10, 16–18, 122, 131; *see also* New York; North Adams, Massachusetts (MASS MoCA)

Val-David, Quebec: fusing art and economy 101–102

Vancouver upper neighborhood 30

Västra Hamnen, Sweden: social sustainability 180, *181*

vehicular traffic *see* traffic, *entries beginning* car

Venice: Burano 94–95

vertical farming 76

Vienna: Holocaust memorial art 134, *135*; urban preservation *161*; walkable green suburb 156–157

Vimy monument, France 133–134

visual impairments 118, 143

Wadsworth, J. 174

walkability 28, 41; establishing sense of place 41–44; Haarlem, Netherlands 48, *49*; and human scale 42–43, *44*; macro measures for 44–47; Sun Juan del Zur, Nicaragua 47–48; Vienna: green suburb 156–157

walking and cycling: safety enhancement for 142–143, 152–154; social value of 149–150

waste, harvesting energy from 198–199, *200*

water conservation 65–67

water and development, Netherlands 58

wellbeing *see* health and wellbeing

Whiteread, R. 134

wildfires 1, *2*

wildlife 53

wind: direction and sun path 53; energy 192, 197; and impact of trees *54*

Windsor, Australia: K2 apartment buildings 180–181, *182*

women and third places 120–121

World Commission on Environment and Development (WCED) *see* Brundtland Commission and report

World Health Organization: aging population 2; definitions of health and obesity 103; Global Action Plan for Physical Activity 104

World Inequality Lab 191–192

xeroscaping 65–67

Yellowstone Park, US 10

Zhouzhuang (Venice of China) 165, *166*

Zoning: contemporary history of 23–25; flexible 172–173; inclusionary 165

Zucker, P. 35–36